NEW DIRECTIONS IN EUROPEAN PRIVATE LAW

This book brings together leading scholars and practitioners to explore contemporary challenges in the field of European private law, identify problems, and propose solutions. The first section reassesses the existing theoretical framework and traditional legal scholarship on which European private law has developed. The book then goes on to examine important and practical topics of geo-blocking and standardisation in the context of recent legislative developments and the CJEU case law. The third section assesses the challenging subject of adequate regulation of online platforms and the sharing economy that has been continuously addressed in recent years by European private law. The fourth section deals with the regulatory challenges brought by an increasing development of artificial intelligence and blockchain technology, as well as the question of liability. The final section examines recent European legislative developments in the area of digital goods and digital content and identifies potential future policy directions in which European private law may develop in the future.

Volume 103 in the Series Modern Studies in European Law

Modern Studies in European Law

Recent titles in this series:

The Interface Between EU and International Law: Contemporary Reflections
Edited by Inge Govaere and Sacha Garben

The Rise and Decline of Fundamental Rights in EU Citizenship
Adrienne Yong

The Court of Justice and European Criminal Law: Leading Cases in a Contextual Analysis
Edited by Valsamis Mitsilegas, Alberto di Martino and Leandro Mancano

The EU as a Global Regulator for Environmental Protection:
A Legitimacy Perspective
Ioanna Hadjiyianni

Citizenship, Crime and Community in the European Union
Stephen Coutts

Critical Reflections on Constitutional Democracy in the European Union
Edited by Sacha Garben and Inge Govaere

Constitutional Law of the EU's Common Foreign and Security Policy:
Competence and Institutions in External Relations
Graham Butler

The Juridification of Individual Sanctions and the Politics of EU Law
Eva Nanopoulos

Sixty Years of European Integration and Global Power Shifts:
Perceptions, Interactions and Lessons
Edited by Julien Chaisse

Fundamental Rights and Mutual Recognition in the Area of Freedom, Security
and Justice: A Role for Proportionality?
Ermioni Xanthopoulou

Law and Judicial Dialogue on the Return of Irregular Migrants from the European Union
Edited by Madalina Moraru, Galina Cornelisse and Philippe De Bruycker

Framing Convergence with the Global Legal Order: The EU and the World
Edited by Elaine Fahey

EU Citizenship at the Edges of Freedom of Movement
Katarina Hyltén-Cavallius

The Internal Market 2.0
Edited by Sacha Garben and Inge Govaere

For the complete list of titles in this series, see
'Modern Studies in European Law' link at
www.bloomsburyprofessional.com/uk/series/modern-studies-in-european-law

New Directions in European Private Law

Edited by
Mateja Durovic
and
Takis Tridimas

•HART•
OXFORD • LONDON • NEW YORK • NEW DELHI • SYDNEY

HART PUBLISHING
Bloomsbury Publishing Plc
Kemp House, Chawley Park, Cumnor Hill, Oxford, OX2 9PH, UK
1385 Broadway, New York, NY 10018, USA
29 Earlsfort Terrace, Dublin 2, Ireland

HART PUBLISHING, the Hart/Stag logo, BLOOMSBURY and the Diana logo are trademarks of Bloomsbury Publishing Plc

First published in Great Britain 2021

A catalogue record for this book is available from the British Library.

Library of Congress Cataloging-in-Publication data

Names: Future of EU private law (2019 : Dickson Poon School of Law). | Durovic, Mateja, editor. | Tridimas, Takis, editor.

Title: New directions in European private law / edited by Mateja Durovic and Takis Tridimas.

Other titles: Future of European Union private law

Description: Oxford, UK ; New York, NY : Hart Publishing, an imprint of Bloomsbury Publishing, 2021. | Series: Modern studies in European law ; volume 103 | "The contributions to this book are based on papers delivered by leading law scholars and practitioners at the conference 'The future of EU Private Law' held at the Centre of European Law, Dickson Poon School of Law, King's College London, in February 2019"—ECIP introduction. | Includes bibliographical references and index.

Identifiers: LCCN 2021000357 (print) | LCCN 2021000358 (ebook) | ISBN 9781509935611 (hardback) | ISBN 9781509949151 (paperback) | ISBN 9781509935635 (pdf) | ISBN 9781509935628 (Epub)

Subjects: LCSH: Civil law—European Union countries—Congresses.

Classification: LCC KJE994.95 .F88 2021 (print) | LCC KJE994.95 (ebook) | DDC 346.24—dc23

LC record available at https://lccn.loc.gov/2021000357

LC ebook record available at https://lccn.loc.gov/2021000358

ISBN: HB: 978-1-50993-561-1
ePDF: 978-1-50993-563-5
ePub: 978-1-50993-562-8

Typeset by Compuscript Ltd, Shannon

CONTENTS

LIST OF CONTRIBUTORS

Oscar Borgogno, Legal Expert, Directorate General for Economics, Statistics and Research, Bank of Italy and PhD Candidate, University of Turin.

Roger Brownsword, Professor of Law, King's College London and Bournemouth University.

Michel Cannarsa, Professor and Dean of Law, Lyon Catholic University (UCLy) Sciences and Humanities Confluence Research Centre.

Menno Cox, Policy Officer with the Directorate-General for Communications Networks, Content and Technology of the European Commission.

Georgios Dimitropoulos, Associate Professor and Associate Dean for Academic Affairs, HBKU College of Law.

Mateja Durovic, Reader in Contract and Commercial Law and Co Director of the Centre for Technology, Ethics, Law and Society (TELOS), King's College London.

Francisco de Elizalde, Associate Professor, IE Law School, IE University.

Valeria Falce, Jean Monnet Professor in EU Innovation Policy and Professor of Regulation, Competition and Intellectual Property, Università Europea di Roma.

Giusella Finocchiaro, Professor of Private and Internet Law, Alma Mater Studiorum, University of Bologna.

Vassilis Hatzopoulos, Professor of EU Law and Policies, Panteion University, Athens and Visiting Professor, College of Europe, Bruges and Barrister, Athens Bar.

Hans W. Micklitz, Professor of Economic Law, Robert Schuman Centre for Advanced Studies, European University Institute and Finland Distinguished Professor, University of Helsinki.

Cristina Poncibo, Professor of Comparative Private Law, Department of Law, University of Turin.

Andrej Savin, Professor in IT Law and Internet Law at CBS LAW, Copenhagen Business School.

Eileen Sheehan, Référendaire (Legal Secretary), Court of Justice of the European Union.

Takis Tridimas, Professor of European Law and Director of the Centre of European Law, King's College London and Professor and Nancy A. Patterson Distinguished Scholar, Pennsylvania State University.

Introduction

I. Background

After some years of growth, European private law has reached a stage of relative maturity as a distinct area of law that brings together elements of private law, regulation, EU law and comparative law. The adoption of numerous directives and several regulations, as well as the development of interesting (though often unsettling) case law, by the CJEU has contributed to a substantial, albeit incomplete, corpus of law at Union level, the *acquis communautaire*. Maturity, however, does not mean stasis. Amid economic, technological and political developments, European private law is undergoing substantial changes. In particular, the rapid, relentless development of new technologies poses new challenges and requires adjustments in policy consensus. This book explores contemporary challenges, identifies problems and proposes solutions in light of the developments in European private law.

The contributions to this book are based on papers delivered by leading law scholars and practitioners at the conference 'The future of EU Private Law', held at the Centre of European Law, Dickson Poon School of Law, King's College London, in February 2019, organised by Mateja Durovic and Takis Tridimas. The first cluster of essays assess the existing theoretical framework and traditional legal scholarship underpinning European private law. The second group of contributions examine the important and current topics of geo-blocking and standardisation in the context of recent legislative developments and the CJEU case law. A third cluster of essays assess the very challenging task of adequate regulation of the collaborative (sharing) economy and of online platforms, issues which European private law has continuously addressed over recent years. The fourth group of chapters deal with the regulatory challenges brought by an increasing development of artificial intelligence and blockchain technology, and the corresponding question of liability. The final group of essays assess recent European legislative developments in the area of goods and digital content, and identify potential future policy directions in which the European private law may develop in the future.

II. Content

In the opening chapter, **Roger Brownsword** examines the future of European private law in light of the impact emerging technologies have on how lawyers and regulators think and reason. How one responds to technology such as artificial intelligence and machine learning, blockchain and cryptocurrency depends on the responder's mindset. In this respect, the author argues that 'regulatory instrumentalist' and 'technocratic mindsets', ie technology-provoked mindsets, challenge the traditional mindset and give rise to an uneasy coexistence between different fractions of the law community. This uneasy coexistence is formed around three tensions which impact on the use of general principles: the use and fitness of rules and standards; accommodation of conflicting and competing interests; and the recognition of fundamental values. In this chapter, the author acknowledges that technology will play a significant part in shaping the future of EU private law, particularly in a disruptive manner. However, the direction taken by European private law will be shaped by the approaches to the current tensions underpinning the mindset of lawyers and regulators.

Francisco de Elizalde examines the issue of standardisation of agreement in EU law by seeking to prove the existence of a 'mass European contract law' (MEUCL). Here, the author claims that EU law is establishing general rules for the formation of contracts by following a radically new approach to procedural fairness. By analysing key EU legislation and case law, the author argues that EU law is transforming the rules on contract formation and validity through the use of legal standards such as the 'average consumer' rather than consideration of the individual characteristics of the contracting parties. By applying this 'contractual position' approach, the author suggests that the development of core EU rules for the formation of contracts could lead to a harmonised mandatory system of MEUCL and a contract law that is technologically more efficient. According to the author, however, the process of MEUCL is ongoing and fraught with various difficulties and complex issues due to the unresolved extent of the EU's competence to harmonise contract law and the relationship between the roles of EU law and national law. Nonetheless, it is claimed that MEUCL has the potential to reinvigorate, from a new angle, studies on harmonisation of European contract law, including harmonisation by mandatory law and the use of legal standards to deal with the intrinsic complexities of EU law as a pluralistic legal system.

Cristina Poncibo and **Oscar Borgogno** reflect upon the future of private law in a challenging environment in which there is a general distrust in the positive force of the law as a vehicle of integration and thus in the means to achieve a new spirit of pacification, cooperation and solidarity in Europe. In their view, legal scholars should respond to the current challenges and be the driving force of private law in Europe. For this purpose, the chapter focuses on identifying the main 'schools of thought' in European private law and their role in the future development of private law. Using the role of 'integration through law' as a starting point, the authors distinguish between the classical schools, which take for granted the subordination of private law to the construction of EU integration and the internal market, and the modern schools, which reject such subordination and search instead for the foundations of private law in Europe. In this latter context, the chapter reflects on the role played by (behavioural) law and economics, giving weight to the argument that EU private law scholarship is driven by the diversity of perspectives as well as sharing ideas, tools and approaches. By taking stock of and analysing the current confusion, the authors furnish preliminary insights into the approaches that have emerged in European private law scholarship and the new directions needed in the future.

Valeria Falce and **Giusella Finocchiaro** assess the extent to which an effective digital ecosystem requires a combination of competition policy and regulation. To this end, the authors examine how the recent Geo-blocking Regulation 2018/302 works in synergy with EU competition rules, consumer protection, e-commerce regulation and data protection to fully unlock e-commerce in the EU and to shape a single European digital ecosystem. In this respect, the authors focus on the common aims of tackling the problem of market partitioning and avoiding discrimination. Following a comprehensive review of the Geo-blocking Regulation, the authors highlight how and the extent to which EU competition policy, especially as applied by the ECJ and the European Commission, combats geo-blocking practices. In a final step, the authors discuss the interplay between the Geo-blocking Regulation, consumer protection, e-commerce regulation and data protection, in particular from the perspective of non-discrimination. Considering that in many Member States national competition authorities will be in charge of supervision of compliance with the geo-blocking rules (including the imposition of fines), the interplay between competition and regulation is expected to be even more fruitful and successful, and the new provisions against geo-factors are likely to enrich what has been happily defined as a 'smart' economic integration through technology, regulation and competition law, thus confirming the need for a direction which takes a 'circular' and integrated approach in applying regulation and competition policy in the digital datasphere.

Eileen Sheehan analyses how ECJ case law on Directive 98/34 (which is now replaced by Directive 2015/1535) has impacted on private relations. The Directive employed a notification/communication and standstill procedure as a means to prevent national standards and regulations from presenting barriers to trade and is thus key to European integration. In the author's view, the impact of the ECJ case law can be seen, on the one hand, in the context of failures by Member States to comply with the Directive's notification/communication and standstill procedure and, on the other, in the way the ECJ defines information society services and thus the Directive's scope of application. In this latter respect, the definition of information society services greatly affects the rules applicable to new technologies and intermediation services. The author points out that the recent judgments of the ECJ in *Asociación Profesional Elite Taxi, Uber France* and *Airbnb* are expected to have considerable implications for private parties depending on how information society services are interpreted, though further legislation or case law is needed to resolve the issue clearly.

Vassilis Hatzopoulos examines the relationship between European private law and a rapidly developing cultural, social and widely unregulated phenomenon, namely the collaborative economy. Described as a contributing factor to a fourth industrial revolution, particular features of the collaborative economy not only disrupt traditional models and raise new legal issues, but can also cause fragmentation within the EU internal market. In his chapter, the author examines the relationship between features of the collaborative economy and the challenges they present for general principles (eg *effet utile*) and key policy areas of European private law (eg consumer protection and data protection). The author argues that legislative outcomes in the form of lacunary regulation and fragmentation are not conducive to the proper application of EU law but are unavoidable in a field as innovative, dynamic and fast-evolving as the collaborative economy. In this context, the author argues that the general principles of EU law may prove crucial both by allowing existing rules to expand and cover original situations and by informing the content of new rules. Accordingly, EU law may need to create a new general principle, enhanced by the interpretative method of analogy, which would be tuned to technological innovation to build a bridge between old (analogue) and new (digital) realities.

Menno Cox explores how the platform economy will drive the future of European private law by analysing the world's first horizontal platform regulation, EU Regulation 2019/1150. The author proceeds from the premise that the online platform business model is overwhelmingly beneficial and requires further support, including through (harmonised) rule setting – of which Regulation 2019/1150 represents a first important step. The chapter starts by introducing Regulation 2019/1150 against the background of the rise of the 'online platform economy', or simply economy – online intermediation being the new normal. It then describes some unique features of online platforms to underline that they are a truly novel phenomenon that warrant an '*ex novo*' approach to regulation. The central section of the chapter covers the novel interplay between government regulation and private law in the inherently cross-border, and frequently global, online platform economy. The author concludes his contribution with a reflection on the future of European private law by being optimistic about its future developments.

George Dimitropoulos examines various legal issues and responses surrounding a revolutionary technological development: blockchain. Although increasing in importance, the legal framework surrounding is especially complex as blockchain not only transcends various different traditional categories of law but also gives rise to a new kind of legal system known as the *lex crytographia*. Accordingly, the author discusses the idea of a new blockchain law, which will serve to enable public and permissionless blockchain, establish new foundations of trust in society, and achieve new interoperability functions between the public and the private, as well as the physical and the digital, world. In the chapter, the author focuses on the nature of the interactions and different phases of development between blockchain technology and the laws of the analogue and digital worlds. A blurred picture emerges of a complex interaction between multiple areas of law, self-regulation and external regulation by ordinary law, which will require the EU to develop new types of laws in order to protect its citizens from the risks of blockchain technology whilst not stifling technological innovation.

Michel Cannarsa addresses the relationship and suitability of national and EU rules governing civil liability to tackle challenges posed by new technologies. Although often overlooked, new technologies pose a variety of challenges and questions for civil liability. If left unanswered, market fragmentation, legal uncertainty and lack of consumer protection would potentially emerge. The chapter considers several core questions, which stem from the underlying issue of whether the legal basis and provisions established by the rules in question in the various Member States and at EU level are fit for the changes under way. In seeking to answer these questions, the author puts forward a number of principles and methods of analysis with a view to identifying some avenues leading towards concrete solutions. In this respect, a response by the EU would offer an environment that would be favourable to the development of new technologies in Europe but would revive thinking on the harmonisation of private law, given that many aspects of it may be affected by the emergence of new technologies.

Andrej Savin examines the broader question of the relationship between private law and the regulation of the Digital Single Market. Using two new EU directives – Directive 2019/770 and Directive 2019/771 on certain aspects concerning contracts for the sale of goods – as a basis, the author questions the extent to which harmonised private law can contribute to achieving the EU Digital Single Market, more specifically its adequacy for addressing problems in the digital world and its ability to adapt to new technology. In the modern world, which moves forward at frightening speed, it may be questioned whether further civil law instruments are needed or what their purpose might be. It is equally important to pose the question whether full harmonisation is preferable to a partial, consumer law-driven approach. At the same time, new developments such as the use of artificial intelligence and the emergence of a data-based economy inevitably challenge the foundations of the traditional law of obligations; they require the rethinking of fundamental concepts such as offer and acceptance, and thus question the extent and role of harmonised EU private law in the digital world.

In the concluding chapter, **Hans Micklitz** adopts different perspectives to approach the fundamental question of the direction(s) that European private law should take. The author begins by presenting seven possible directions, ranging from conceptual to doctrinal, and from technological to ecological, and viewing European private law in each of these contexts. In a second step, the author addresses the development of European private law scholarship, identifying three distinct phases, but hinging the success of the search for new directions on self-critical legal scholarship. In a third step, the author reflects on the role of European private law as European economic law. On the basis of the contributions to this volume, the author identifies three different options to handle the search for a self-critical direction in European private law as European economic law. Moreover, the author proposes a particular methodology and technique that could serve as a starting point for considering possible 'new directions': identifying the different constituent elements in the pre- and post-contractual stages of a contract shows how the EU uses not only private law, but also codes of conducts and technical standards. Although the search for new directions depends on who is searching for what, the author reinforces the critical role that legal scholars will play in the future direction of European private law.

1

Political Disruption, Technological Disruption and the Future of EU Private Law

ROGER BROWNSWORD

I. Introduction

For Europeans, these are challenging times. According to Guido Montani, the surge in populist politics reflects a widespread sense of discontent about the EU's ability 'to offer a credible response to the challenges of globalisation, the rise of multinationals, new technologies and uncontrolled migration flows'.[1] In this unsettled context, while we cannot predict the future of European law with any degree of confidence, we can be confident that its future will be shaped, to a considerable extent, by the ways in which Europeans respond to these challenges, including the ways in which, both within and without the EU, they respond to Brexit.[2]

Against this background, the focus of this chapter is on the challenges presented to Europeans by emerging technologies – technologies such as artificial intelligence (AI) and machine learning, robotics, blockchain and cryptocurrencies. In the recent past, Europeans have found themselves seriously divided about the regulation of biotechnologies (concerning both genetically modified organisms and human genetics),[3] and it seems likely that the latest raft of technologies will generate further divisions, particularly about the extent to which it is acceptable to

[1] G Montani, 'Social Discontent and Democracy in the EU' (*Social Europe*, 19 February 2019, www.socialeurope.eu/democracy-in-the-eu). On the last of these elements ('uncontrolled migration flows'), cp D Murray, *The Strange Death of Europe* (London, Bloomsbury, 2018) 8, arguing that 'while the likelihood of cultural erosion remains irresistible the options for cultural defence continue to be unacceptable'.

[2] See, eg C MacMillan, 'The Impact of Brexit upon English Contract Law' (2016) 27 *King's Law Journal* 420; for a range of Brexit-related questions, see the special issue of the *King's Law Journal* (volume 27, issue 3).

[3] See R Brownsword, *Rights, Regulation and the Technological Revolution* (Oxford, Oxford University Press, 2008).

take humans out of the loop by automating processes in health, criminal justice, financial services and so on.

Although the future of law in Europe will surely be shaped by the nature of the responses to these new technologies, this chapter is specifically about the likely trajectory of EU private law;[4] and, in particular, it is about the disruptive impact of technologies on the ways in which lawyers and regulators think and reason. The central point is that the 'coherentist' way in which private lawyers traditionally think and reason is already, and will continue to be, challenged by two technology-provoked mindsets – one of these mindsets is 'regulatory instrumentalist', the other more 'technocratic'. There is currently an uneasy coexistence between these mindsets – not so much an uneasy coexistence between the technology community and the law community,[5] but between and within different fractions of the law community itself.

This uneasy coexistence is formed around the following three tensions. First, there is a tension between traditional coherentist reasoning (which is characteristic of private law and centres on the application of general legal principles) and regulatory instrumentalist thinking (which is guided by whether the law is fit for purpose and centres on serving regulatory policies). The second tension is between legal reasoning, which relies on rules and standards as its regulatory instruments, and regulatory reasoning, which relies on technological instruments and technical solutions. The latter reasoning goes beyond raising questions about the fitness for purpose of particular rules of private law; it raises the question of whether the rules and standards themselves are fit for purpose as regulatory instruments. The third tension, introducing a further dimension of difference, is between a regulatory approach that engages with a plurality of conflicting and competing interests by seeking out a reasonable balance or an acceptable accommodation of those interests and a renewed form of (constitutional) coherentism that cross-checks the integrity of regulatory interventions relative to fundamental values.

While no one will doubt that technology will play a significant part in shaping the future of EU private law, this chapter highlights three areas to watch: first, the extent to which traditional coherentist thinking survives in the face of digital market-making regulatory instrumentalist thinking – and, concomitantly, whether revisions to the rules reflect a coherentist adjustment or a regulatory instrumentalist correction; secondly, whether the rules of private law are superseded by technological instruments and solutions; and, thirdly, whether a renewed coherentism, supporting distinctively European basic values (such as respect for human rights and human dignity), is able to stand its ground against a technocratic instrumentalism that defaults to balancing, accommodation and underlying utilitarian efficiency.

[4] I am treating 'private law' as that part of the law that relates to relations, interactions and transactions between private citizens.

[5] K Yeung, 'Regulation by Blockchain: The Emerging Battle for Supremacy between the Code of Law and Code as Law' (2019) 82 *MLR* 207.

The chapter is in three parts: first, I deal with the tension between traditional coherentist and regulatory instrumentalist reasoning; next, I focus on the tension between rule-based regulatory thinking and regulatory thinking that relies on technological instruments; and, finally, I consider the tension between a renewed coherentism and a technocratic approach that flattens interests and is underwritten by utilitarian reasoning.

II. The First Tension

Technological developments in the last two centuries have provoked a number of revisions and corrections to a transactional model of contract law that is predicated on a subjective meeting of minds and gives effect to the intentions of the parties. First, subjectivism gave way to a more objective approach; secondly, reasonableness impinged on intention; and, thirdly, the public policy limits on freedom of contract were materially extended.[6] Thus, when contract law abandoned a pure transactional theory of contractual rights and obligations in favour of an objective theory of agreement, this served to shield carriers against otherwise crippling claims for compensation (when valuable packages were lost or when there were accidents on the railways); and when, in the middle years of the last century, a mass consumer market for new technological products (cars, televisions, kitchen appliances and so on) was developing, a fundamental correction to freedom and sanctity of contract was needed to protect consumers against the small print of suppliers' standard terms and conditions.

While these modifications to the law reflected some disturbance to the surface of legal doctrine, a deeper disruption was also taking place. This deeper disruption was to traditional coherentist thinking, for coherentism now found itself in tension with a quite different form of legal reasoning – one that was represented by regulatory instrumentalist thinking.[7] These two forms of legal thinking and the tension between them are elaborated in this part of the chapter.

A. Coherentism

For present purposes, we can treat coherentist thinking as being defined by the following five characteristics.[8]

[6] cp R Brownsword, 'Remedy-Stipulation in the English Law of Contract: Freedom or Paternalism?' (1977) 9 *Ottawa Law Review* 95; R Brownsword, *Contract Law: Themes for the Twenty-First Century* (Oxford, Oxford University Press, 2006).

[7] For a fine example of principled contractual thinking (concerning the doctrine of privity of contract) coming into tension with regulatory reasoning (concerning the need to protect the railway companies), see C MacMillan, 'The Mystery of Privity: *Grand Trunk Railway Company of Canada v Robinson* (1915)' (2015) 65 *University of Toronto Law Journal* 1.

[8] See R Brownsword, 'After Brexit: Regulatory Instrumentalism, Coherentism, and the English Law of Contract' (2018) 35 *Journal of Contract Law* 139.

First, for coherentists, what matters above all is the integrity and internal consistency of legal doctrine. This is viewed as desirable in and of itself. Secondly, coherentists are not concerned with the fitness of the law for its regulatory purpose. Thirdly, coherentists approach new technologies by asking how they fit within existing legal categories (and then try hard to fit them in). Fourthly, coherentists believe that legal reasoning should be anchored to guiding general principles of law. In the case of questions about the enforcement or non-enforcement of transactions, the foundational principles are that parties should be free to make their own deals and that it is the fact that parties have freely agreed to a deal that justifies holding them to the bargain. Fifthly, the function of private law, together with its guiding principles, is largely concerned with ex post correction and compensation.

Coherentism is thus the natural language of litigators and judges, who seek to apply the law in a principled way.[9] It is also the default mode of thinking for many lawyers who take it that being trained 'to think like a lawyer' is synonymous with being trained to apply general principles of law to situations and phenomena both familiar and novel.[10]

So, for example, developments in modern biotechnology have raised questions about the patentability of products and processes the working of which cannot be demonstrated by taking model machines into patent offices;[11] and these same developments, like developments in both information technology and blockchain, have raised questions about the way in which fundamental concepts and distinctions in property law map onto a range of 'things', such as cell lines,[12] gametes,[13] personal data[14] and cryptoassets.[15]

[9] For a somewhat similar view, presented as a 'legalistic approach' to emerging technologies, see N Petit, 'Law and Regulation of Artificial Intelligence and Robots: Conceptual Framework and Normative Implications', https://papers.ssrn.com/sol3/papers.cfm?abstract_id=2931339.

[10] Compare the much-debated view in FH Easterbrook, 'Cyberspace and the Law of the Horse' [1996] *University of Chicago Legal Forum* 207. For my take on this, see R Brownsword, 'Law Disrupted, Law Re-imagined, Law Re-invented' (2019) 1 *Technology and Regulation* 10. On refocusing both legal teaching and legal scholarship, see R Brownsword, 'Teaching the Law of Contract in a World of New Transactional Technologies' in W Swain and D Campbell (eds), *Reimagining Contract Law Pedagogy: A New Agenda for Teaching (Legal Pedagogy)* (Abingdon, Routledge, 2019) 112; R Brownsword, '3D Printing, Transformative Technologies, and Responsive Legal Scholarship' in D Mendis, M Lemley and M Rimmer (eds), *3D Printing and Beyond: The Intellectual Property and Legal Implications Surrounding 3D Printing and Emerging Technology* (Cheltenham, Edward Elgar Publishing, 2019) 137.

[11] A Pottage and B Sherman, *Figures of Invention: A History of Modern Patent Law* (Oxford, Oxford University Press, 2010).

[12] Famously, see the John Moore case, *Moore v Regents of the University of California* 51 Cal 3d 120; 271 Cal Rptr 146; 793 P2d 479. For a discussion of *Moore* and subsequent cases on the same point, see R Brownsword, 'Property in Human Tissue: Triangulating the Issue' in M Steinman, P Sykora and U Wiesing (eds), *Altruism Reconsidered: Exploring New Approaches to Property in Human Tissue* (Aldershot, Ashgate, 2009) 93. Generally, see RT Hardcastle, *Law and the Human Body: Property Rights, Ownership and Control* (Oxford, Hart Publishing, 2007).

[13] See *Yearworth v North Bristol NHS Trust* [2009] EWCA Civ 37.

[14] See, eg the argument in J Lanier, *Who Owns the Future?* (New York, Simon & Schuster, 2013).

[15] See, eg KFK Low and EGS Teo, 'Bitcoins and Other Cryptocurrencies as Property?' (2017) 9 *Law, Innovation and Technology* 235.

However, according to Edward Rubin, the days of coherentism are numbered. Nowadays, Rubin claims, we live in the age of modern administrative states where the law is used 'as a means of implementing the policies that [each particular state] adopts. The rules that are declared, and the statutes that enact them, have no necessary relationship with one another; they are all individual and separate acts of will.'[16] In the modern administrative state, the 'standard for judging the value of law is not whether it is coherent but rather whether it is effective, that is, effective in establishing and implementing the policy goals of the modern state'.[17]

In contrast to such modern regulatory thinking, coherentism presupposes a world of, at most, leisurely change. It is not geared for making agile responses to rapidly emerging and highly disruptive technologies. When they are called on to respond to new technological developments, lawyers who reason like coherentists tend to try to classify the new phenomena within existing legal categories. For example, while the initial response to embryonic e-commerce was clearly driven by a regulatory concern that e-transactions should be legally recognised and supported, there was, and still is, a distinctly coherentist response that tries to apply the legal template for offline contracts and the principles of contract law to the emerging world of online transactions.[18]

Similarly, in the case of blockchain, one of the principal topics of coherentist conversation is whether a smart contract is to be regarded as, in principle, a legally enforceable contract (as per the law of contract).[19] To be sure, some of the examples that might be given to illustrate the nature of smart contracts do not sit easily with the template for fiat contracts. Nevertheless, even with unhelpful examples out of the way, there will still be some puzzlement. In particular, coherentists will wonder where we find the offer, the acceptance and the consideration when all that we have is a piece of software that is coded to transfer a specified value from A's wallet to B's wallet on the occurrence of some specified event. Moreover, because the technology is designed to guarantee that, on the occurrence of the specified event, the value is duly transferred from A to B, coherentists will wonder whether it is possible to apply doctrines that allow for the avoidance of a transaction – for example, doctrines such as duress and undue influence, or misrepresentation – to a smart contract; or how, in the event that the technology fails to perform, we should

[16] E Rubin, 'From Coherence to Effectiveness' in R van Gestel, H-W Micklitz and EL Rubin (eds), *Rethinking Legal Scholarship* (New York, Cambridge University Press, 2017) 311.

[17] ibid 328.

[18] For a discussion, see R Brownsword, 'The e-Commerce Directive, Consumer Transactions, and the Digital Single Market: Questions of Regulatory Fitness, Regulatory Disconnection and Rule Redirection' in S Grundmann (ed), *European Contract Law in the Digital Age* (Antwerp, Intersentia, 2017) 165.

[19] See R Brownsword, 'Regulatory Fitness: Fintech, Funny Money, and Smart Contracts' (2019) 20 *European Business Organization Law Review* 5; R Brownsword, 'Smart Contracts: Coding the Transaction, Decoding the Legal Debates' in Philipp Hacker, Ioannis Lianos, Georgios Dimitropoulos and Stefan Eich (eds) *Regulating Blockchain: Techno-Social and Legal Challenges* (Oxford, Oxford University Press, 2019) 311. Generally, see P De Filippi and A Wright, *Blockchain and the Law* (Cambridge, MA, Harvard University Press, 2018) 74 et seq.

determine whether there has been a breach (and, if so, how we are to decide upon the nature of the breach and the appropriate remedy).[20] Furthermore, coherentists will doubt that a smart contract can be viewed as a contract when the terms and conditions are not written in natural language and when there are no humans in the blockchain loop. To the coherentist, the idea that a smart contract can be likened to an agreement for the supply of goods or services (the staple of the law of contract) will be perplexing indeed.[21]

B. Regulatory Instrumentalism

In contrast with coherentism, we can treat regulatory instrumentalism as being defined by the following six features.[22]

First, as Rubin explains, regulatory instrumentalism is not concerned with the internal consistency of legal doctrine. When regulatory instrumentalists raise questions about consistency, they are typically making sure that particular regulatory interventions will complement others in serving specified regulatory objectives.[23] Secondly, it is entirely focused on whether the law is instrumentally effective in serving specified regulatory purposes. Regulatory instrumentalists do not ask whether the law is 'coherent' – other than in the sense of asking whether a group of related interventions pushes in the required regulatory direction – but whether it works. Thirdly, regulatory instrumentalism has no reservation about enacting new bespoke laws if this is an effective and efficient response to a question raised by new technologies. Fourthly, the anchoring points for regulatory instrumentalists are not the general principles that are established in the jurisprudence, but current policy purposes and objectives. It follows that, for regulatory instrumentalists, the enforcement or non-enforcement of transactions should turn on how the options stand relative to relevant regulatory purposes; and the justification for taking one option rather than the other is that this is judged to be in line with regulatory policy. Fifthly, alongside its policy focus, regulatory instrumentalism in relation to new technologies tends to be orientated towards striking an acceptable balance between benefits and risks. Sixthly, the risk-management mindset that goes with regulatory instrumentalism is geared towards ex ante prevention rather than ex post correction.

[20] Compare the UK Jurisdiction Taskforce of the LawTech Delivery Panel's consultation paper on 'The Status of Cryptoassets, Distributed Ledger Technology and Smart Contracts under English Private Law' (May 2019) para 3.2: 'if smart contracts are capable of giving rise to binding legal obligations, it will be important for parties to be aware of the circumstances in which this will be the case (notably if the parties' intention is not to create legal relations). It will also be important for parties to know if and how their rights might be enforced in the event that technology does not work as expected.'

[21] See, eg the discussion in K Werbach and N Cornell, 'Contracts *Ex Machina*' (2017) 67 *Duke Law Journal* 313, 338 et seq.

[22] For other dimensions of coherentism, see Brownsword 'After Brexit' (n 8).

[23] See, eg the European Commission's remarks in the Explanatory Memorandum to the proposal for a new copyright Directive, COM (2016) 593 final, 3–4; see also the concluding remarks on coherence in the European Commission's Staff Working Document, SWD (2017) 209 final, s 7.3.

Regulatory instrumentalism is thus the (democratically) mandated language of legislators, policy-makers and regulatory agencies.[24] Conversely, while judges might have some responsibility for applying the spirit of policy-driven legislation, it is precisely the setting of regulatory policy that we think falls beyond the mandate of unaccountable judges.[25]

From the industrial revolution onwards – at any rate, in the common law world – the direction of travel in criminal law, torts and contracts has been away from coherentism and towards regulatory instrumentalism. While intentionality and fault were set aside in the regulatory parts of criminal law and torts, as we have already noted, classical transactionalist ('meeting of the minds') ideas of consent and agreement were marginalised, being replaced in the mainstream of contract law by 'objective' tests and standards set by reasonable business practice. As Morton Horwitz puts it, there was a dawning sense that 'all law was a reflection of collective determination, and thus inherently regulatory and coercive'.[26]

What we see across these developments is a pattern of disruption to legal doctrines that were organically expressed in smaller-scale non-industrialised communities. Here, the legal rules presuppose very straightforward ideas about holding to account those who engage intentionally in injurious or dishonest acts, about expecting others to act with reasonable care and about holding others to their word. Once new technologies disrupt these ideas, we see the move to strict or absolute criminal liability without proof of intent, to tortious liability without proof of fault and to contractual liability (or limitation of liability) without proof of actual intent, agreement or consent. Even if the development in contract is less clear at this stage, in both criminal law and torts we can see the early signs of a risk management approach to liability. Moreover, we also see the early signs of doctrinal bifurcation, with some parts of criminal law, tort law and contract law resting on traditional principles (and representing, so to speak, 'real' crime, tort and contract), while others deviate from these principles – often holding enterprises to account more readily, but also sometimes easing the burden on business for the sake of beneficial innovation[27] – in order to strike a more acceptable balance of the benefits and risks that technological development brings with it.

[24] For example, the UK Financial Conduct Authority is conspicuously sensitised to 'reg tech' (in the sense of utilising information technologies to enhance regulatory processes with a particular emphasis on monitoring, reporting and compliance): see FCA Press Release, 'FCA Launches Call for Input on the Use of Technology to Achieve Smarter Regulatory Reporting' (20 February 2018), www.fca.org.uk/news/press-releases/fca-launches-call-input-use-technology-achieve-smarter-regulatory-reporting.

[25] Seminally, see R Dworkin, *Taking Rights Seriously*, rev edn (London, Duckworth, 1978); cp S Waddams, *Principle and Policy in Contract Law – Competing or Complementary Concepts?* (Cambridge, Cambridge University Press, 2011).

[26] MJ Horwitz, *The Transformation of American Law 1870–1960* (Oxford, Oxford University Press, 1992) 50.

[27] For example, in the United States, the interests of the farming community were subordinated to the greater good promised by the development of the railroad network: see MJ Horwitz, *The Transformation of American Law 1780–1860* (Cambridge, MA, Harvard University Press, 1977).

For regulatory instrumentalists, the basic question is: what works, what will serve certain specified purposes? When a regulatory intervention does not work, it is not enough to restore the status quo; rather, further regulatory measures should be taken, learning from previous experience, with a view to realising the regulatory purposes more effectively. Hence, the purpose of the criminal law is not simply to respond to wrongdoing (as corrective justice demands), but to reduce crime by adopting whatever measures of deterrence promise to work.[28] Similarly, in a safety-conscious community, the purpose of tort law is not simply to respond to wrongdoing, but to deter practices and acts where agents could easily avoid creating risks of injury and damage. For regulatory instrumentalists, the path of the law should be progressive: we should be getting better at regulating crime and improving levels of safety.[29]

While the simple idea of holding co-contractors to their word was still central to much trading in the last century, as I have said, this needed to be qualified in the embryonic consumer markets for cars, electrical appliances, package holidays and so on. Here, there was widespread legislative intervention to ensure that the balance between the interests of suppliers and the interests of consumers was fair and reasonable.[30] Moreover, the correction that was already underway in English law was consolidated by a stream of EC directives recognising a raft of consumer rights.[31] Today, at any rate in English law, following the Consumer Rights Act 2015, we can say that consumers engage not so much in contracts as in regulated transactions; that there is a clear bifurcation between the treatment of commercial (business to business) contracts and consumer contracts; and that this latter branch of the law is dominated by a regulatory instrumentalist mindset.

Turning to today's emerging transactional technologies, a regulatory instrumentalist conversation will not focus (as is the case with a coherentist approach) on the application of the general principles of the law of contract to smart contracts. Rather, against the backcloth of relevant economic and social policies, the conversation will seek to identify the potential benefits and risks of committing transactions (or parts of transactions) to a blockchain and regulators will

[28] cp David Garland, *The Culture of Control: Crime and Social Order in Contemporary Society* (Oxford, Oxford University Press, 2001); A Marks, B Bowling and C Keenan, 'Automatic Justice? Technology, Crime, and Social Control' in R Brownsword, E Scotford and K Yeung (eds), *The Oxford Handbook of Law, Regulation and Technology* (Oxford, Oxford University Press, 2017) 705.

[29] The parallel development of a risk-management ideology in both criminal law and tort is noted by M Feeley and J Simon, 'Actuarial Justice: The Emerging New Criminal Law' in D Nelken (ed), *The Futures of Criminology* (London, Sage, 1994) 173.

[30] cp H Collins, *The European Civil Code* (Cambridge, Cambridge University Press, 2008) 26: 'Instead of talking about *caveat emptor* (let the buyer beware) as in the past, today we speak of ensuring that consumers receive good-quality goods that meet their expectations in return for a fair competitive price.'

[31] Directives have been issued dealing with such matters as doorstep selling, consumer credit, product liability, package holidays, unfair terms in consumer contracts, distance selling, and the sale of consumer goods and associated guarantees.

then strive to find an acceptable balance between management of the risks and not stifling enterprise. In other words, the challenge is to find the regulatory sweet spot, neither over-regulating (and stifling innovation) nor under-regulating and exposing parties to unacceptable risks.[32]

C. Tension, Coexistence and the Direction of Travel

Although there is a tension between coherentist and regulatory instrumentalist approaches, they can coexist. For example, Christian Twigg-Flesner has noted both coherentist (contract principles) and regulatory instrumentalist (market-making) elements in the proposed (and now adopted) Regulation on business-to-business (B2B) platforms;[33] and in the much-debated General Data Protection Regulation (GDPR),[34] we might detect a fault line that separates a traditional (coherentist) reliance on the consent of the data subject (which implies transactionalist thinking) and a much more regulatory balancing of the interests of data subjects with the legitimate interests of others in accessing and processing personal data. Nevertheless, where different logics are in play, there will be cases where the tension leads to some uncertainty and turbulence in private law doctrine.[35]

What is the direction of travel here? From a long time ago, my reading of the Commission's mindset is that it is essentially regulatory instrumental – first the Commission's primary policy focus was the making of the European Single Market and now it is the making of the Digital Single Market; in both phases, the interests and rights of consumers are secondary to the primary objective. It is precisely because the Commission's approach is so regulatory that it has caused tensions with the coherentist traditions of Member States – here, we might recall the familiar complaint made by EU private lawyers that too many directives have sliced into national legal cultures without any regard for their integrity.[36] The EU is not just a multilevel legal system: it brings national coherentist and regional

[32] Compare the excellent discussion of the regulation of 'TechFins' in DA Zetzsche, RP Buckley, DW Arner and JN Barberis, 'From FinTech to TechFin: The Regulatory Challenges of Data-Driven Finance' (European Banking Institute, 2017) EBI Working Paper Series 2017 – No 6, 31 et seq.

[33] Regulation (EU) 2019/1150: on which, see C Twigg-Flesner, 'The EU's Proposals for Regulating B2B Relationships on Online Platforms: Transparency, Fairness and Beyond' (2018) 7 *Journal of European Consumer and Market Law* 222. See, too, D Mendis, 'In Pursuit of Clarity: The Conundrum of CAD Software and Copyright – Seeking Direction through Case Law' (2018) 40 *European Intellectual Property Law Review* 694.

[34] Regulation (EU) 2016/679.

[35] cp R Brownsword, R van Gestel and H-W Micklitz, 'Contract and Regulation: Changing Paradigms' in R Brownsword, R van Gestel and H-W Micklitz (eds), *Contract and Regulation* (Cheltenham, Edward Elgar Publishing, 2017) 1; R Brownsword, 'Automated Transactions and the Law of Contract: When Codes Are Not Congruent' (Routledge 2020) ch 6.

[36] See, eg L Niglia, *The Transformation of Contract in Europe* (The Hague, Kluwer Law International, 2002); W van Gerven, 'Private Law in a Federal Perspective' in R Brownsword, H-W Micklitz, L Niglia and S Weatherill (eds), *The Foundations of European Private Law* (Oxford, Hart Publishing, 2011) 337.

regulatory instrumentalist thinking into acute and chronic tension.[37] The direction of travel, it seems, is towards more regulatory instrumentalism.[38]

III. The Second Tension

Shortly before Christmas 2018, an unauthorised drone was sighted in the vicinity of the airfield at the London Gatwick airport. As a precautionary measure, all flights were suspended, and, for two days, the airport was closed.[39] Following this incident, some exhorted the government to change the rules, particularly by providing for an extended drone no-fly zone around airports – in response to which, the government announced that the police would be given new powers to tackle illegal drone use,[40] and that the drone no-fly zone would be extended to three miles around airports.[41] Others, however, focused, not on fixing the rules, but on the possibility of finding a technological fix, ideally one that rendered it impossible in practice for a drone to be flown near an airport (or, failing that, a technology for disabling and bringing down unauthorised drones).[42]

Similarly, in its recent White Paper on the regulation of harmful online content – ranging broadly across content that is harmful to national security, to politicians, to children and so on – the UK government has outlined a two-pronged strategy.[43] While one prong of the proposed response focuses on rendering the rules fit for purpose in the digital age (notably by establishing a new statutory duty of care on Internet companies 'to take reasonable steps to keep their users safe and tackle illegal and harmful activity on their services'[44]), the other prong aspires to make 'technology itself [a] … part of the solution'.[45]

In these two responses, focusing on both rule changes and technological solutions, we see the disruption of law represented in two ways. First, there is the thought that the rules are not fit for (regulatory) purpose, this reflecting a sense

[37] cp R Michaels, 'Of Islands and the Ocean: The Two Rationalities of European Private Law' in Brownsword et al (ibid) 139, esp 144–49 (contrasting the ideal-type of 'juridical private law' with that of 'instrumentalist private law').

[38] See, eg the Commission, 'A New Deal for Consumers' (Communication) COM (2018) 183 final.

[39] See, eg 'Gatwick Airport: How Countries Counter the Drone Threat' (*BBC News*, 21 December 2018), www.bbc.co.uk/news/technology-46639099.

[40] See 'Police to Get New Powers to Tackle Illegal Drone Use' (*BBC News*, 7 January 2019) www.bbc.co.uk/news/uk-46787730.

[41] See 'Drone No-Fly Zone to Be Widened after Gatwick Chaos' (*BBC News*, 20 February 2019) www.bbc.co.uk/news/business-47299805.

[42] It has also been reported that the Home Office is testing new counter-drone technologies (see n 40).

[43] HM Government, *Online Harms White Paper* (CP No 57, April 2019).

[44] ibid 42 (para 3.1).

[45] ibid 6 (para 10) – so, eg at 13 (para 1.12) we read that it is 'vital to ensure that there is the technology in place to automatically detect and remove terrorist content within an hour of upload, secure the prevention of re-upload and prevent, where possible, new content being made available to users at all'. For the various ways in which the government proposes to encourage the search for technological solutions, see Part 4 of the White Paper.

of the inadequacy of existing legal rules. Secondly, there is the thought that the most effective regulatory response might be to rely on technological instruments rather than rules, this being at odds with the assumption that social order is to be maintained by the use of rules (and, concomitantly, heightening our appreciation of the potential use of both technological instruments other than legal rules and smart machines rather than human agents). If the former views technology as a disruptive problem, the latter sees technology as part of the solution. If the former is characteristic of disruption that goes back to the early years of industrialisation, the latter is more characteristic of the new millennium.

In this part of the chapter, I focus on the tension between regulatory thinking, which relies on rules and standards as its instruments to channel and direct human conduct, and regulatory thinking, which relies on technological instruments, first in support of rules and standards, but then superseding rules and standards as it assumes the form of technological management. I start with the spectrum of techno-regulation and then address technological management at the hard end of this spectrum.

A. The Spectrum of Techno-regulation

Famously, Lawrence Lessig drew a contrast between the regulatory (rule-based) style of the East Coast (of the United States) and the regulatory (technology-based) style of the West Coast.[46] To this, we should add the contrast between tools that might play an assistive or advisory role (for both regulators and regulatees) and tools that take over and constitute the regulatory environment.[47]

West Coast-style techno-regulation can be charted on a spectrum running from soft to hard.[48] At the soft end of the spectrum, the technologies are employed in support of the legal rules. For example, the use of surveillance technologies and/or identification technologies signals that rule-breaking is more likely to be detected; other things being equal, compliance with the rules is assisted and encouraged; but the strategy is still rule-based and the practical option of non-compliance remains. By contrast, at the hard end of the spectrum, the focus and the ambition are different. Here, measures of 'technological management' focus on limiting the practical (not the paper) options of regulatees;[49] and, whereas legal rules back their prescriptions with ex post penal, compensatory or restorative measures, the focus of technological management is entirely ex ante, aiming to anticipate and prevent

[46] Seminally, see L Lessig, *Code and Other Laws of Cyberspace* (New York, Basic Books, 1999). See, too, R Brownsword, 'Code, Control, and Choice: Why East Is East and West Is West' (2005) 25 *Legal Studies* 1.

[47] See, eg M Hildebrandt, 'Legal and Technological Normativity: More (and Less) than Twin Sisters' (2008) 12(3) *Techné* 169.

[48] See, eg P O'Malley, 'The Politics of Mass Preventive Justice' in A Ashworth, L Zedner and P Tomlin (eds), *Prevention and the Limits of the Criminal Law* (Oxford, Oxford University Press, 2013) 273.

[49] See, eg R Brownsword, 'Law, Liberty and Technology' in Brownsword et al (n 28) 41.

'wrongdoing' (in the sense of acts that are contrary to the regulatory purposes) rather than punish or compensate after the event. As Lee Bygrave has put it in the context of the design of information systems and the protection of both intellectual property rights and privacy, the assumption is that, by embedding norms in the architecture, there is 'the promise of a significantly increased *ex ante* application of the norms and a corresponding reduction in relying on their application *ex post facto*'.[50]

This evolution in regulatory thinking is not surprising. Having recognised the limited fitness of traditional legal rules, and having taken a more regulatory approach, the next step surely is not just to think in terms of risk assessment and risk management, but also to be mindful of the technological instruments that increasingly become available for use by regulators. In this way, the regulatory mindset is focused not only on the risks to be managed, but also on how best to manage those risks (including making use of technological tools).

For example, when individuals operate in online environments, they are at risk in relation to both their 'privacy' and the fair processing of their personal data. Initially, regulators assumed that 'transactionalism' would suffice to protect individuals: in other words, it was assumed that, unless the relevant individuals agreed to, or consented to, the processing of their details, it would not be lawful. However, once it was evident that consumers in online environments routinely signalled their agreement or consent in a mechanical way, without doing so on a free and informed basis, a more robust risk-management approach invited consideration. Such an approach might still be rule-based, but the management might also be technological. In other words, once we are thinking about the protection of the autonomy of Internet users or about the protection of their privacy, why not also consider the use of technological instruments in service of the regulatory objectives? Indeed, in Europe, this is just what we find in the GDPR and, similarly, in the new Copyright Directive.[51] While talk of 'privacy enhancing technologies' and 'privacy by design' has been around for some time,[52] in the GDPR we see that this is more than talk; it is not just that the regulatory discourse is more technocratic, there are signs that this particular form of disruption is beginning to impact on regulatory practice.

[50] LA Bygrave, 'Hardwiring Privacy' in Brownsword et al (n 28) 754, 755.

[51] Regulation (EU) 2016/679. See, eg Recital 78, which enjoins data controllers to take 'appropriate technical and organisational measures' to ensure that the requirements of the Regulation are met; similarly, in the body of the GDPR, see Art 25 (concerning data protection by design and by default); Art 17 of Directive 2019/790 (where content recognition technologies and further development of such technologies are treated as central to cooperative arrangements between copyright holders and information society service providers).

[52] See Bygrave (n 50); A Cavoukian, *Privacy by Design: The Seven Foundational Principles*, rev edn (Information and Privacy Commissioner of Ontario, 2011), www.ipc.on.ca/images/Resources/7foundationalprinciples.pdf. Compare, too, the highly relevant argument for a design agenda for privacy law in W Hartzog, *Privacy's Blueprint* (Cambridge, MA, Harvard University Press, 2018), which comes down to the 'one simple idea [that] the design of popular technologies is critical to privacy, and the law should take it more seriously' (7).

With artificial intelligence (AI) tools now coming onto the radar, there promises to be a significant enhancement in the regulatory repertoire. Accordingly, we need to be alert to the transition from soft to hard use of these new instruments. The key indicators here include: whether AI tools merely assist humans (for example, to help regulatees to be clear about the legal position specified by a regime of rules[53]) or whether they take over the functions of the rules; whether humans are still in the loop or not; and whether AI is employed in the service of ex ante prevention rather than traditional ex post correction. The more that regulatory processes are automated, the less that humans are in the loop and the more that the focus shifts to prevention and pre-emption, the thicker the technological wedge becomes.[54]

If this is the direction of travel, the regulation of markets and private relationships will not just become more intense and micromanaged; it will become increasingly technologically mediated and technologically managed rather than reliant on rules.

B. Technological Management

In response to the demand that 'there needs to be a law against this' or the complaint that the law is not fit for purpose, the technocratic mindset, rather than drafting new rules, looks for technological solutions. Such a mindset was nicely captured by Joshua Fairfield when, writing in the context of non-negotiable terms and conditions in online consumer contracts, he remarked that 'if courts [or, we might say, the rules of contract law] will not protect consumers, robots will'.[55]

We should not assume, however, that technocratic solutions will be accepted without resistance. Famously, in the USA, a proposal to design vehicles so that cars were simply immobilised if seat belts were not worn was eventually rejected.[56] Although the (US) Department of Transportation estimated that the so-called interlock system would save 7000 lives per annum and prevent 340,000 injuries,

[53] See, eg B Alarie, 'The Path of the Law: Toward Legal Singularity' (2016) 66 *University of Toronto Law Journal* 443 (on the question of whether a worker will be classified as an employee or as an independent contractor). For an application of new technological tools to the regulation of unfair terms in consumer contracts, see H-W Micklitz, P Palka and Y Panagis, 'The Empire Strikes Back: Digital Control of Unfair Terms of Online Services' (2017) 40 *Journal of Consumer Policy* 367. Similarly, but with machine learning applied to flag up provisions in online privacy policies that are problematic relative to the GDPR, see G Contissa, K Docter, F Lagioia, M Lippi, H-W Micklitz, P Palka, G Sartor and P Torroni, 'Claudette Meets GDPR: Automating the Evaluation of Privacy Policies Using Artificial Intelligence' (2 July 2018), https://ssrn.com/abstract=3208596.

[54] cp R Brownsword, 'Artificial Intelligence and Legal Singularity: The Thin End of the Wedge, the Thick End of the Wedge, and the Rule of Law' in S Deakin and C Markou (eds), *Is Law Computable?* (Oxford: Hart, 2020) 135–160.

[55] J Fairfield, 'Smart Contracts, Bitcoin Bots, and Consumer Protection' (2014) 71 *Washington and Lee Law Review Online* 36, 39.

[56] See JL Mashaw and DL Harfst, *The Struggle for Auto Safety* (Cambridge, MA, Harvard University Press, 1990) ch 7.

'the rhetoric of prudent paternalism was no match for visions of technology and "big brotherism" gone mad'.[57] Taking stock of the legislative debates of the time, Jerry Mashaw and David Harfst remarked:

> Safety was important, but it did not always trump liberty. [In the safety lobby's appeal to vaccines and guards on machines] the freedom fighters saw precisely the dangerous, progressive logic of regulation that they abhorred. The private passenger car was not a disease or a workplace, nor was it a common carrier. For Congress in 1974, it was a private space.[58]

Today, similar debates might be had about the use of mobile phones, even hands-free mobile phones,[59] by motorists. There are clear and dramatic safety implications, but many drivers persist in using their phones while they are in their cars. If we are to be technocratic in our approach, perhaps we might seek a design solution that disables phones within cars, or while the user is driving. However, once automated vehicles relieve 'drivers' of their safety responsibilities, it seems that the problem will drop away – rules that penalise humans who use their mobile phones while driving will become redundant; humans will simply be transported in vehicles and the one-time problem of driving while phoning will no longer be an issue. Not only that: even if, in an age of autonomous vehicles, there continue to be road traffic accidents, it surely will not be the law of negligence that we will rely upon to determine compensatory entitlements.

With rapid developments in AI, machine learning and blockchain, a question that will become increasingly important is whether – and, if so, how far – a community sees itself as distinguished by its commitment to regulation by rule rather than by technological management.[60] In some smaller scale communities or self-regulating groups, there might be resistance to a technocratic approach because compliance that is guaranteed by technological means compromises the context for trust – this might be the position, for example, in some business communities (where self-enforcing transactional technologies are rejected).[61] Or, again, a community might prefer to stick with regulation by rules because rules (unlike technological measures) allow for some interpretive flexibility, or because it values public participation in setting standards and is worried that this might be more difficult if the debate were to become technocratic.[62]

[57] ibid 135.

[58] ibid 140.

[59] 'Hands-Free Phone Ban for Drivers "Should Be Considered"' (*BBC News*, 13 August 2019), www.bbc.co.uk/news/uk-49320473.

[60] cp De Filippi and Wright (n 19) 210: 'If blockchain technology matures, we may need to ask ourselves whether we would rather live in a world where most of our economic transactions and social interactions are constrained by rules of law – which are universal but also more flexible and ambiguous, and therefore not perfectly enforceable – or whether we would rather surrender ourselves to the rules of code.'

[61] See the excellent discussion in KEC Levy, 'Book-Smart, Not Street-Smart: Blockchain-Based Smart Contracts and the Social Workings of Law' (2017) 3 *Engaging Science, Technology, and Society* 1.

[62] cp JA Kroll, J Huey, S Barocas, EE Felten, JR Reidenberg, DG Robinson and H Yu, 'Accountable Algorithms' (2017) 165 *University of Pennsylvania Law Review* 633, 702–04.

While the contrast between a technocratic approach and coherentism is sharp – the former not being concerned with doctrinal integrity and not being entirely focused on restoring the status quo prior to wrongdoing – the contrast with regulatory instrumentalism is more subtle. For both regulatory instrumentalists and technocrats, the law is to be viewed in a purposive and policy-orientated way; indeed, as I have said, the latter can be regarded as a natural evolution from the former. In both mindsets, it is a matter of selecting the tools that will best serve desired purposes and policies; and, so long as technologies are being employed as tools that are designed to assist with a rule-based regulatory enterprise – as is the case with the examples of drones at Gatwick Airport and harmful online content that I mentioned earlier in the chapter – the technocratic approach might be viewed as merely an offshoot from the stem of regulatory instrumentalism.

That said, once technocrats contemplate interventions at the hard end of the spectrum, their thinking departs from order based on rules to order based on technological management, from correcting and penalising wrongdoing to preventing and precluding wrongdoing, and from reliance on rules and standards to employing technological solutions. At this point, the technocratic mindset reflects a new paradigm.

IV. The Third Tension

While coherentist thinking tends towards the maintenance of settled principles, both regulatory instrumentalism and technocratic thinking are focused on serving agreed regulatory objectives. However, in each case, the legal or regulatory logic starts with *agreed* principles or policies. Where principles or policies are heavily contested, as they often are in modern pluralistic societies, these approaches have no obvious strategy to find their starting position. Faced with pluralism, a stock response is to advocate inclusive consultation and the identification of relevant interests, and then the articulation of an acceptable accommodation of those interests. We can call this a 'balancing' approach.

The problem with the balancing approach is that it tends to flatten the interests to be considered without privileging whatever red lines or fundamental values are recognised in a particular community. In EU law, there are some very explicit red lines and fundamental values, notably those expressed in the EU Charter on Fundamental Rights.[63] Quite simply, our third tension is between a simple balancing approach to plurality and an approach that recognises not only the red lines and fundamental values that are recognised in Europe, but also the need to protect the conditions that are presupposed by any kind of viable human community.

[63] 2000/C 364/01, available at www.europarl.europa.eu/charter/pdf/text_en.pdf.

Accordingly, I start with the balancing approach; then I place this in the bigger picture of regulatory responsibilities; after that, I say more about the red lines; before, in the final section of this part of the chapter, drawing out the tensions between a regulatory balancing of interests and a renewed coherentism that insists on the priority of fundamental values and which demands that regulatory positions and strategies have an integrity relative to such values.

A. Balancing, Red Lines and Basic Values

In the context of emerging technologies, there are, of course, many views about how permissive or restrictive, how incentivising or disincentivising, the regulatory position should be. Some of these differences are straightforwardly prudential, but there are also moral differences in some cases. The question is: how are we to avoid, on the one side, over-regulating (which might stifle innovation or lead to new beneficial technologies being developed elsewhere) while also avoiding, on the other side, under-regulating (which might expose regulatees to unacceptable risks or compromise important values)? In other words, how are the interests in pushing forward with potentially beneficial technologies to be reconciled with the heterogeneous interests of the concerned who seek to push back against them?

A stock answer to this question is that regulators should seek an accommodation or a balance of interests that is broadly 'acceptable'. If the issue is about risks to human health and safety, then regulators (having assessed the risk) should adopt a management strategy that confines risk to an acceptable level; and, if there is a tension between, say, the interest of health-care researchers in accessing personal data and the interest of individuals in both their privacy and the fair processing of their personal data, then regulators should accommodate these interests in a way that is reasonable – or, at any rate, not manifestly unreasonable.

There are several problems with this balancing approach. For example, it is not at all clear where the onus of justification lies (is it for those who wish to push forward or for those who wish to push back to make the case?) any more than it is clear what the burden of proof is; and, because the simple balancing approach allows a broad margin for 'acceptable' accommodation, there are likely to be several regulatory positions that can claim to be reasonable while, conversely, we have no particular reason to favour one such reasonable accommodation over another. More seriously, though, the balancing approach encourages two misleading assumptions: one is the assumption that whatever particular principles, purposes or interests are taken to be guiding, they are in the final analysis contestable; the other is that there is no defensible hierarchy or ranking of interests to which regulators can refer to resolve conflicts.

Now, I do not want to suggest that the balancing approach is never appropriate. In some cases, this might be the best that regulators can do. However, it should not be treated as the default response; and it should not be adopted without a proper understanding of the bigger picture of the state's responsibilities.

B. A Bigger Picture of the State's Responsibilities

In the bigger picture – and I emphasise that this bigger picture applies wherever we are dealing with humans, whether in relation to new technologies or any other matter – the state has responsibilities that go beyond simple balancing. Moreover, these are responsibilities that not only introduce some hierarchy into a regime of human interests, but also correct the idea that there are no interests that stand on rational foundations and that, as such, provide an apodictic reference point for assessing the legitimacy of state action.

We introduce the idea of hierarchy as soon as we demand that regulators should be responsive to whatever red lines and basic values are recognised as distinctive of the particular community. Any claimed interest or proposed accommodation of interests that crosses these red lines or that is incompatible with the community's basic values is 'unacceptable' – but this is for a different reason to that which applies where a simple balancing calculation is undertaken. While certain preferences or interests might prevail in a particular balancing judgment, basic values (by definition) are privileged in the sense that they should prevail every time against any simple preference or interest – regardless of whether this is a preference or interest of an individual, group or majority.

Most fundamentally, however, what the bigger picture highlights is that regulators have a stewardship responsibility in relation to the anterior conditions for humans to exist and for them to function as a community of agents.[64] We should certainly say that any claimed interest or proposed accommodation of interests that is incompatible with the maintenance of these conditions is totally 'unacceptable' – but it is more than that. Unlike the red lines or basic values to which a particular community commits itself – red lines and basic values which may legitimately vary from one community to another – the essential preconditions for human social existence are not contingent or negotiable. For human agents, to compromise the conditions – the commons' conditions – upon which human existence and agency is itself predicated is simply unthinkable.

Accordingly, I suggest that we frame our thinking by articulating three tiers of regulatory responsibility, the first tier being foundational, and the responsibilities being ranked in three tiers of importance.

The responsibilities of the first tier are cosmopolitan and non-negotiable (the red lines here are hard); the responsibilities of the second and third tiers are contingent, depending on the fundamental values and the interests recognised in each particular community. Conflicts may arise both vertically (between responsibilities and interests of different tiers) and horizontally (between responsibilities and interests within the same tier). In the former case, conflicts are to be resolved by reference to the tiers of importance: responsibilities and interests that are engaged

[64] R Brownsword, 'Responsible Regulation: Prudence, Precaution and Stewardship' (2011) 62 *Northern Ireland Legal Quarterly* 573.

by a higher tier always outrank those of a lower tier. In the latter case, there might be some understanding about the relative importance of the interests at issue but this might not be well articulated or developed, in which case the resolution of conflicts will need to be more than usually provisional and reviewable.

C. Red Lines

The paramount concern of regulators is the discharge of their fundamental stewardship responsibilities. However, regulators are also responsible for ensuring that the basic values of their particular community are respected. Just as each individual human agent has the capacity to develop their own distinctive identity, the same is true if we scale this up to communities of human agents. There are common needs and interests, but also distinctive identities.

From the middle of the twentieth century, many nation states have expressed their basic (constitutional) values in terms of respect for human rights and human dignity.[65] These values clearly intersect with the commons conditions, and there is much to debate about the nature of this relationship and the extent of any overlap – for example, if we understand the root idea of human dignity in terms of humans having the capacity freely to do the right thing for the right reason,[66] then human dignity reaches directly to the commons' conditions for moral agency.[67] However, those nation states that articulate their particular identities by the way in which they interpret their commitment to respect for human dignity are far from homogeneous.

Put somewhat bluntly, whereas, in some communities, the emphasis of human dignity is on individuals having the right to make their own choices, in others, it is on the constraints (in particular, relating to the sanctity, non-commercialisation, non-commodification and non-instrumentalisation of human life) that serve to limit individual choice.[68] These differences in emphasis mean that we frequently encounter the protagonists on both sides of the debate invoking human dignity in support of their positions; puzzlingly, according to some, there is dignity in dying (choosing to die), while, according to others, there is dignity in living (life being

[65] See R Brownsword, 'Human Dignity from a Legal Perspective' in M Duwell, J Braarvig, R Brownsword and D Mieth (eds), *Cambridge Handbook of Human Dignity* (Cambridge, Cambridge University Press, 2014) 1.

[66] For such a view, see R Brownsword, 'Human Dignity, Human Rights, and Simply Trying to Do the Right Thing' in C McCrudden (ed), *Understanding Human Dignity*, Proceedings of the British Academy 192 (Oxford, The British Academy and Oxford University Press, 2013) 345; R Brownsword, 'Developing a Modern Understanding of Human Dignity' in D Grimm, A Kemmerer and C Möllers (eds), *Human Dignity in Context* (Baden-Baden, Nomos/Oxford, Hart Publishing, 2018) 299.

[67] See R Brownsword, 'From Erewhon to Alpha Go: For the Sake of Human Dignity Should We Destroy the Machines?' (2017) 9 *Law, Innovation and Technology* 117.

[68] See D Beyleveld and R Brownsword, *Human Dignity in Bioethics and Biolaw* (Oxford, Oxford University Press, 2001); T Caulfield and R Brownsword, 'Human Dignity: A Guide to Policy Making in the Biotechnology Era' (2006) 7 *Nature Reviews Genetics* 72; Brownsword, *Rights, Regulation* (n 3).

maintained). This also means that communities articulate in very different ways on a range of beginning of life and end of life questions, as well as questions of human enhancement, the use of human embryos for research, property rights in detached human body parts and so on.[69]

It is, of course, essential that, whatever the basic values to which a particular community commits itself, they should be consistent with (or cohere with) the commons' conditions. In the first instance, the commons set the stage for community life; and then, without compromising that stage, the particular communities form and self-identify with their own distinctive values.

D. Tensions

The headline tension arising from a plurality of prudential and moral viewpoints is between, on the one side, those forms of legal and regulatory thinking that favour a simple balancing of stakeholders' interests or that default to a utilitarian calculus and, on the other, those forms that recognise that the balancing or the calculus should be constrained by the array of basic values to which a community (such as the EU) is committed. While traditional coherentist thinking is not focused on the integrity of doctrine relative to basic values, a renewed form of coherentist thinking could subject regulatory instrumentalist and technocratic impulses to this discipline. However, there are at least three ways in which the development of a renewed coherentism might be challenged.

First, new coherentism presupposes a clear understanding that fundamental values are privileged over simple interests. Accordingly, when, within a plurality of viewpoints, fundamental values are engaged, they take priority. So far so good, but this understanding is challenged where the relationship between fundamental values and simple interests is blurred. For example, in the *Google Spain* case,[70] where the CJEU accepted that a right to be forgotten is implicit in the conjunction of Articles 7 (respect for private life) and 8 (protection of personal data) of the EU Charter of Fundamental Rights together with Articles 12(b) and 14(a) of the Data Protection Directive, we find many references to a 'balancing of interests' that leave the precise basis of the right unclear. If the right is derived from Articles 7 and 8 of the Charter, then, as the Court observes, it belongs to a privileged class of rights that 'override, as a rule, not only the economic interests of the operator of the search engine but also the interest of the general public in finding that information upon a search relating to the data subject's name'.[71]

[69] See R Brownsword, 'Human Dignity, Ethical Pluralism, and the Regulation of Modern Biotechnologies' in T Murphy (ed), *New Technologies and Human Rights* (Oxford, Oxford University Press, 2009) 19; R Brownsword, 'Developing a Modern Understanding of Human Dignity' (n 66).

[70] Case C-131/12 *Google Spain SL, Google Inc v Agencia Española de Protection de Datos (AEPD), Mario Costeja González* [2014], http://curia.europa.eu/juris/document/document_print.jsf?doclang=EN&docid=152065.

[71] ibid para 97.

In other words, it would only be other, conflicting, fundamental rights (such as the fundamental right to freedom of expression that is recognised by Article 11 of the Charter) that could be pleaded against such an overriding effect. Immediately after saying this, though, the CJEU muddies the waters by suggesting that the right to be forgotten would not have overriding effect if

> it appeared, *for particular reasons*, such as the role played by the data subject in public life, that the interference with his fundamental rights is justified by the preponderant interest of the general public in having, on account of inclusion in the list of results, access to the information in question.[72]

Clearly, care needs to be taken that the only reasons that qualify as 'particular reasons' here are that fundamental rights are implicated. If, on the other hand, the right to be forgotten rests on the rights in Articles 12(b) and 14(a) of the Directive, it would not be privileged in the way that fundamental rights are and a general balancing of interests (seeking an acceptable or reasonable accommodation of relevant interests) would be appropriate. On this analysis, the particular reasons relied on against the right to be forgotten could be much broader – or, at any rate, this would be so unless we read the more particular provisions of Article 8 of the Charter as elevating the specific rights of the Directive to the status of fundamental rights.

Secondly, where more than one basic value (such as a fundamental right) is engaged, with one value (or right) conflicting with another, it is important that both values are taken into consideration. In other words, new coherentism will be challenged unless it is understood that all relevant values should be considered. Recently, a trio of copyright references made by Germany to the CJEU – *Funke Medien* (the Afghanistan papers case),[73] *Pelham* (the Kraftwerk sampling case)[74] and *Spiegel Online*[75] – have given rise to concerns about the Opinions given by Advocate-General Szpunar. In a critical Opinion by the European Copyright

[72] ibid para 97 (emphasis added).

[73] Case C-469/17.

[74] Case C-476/17.

[75] Case C-516/17. The Grand Chamber handed down its judgment on 29 July 2019, http://curia.europa.eu/juris/document/document.jsf;jsessionid=73A2FD1C1C1C7A89D0952D27E170642C?text=&docid=216543&pageIndex=0&doclang=en&mode=lst&dir=&occ=first&part=1&cid=7379109. Summarising its ruling on what, for present purposes, is the key question, the Court said: 'Freedom of information and freedom of the press, enshrined in Article 11 of the Charter of Fundamental Rights of the European Union, are not capable of justifying, beyond the exceptions or limitations provided for in Article 5(2) and (3) of Directive 2001/29, a derogation from the author's exclusive rights of reproduction and of communication to the public, referred to in Article 2(a) and Article 3(1) of that directive respectively.' If the balance that is struck in the Directive is simply between, on the one hand, the interests of the press and the public and, on the other, the interests of an author, then the exclusion of appeal to the fundamental values of the Charter is surely problematic. However, in the body of its judgment, the Court presents the balance struck in the Directive in somewhat different terms, as being one between the interests of authors and their IP rights as guaranteed by Art 17(2) of the Charter and the interests of users of protected matter as guaranteed by Art 11 of the Charter. In other words, the fair balance struck by the Directive is already an implicit balancing of the conflicting Charter rights.

Society,[76] concerns are expressed about both the Advocate-General's view that fundamental rights can override legislatively agreed intellectual property balances only in exceptional circumstances[77] and about a failure to recognise 'the need to secure a "fair balance" between competing [fundamental] rights'.[78] Whether or not the Court's judgment in *Spiegel Online* will assuage these concerns remains to be seen.[79]

Thirdly, new coherentism will be challenged if the commitment to a particular set of basic values (such as fundamental rights) is compromised or clouded by a competing set of values. In the EU, the Charter value of dignity (to which the opening chapter of the instrument is dedicated) invites a rights-based reading that supports individual agents making their own informed choices and having as much choice as possible but also a more conservative duty-based reading that focuses on constraining the choices available to individuals. To say that the latter has a foothold in EU jurisprudence would be something of an understatement. As the much-debated *Brüstle*[80] case vividly highlights, this is how the CJEU interprets the morality exclusion in Directive 98/44/EC on the Legal Protection of Biotechnological Inventions.[81] Moreover, there are some signs that the European Court of Human Rights, too, is willing to tolerate conservative dignitarian values,[82] seemingly diluting its commitment to a regime of fundamental rights.

To be sure, decisions about the right to be forgotten, about copyright or about the patentability and use of modern biotechnologies might be some way from typical private law issues. Nevertheless, in the EU, we cannot be entirely confident about the prospects for a renewed coherentism, preserving the community's fundamental values against the logic of regulatory instrumentalism or against technological management that proceeds on utilitarian values that favour efficiency and economy over humanity.

V. Conclusion

Summing up, in uncertain times, and in the context of both political and technological disruption, it is hard to know what the future holds for European private law. Nevertheless, I have identified three things to look out for.

[76] See L Bently, S Dusollier, C Geiger, J Griffiths, A Metzger, A Peukert and M Senftleben, 'Sound Sampling, a Permitted Use under EU Copyright Law? Opinion of the European Copyright Society in Relation to the Pending Reference before the CJEU in Case C-476/17, *Pelham GmbH v Hütter*' (2019) 50 *International Review of Intellectual Property and Competition Law* 467.

[77] ibid ff 4.

[78] ibid 470.

[79] See n 75.

[80] Case C-34/10 *Oliver Brüstle v Greenpeace eV* (Grand Chamber, 18 October 2011).

[81] For a discussion, see R Brownsword, *Law, Technology and Society – Re-imagining the Regulatory Environment* (Abingdon, Routledge, 2019) ch 6.

[82] See the judgment of the Grand Chamber at the European Court of Human Rights in the case of *SH v Austria* App no 57813/00 (3 November 2011). There, the Court seems to permit Austria to rely

First, as technologies continue to disrupt the law, provoking the thought that the law is not fit for purpose, we might wonder whether traditional coherentist reasoning will be of any relevance. On the face of it, it seems likely that the content of the revised rules of private law will largely reflect policy-focused regulatory instrumentalist thinking with only faint echoes of coherentist thinking. Moreover, where policy is implemented through regulations or maximum harmonisation directives, these echoes will be even fainter.

Secondly, as new technologies increasingly offer themselves as regulatory tools, leading in some cases to full-scale technological management, we need to watch whether the *rules* of private law become less relevant. Again, we might expect many of these traditional rules to become redundant, with rules (such as they are) being redirected to those who design, manufacture and produce transactional technologies and automated processes and products.[83]

Thirdly, we should also monitor whether the dominant regulatory discourse is one that seeks to manage risk effectively, to establish an acceptable balance of interests and to promote the collective utility. If so, to what extent are these regulatory imperatives constrained by red lines that protect fundamental values such as human rights and human dignity? Here, I am not sure what to expect. Are basic values in the EU too fractured to stand firm against utilitarian efficiency? To find our last-ditch defence of humanity, to maintain human-centric regulatory regimes, do we have to go deeper – to the maintenance of the conditions that are prerequisites for any form of human social existence? If so, the sooner that regulators have a clearer sight of their regulatory responsibilities, especially their stewardship responsibilities, the better for all Europeans, whether they are citizens of the EU or of some other European state.[84]

on conservative dignitarian values to justify its restrictive in vitro fertilisation laws (prohibiting third-party donation of gametes). For a critique, see R Scott, 'Reproductive Health: Morals, Margins and Rights' (2018) 81 *MLR* 422.

[83] See further Brownsword, 'The e-Commerce Directive' (n 18).

[84] I am conscious that, having started this chapter with some remarks about the non-ideal state of Europe, I am finishing on a somewhat idealistic note. I take some comfort from knowing that I am not alone in thinking such thoughts about global stewardship or the like; but I also heed Jan Klabbers's warning that 'regular politics and morality are messy affairs': see J Klabbers, 'On Responsible Global Governance' in J Klabbers, M Varaki and G Vasconcelos Vilaca (eds), *Towards Responsible Governance* (Helsinki, University of Helsinki, 2018) 11, 28 (see esp 24–28).

2

Standardisation of Agreement in EU Law. An Adieu to the Contracting Parties?

FRANCISCO DE ELIZALDE*

I. Introduction

2014 will probably be remembered as the year in which the process to harmonise European contract law was abandoned. The withdrawal of the Proposal for a Regulation on a Common European Sales Law (CESL),[1] which occurred that year, interrupted a continuous trend of efforts to achieve a common private law instrument that had been going on for more than three decades. In short, the recent history of European contract law goes back to the Principles of European Contract Law (PECL) that the Commission on European Contract Law drafted, chaired by Ole Lando, which began its work in 1982 and completed it in 2003.[2] Subsequently, three important communications from the European Commission (on European contract law,[3] an action plan[4] and the way forward[5]) paved the way for the Draft Common Frame of Reference (DCFR) in 2009, prepared by the Study Group on a European Civil Code, led by Christian von Bar, and the

* This chapter is an output of the EU Jean Monnet Module 'Liability of Robots: a European Vision for a New Legal Regime' and of the research project (Spain) DER 2017-84947-P. I would like to thank Beatriz Gregoraci for comments on an earlier draft and to the students Bárbara Gómez Cortés and Elena Sabau for their research assistance. The usual disclaimer applies.

[1] Commission, 'Proposal for a Regulation of the European Parliament and of the Council of 11 October 2011 on a Common European Sales Law' COM (2011) 635 final. It was withdrawn by the Commission, 'Commission Working Programme 2015' COM (2014) 910 final, Annex 2.

[2] O Lando and H Beale (eds), *The Principles of European Contract Law*, Parts I and II (combined and revised) (The Hague, Kluwer, 2000).

[3] Commission, 'On European Contract Law' (Communication) COM (2001) 398 final.

[4] Commission, 'A More Coherent European Contract Law – An Action Plan' (Communication) COM (2003) 68 final.

[5] Commission, 'European Contract Law and the Revision of the Acquis: The Way Forward' (Communication) COM (2004) 651 final.

Research Group on Existing EC Private Law, chaired by Hans Schulte-Nölke.[6] A Feasibility Study succeeded the DCFR in 2011,[7] resulting in the CESL produced by an Expert Group.[8]

The breadth of the proposals ranged from model rules for a unified European general contract law (PECL) to an ambitious project to harmonise contracts and other areas of private law (DCFR) and an optional instrument for sales (CESL). However, they all had in common that they were backed by the European Commission, were prepared by networks of academics from the Member States (*Professorenrecht*) and had at their bases a thorough comparative law analysis. The consumer law *acquis communautaire* was also present in some of the proposals.

This is not the place to assess the success of the proposals, a task that has largely already been undertaken.[9] Among their merits, the model rules impacted the modernisation of national contract laws, including the reform of the German and French civil codes, and have been used to refresh the interpretation, by courts, of other civil codes (such as Spain's) that have not undergone reform.[10] A certain alignment in terms of legal thought of national general contract law and the proposals to harmonise European contract law could justify the latter's impact over the former. For the purposes of this chapter, it is important to highlight, with qualifications, the liberal stance on contract law, with the individual and corrective justice as cornerstones.[11] This standpoint explains the rules for the life cycle of contracts, which revolve around freedom of contract: formation (offer and acceptance), validity (defects of consent), interpretation (subjective or objective), terms (express and implied) and remedies (individual, private enforcement).

[6] C von Bar and H Schulte-Nölke (eds), *Principles, Definitions and Model Rules on European Private Law: Draft Common Frame of Reference (DCFR)*, outline edn (Munich, Sellier, 2009).

[7] See 'A European Contract Law for Consumers and Businesses: Publication of the Results of the Feasibility Study Carried Out by the Expert Group on European Contract Law for Stakeholders' and Legal Practitioners' Feedback', ec.europa.eu/justice/contract/files/feasibility_study_final.pdf.

[8] For a detailed account, see H Beale, 'The Story of EU Contract Law – from 2001 to 2014' in C Twigg-Flesner (ed), *Research Handbook on EU Consumer and Contract Law* (Cheltenham, Edward Elgar Publishing, 2016) 432–62.

[9] S Grundmann, 'European Contract Law (s) of What Colour?' (2005) 1 *European Review of Contract Law* 184; S Vogenauer and S Weatherill (eds), *The Harmonisation of European Contract Law. Implications for European Private Law, Business and Legal Practice* (Oxford, Hart Publishing, 2006); H Eidenmüller, F Faust, HC Grigoleit, G Wagner and R Zimmermann, 'The Common Frame of Reference for European Private Law. Policy Choices and Codification Problems' (2008) 28 *OJLS* 659; HW Micklitz and F Cafaggi (eds), *European Private Law after the Common Frame of Reference* (Cheltenham, Edward Elgar Publishing, 2010); G Howells, 'European Contract Law Reform and European Consumer Law – Two Related but Distinct Regimes' (2011) 7 *European Review of Contract Law* 173; N Jansen and R Zimmermann (eds), *Commentaries on European Contract Laws* (Oxford, Oxford University Press, 2018); F de Elizalde (ed), *Uniform Rules for European Contract Law? A Critical Assessment* (Oxford, Hart Publishing, 2018).

[10] E Roca Trías, 'The Modernisation of the Law of Obligations Using the Principles of European Contract Law' in de Elizalde (ibid) 83–90; T Ackermann, 'Uniform Rules as Guidelines for National Courts and Legislatures: The German Experience' in de Elizalde (ibid) 91–102; B Fauvarque-Cosson, 'National Reforms: New Instruments towards Converging Rules within Europe? The Example of the French Contract Law Reform (2016)' in de Elizalde (ibid) 103–14.

[11] G Brüggemeier et al, 'Social Justice in European Contract Law: A Manifesto' (2004) 10 *European Law Journal* 653.

In parallel to the academic endeavours to harmonise contract law, a less noticeable movement seems to have advanced in the same direction, albeit with different means, methodology and philosophy. I refer to it as 'mass EU contract law' (MEUCL).

It is the working hypothesis of this chapter that EU law is developing core rules for the formation of contracts that could end up in a harmonised system (MEUCL), yet one that is of a different colour to the previous academic proposals in the field. These rules are enshrined in legislative instruments (mainly directives) that are later advanced by the Court of Justice of the European Union (CJEU) interpretation when resolving requests for preliminary rulings from national courts (Art 267 TFEU). Different to the proposals, MEUCL does not produce soft law model rules but mandatory law.

The system is under construction. Unified EU general contract laws have not been put in place and the controversy over the competences of the EU to pursue harmonisation in contract law remains unsolved, while the Union advances almost imperceptibly. Moreover, the horizontal relationship (cross-directive) between the diverse legal sources is unclear and their impact over contract law is heterogeneous. Therefore, the alleged harmonisation is close to spontaneous, which makes the case harder to prove. Complexity also arises from the pluralistic and multilayered character of EU law, on which the Union enshrines the rights and the Member States design the remedies for their infringement, following procedural autonomy, with limitations arising from the principles of effectiveness, equivalence, proportionality and dissuasiveness.[12]

Despite said complexities, this chapter claims that EU law is establishing general rules for the formation of contracts by following a radically new approach to procedural fairness. Agreement, the core element in contract formation, is being transformed by becoming standardised as it ignores the characteristics of the contracting parties. The transformation results from the use of legal standards to determine valid contract formation. Those legal standards include the 'average consumer' and the 'average retail (investment) client', which ignore individual knowledge, expertise and causation – a radical shift from traditional contract law. MEUCL treats all members of the class alike. It is claimed here that this transformation is occurring despite the recurrent affirmation that EU law is without prejudice 'to contract law and, in particular, to the rules on the validity, formation or effect of a contract'.[13]

[12] N Reich, 'The Principle of Effectiveness and EU Private Law' in U Bernitz, X Groussot and F Schulyok (eds), *General Principles of EU Law and European Private Law* (Alphen aan den Rijn, Wolters Kluwer, 2013) 301; F Cafaggi and P Iamiceli, 'The Principles of Effectiveness, Proportionality and Dissuasiveness in the Enforcement of EU Consumer Law: The Impact of a Triad on the Choice of Civil Remedies and Administrative Sanctions' (2017) 25 *European Review of Private Law* 575.

[13] See Art 3(2) of Directive 2005/29/EC of the European Parliament and of the Council of 11 May 2005 concerning unfair business-to-consumer commercial practices in the internal market and amending Council Directive 84/450/EEC, Directives 97/7/EC, 98/27/EC and 2002/65/EC of the European

The claimed evolution of EU law has a direct impact on corrective justice, which becomes highly dependent on the pursuit of societal aims through market regulation. From the perspective of legal philosophy, MEUCL looks utilitarian and instrumental as it aims to improve the functioning of the internal market – most of its legal provisions being justified in Article 114 TFEU, which serves as a basis for EU legislative action in private law.[14] This would be a fundamental change for traditional private law, which is set to face increased pressure from public policies,[15] with even its autonomy being challenged.[16] EU private law would thus have a unique character. The legal transformation affects the cornerstone of contract formation (agreement), with further consequences on freedom of choice, freedom to conduct a business, individual responsibility and market behaviour. Moreover, it might be the case that a standardised approach to agreement is already old-fashioned at the time of its conception against the backdrop of big data and artificial intelligence (AI), which allow personalisation in the online mass contracting of goods and services.[17]

This chapter aims to prove the existence of MEUCL and its innovative character. First, the chapter will briefly address agreement and the validity of contracts in national law, including references to the soft law proposals to harmonise European contract law. Then it will define the scope of MEUCL and reflect on the 'contractual logic' position of modern private law as opposed to the more homogeneous approach of traditional law. Within that framework, the chapter will delve into the use of legal standards in contract formation under EU law, which stems from a cross-legislative assessment.

Parliament and of the Council and Regulation (EC) 2006/2004 of the European Parliament and of the Council [2005] OJ L149/22; Recital 14 of Directive 2011/83/EU of the European Parliament and of the Council of 25 October 2011 on consumer rights, amending Council Directive 93/13/EEC and Directive 1999/44/EC of the European Parliament and of the Council and repealing Council Directive 85/577/EEC and Directive 97/7/EC of the European Parliament and of the Council [2011] OJ L304/64; Art 3(10) of Directive (EU) 2019/770 of the European Parliament and of the Council of 20 May 2019 on certain aspects concerning contracts for the supply of digital content and digital services [2019] OJ L136/1; Recital 18 of Directive (EU) 2019/771 of the European Parliament and of the Council of 20 May 2019 on certain aspects concerning contracts for the sale of goods, amending Regulation (EU) 2017/2394 and Directive 2009/22/EC, and repealing Directive 1999/44/EC [2019] OJ L136/28.

[14] K Gutman, *The Constitutional Foundations of European Contract Law. A Comparative Analysis* (Oxford, Oxford University Press, 2014); M Hesselink, 'Contract Theory and EU Contract Law' (2015) Amsterdam Legal Studies Research Paper No 2015-39, 1, 9, papers.ssrn.com/sol3/papers.cfm?abstract_id=2674508; R Schulze and F Zoll, *European Contract Law* (Munich, CH Beck/Oxford, Hart Publishing/Baden Baden, Nomos, 2016) 13.

[15] HW Micklitz, *The Politics of Justice in European Private Law. Social Justice, Access Justice, Societal Justice* (Cambridge, Cambridge University Press, 2018) 22–24.

[16] HW Micklitz, Y Svetiev and G Comparato, 'European Regulatory Private Law – The Paradigms Tested' (2014) EUI Law Working Paper 2014/04, cadmus.eui.eu/handle/1814/31137.

[17] See A Porat and L Starhilevitz, 'Personalising Default Rules and Disclosure with Big Data' (2014) 112 *Michigan Law Review* 1417; C Busch, 'Implementing Personalized Law: Personalized Disclosures in Consumer Law and Data Privacy Law' (2019) 86 *University of Chicago Law Review* 309.

II. The Formation of Contracts under National Law. The Proposals to Harmonise European Contract Law

A. Agreement and Its Interpretation

It is a shared tradition in national contract law of the Member States of the EU (although not to a uniform one) that a contract is formed by an agreement, represented as an offer, which contains sufficient and definite terms to bring about an acceptance.[18] Two possible approaches to agreement diverge therefrom: an 'objective' one, prevailing in the common law tradition, and a 'subjective' one, existing in the civil law tradition, although not exclusively.

According to the objective approach, the offeror is bound by its offer based on the reliance that it creates upon a reasonable person.[19] In this way, the offeror may be bound even though in fact it had no such intention insofar as the offeree was ignorant about it.[20] From the perspective of the interpretation of express terms, which concerns the meaning of agreement and hence completes the picture of it, the objective criterion also reigns. In this context, it is further defined that the reasonable person is put in the position of the parties and has 'all the background knowledge which is reasonably available to the person or class of persons to whom the document is addressed'.[21]

In civil law, agreement (*consensus ad idem*) is usually explained as the meeting of the parties' minds, an expression that highlights the need for an actual common intention. The subjectivity inherent in this approach is further reflected in the interpretation of the terms agreed by the parties. Civil codes provide for canons of interpretation according to which the true intention of the parties prevails when in contradiction with the literal meaning of the declaration of intent (eg in France, Article 1188 of the Code civil (CC)). Nevertheless, civil law is not purely subjective. Objective criteria that address the protection of reliance are also present, including determining the existence and meaning of agreement according to good faith and usages (eg in Germany, § 157 of the Bürgerliches Gesetzbuch (BGB)). The exact balance between subjective and objective criteria varies from country to country and remains a controversial issue in many jurisdictions.

Beyond a different stance on agreement (objective or subjective), national laws share the fact that agreement and the interpretation of it is restricted to the

[18] H Beale, B Fauvarque-Cosson, J Rutgers, D Tallon and S Vogenauer, *Cases, Materials and Text on Contract Law* (Oxford, Hart Publishing, 2010) 241.

[19] M Chen-Wishart, 'Formation of Contract' in H Beale (ed), *Chitty on Contracts* (London, Sweet & Maxwell, 2015) 193–94.

[20] ibid.

[21] G Treitel and E Peel, *The Law of Contract* (London, Sweet & Maxwell, 2011) 241.

contracting parties. The task of courts is to ascertain if a contract has come into existence by looking at the actual contracting parties and the 'meaning of the language that the parties have chosen to express their agreement'.[22] It is thus possible to consider this approach as 'individual' or 'particular' in contrast to a model that primarily looks beyond the parties. Moreover, this classic (national) way to address agreement is largely designed for negotiated contracts; the *contra proferentem* rule, according to which obscure terms are to be interpreted against their drafter, later extended to standard form contracts, was also created for bargained-for contracts.

The soft law proposals to harmonise European contract law adhere to the perspective of national law, which ascertains agreement focusing on the contracting parties. They also consider sufficient agreement to be the basis for a valid contract and, as regards interpretation of the agreed terms, the proposed model rules search for the common intention of the parties – opting for the subjective approach, in the first place, which is supplemented by objective criteria (Articles 5:101 PECL, II.8:101 DCFR and 58 CESL).

B. Validity of Contracts

National law recognises the binding force of agreements based on freedom of contract or party autonomy, which is a general principle enshrined as such in the proposals to harmonise European contract law (Articles 1:102 PECL and II.1:102 DCFR). Freedom of contract requires procedural fairness, ie that agreement was formed with actual freedom and intent. Such procedural fairness is traditionally controlled with the 'vices' or 'defects' of consent (mistake, misrepresentation, undue influence, etc), which lead to invalidity of contracts, on occasion coupled with damages. Only in more recent times, and recurrently following the implementation of the Unfair Contract Terms Directive (UCTD)),[23] have national laws of the Member States introduced a substantive control of terms (beyond the historical institution of *laesio enormis*, existent in some jurisdictions such as Austria, §934 of the Allgemeines bürgerliches Gesetzbuch), usually restricted to standard form contracts and mostly in the context of business-to-consumer (B2C) relationships.

The assessment of the validity of contracts in national law is largely consistent with the approach that a particular jurisdiction adopts towards agreement. Jurisdictions that rely on an objective criterion (eg England and Wales) are normally more reluctant to rescind a contract under a defect of consent, unless the reliance that the non-aggrieved party has placed on the contract does not deserve protection. Again, the 'reasonable person' test appears, as in the case

[22] *Wood v Capita Insurance Services* [2017] UKSC 24.

[23] Council Directive 93/13/EEC of 5 April 1993 on unfair terms in consumer contracts [1993] OJ L95/29.

of misrepresentations in English law, to determine the objective meaning of statements.[24] A parallel, yet different scenario is visible in civil law. There, too, the vices of consent relate to the stance that national law takes on agreement, which primarily refers to the common intention of the parties. A vitiated agreement should give the affected party the remedy to invalidate it – the actual understanding of the parties being the paradigm to assess the validity of the contract. However, this is not at all straightforward because, as stated, civil law balances actual intention (subjective approach to agreement) with the reliance placed by the parties (resorting to objective criteria). Therefore, for example, an action for mistake is not granted if the error was inexcusable for the mistaken party (eg Article 1132 CC).

Replicating what occurs with the existence of agreement and the interpretation of the terms created by it, national laws coincide in analysing the defects of consent 'individually', ie restricted to the contracting parties. In addition to other requirements, an action for invalidity does not succeed if the consent of one of the parties (or both) is actually not vitiated. This happens, for example, when one party does not rely on the incorrect information given by the other.[25] Moreover, the analysis of invalidity includes the personal characteristics of the aggrieved party. This is considered, for example, to assess an action for misrepresentation under English law ('the known characteristics of the actual representee')[26] or an action for mistake in civil law. A similar, individual approach is the one underlying the soft law proposals to harmonise European contract law (Articles 4:103 PECL and II.7:201 DCFR).

III. The Bases of MEUCL

A. Overview

The hypothesis underlying this chapter is that partial harmonisation of EU law is ongoing, which stems from a radically new understanding of agreement and contractual validity – core elements in the formation of contracts. It is claimed here that legal standards are replacing agreement to determine procedural fairness (the process that leads to a valid contract), which would entail an innovative intervention of EU law to alter the long-established framework of contract formation. The change would arise from the fact that, under MEUCL, agreement appears not to be individually assessed (party-based), but instead is benchmarked against objective legal standards that determine the validity of contracts: the 'average consumer' and the 'average (investment) client'. The change would be even more significant

[24] Treitel and Peel (n 21) 361.
[25] ibid.
[26] ibid.

if, as the CJEU has decided, the legal standard ignores individual knowledge and expertise, which represents a 180-degree shift from traditional contract law.

The transformation of the rules on contract formation, beyond more express intervention of EU law, seems restricted to what this chapter calls 'protective' or 'asymmetric' contracts. These are contracts in which one of the parties is in an asymmetric position vis-à-vis its business counterparty. Protective contracts include not only B2C contracts,[27] but also other private law relationships such as those arising from investment law (eg the Markets in Financial Instruments Directive (MiFID) regime).

MEUCL is EU mandatory law that stems from a cross-directive interpretation of the regulation of protective contracts and is completed with the remedies recognised in national law. Hans Micklitz and his research group on European regulatory private law (ERPL) should probably be credited for stressing the private law elements in a variety of markets regulated by EU legislative instruments.[28] However, they consider each market's vertical regulation isolated from the rest (a 'silo').[29] In consequence, ERPL would reject general rules in EU private law that apply horizontally across sectors. In an assessment of ERPL, Martijn Hesselink opposed this view and flagged the Unfair Contract Terms Directive (UCTD) as an example of EU law that applies horizontally to all markets to control unfair terms in B2C standard form contracts.[30] This chapter shares this assumption, ie that it is possible to recognise contract rules in EU law that apply horizontally, with the said extended scope beyond the boundaries of consumer law.

Having stated this, the word 'mass' (of the acronym MEUCL) and its relationship with the formation of contracts needs further explanation. Classic general contract rules from national law were designed for individual transactions, according to the reality of the time. As mentioned, the soft law proposals to harmonise European contract law shared that assumption. Instead, the contract law system that is allegedly being built in the EU seems designed for mass, asymmetric transactions, which are customary in today's economies of scale. This does not mean that the application of EU law always requires repetitive contracts,[31] but, instead, that regulation is planned for contracts that are directed towards a broad number of people. The disruptive character of EU private law (and the partial harmonisation in the formation of contracts stemming from MEUCL) is perceived in its innovative approach to a binding agreement, which, as stated, shifts away from a millenary understanding.

[27] See V Roppo, 'From Consumer Contracts to Asymmetric Contracts: A Trend in European Contract Law' (2009) 5 *European Review of Contract Law* 304, 310 ff.

[28] See HW Micklitz, 'The Visible Hand of European Regulatory Private Law – The Transformation of European Private Law from Autonomy to Functionalism in Competition and Regulation' (2009) 28 *Yearbook of European Law* 3, 21–29.

[29] Micklitz et al (n 16).

[30] M Hesselink, 'Private Law, Regulation and Justice' (2016) 22 *European Law Journal* 681, 683.

[31] Case C-388/13 *Nemzeti Fogyasztóvédelmi Hatóság v UPC Magyarország kft* ECLI:EU:C:2015:225, para 41.

Agreement has been the historical cornerstone in the formation of a valid contract, which is a requirement shared (with variations) by diverse legal traditions. Starting from a restricted application in classical Roman law, agreement went on to become the basis for a valid contract, and the criterion for corrective justice. Following the expansion of economies of scale and the standardisation of contracts, legal systems intervened in the twentieth century to control the substantive fairness of terms in standard form contracts: the assessment of unfair terms. However, in EU law, the control did not reach contract formation (procedural fairness). Additionally, the essential elements of the contract (the definition of the subject matter and the adequacy of price in relation to the product or service, Article 4.2 UCTD) were also left to party autonomy (agreement) and competition.[32] Respect for agreement has characterised EU private law, even beyond standard form contracts. Arguably, EU law has assumed a classic economic analysis (parties as rational agents) that revolves around agreement, with legal intervention being mostly restricted to correct traditional market failures such as information problems.[33]

As stated, the hypothesis underlying this chapter is that the concept of agreement, as it has been understood for centuries, is being disrupted by legal standards that determine procedural fairness in contract formation, ie the 'average consumer' and the 'average retail (investment) client'. The average consumer and the average retail client are legal standards that apply following a contractual-position logic, be it B2C or investment firm/client, that remain alien to the actual agreement and would disregard individual knowledge and expertise. As will be explained in the following section, MEUCL protects all members of the class alike, which represents a regulatory policy of 'maximum welfarism' (ie one that is not targeted).[34]

The use of a legal standard (the 'average') to assess the formation of contracts, if proven, would represent a major shift from traditional private law. In terms of validity of contracts, the classic 'vices' or 'defects' of consent look at flaws in the agreement of the actual contracting parties. To that end, for example, actual non-reliance of the claimant on the pre-contractual information provided by the defendant bars the action of the former. EU law replaces defects of consent with, among others, the notion of 'lack of transparency', according to the understanding of an 'average consumer' – ignoring the actual knowledge of the parties, which is immaterial to the claim. Thus, even the person who understood or was capable of understanding the pre-contractual information of a term, ie was above 'average', would be protected. This has never been the case from a comparative perspective, not even in a system like English law, which adopts an objective approach to

[32] AG Trstenjak in Case C-484/08 *Caja de Ahorros y Monte de Piedad de Madrid v Ausbanc* ECLI:EU:C:2009:682.

[33] G Howells, 'The Potential and Limits of Consumer Empowerment by Information' (2005) 32 *Journal of Law and Society* 349.

[34] C Willet, *Fairness in Consumer Contracts. The Case of Unfair Terms* (Aldershot, Ashgate, 2007) 377–78.

agreement. Therefore, the validity of contracts in EU law would become standardised for the first time, leading to a major shift from traditional rules.

B. The Contractual Position Logic

An important characteristic of contract law today is the logic of the 'contractual position'. Modern contract law increasingly takes the condition of the parties into consideration in applying one set of rules or another.[35] The most extended application of this logic is the classification of contract rules following the B2B, B2C and C2C distinction.

The variety of rules is not at all new and is well documented in history. The special status for merchants is a good example of it. However, general contract law beyond a specific status (eg the rules contained in civil codes) was meant to apply equally to all. A political purpose underlying liberal contract law was precisely freedom of contract for parties that were assumed to be equal, with equally applicable rules.

The recognition of asymmetries in the bargaining power of the parties as well as information asymmetries have put an end to homogeneity in private law. The result, in national law, is usually a mixed system of general contract law, with rules that take the position of the parties into consideration (clearly, consumer law) and others that do not (eg unreformed provisions in civil codes). For example, English law has two layers of liability for the seller of a good: no liability unless otherwise agreed in C2C contracts (*caveat emptor*) and an implied term of satisfactory quality in B2B and B2C contracts (Sale of Goods Act 1979, section 14 and Consumer Rights Act 2015, section 9 – non-mandatory in the former, mandatory in the latter). In French law and other systems from the civil law tradition (not German law due to the 2001 reform), the Roman system of latent defects (B2B, C2C) coexists with the principle of conformity (B2C), which was introduced by the Consumer Sales Directive.[36]

EU contract law, which started to develop in the late twentieth century, already follows the modern conception of contract rules. Accordingly, EU contract law 'almost never addresses contracting parties simply as persons, as [traditional] private law normally does, but always as members of a certain category, in particular consumers and professionals'.[37] Consumer law, for example, is the

[35] Hesselink, 'Contract Theory' (n 14) 11.

[36] Directive 1999/44/EC of the European Parliament and of the Council of 25 May 1999 on certain aspects of consumer goods and associated guarantees [1999] OJ L171/12. In French law, the system of latent defects survives in Art 1641 CC. For a comparative approach, see F de Elizalde, 'Should the Implied Term Concerning Quality Be Generalized? Present and Future of the Principle of Conformity in Europe' (2017) 25 *European Review of Private Law* 71.

[37] Hesselink, 'Contract Theory' (n 14) 11. See also F Cafaggi, 'From a Status to a Transaction Based Approach? Institutional Design in European Contract Law' (2013) 50 *CML Rev* 311.

clear result of B2C. But other legislative interventions in the field, such as the Commercial Agents Directive[38] and the Late Payment Directive,[39] are exclusively aimed at regulating B2B relationships. In other legislative instruments, such as the e-Commerce Directive,[40] distinctions are made for consumers with an added reference to the general framework of consumer protection. In investment law, the MiFID regime[41] classifies investors in retail, professionals and eligible counterparties, with a different level of protection.[42]

A special characteristic of the contractual-position logic, in EU private law, is that belonging to a certain category is objectively defined.[43] The corresponding EU legal instruments determine the category of persons that are included in its scope of application, ignoring individual circumstances. Usually the business is defined in a positive way, while the protected party (the consumer or the retail investor) is negatively defined. For example, under the UCTD, a 'seller or supplier' means any natural or legal person who 'is acting for purposes relating to his trade, business or profession' (Article 2c UCTD); while a consumer means any natural person who 'is acting for purposes which are outside his trade, business or profession' (Article 2b UCTD). Similar definitions can be found in the Unfair Commercial Practices Directive (UCPD, Article 2a and b)[44] and the Consumer Rights Directive (CRD, Article 2[1] and [2]).[45] It is not surprising that in *Kamenova* the CJEU decided that the concept of 'trader' under the UCPD and the CRD, which are almost identical, should be interpreted uniformly as, additionally, both instruments are based in the same treaty provision (Article 114 TFEU – the predecessor of which also justified the UCTD).[46]

Furthermore, in *Costea*, the CJEU clarified that the category of consumer (and the protection arising therefrom under the UCTD) is to be determined solely by the purpose of the contract, with the actual knowledge or expertise of the actual

[38] Council Directive 86/653/EEC of 18 December 1986 on the coordination of the laws of the Member States relating to self-employed commercial agents [1986] OJ L382/17.

[39] Directive 2011/7/EU of the European Parliament and of the Council of 16 February 2011 on combating late payment in commercial transactions [2011] OJ L48/1.

[40] Directive 2000/31/EC of the European Parliament and of the Council of 8 June 2000 on certain legal aspects of information society services, in particular electronic commerce, in the Internal Market [2000] OJ L178/1.

[41] Directive 2014/65/EU of the European Parliament and of the Council of 15 May 2014 on markets in financial instruments and amending Directive 2002/92/EC and Directive 2011/61/EU [2014] OJ L173/349 (MiFID II) and Level 2 Provisions.

[42] M Kruithof, 'A Differentiated Approach to Client Protection: The Example of MiFID' in S Grundmann and Y Atamer (eds), *Financial Services, Financial Crisis, and General European Contract Law: Failures and Challenges of Contracting* (Alphen aan den Rijn, Wolters Kluwer, 2011) 114–15. See also D Busch and G Ferrarini (eds), *Regulation of the EU Financial Markets: MiFID II and MiFIR* (Oxford, Oxford University Press, 2017).

[43] E Terryn, 'Consumers, By Definition, Include Us All' … But Not For Every Transaction' (2016) 24 *European Review of Private Law* 271, 273–74.

[44] Directive 2005/29/EC (UCPD).

[45] Directive 2011/83/EU (CRD).

[46] Case C-105/17 *Komisia za zashtita na potrebitelite v Evelina Kamenova* ECLI:EU:C:2018:808, paras 27–29.

consumer being immaterial.[47] The claimant of the case was a commercial lawyer who challenged the validity of a credit agreement into which he had entered for non-professional purposes. Therefore, at least under the UCTD, a consumer is treated and protected as such even if he is, in fact, a knowledgeable and experienced person. The CJEU interpreted the notion of consumer in the same way under the Brussels Regulation in *Schrems*[48] and *Jana Petruchová*.[49]

I have called this 'contractual-position' logic and not 'status-based' logic because the applicable rules of EU law vary depending on the type and purpose of the contract. They are functional.[50] Following the example of Mr Costea, he would be treated as a consumer when he concludes a credit agreement for non-professional purposes or when he shops at the supermarket, but he would be classified as a professional when acting as an attorney and as a retail investor (with a high level of protection) if he invests in a financial market (not being a professional client under MiFID II).

The contractual-position logic is fundamental to MEUCL. The recognition of categories of legally protected parties to a contract (consumers, retail investors, etc), which are objectively defined, results in the same legal treatment for all members of the class. *Costea* is clear in this sense. Even a knowledgeable and experienced person deserves consumer protection when acting for non-professional purposes.

If we apply the contractual-position logic to the formation of contracts, it points to a radical change. The existence and validity of contracts, according to classic contract law, pivots on the actual contracting parties (not on categories of parties), and on their actual knowledge and expertise. For example, any incorrect statement made while bargaining is to be assessed against that backdrop to determine a possible defect of consent. For those purposes, it is certainly not the same situation with an experienced party as with a layperson. However, if all members of the class are to be treated alike during contract formation, the outcome could be a standardised criterion to determine the validity of contracts. The contractual-position logic would therefore be fertile terrain for the development of a legal standard in the formation of contracts. The hypothesis of this chapter is that the standards of the 'average consumer' and the 'average retail (investment) client' serve that function to the detriment of agreement.

[47] Case C-110/14 *Horaţiu Ovidiu Costea v SC Volksbank România SA* ECLI:EU:C:2015:538, para 21.

[48] Case C-498/16 *Maximilian Schrems v Facebook Ireland Limited* ECLI:EU:C:2018:37, para 39. It was solved under Council Regulation (EC) No 44/2001 of 22 December 2000 on jurisdiction and the recognition and enforcement of judgments in civil and commercial matters [2001] OJ L12/1 (Brussels I Regulation).

[49] Case C-2018/18 *Jana Petruchová v FIBO Group Holdings Limited* ECLI:EU:C:2019:825, para 55. It was solved under Regulation (EU) No 1215/2012 of the European Parliament and of the Council of 12 December 2012 on jurisdiction and the recognition and enforcement of judgments in civil and commercial matters [2012] OJ L351/1 (Brussels I Regulation recast).

[50] N Reich, HW Micklitz, P Rott and K Tonner, *European Consumer Law* (Cambridge, Intersentia, 2014); Terryn (n 43) 280–81.

As noted, EU law has frequently resorted to the contractual-position logic as an instrument of protection of the weaker party in asymmetric contracts, be it a consumer or a retail investor (Recital 86 MiFID II). It is only in respect of them ('protective contracts') that MEUCL operates. A general contract law, applicable to all contracts in the same way (an assumption that underlay the soft law proposals to harmonise European contract law) is currently not the driving force of EU hard law. Beyond 'protective' or 'asymmetric' contracts, the interference of EU law instruments with traditional rules on the formation of contracts is minimal and mostly restricted to the introduction of information duties.[51] In respect of negative harmonisation, EU law, at the most, introduces limitations to freedom of contract, with competition law being a good example of this (Articles 101 and 102 TFEU).

IV. The Legal Standard: The 'Average'

The EU legislative *acquis* remains piecemeal despite certain shared concepts and some overarching instruments that provide it with at least partial coherence.[52] Systematisation is enhanced by the CJEU through its concern for the consistency of the *acquis*.[53] Despite this, the chapter aims to prove that harmonisation of the rules on formation of 'protective contracts' arises from a cross-EU secondary law analysis.[54] To achieve that objective, the chapter will assess the main legislative instruments that impact the formation of contracts.

EU law is notoriously frugal in defining how a contract comes into existence.[55] Unlike national law, references to the process of formation as a result of acceptance mirroring an offer are scarce. This is a logical outcome of the lack of express competences of the Union to regulate contract law as such. The measures undertaken in this field are justified, to a large extent, in a better functioning of the internal market (Article 114 TFEU).

[51] See, eg the e-Commerce Directive and the Prospectus Regulation (Regulation (EU) 2017/1129 of the European Parliament and of the Council of 14 June 2017 on the prospectus to be published when securities are offered to the public or admitted to trading on a regulated market, and repealing Directive 2003/71/EC [2017] OJ L168/12.

[52] S Weatherill, 'The Relationship of the Unfair Commercial Practices Directive to European and National Contract Laws' in S Weatherill and U Berniz (eds), *The Regulation of Unfair Commercial Practices under EC Directive 2005/29. New Rules and New Techniques* (Oxford, Hart Publishing, 2007) 122; Hesselink, 'Private Law' (n 30) 685.

[53] See Case C-694/17 *Pillar Securitisation Sàrl v Hildur Arnadottir* ECLI:EU:C:2019:345, para 34.

[54] In respect of this methodology, see V Mak, 'Harmonisation through 'Directive-Related' and 'Cross-Directive' Interpretation: The Role of the ECJ in the Development of European Consumer Law' (2008) Tilburg Institute of Comparative and Transnational Law Working Paper 2008/8, ssrn.com/abstract=1276191. See also A Johnston and H Unberath, 'European Private Law by Directives: Approach and Challenges' in C Twigg-Flesner (ed), *The Cambridge Companion to European Union Private Law* (Cambridge, Cambridge University Press, 2010) 85.

[55] Schulze and Zoll (n 14) 118.

The CJEU assumed that a contract is formed by means of offer and acceptance in *Rudolf Gabriel*, in the context of the Brussels Convention.[56] Therein the Court decided that a contract came into existence when the consumer ordered the goods that had been offered by the business, 'thereby demonstrating his acceptance of the offer – including all conditions attaching thereto – which that company had sent to him in person'.[57] Consumer legislation sometimes refers to the conclusion of the contract via offer and acceptance, although not in such clear terms. For example, Article 8(6) CRD states that when a contract is to be concluded by telephone, 'Member States may provide that the trader has to confirm the offer to the consumer who is bound only once he has signed the offer or has sent his written consent' – so that the signature or written consent entails an acceptance.[58] Either by express reference in EU law or as a result of national law, European contract law still relies on the theoretical model of offer and acceptance (with options of protective nature),[59] which results in agreement.

Despite this basis, it is claimed here that agreement and validity of contracts are being disrupted by the application of the legal standards of the average consumer and the average retail investment client. This section is aimed at proving that. Additionally, it traces signs of the new remedies (at an EU level) to control invalid contract formation, showcasing how the traditional ones could be affected. The analysis includes three main B2C horizontal (cross-sectorial) directives: the Unfair Contract Terms Directive (UCTD), the Unfair Commercial Practices Directive (UCPD) and the Consumer Rights Directive (CRD). It also showcases contract formation in other non-consumer protective contracts, such as those regulated by the Markets in Financial Instruments Directive (MiFID regime).

A. The Unfair Contract Terms Directive

One of the pillars of EU private law is the control of unfair terms, as established in the UCTD[60] and following the interpretation of the CJEU. The UCTD controls the

[56] 1968 Brussels Convention on jurisdiction and the enforcement of judgments in civil and commercial matters [1972] OJ L299/32.

[57] Case C-96/00 *Rudolf Gabriel* ECLI:EU:C:2002:436, para 48.

[58] However, the time of formation of the contract remains uncertain. See G De Cristofaro, 'After the Implementation of the Consumer Rights Directive in the Member States. Are the National Provisions on Consumer Sales Effectively Harmonised?' in G De Cristofaro and A De Franceschi (eds), *Consumer Sales in Europe. After the Implementation of the Consumer Rights Directive* (Cambridge, Intersentia, 2016) 11.

[59] I am referring here to the binding effect of public statements, which in many jurisdictions are considered as mere invitations to treat. See Beale et al (n 18) 252 ff. Instead, on occasion, EU law makes public statements binding, eg Art 6(1) of Directive (EU) 2015/2302 of the European Parliament and of the Council of 25 November 2015 on package travel and linked travel arrangements, amending Regulation (EC) No 2006/2004 and Directive 2011/83/EU of the European Parliament and of the Council and repealing Council Directive 90/314/EEC [2015] OJ L326/1 (Package Travel Directive); Art 7(1)d of Directive 2019/770 (Consumer Sales Directive).

[60] Hesselink, 'Private Law' (n 30) 684–85.

substantive fairness of non-negotiated B2C contracts, which constitutes a major inroad into traditional contract law.

The UCTD follows the above-stated logic of regulation by contractual position – B2C in this case. The aim of the UCTD is to re-establish the equality between the parties by correcting the imbalance that exists between the consumer and the seller/supplier due to the weaker position of the former as regards its bargaining power and level of knowledge.[61] It also includes the 'mass' aspect of MEUCL as it deals exclusively with non-negotiated terms, which is a characteristic of mass contracting.

The UCTD controls the substantive fairness of ancillary terms included in standard-form contracts directly if grey-listed in the Annex or when they reunite the characteristics of the general criteria set forth in Article 3(1) UCTD (contrary to good faith, the term causes a significant imbalance in the rights and obligations of the parties, to the detriment of the consumer). This type of control, which was certainly an inroad into freedom of contract, did not affect procedural fairness. Moreover, agreement remained unaltered in respect of the *essentialia negotii* as the control of terms under the UCTD does not reach the 'essential obligations under the contract', namely, 'the definition of the main subject matter of the contract nor to the adequacy of the price and remuneration, on the one hand, as against the services or goods supplied in exchange' (Article 4(2) UCTD). This was an amendment to the original draft of the UCTD, as a sign of respect for agreement and competition.[62] This chapter suggests that the approach to agreement is now changing.

Those essential obligations under the contract can be controlled if they are not drafted in 'plain intelligible language' (Article 4(2) UCTD), which is the requirement of transparency and is additionally set forth in Article 5 UCTD for all terms (ancillary or main). The CJEU advanced the interpretation of the UCTD by defining that transparency has the same substantive meaning throughout the UCTD (*CIB Bank, Gutiérrez Naranjo, Kásler, Matei*),[63] which exceeds mere grammatical control. Moreover, the Court has decided that this substantive interpretation depends on the capacity of an 'average consumer' to understand the legal and

[61] *Costea* (n 47) para 18, among many.

[62] S Cámara Lapuente, 'The Innovative Role of the CJEU's Case Law in the Review of Price-Related Terms in Standard Form Contracts' in Y Atamer and P Pichonnaz (eds), *Control of Price Terms in Standard Form Contracts* (Cham, Springer, 2019) 72. For a critic of the formalistic approach of the CJEU in the definition of a core term, see F Gómez Pomar, 'Core versus Non-core Terms and Legal Controls over Consumer Contract Terms: (Bad) Lessons from Europe?' (2019) 15 *European Review of Contract Law* 177, 189–93.

[63] Case C-621/17 *Gyula Kiss and CIB Bank Zrt. v Emil Kiss and Gyuláné Kiss* ECLI:EU:C:2019:820, para 36; Joined Cases C-154, 307 and 308/15 *Francisco Gutiérrez Naranjo v Cajasur Banco SAU; Ana María Palacios Martínez v Banco Bilbao Vizcaya Argentaria SA (BBVA) and Banco Popular Español SA v Emilio Irles López and Teresa Torres Andreu* ECLI:EU:C:2016:980, para 49; Case C-26/13 *Árpád Kásler, Hajnalka Káslerné Rábai v OTP Jelzálogbank Zrt* ECLI:EU:C:2014:282, para 69; Case C-143/13 *Bogdan Matei and Ioana Ofelia Matei v SC Volksbank România SA* ECLI:EU:C:2015:127, para 73.

economic implications of a term – a major definition which was introduced in *Kásler*.[64]

The 'average consumer' benchmark was developed by the CJEU and is already decades old.[65] It refers to that consumer that is 'reasonably well-informed, reasonably observant and circumspect'.[66] The achievement of this benchmark requires businesses to adequately inform the consumer,[67] which is an obligation that the Court developed,[68] despite the existing challenges arising from behavioural literature to the effectiveness of mandated information duties.[69]

The average consumer is not a statistical conception but a legal standard.[70] When applying the benchmark in the context of the UCTD, judges should take into consideration 'the nature of the goods or services for which the contract was concluded and … all the circumstances attending the conclusion of the contract' (Article 4(1) UCTD).[71] Therefore, the standard is contextualised.

The UCTD provides a valuable insight into the validity of non-negotiated contracts, which are customary in mass contracting (and hence form the basis of MEUCL). Beyond the substantive control of ancillary terms, the current interpretation of transparency that the CJEU developed impacts on the formation of contracts, affecting procedural justice. The purpose of transparency is to enable the comparison between offers in the market,[72] which prevents the consumer from entering into a contract in error.[73] To avoid an unwanted choice, businesses are additionally required to provide information.[74] These are all concepts that, in

[64] *Kásler* (n 63) paras 71–75.

[65] M Durovic, *European Law on Unfair Commercial Practices and Contract Law* (Oxford, Hart Publishing, 2016) 24 ff; V Mak, 'Standards of Protection: in Search of the "Average Consumer" of EU Law in the Proposal for a Consumer Rights Directive' (2010) TISCO Working Paper Series on Banking, Finance and Services 4/10, 4 ff, papers.ssrn.com/sol3/papers.cfm?abstract_id=1626115.

[66] *Kásler* (n 63) para 74.

[67] Case C-92/11 *RWE Vertrieb AG v Verbraucherzentrale Nordrhein-Westfalen e V* ECLI:EU:C:2013:180, para 50.

[68] HW Micklitz and N Reich, 'The Court and Sleeping Beauty: The Revival of the Unfair Contract Terms Directive (UCTD)' (2014) 51 *CML Rev* 771, 786.

[69] Howells (n 31); O Ben-Shahar and C Schneider, 'The Failure of Mandated Disclosure' (2011) 159 *University of Pennsylvania Law Review* 647; O Ben-Shahar and C Schneider, *More Than You Wanted to Know. The Failure of Mandated Disclosure* (Princeton, Princeton University Press, 2014); O Seizov, AJ Wulf and J Luzak, 'The Transparent Trap: A Multidisciplinary Perspective on the Design of Transparent Online Disclosures in the EU' (2019) 42 *Journal of Consumer Policy* 149.

[70] Recital 18 of Directive 2005/29 (UCPD). See V Mak, 'Standards in European Private Law. A Model for European Private Law Pluralism' (2013) Tilburg Law School Legal Studies Research Paper Series 15/20129', papers.ssrn.com/sol3/papers.cfm?abstract_id=2302562, 18. On the use of empirical evidence, see BB Duivenvoorde, *The Consumer Benchmarks in the Unfair Commercial Practices Directive* (Cham, Springer, 2015) 20 ff.

[71] Case C-186/16 *Ruxandra Paula Andriciuc and Others v Banca Românească SA* ECLI:EU:C:2017:703, para 47.

[72] Cámara Lapuente, 'The Innovative Role' (n 62) 78.

[73] Case C-191/15 *Verein für Konsumenteninformation v Amazon EU Sàrl* ECLI:EU:C:2016:612, para 71.

[74] *RWE Vertrieb* (n 67) para 50.

national law, relate to the formation and validity of contracts. It is therefore possible to argue that the Court's stance towards agreement and its validity is enshrined in the concept of transparency, at least in the context of the UCTD, with transparency being benchmarked against the legal standard of the 'average consumer'.

Therefore, if an average consumer were unable to understand a term, it would be non-binding[75] and, if the term were a main one, it could even result in the invalidity of the contract due to a 'lack of transparency', which is to be objectively asserted, following the CJEU in *Pereničová*.[76] Moreover, as mentioned above, the CJEU decided in *Costea* that the actual knowledge and expertise of the contracting consumer is immaterial to the claim.[77]

If the concept of 'consumer' is analysed against the backdrop of the requirement of transparency, the result is that the application of the 'average consumer' test cannot take actual knowledge into account. Hence, a term and also a contract could be invalid, in the absence of transparency, even if an actual consumer understood and could foresee the consequences of the term.

This is a radically different outcome to agreement and validity compared to national law, where no action for invalidity is granted if agreement is not actually vitiated because one party did not or could not rely on the information received from its counterparty. This was assessed subjectively or objectively, but always in the position of the actual contracting parties. This is not the case for the average consumer under the UCTD, which makes the approach to agreement and validity innovative and particular to EU law.

However, it should be noted that in a more recent thread of cases under the UCTD (*Banco Primus*,[78] *Dunai*[79] and *GT v HS*[80]), the Court related the transparency control with the general substantive unfairness assessment (Article 3(1) UCTD). This could imply that the assessment of transparency of main terms is moving along the timeline of the life cycle of contracts: from formation to the content of contracts (terms).[81] According to some, the Court could have overstepped its constitutional boundaries in granting a remedy that remained in the realm of procedural autonomy.[82] Moreover, the CJEU could be interpreting the

[75] On the similarities of this remedy with invalidity, see C Leskinen and F de Elizalde, 'The Control of Terms That Define the Essential Obligations of the Parties under the Unfair Contract Terms Directive: Gutiérrez Naranjo' (2018) 55 *CML Rev* 1595, 1607–10.

[76] Case C-453/10 *Jana Pereničová and Vladislav Perenič v SOS financ spol. s.r.o.* ECLI:EU:C:2012:144, paras 31–34.

[77] *Costea* (n 47) para 21.

[78] Case C-421/14 *Banco Primus SA v Jesús Gutiérrez García* ECLI:EU:C:2017:60, para 64.

[79] Case C-118/17 *Zsuzsanna Dunai v ERSTE Bank Hungary Zrt* ECLI:EU:C:2019:207, para 49.

[80] Case C-38/17 *GT v HS* ECLI:EU:C:2019:461, para 37.

[81] As anticipated by P Nebbia, *Unfair Contract Terms in European Law* (Oxford, Hart Publishing, 2007) 137.

[82] S Cámara Lapuente, 'Un examen crítico de la STJUE de 21 diciembre 2016: nulidad retroactiva sí, falta de transparencia 'abusiva' de las cláusulas suelo no' (2017) 9 *Cuadernos de Derecho Transnacional* 383, 389–91. On the lack of harmonisation, see M Ebers, 'Unfair Contract Terms Directive (93/13)' in

Directive through the lens of German law (§ 307.1 BGB, which, according to the prevailing interpretation, links transparency with the general assessment test) and not through the UCTD.[83]

This interpretation diverges from the more recent regulation of standard terms in EU law, more specifically B2B contracts in the context of online intermediation services, according to which a non-transparent term is null and void.[84] In any case, the interpretation of the CJEU does not necessarily imply a change in national law as the UCTD seeks minimum harmonisation, and Member States could raise the level of protection by sanctioning non-transparency directly; thus remaining an issue of formation of contracts.[85]

B. The Unfair Commercial Practices Directive

The UCPD is an important instrument in the consumer *acquis* as it sets the standard of commercial behaviour horizontally (Article 3(1) UCPD). The scope of application of the UCPD *ratione materiae* is broad: 'any act, omission, course of conduct or representation, commercial communication including advertising and marketing, by a trader, directly connected with the promotion, sale or supply of a product to consumers' (Article 2(d) UCPD).[86] The CJEU has confirmed this broad meaning by interpreting the UCPD as applying to all commercial practices that distort consumers' economic behaviour.[87]

The UCPD regulates commercial behaviour in the pre-contractual stage; during the formation and performance of a contract; and at the post-contractual phase.[88] As in the case of the UCTD, the UCPD also assumes the contractual-position logic, limiting its scope of application to B2C relationships (Article 3(1) UCPD).

The unfairness assessment of a commercial practice should follow a three-step hierarchical mechanism.[89] The first step is to check whether the commercial

H Schulte-Nölke, C Twigg-Flesner and M Ebers (eds), *EC Consumer Law Compendium. The Consumer Acquis and its Transposition in the Member States* (Munich, Sellier, 2008) 201–02. See also Commission, 'Report from the Commission on the Implementation of Council Directive 93/13/EEC, of 5 April 1993, on Unfair Terms in Consumer Contracts' COM (2000) 248 final, 18–19.

83 Cámara Lapuente, 'The Innovative Role' (n 62) 93.

84 Art 3.3 of Regulation (EU) 2019/1150 of the European Parliament and of the Council of 20 June 2019 on promoting fairness and transparency for business users of online intermediation services [2019] OJ L186/57.

85 See Commission, 'Guidance on the Interpretation and Application of Council Directive 93/13/EEC of 5 April 1993 on unfair contract terms in consumer contracts' (Notice) C (2019) 5325 final, 18 and 37.

86 See also *UPC Magyarország* (n 31) para 34.

87 Case C-281/12 *Trento Sviluppo srl and Centrale Adriatica Soc. coop. arl v Autorità Garante della Concorrenza e del Mercato* ECLI:EU:C:2013:859, para 32.

88 S Whittaker, 'The Relationship of the Unfair Commercial Practices Directive to European and National Contract Laws' in Weatherill and Berniz (n 52) 155.

89 Durovic, *European Law* (n 65) 12.

practice is included in the blacklist of the UCPD (Annex I). If it is not, the practice must be assessed against the backdrop of three clauses on misleading actions, misleading omissions and aggressive practices (Articles 6–9 UCPD). In these scenarios, the commercial practice would be unfair if it causes or is likely to cause an 'average consumer' to take a 'transactional decision' (defined in Article 2(k) UCPD) that he would not have otherwise taken.[90]

Lastly, if the practice passes the two first tests, the general clause applies: the commercial practice is unfair if

> it is contrary to the requirements of professional diligence and it materially distorts or is likely to materially distort the economic behaviour with regard to the product of the average consumer whom it reaches or to whom it is addressed, or of the average member of the group when a commercial practice is directed to a particular group of consumers.[91]

In the case of consumers who are vulnerable (for reasons of 'mental or physical infirmity, age or credulity'), the assessment is conducted from the perspective of the average member of that group (Article 5(3) UCPD).

Article 3(2) UCPD splits unfair commercial practices from their consequences in contracts, stating that 'This Directive is without prejudice to contract law and, in particular, to the rules on the validity, formation or effect of a contract'. Concurrent reasons could explain this provision, which, although reasonable from a traditional private law perspective, departs from a twofold enforcement (private and public), which is frequent in the consumer *acquis*.[92]

However, as was advanced at the time of the enactment of the UCPD[93] and confirmed 10 years later,[94] the UCPD has had a strong impact on contractual relationships, at both the national and EU level. In fact, all three general clauses of the UCPD (misleading actions, misleading omissions and aggressive commercial practices) require that the practice affects or is likely to affect a 'transactional decision' of the consumer. A transactional decision is defined as

> any decision taken by a consumer concerning whether, how and on what terms to purchase, make payment in whole or in part for, retain or dispose of a product or to exercise a contractual right in relation to the product, whether the consumer decides to act or to refrain from acting.[95]

In other words, it relates to those decisions that affect the life cycle of contracts, including formation.

[90] *Trento Sviluppo* (n 87) para 36.
[91] Art 5(2) UCPD.
[92] Whittaker (n 88) 140–41.
[93] ibid 143–45.
[94] M Durovic, 'The Subtle Europeanization of Contract Law. The Case of Directive 2005/29 EC on Unfair Commercial Practices' (2015) 23 *European Review of Private Law* 715, 716.
[95] Art 2(k) UCPD.

Misleading actions (Article 6 UCPD), including communicating wrong or deceptive information, as well as misleading omissions of material information (Article 7 UCPD), are typical situations of defects of consent in national law (mistake, misrepresentation), whereas the aggressive commercial practices of coercion and undue influence (Articles 8 and 9 UCPD) are also usual instances of defects of consent (duress, undue influence).[96] Therefore, the UCPD impacts the national law of those Member States which have, in fact, resorted to these remedies directly or indirectly, or have even created specific contractual remedies for the breach of the UCPD.[97]

However, all those practices require that unfairness is benchmarked against the 'average consumer' or the 'average member of the group' when the practice is aimed at them, or the 'vulnerable consumer', in the conditions defined. Therefore, unlike the technique of the defects of consent, the actual parties are immaterial in the determination of the validity of the contract. Hence, the defects of consent might not be effective remedies to deal with infringements of the UCPD unless the UCPD is seriously disrupted.[98] The same could be argued in respect of any remedy that involves causation, as is the case in the UK, where individual redress against an unfair commercial practice requires that the practice was 'a significant factor in the consumer's decision to enter into the contract'.[99] The benchmark of the 'average consumer' ignores the subtleties of an individual decision.

Standardisation is enhanced by the new remedies that Directive 2019/2161 has incorporated into the UCPD[100] as a result of the reform that was planned under the New Deal for Consumers.[101] Following the recommendations of the Fitness Check,[102] the reform introduced remedies for individual redress into the UCPD. The new Article 11a UCPD foresees private law remedies to cure a breach of the UCPD, including damages and, 'where relevant', reduction of price or termination of the contract. At least the latter are clear contractual remedies (damages could follow a contract or, instead, be grounded in tort or unjust enrichment).

[96] Whittaker (n 88) 152; Durovic, 'The Subtle Europeanization' (n 94) 743.

[97] Durovic, 'The Subtle Europeanization' (n 94) 743–46; FP Patti, '"Fraud" and "Misleading Commercial Practices": Modernising the Law of Defects in Consent' (2016) 12 *European Review of Contract Law* 307, 319–25; Civic Consulting for the European Commission, 'Study for the Fitness Check of EU Consumer and Marketing Law' (2017), ec.europa.eu/newsroom/just/item-detail.cfm?item_id=59332.

[98] H Collins, 'EC Regulation of Unfair Commercial Practices' in H Collins (ed), *The Forthcoming EC Directive on Unfair Commercial Practices* (Alphen aan den Rijn, Wolters Kluwer, 2005) 37; Durovic, *European Law* (n 65) 161.

[99] Consumer Protection from Unfair Trading Regulations 2008, s 27A(6). See also S Whittaker, 'Consumer Contracts' in H Beale (ed), *Chitty on Contracts*, II (London, Sweet & Maxwell, 2015) 1022.

[100] Directive (EU) 2019/2161 of the European Parliament and of the Council of 27 November 2019 amending Council Directive 93/13/EEC and Directives 98/6/EC, 2005/29/EC and 2011/83/EU of the European Parliament and of the Council as regards the better enforcement and modernisation of Union consumer protection rules [2019] OJ L328/7.

[101] Commission, Council and the European Economic and Social Committee, 'A New Deal for Consumers' (Communication) COM (2018) 183 final.

[102] n 97.

The reform of the UCPD has bridged the gap between unfair commercial practices and contract law. In respect of the formation of contracts, this seems to reinforce the claim that agreement has become standardised. If the breach of the UCPD is to be benchmarked against the 'average consumer' (or the alternative legal standards), an effective design of the contractual remedies should not depart from that standard. Even though Article 11a UCPD dictates that 'Member states may determine the conditions for the application and effects of those remedies', national procedural autonomy should comply with the principle of effectiveness of EU law.[103] Arguably, it would be ineffective to deny a remedy when a breach of the UCPD affects the transactional decision of the average consumer (Articles 5–9 UCPD), even though an individual consumer is not influenced by the unfair practice.[104] However, it cannot be omitted that the reform did not address individual causation, which leaves the control of effectiveness in the realm of the judiciary.

In that respect, it could be argued that the standardised understanding of agreement under the UCPD is further supported by the concept of 'consumer'. In a similar vein to other legislative instruments of the *acquis*, the UCPD defines who a consumer is in an objective manner, stating that it is any natural person who acts for purposes outside of his trade, craft, business or profession (Article 2a UCPD).

The CJEU has not yet had the opportunity to rule on the specific question of whether the knowledge and experience of a particular consumer justifies a departure from its protection under the UCPD. The answer to this question is important because, if personal circumstances were deemed irrelevant, it would entail an insurmountable barrier to the application of the defects of consent (at least in their traditional shape) to control infringements of the UCPD. It would also mean that the new contractual remedies of the UCPD would be granted even if a consumer could not have been affected by an unfair commercial practice because of its higher knowledge or expertise. It should be recalled that in *Costea* the Court rejected taking personal knowledge and expertise into account, in the context of unfair contract terms.[105] A consistent interpretation of EU law[106] would presumably extend the stare decisis of *Costea* to the UCPD. There does not seem to be a justifiable divergence in the definition of the consumer in the UCTD and the UCPD, unlike what could be said of the type of control that each directive aims at.[107]

[103] See n 12.

[104] *cf* M Loos, 'The Modernization of European Consumer Law (Continued): More Meat on the Bone After All' (2019) Amsterdam Law School Legal Studies Research Paper 2019-32, 4, https://papers.ssrn.com/sol3/papers.cfm?abstract_id=3445448.

[105] *Costea* (n 47) para 21.

[106] Whittaker (n 88) 150; *Kamenova* (n 46) paras 25–29.

[107] *Pereničová* (n 76) para 43; Case C-109/17 *Bankia SA v Juan Carlos Mari Merino and Others* ECLI:EU:C:2018:735, para 36.

In support of this argument, in *Kamenova*, the Court gave a uniform interpretation for the UCPD and the CRD to the concept of 'trader',[108] the 'B' party of the B2C contract who, unlike the consumer, acts for purposes relating to his trade, business, craft or profession. The 'trader' is defined in a positive way (who it is) and is the other side of the coin of the 'consumer', who is negatively defined (it is not a trader). The argument of the Court was that both the UCPD and the CRD are based on Article 114 TFEU and, as such, pursue the same objectives of contributing to the proper functioning of the internal market and ensuring a high level of consumer protection.[109]

The UCTD, in the context of which *Costea* was decided, has the same constitutional basis as the UCPD: Article 100A EEC Treaty (Recital 1), which is the predecessor of Article 114 TFEU.[110] Moreover, both the UCTD and the UCPD share the assumption that the consumer is in a weak position vis-à-vis the trader.[111] Therefore, it seems reasonable that the uniform interpretation of who a trader is will be shared. Consequently, the concept of the counterparty to the contract (ie the consumer, who is not a trader) would also become harmonised, with all its implications. Thus, it is sensible for the Court to extend *Costea* to the UCPD and ignore the personal circumstances of a particular consumer. This outcome would reinforce the doubts concerning the 'defects of consent' (or any other remedy that takes personal circumstances into account) as an effective remedy to cure an unfair commercial practice. It would also enable the interpretation of the contractual remedies of the UCPD without resorting to individual causation.

C. The Consumer Rights Directive

The CRD regulates duties to provide pre-contractual information in B2C contracts horizontally. The CRD contains a pointillist list of information that should be disclosed in contracts other than distance and off-premises ones (Article 5(1) CRD), both of which have a specific regulation within the CRD (Articles 6–16 CRD), as they proceeded from previous EU legal instruments. However, the duty to disclose pre-contractual information is also set forth for those contracts (Article 6(1) CRD).

The obligation imposed upon the trader to provide information to the consumer before it is bound by a contract completes the legal framework of contract formation horizontally in B2C contracts, which is also composed by the UCTD and the UCPD. However, in line with the latter, Article 3(5) CRD states that 'This Directive shall not affect national general contract law such as the rules

[108] *Kamenova* (n 46) para 29.
[109] ibid para 28.
[110] S Weatherill and U Berniz, 'Introduction' in Weatherill and Berniz (n 52) 1.
[111] *UPC Magyarország* (n 31) para 53; *Pereničová* (n 76) para 27.

on the validity, formation or effect of a contract, in so far as general contract law aspects are not regulated in this Directive'. Consistent with this approach, remedies for the breach of the pre-contractual duty to provide information were left to the procedural autonomy of Member States, the efficacy of which should be assessed according to the interpretation given to the CRD.[112] The referral to national law remedies is restricted to contracts other than distance and off-premises ones. In respect of distance and off-premises contracts, the CRD does foresee some specific remedies.[113] Moreover, for these, the information that the trader must disclose becomes an 'integral part of the contract' (Article 6(5) CRD), which leads to contractual remedies in the event of breach.[114]

Unlike the UCPD, the CRD does not resort to general clauses but, instead, lists the information that the trader ought to disclose. The existence of a list could explain why there was no need to benchmark the obligation to inform against the 'average consumer'. However, the quality of that information and the way in which it is presented do require a benchmark. Should the information be comprehensible for an actual consumer, taking its personal characteristics into account? Or, instead, should it be understandable for an average consumer? The answer is important in analysing agreement and determining if the stance of EU law remains within classic economics (information duties to correct market failures) or instead whether agreement has ceased to be the criterion to determine a valid contract formation.

Unlike the UCPD, there is no express reference in the CRD to the 'average consumer'. Also unlike the UCPD, the CRD does not foresee categories of addressees of the information (average consumer, vulnerable consumer, targeted consumer). However, in Recital 34 CRD it is stated that the trader should give 'clear and comprehensible information', taking into account the specific needs of vulnerable consumers, the definition of whom is identical to the one enshrined in Article 5(3) UCPD. Therefrom, it has been interpreted that the 'vulnerable consumer' represents a subsidiary benchmark to assess the information required under the CRD (as in the UCPD) and that, consequently, the 'average consumer' would be the main benchmark.[115]

In fact, the CRD requires that the information be provided in a 'clear and comprehensible manner' (Article 5(1) CRD). Furthermore, as a formal requirement for off-premises contracts, the information should be given on paper or another durable medium, in a way that is 'legible, and in plain intelligible

[112] Art 23(1) CRD. De Cristofaro (n 58) 11–13.

[113] Arts 6(6), 10(1) and 14(1) CRD. See E Hall, G Howells and J Watson, 'The Consumer Rights Directive – An Assessment of Its Contribution to the Development of European Consumer Contract Law' (2012) 8 *European Review of Contract Law* 139, 152–53; L Tigelaar, 'How to Sanction a Breach of Information Duties of the Consumer Rights Directive?' (2019) 27/1 *European Review of Private Law* 27, 34 ff.

[114] A Nordhausen Scholes, 'Information Requirements' in G Howells and R Schulze, *Modernising and Harmonising Consumer Contract Law* (Munich, Sellier, 2009) 225.

[115] Durovic, 'The Subtle Europeanization' (n 94) 721.

language' (Article 7(1) CRD). For distance contracts, the information must be made available to the consumer in a way appropriate to the means of distance communications used 'in plain intelligible language' (Article 8(1) CRD). Insofar as that information is provided in a durable medium, it should be 'legible' (Article 8(1) CRD). If a distance contract is to be concluded by electronic means and places the consumer under an obligation to pay, some of the information listed should be given in a 'clear and prominent manner' (Article 8(2) CRD).

The terminological conundrum ('clear and comprehensible manner', 'legible', 'plain intelligible language', 'clear and prominent') has rightfully been criticised.[116] In the absence of definitions, it confuses (creating different standards?) and sheds no light on the quality of the information that has to be provided. However, the CJEU in *Purely Creative* used some of those terms in the context of the UCPD in relation to the 'average consumer', even though they are not mentioned therein, which could reinforce the argument of a uniform meaning of transparency in consumer contracts.[117]

Furthermore, in *Verbraucherzentrale Berlin*, the CJEU introduced the benchmark of the 'average consumer' into the CRD to ascertain whether a stand at a trade fair should be classified as 'business premises' (within the meaning of Article 2(9) CRD).[118] In *Walbusch*, the Court extended its use to the provision of information. Specifically, in the interpretation of Article 8(4) CRD, the Court referred to the criterion of the 'average consumer targeted by that communication' to assess whether in a specific case the complete list of information requirements of the CRD (Article 6(1) CRD) could be displayed.[119] *Walbusch* could have far-reaching consequences in filling in the existing gaps of the CRD. The 'average consumer targeted by that communication' could be the standard 'average consumer' or a particular group of consumers targeted by the communication. Finally, it could be the vulnerable consumer if the communication targets that group, which is referred to in Recital 34 CRD.

If, following *Kamenova*, the concept of trader in the CRD and the UCPD is uniform[120] and, inversely, the concept of consumer should also be uniform, the CRD could make headway in the interpretation of the quality and format of the information disclosed according to the 'average consumer'. Furthermore, considering the shared constitutional justification of the CRD and the UCTD (Article 114 TFEU), and the common approach to consumer protection,[121] the

[116] Hall et al (n 113) 150–51.

[117] Case C-428/11 *Purely Creative Ltd and Others v Office of Fair Trading* ECLI:EU:C:2012:651, paras 55–56.

[118] Case C-485/17 *Verbraucherzentrale Berlin eV v Unimatic Vertriebs GmbH* ECLI:EU:C:2018:642, para 43.

[119] Case C-430/17 *Walbusch Walter Busch GmbH & Co. KG v Zentrale zur Bekämpfung unlauteren Wettbewerbs Frankfurt am Main eV* ECLI:EU:C:2019:47, para 47.

[120] *Kamenova* (n 46) para 29.

[121] ibid para 28.

concept of consumer defined in *Costea* (objective, disregarding experience and knowledge)[122] could be extended to the CRD.

The 'average consumer' benchmark to assess the quality of information was used in *Romano* in the context of Directive 2002/65/EC, which regulates distance consumer contracts for financial services (excluded from the CRD, ex Article 3(3)(d)).[123] In parallel to the CRD, this directive sets forth a list of information that the business must disclose prior to the contract, also (as in Articles 5(1) and 6(1) CRD) 'in a clear and comprehensible manner' (Articles 3(1) and (2) Directive 2002/65/EC). As in the CRD, there is no benchmark against which to assess the quality of the information that should be disclosed. In *Romano*, the Advocate General understood that the definition of consumer in the UCTD, the UCPD and Directive 2002/65/EC (Article 2 (d)) is uniform, and includes the benchmark of the 'average consumer' as defined by the CJEU for the UCTD and the UCPD.[124] The CJEU followed the Advocate General.[125]

Therefore, it seems that this benchmark is the one that should be used to assess the quality and format of the information disclosed under the CRD. Information that is not comprehensible to an average consumer, if central to the contract, could result in invalidity (due to lack of transparency?) even if the claimant is experienced or knowledgeable. The use of the average consumer to benchmark information could minimise the criticism directed at mandatory disclosure, as transparency is different to mere disclosure of information. The model of the 'average consumer' (rational or, instead, including behavioural aspects) could determine the change in contract formation from a rational individual to a more realistic criterion, but in either case standardised.

D. The MiFID Regime

Disruption in the formation of 'protective' or 'asymmetric' (mass) contracts is not restricted to B2C relationships. This section will explore the traces of MEUCL in sectorial legislation beyond consumer protection – more precisely, in investment law under the MiFID regime.

The MiFID framework provides a high level of harmonised investor protection (Recital 70 MiFID II). It comprises not only the MiFID II, but also the MiFIR[126] and a significant number of implementing instruments (Level 2 provisions) of which, for the purposes of this chapter, the Commission Delegated

[122] *Costea* (n 47) para 21.
[123] Case C-143/18 *Antonio Romano and Lidia Romano v DSL Bank* ECLI:EU:C:2019:701.
[124] Opinion of AG Pitruzzella in Case C-143/18 *Romano* ECLI:EU:C:2019:273, para 78–79.
[125] *Romano* (n 123) paras 54–55.
[126] Regulation (EU) No 600/2014 of the European Parliament and of the Council of 15 May 2014 on markets in financial instruments and amending Regulation (EU) No 648/2012 [2014] OJ L173/84 (MiFIR).

Regulation (EU) 2017/565 is of importance.[127] The current regime replaced the MiFID I[128] legislative framework and tightened it in the aftermath of the 2008 financial crisis.[129]

The MiFID II (as did the MiFID I) classifies investors into three categories with a decreasing degree of protection: retail clients, professional clients and eligible counterparties. A retail client is defined in a negative way (as EU law does with consumers) as he 'who is not a professional client' (Article 4(1)(11) MiFID II). Professional clients are listed: regulated or authorised professional participants in financial markets, large undertakings meeting the established criteria, major public entities and other (non-regulated) institutional investors (Article 4(1)(10) and Annex II MiFID II).[130] An investor that is not automatically classified as professional may request to be treated as such if it meets qualitative and quantitative requirements, specified in MiFID II, that prove that it 'possesses the experience, knowledge and expertise to make its own investment decisions and properly assess the risks that it incurs' (Annex II MiFID II).[131] Lastly, the eligible counterparties (open) listed receive the least degree of protection (Article 30 MiFID II).

In respect of the investment firm–client relationship, the MiFID II adopts the contractual-position logic (that is the basis of MEUCL) by providing different rules according to the category of client, which does not follow the already more established B2B, B2C, C2C model. Retail clients include consumers, but also small and medium-sized enterprises (SMEs) and other legal entities that are not listed as professional clients nor eligible counterparties.[132] Thus, the subjective scope of those treated as retail clients and, hence, that receive the highest level of protection under MiFID II is broader than that envisaged in consumer law.

Investment firms have the obligation to act 'honestly, fairly and professionally in accordance with the best interests of their clients'.[133] The key provisions specifying this duty are:[134] the obligation of investment firms to adequately inform their clients or potential clients (Article 24(3)–(7) MiFID II) and, when required, to

[127] Commission Delegated Regulation (EU) 2017/565 of 25 April 2016 supplementing Directive 2014/65/EU of the European Parliament and of the Council as regards organisational requirements and operating conditions for investment firms and defined terms for the purposes of that Directive [2017] OJ L87/1 (CDR).

[128] Directive 2004/39/EC of the European Parliament and of the Council of 21 April 2004 on markets in financial instruments amending Council Directives 85/611/EEC and 93/6/EEC and Directive 2000/12/EC of the European Parliament and of the Council and repealing Council Directive 93/22/EEC [2004] OJ L145/1 (MiFID I).

[129] Busch and Ferrarini (n 42) v.

[130] Kruithof (n 42) 116–17.

[131] ibid; R Steennot, 'Protecting Investors through Information Requirements' (2011) 4 *International Journal of Private Law* 111, 114–15.

[132] Kruithof (n 42) 121–23.

[133] L Enriques and M Gargantini, 'The Overarching Duty to Act in the Best Interest of the Client in MiFID II' in Busch and Ferrarini (n 42) 85–122.

[134] ibid 89.

conduct the suitability and appropriateness tests of a service or product ('know-your-customer' duties, Article 25 MiFID II). The European Commission identified these duties as being among the ones that are most likely to be found in private claims against investment firms.[135]

Private enforcement of the MiFID regime was not expressly foreseen in MiFID I, which only set forth administrative sanctions (Article 51). However, when deciding on the non-compliance of know-your-customer duties under MiFID I, the CJEU in *Genil* interpreted it thus:

> In the absence of EU legislation on the point, it is for the internal legal order of each Member State to determine the contractual consequences of non-compliance with those obligations, subject to observance of the principles of equivalence and effectiveness.[136]

Thus, the prevailing view thereon was that Member States could choose the private law remedy but should necessarily recognise one.[137]

The last paragraph of Article 69(2) MiFID II reinforces this understanding:

> Member States shall ensure that mechanisms are in place to ensure that compensation may be paid or other remedial action be taken in accordance with national law for any financial loss or damage suffered as a result of an infringement of this Directive or of [MiFIR].

This remedy is subject to the principles of effectiveness and equivalence, and coexists with public enforcement of the MiFID regime (Article 70 MiFID II).[138]

For the purposes of MEUCL, it is important to determine whether the MiFID regime provides a benchmark against which to assess the effectiveness of a private law remedy recognised in national law. In the context of contract formation, which is under analysis, the assessment has to relate to the overarching information duties imposed upon investment firms. Information, especially about the risks associated with a certain investment service or product, is crucial in the decision of an investor to enter into a contract.[139] Therefore, non-compliance with those duties has a direct impact on a valid contract formation.

Article 24(3) MiFID II requires that all information, including marketing communications, that an investment firm addresses to clients or potential

[135] Commission, 'Public Consultation: Review of the Markets in Financial Instruments Directive', 8 December 2010 (Review of Markets in Financial Instruments).

[136] Case C-604/11 *Genil 48 SL and Comercial Hostelera de Grandes Vinos SL v Bankinter SA and Banco Bilbao Vizcaya Argentaria SA* ECLI:EU:C:2013:344, para 57.

[137] S Grundmann, 'The Bankinter Case on MiFID Regulation and Contract Law' (2013) 9 *European Review of Contract Law* 267, 278; D Busch, 'The Private Law Effect of MiFID: Genil and Beyond' (2017) 13 *European Review of Contract Law* 70, 73–74.

[138] Busch (n 137) 74.

[139] M Wallinga, 'Why MiFID & MiFID II Do (Not) Matter to Private Law: Liability to Compensate for Investment Losses for Breach of Conduct of Business Rules' (2019) 27 *European Review of Private Law* 515, 519–20.

clients is 'fair, clear and not misleading'. Article 24(4) MiFID II establishes that 'Appropriate information shall be provided in good time to clients or potential clients with regard to the investment firm and its services, the financial instruments and proposed investment strategies, execution venues and all costs and related charges', and adds details to this respect. Article 24(5) MiFID II states that such information

> shall be provided in a comprehensible form in such a manner that clients or potential clients are reasonably able to understand the nature and risks of the investment service and of the specific type of financial instrument that is being offered and, consequently, to take investment decisions on an informed basis.

Additionally, 'Member States may allow that information to be provided in a standardised format' (Article 24(5) MiFID II).

However, against which benchmark should it be assessed that the information is 'fair, clear and not misleading', 'appropriate' and 'provided in a comprehensible manner'? An individual investor or an average one according to the classification of clients set forth in MiFID II?

The answer is hidden in the Commission Delegated Regulation (EU) 2017/565 (CDR), a Level 2 instrument of the MiFID regime. Article 44 CDR gives guidance in respect of the benchmark against which the information should be assessed. It specifies the conditions that the information must meet in order to be 'fair, clear and not misleading' (as required by Article 24 MiFID II) when investment firms disseminate it to 'retail or professional clients' or 'potential retail or professional clients'. As regards the quality of that information, Article 44(2)(d) CDR states that the information must be 'sufficient for, and presented in a way that is likely to be understood by, the average member of the group to whom it is directed, or by whom it is likely to be received' – ie the average retail client or the average professional client.[140]

Furthermore, in the provision of non-complex services, reference is made to the standard of the average investor, which in that case is the 'average retail client'. A financial instrument is non-complex if, among other things,

> adequately comprehensive information on its characteristics is publicly available and is likely to be readily understood so as to enable the average retail client to make an informed judgment as to whether to enter into a transaction in that instrument.[141]

Therefore, it seems that for a national private law remedy to effectively cure an infringement of MiFID in the formation of contracts, a requirement that stems from the CJEU case *Genil* and the last paragraph of Article 69(2) MiFID II,[142] it must be benchmarked against the standard of the group targeted by the

[140] *cf* Steennot (n 131) 115.
[141] Art 57(f) CDR.
[142] See n 137.

information – an average retail client or an average professional client. As retail clients are defined in an objective manner (who is not a professional client), the particular knowledge or expertise of the investor might not be taken into account so as not to hinder the protection enshrined in MiFID II, which is one of the key objectives of the directive (Recital 70).[143] This is the same reasoning that the CJEU developed in *Costea*,[144] yet in a different protective context: that of B2C contracts. Hence, a remedy in national law (as a defect of consent) that requires investigation of the particular knowledge or expertise of the investor might not be effective, even though guidance from the CJEU, in the specific context of MiFID II, has not yet been given.[145] Against this, it could be argued that it is not possible to define a homogeneous standard for retail investors as such, as it is a class that encompasses heterogeneous parties – from consumers to SMEs.

The solution could be more straightforward when the investor is a consumer and the non-compliance by the investment firm with its information duties causes or is likely to cause the average consumer to take a transactional decision that it would not otherwise have taken. This would entail an unfair commercial practice (Articles 7(1) and 7(5) and Annex II UCPD; Article 94 MiFID II),[146] with the envisaged contractual law consequences. This express cross-reference reinforces the argument of a harmonised system for contract formation arising from a cross-directive interpretation.

V. Conclusion

The information model has been the hallmark of EU private law, following a classic economic analysis (parties as rational agents) that revolves around agreement. It uses mandated disclosure to correct market failures arising from information asymmetries. If applied to individual transactions, it interacts easily with traditional general contract law. While requiring the strong party to disclose information indicates an inroad into the rules on formation of contracts (especially in the common law), it does not impact the assumption that agreement is the parameter of validity in the formation of contracts.

Instead, the ongoing transformation of EU law, which standardises contract formation, implies a radically new understanding of agreement and contractual validity. The use of a legal standard (the 'average') to determine procedural fairness entails an innovative intervention of EU law. Indeed, the common thread that can be found in several EU law instruments shapes general contract law in a manner that is new and, at the same time, seems incompatible with traditional contract

[143] Busch (n 137) 88.
[144] *Costea* (n 47) para 21.
[145] Busch (n 137) 89.
[146] Steennot (n 131) 115–16.

rules. Reframing agreement could also affect how consent is interpreted in other (not necessarily contractual) areas, such as data protection.

MEUCL is still an untidy patchwork and it is therefore too early to call it a 'system'. Some legal instruments show a more defined picture than others. It is a work in progress, but it is, indeed, in progress. Rules that were aimed to intertwine with national law are being reshaped by the CJEU in a way that pushes the boundaries of national law backwards. A standardised, average-dependent EU contract law casts doubt on the effectiveness of traditional contract law remedies, which pivot around agreement and take individual knowledge and expertise into account. Unsurprisingly, the CJEU has been creating new remedies leading to invalidity, which are benchmarked against the average consumer.

The common design of EU law for mass contracting reaches exclusively relationships in need of particular protection, precisely those in which agreement was underperforming. Therefore, MEUCL does not lead to full harmonisation of European contract law. Although partial in its scope, MEUCL has the potential to reinvigorate, from a new angle, studies on harmonisation of European contract law, including harmonisation by mandatory law and the use of legal standards to deal with the intrinsic complexities of EU law as a pluralistic legal system.[147]

The standardised criterion to assess valid contract formation would lead to a system of contract law that is technologically more efficient. Standardisation enhances legal solutions that are more homogeneous and produce less varied big data, which increases the reliability of the outcomes that AI produces from that data. Disrupting contract law in this manner could be a game changer in the global competition for supremacy in AI, placing EU law at the forefront of innovation in law.

MEUCL could also enhance collective enforcement of EU law, a task that the EU has undertaken under the New Deal for Consumers.[148] Standardised rules would make EU law more apt for collective redress as the requirement of commonality (a shared question of law or fact that predominates over individual issues) is easier to meet than agreement, which necessarily has to be individually assessed.

However, concerns about the pressures of the instrumental character of MEUCL (which aims at the improved functioning of the internal market) on corrective justice would probably arise under Article 16 of the Charter of Fundamental Rights of the EU ('Freedom to conduct a business'), which is increasingly referred to in decisions of the CJEU concerning private law.[149] The debate should probably be framed within a broader discussion on the

[147] See n 70.

[148] See n 101.

[149] *Walbusch* (n 119) para 42; Case C-649/17 *Bundesverband der Verbraucherzentralen und Verbraucherverbände – Verbraucherzentrale Bundesverband eV v Amazon EU Sàrl* ECLI:EU:C:2019:576, para 44.

relationship between law and efficiency, which is not limited to the established analysis of economic efficiency but, instead, should comprise technological efficiency as well. It should also consider private autonomy, freedom of choice and individual responsibility against the backdrop of market regulation and consumer protection. The disruption of such a core notion of contract law as agreement opens a number of topics up that require further reflection. Hopefully, this chapter will serve as a springboard to some of them.

3

Schools of Thought in European Private Law

CRISTINA PONCIBÒ AND OSCAR BORGOGNO*

I. Introduction

The expression 'European private law' is relatively new and has various meanings according to the scholarship that has appeared in recent decades. The expression concerns the contributions of scholars from different legal and cultural backgrounds. The concept cannot be analysed according to the paradigms to which legal scholars used to be accustomed, because EU private law is not domestic law or supranational law; rather, it is both together and something more.[1] In the words of one author: 'When we speak of European private law we use a highly evocative term, because it refers to Europe that is a myth, a geographical expression, an economic and social idea, and finally a political expression.'[2]

Currently, the European private law field of study – that is, studies in EU private law traditionally supporting and consolidating the integration of the internal market – is in difficulties.[3] The EU seems to have lost law as a vector of dynamism and cohesion. This should result in the worrying question for scholars today about the future of private law in Europe. More generally, the process of European integration has undoubtedly encountered many other difficulties. What is striking about recent events (specifically Brexit and the rise of nationalism), however, is a general distrust in the positive force of law as a vehicle of integration.[4]

* Author of sub-sections IIIB and C. Any opinions expressed in this paper by the Authors are personal and are not to be attributed to the Bank of Italy.

[1] We think, for example, of the Directive on the manufacturer's liability for damage caused by product defects to users and consumers (85/374 EEC): it was issued by the Community bodies, implemented within the framework of the state regulations of the member countries of the Union, has given rise to a series of case law applications, introduced new terms, codified a principle – objective responsibility of the manufacturer – and led to the approximation of the provisions that in the individual orders already regulated the matter. The case is commented on by G Alpa, 'Il diritto privato europeo' [2019] *Federalismi* 1, 3.

[2] Alpa (ibid).

[3] J Habermas, *The Crisis of the European Union. A Response* (Cambridge, Polity, 2012).

[4] L Azoulai, '"Integration through Law" and Us' (2016) 14 *ICON* 449.

The legal form is no longer seen as the means to achieve a new spirit of pacification, cooperation and solidarity in Europe. EU private law is perceived as the vehicle of economic forces and government apparatuses at the origin of processes of restructuring national societies and their remaining welfare states. At this juncture, two authors have urged reconsideration of the EU's legal and political construction.[5] We note that the challenge is twofold: it is both substantive and methodological. The former concerns the scope of EU private law and its meaning; the latter concerns how to approach it. Although these issues are closely related, this chapter focuses on the latter.

In light of the foregoing discussion, we believe that legal scholarship should drive the future of private law in Europe.[6] Consequently, in what follows, we attempt to take stock of and analyse the current confusion, an exercise we deem necessary in these troubled times.[7] This will not be enough to resolve the issue, which is far too complicated, but we hope to furnish some preliminary insights into the approaches that have emerged in EU private law scholarship. First, we describe the main schools of thought, or intellectual traditions, in European private law, ie groups of scholars who share an opinion or a similar outlook on European private law. Secondly, we argue that such schools may be classified into classical and modern because of a shift of paradigm in understanding the relationship between private law and EU integration. The classical schools expressly admitted the subordination of private law to the construction of EU integration, while the modern schools have not followed the same path while searching for the foundations of private law in Europe.

For the purposes of this chapter, a school of thought is 'a community of expertise which considers itself a comparatively self-contained, teachable and knowable domain', while the act of 'disciplining' is the enforcement of circumscribed, usually conservative, views of such discipline.[8]

On this basis, we deal with the merits of a polyphonic engagement between the main theories that have been propounded to address the present challenges. We argue that if EU private law scholarship is to become a more productive and inclusive academic field, it should open itself up to critical self-reflection, which – surprisingly – is almost non-existent in the field,[9] and overcome the

[5] C Joerges and C Kreuder-Sonnen, 'European Studies and the European Crisis: Legal and Political Science between Critique and Complacency' (2017) 23 *European Law Journal* 118.

[6] R van Caenegem, *Judges, Legislators & Professors: Chapters in European Legal History* (Cambridge, Cambridge University Press, 1987).

[7] R van Gestel, HW Micklitz and EL Rubin (eds), *Rethinking Legal Scholarship: A Transatlantic Dialogue* (Cambridge, Cambridge University Press, 2017). H Schepel, 'Law, Lawyers and Legal Integration' (2004) 4(17) *EUSA Review* 1.

[8] I Manners, 'Normative Power Europe: A Transdisciplinary Approach to European Studies' in C Rumford (ed), *Handbook of European Studies* (New York, Sage, 2009).

[9] A notable exception is C Jorges and C Kreuder-Sonnen, 'Europe and European Studies in Crisis, Inter-disciplinary and Intra-disciplinary Schisms in Legal and Political Science' (2016) Berlin Social Science Centre Discussion Paper No 109. The authors conclude their contribution by saying: 'We are confident that contestation and critique will generate new ideas and perspectives for a European future beyond the present emergency politics.'

confusion of the present. Accordingly, the chapter benefits from a dialogue conducted between a researcher studying law and economics and its current developments and a researcher in comparative private law, in order to identify the main schools of thought from classical to modern and their role in the future evolutionary path of European private law.[10]

II. Classical Schools of Thought

A. Integration through Private Law Scholarship

The 'Integration through Law' school has been one of the most influential narratives of European integration.[11] In *Integration Through Law: Europe and the American Federal Experience*, the authors stressed that 'integration is fundamentally a political process' and law is 'but one of the many instruments' harnessed to achieve the objectives of integration, while 'law has a vital role to play in the process'.[12] Accordingly, the European Community has often been presented as

> a juristic idea; the written constitution as a sacred text; the professional commentary as a legal truth; the case law as the inevitable working out of the correct implications of the constitutional text; and the constitutional court as the disembodied voice of right reason and constitutional theology.[13]

The traditional role of a court of law is to interpret law already in effect, but the European Court of Justice (now the CJEU) has declared itself to be a 'new legal order of international law'.[14] In this respect, we underline that legal scholars have always been fascinated by the role played by the CJEU in dealing with national legal traditions (and specifically private law issues) in a more express or implicit way.[15] It has been stressed that the above-mentioned project viewed law as both an object and an agent of integration: while law is a product of the polity, the polity is

[10] R Zimmermann, 'Civil Code and Civil Law: The "Europeanization" of Private Law within the European Community and the Re-emergence of a European Legal Science' (1994–1995) 1 *Columbia Journal of European Law* 63.

[11] M Cappelletti, M Seccombe and J Weiler, 'A General Introduction' in M Cappelletti, M Seccombe, J Weiler (eds), *Integration through Law: Europe and the American Federal Experience* (Brussels, De Gruyter, 1985) 3–15 (describing the project as aimed at examining 'how law can be used to promote … economic integration').

[12] Cappelletti et al, *Integration through Law* (ibid).

[13] M Shapiro, 'Comparative Law and Comparative Politics' (1980) 53 *Southern California Law Review* 537.

[14] A Stone Sweet, *The Judicial Construction of Europe* (Oxford, Oxford University Press, 2014). See also JH Weiler, 'Community, Member States and European Integration: Is the Law Relevant?' (1982) 21 *Journal of Common Market Studies* 56.

[15] F Nicola, 'National Legal Traditions at Work in the Jurisprudence of the Court of Justice of the European Union' (2016) 64 *American Journal of Comparative Law* 865.

also to some extent a creature of the law.[16] This mutual conditioning of legal structure and political process explains the project for integration of and through law in the European Union. On the one hand, this school of thought has capitalised on the instrumental role of (statutory) law in integrating modern societies characterised by a complex differentiation of functional spheres of social reproduction (politics, economics, culture, etc). On the other hand, it has imbued European legal integration with a broader normative vision of 'convergence' that should lead to the emergence of a common European identity.

Unfortunately, the instrumental role of statutory law has been perceived as an appendage to EU economic forces and governmental mechanisms that undermine the social structures of the Member States, producing social commodification and cultural standardisation. The question of integration has now to be defined as a process that is legally structured not only by alleged homogeneity, equality and inclusion, but also by increased forms of heterogeneity, inequality and exclusion.[17]

Private law has indubitably played a significant role on the political agenda of this school and, particularly, in establishing and removing the barriers to the internal market of the EU.

In other words, the rationality of EU private law, focused as it is on the integration of the internal market, can be regarded as primarily instrumentalist. Consequently, private law was initially conceived as an instrument with which to achieve the policy objectives of the EU. These objectives were primarily related to the integration of the internal market, and the framework within which the discipline was perceived was, therefore, one of pragmatic and purposive rulemaking based on statutory law (ie regulations, directives). In particular, one author has demonstrated that private, as opposed to public, law played a central part in European integration.[18]

While the idea remains valid, the context has dramatically changed in Europe. The dichotomy between EU and domestic legal cultures in private law created by the market-driven EU private law has significantly contributed to the failures now apparent. An example is the key role assigned to the discipline of consumer contract law that, evidently, is important for the establishment and functioning of the internal market in the EU.[19] After the adoption of various consumer law measures, the EU decided to conduct a profound review of the consumer *acquis*, and proposed major reforms. Initially, the EU's activities were based on a minimum harmonisation approach which allowed Member States to adopt more protective rules. In the past decade, activities have revealed the change in the EU's

[16] D Augenstein, *"Integration through Law" Revisited. The Making of the European Polity* (Farnham, Ashgate, 2012).

[17] Jorges and Kreuder-Sonnen (n 9).

[18] D Caruso, 'The Missing View of the Cathedral: The Private Law Paradigm of European Legal Integration' (1997) 3 *European Law Journal* 3.

[19] S Weatherill, *EU Consumer Law and Policy* (Cheltenham, Edward Elgar Publishing, 2005).

approaches, since measures have been based on a full harmonisation approach, removing Member States' freedom to rule by favouring more protection rules in the areas covered by those measures.[20]

Indeed, the notion of 'integration through law' has proved to be an extremely powerful concept providing a group of scholars, civil servants from the Community institutions and CJEU judges with 'a flattering self-image and a *raison d'être* expressed in three little words'.[21]

B. Market-Driven Private Law Scholarship

Private law has indubitably had a significant role on the political agenda of the school of thought of Cappelletti and others and, particularly, in establishing and removing the barriers to the internal market of the EU.[22]

For example, legal scholars have noted that France reacted fiercely to the Product Liability Directive[23] with what can be called national resistance. The transformation of this directive into a full harmonisation measure occurred through the CJEU's interpretation in a number of infringement proceedings. In France, in particular, resistance was raised by two actors on the legal scene: the legislator and legal scholars.[24] The example shows that EU private law has been 'applied' as an instrument with which to achieve the policy objectives of the EU. These objectives primarily concern integration of the internal market, and the framework within which the discipline has been perceived is therefore one of pragmatic and purposive rulemaking. This approach implies that EU private law has had a limited doctrinal autonomy and is focused on specific sectors of the market according to EU policy goals.

C. The Enchantment with Full Harmonisation and Codification

Our contention here is that EU private law scholarship has focused on the goal of European integration and, for this reason, has supported EU institutions in a process of 'Europeanisation by imposition' grounded on harmonised rules

[20] M Loos, 'Full Harmonisation as a Regulatory Concept and its Consequences for the National Legal Orders: The Example of the Consumer Rights Directive' (2010) Centre for the Study of European Contract Law Working Paper Series No 3.

[21] R Byberg, 'The History of the Integration through Law Project: Creating the Academic Expression of a Constitutional Legal Vision for Europe' (2017) 18 *German Law Journal* 1531.

[22] Caruso (n 18).

[23] Council Directive 85/374/EEC of 25 July 1985 on the approximation of the laws, regulations and administrative provisions of the Member States concerning liability for defective products [1985] OJ L210/29.

[24] Caruso (n 18).

(ie regulations, directives) and/or a codified EU private law. One author has argued that, on the contrary, there was a tension between the objectives of the original integration through law-project and its reliance on a positivist conception of law.[25]

Nevertheless, the turn to positivism occurred, and it took place either in piecemeal fashion, by way of harmonising directives, or in the comprehensive style of a supranational civil code.

On the one hand, it is well known that the harmonisation of private law had the objective of establishing an equivalent or even uniform set of rules in private law, with the effect of 'approximating', ie bringing closer together, the heterogeneous legal systems in the EU. One way to approximate national laws is to set minimum standards (minimum harmonisation), thus enabling Member States to maintain or introduce more stringent measures of protection above the limit. Another approach is that of maximum harmonisation, which gives no room for manoeuvre to Member States, since the measure fixes an upper limit.[26] The terminology is confused, since terms such as 'complete, total or full harmonisation' are also used. For example, legal scholars usually indicate the Unfair Commercial Practices Directive as an example of full harmonisation containing more hardcore measures of maximum harmonisation providing expressly for uniform rules.[27]

On the other hand, legal scholars then focused on the codification of EU private law to absolve a prominent 'state-making function' for the EU. This view was grounded on the role that codification played in eighteenth- and nineteenth-century continental Europe. Napoleon's imperial vision relied on both military victories and the success of his codification.[28] Like France, many other European nations linked the definition of a coherent body of private law to state unity, constitutional breakthroughs and national identity.[29] In contrast, we agree with the scholarship noting that

> private law codification is not as indispensable to continental legal culture as standard legal histories would have us believe. Law was modernizing roughly at the same time, and in the same way, in Western countries that did not codify private law, including the common law world and Scandinavia.[30]

Unfortunately, mainstream legal scholarship has mainly relied on the imposition of positive law and full harmonisation of domestic private law. Moreover, it

[25] C MacAmhlaigh, 'Concepts of Law in Integration through Law' in Augenstein (n 16) 69.

[26] G Howell, 'European Consumer Law – The Minimal and Maximal Harmonization Debate and Pro Independent Consumer Law Competence' in S Grundmann and J Stuyck (eds), *An Academic Green Paper on EU Contract Law* (The Hague, Kluwer Law International 2002) 73–80.

[27] H Collins, 'Harmonization by Example: European Laws against Unfair Commercial Practices' (2010) 73 *MLR* 89. The authors claimed (118) that this directive represented a 'much more aggressive approach to harmonization'.

[28] J Gordley, 'Myths of the French Civil Code' (1994) 42 *American Journal of Comparative Law* 459.

[29] Caruso (n 18).

[30] H Pihlajamäki, 'Private Law Codification, Modernization and Nationalism: A View from Critical Legal History' (2015) 2 *Critical Analysis of Law* 135.

has embraced the myth of developing a civil code to support the making of the EU. Indeed, such a descriptive and normative approach was very successful for decades, with few exceptions (see sub-section IIID), until its recent failure.[31] There is no need to stress that Legrand was among the first leading academics in the field to maintain that merely drafting uniform rules does not result in uniform law.[32] Law is, after all, much more than just formally uniformed rules: the meaning of a particular rule in a particular cultural and national context can only be established after studying that context. This context differs among the various cultures. According to Legrand, the contexts were also irreconcilable in the case of civil law and English law.[33] He put forward other arguments as well: the whole idea of a European codification is arrogant in his view, because it imposes on common lawyers the supposedly superior worldview of continental lawyers. They each offer different accounts of reality and those preaching codification of private law consider the Anglo-American reality as being without merit.

Legrand noted that the project of a European Civil Code was primarily in the interests of the development of the internal market. Furthermore, he also stressed that the suggestion that Europe would return to the golden age of the *Ius Commune* was misleading, because English law was never part of it.

Notwithstanding the above, the enchantment of certain legal scholars with full harmonisation and then the codification of private law has flourished until recently.[34] Specialised academic journals have been launched and many tomes on 'European' tort and contract law have appeared; courses and modules are offered throughout the continent and the UK; chairs and graduate schools are dedicated to the subject; and a variety of lavishly funded transnational research projects have produced libraries full of works: the *Ius Commune* school has identified common principles through a series of casebooks and the 'Trento' Group has gradually distinguished the common core of European private law.[35] In addition, it is well known in academia that the 'Lando Commission' has produced its 'Principles of European Contract Law' and the Study Group on a European Civil Code has worked away on its draft articles and comparative studies.[36]

[31] C Von Bar, 'From Principles to Codification: Prospects for European Private Law' (2002) 8 *Columbia Journal of European Law* 379, 385.

[32] P Legrand, 'European Legal Systems Are Not Converging' (1996) 45 *International and Comparative Law Quarterly* 52; P Legrand, 'Against a European Civil Code' (1997) 60 *MLR* 45. See also BS Markesinis (ed), *Gradual Convergence: Foreign Ideas, Foreign Influence and English Law on the Eve of the 21st Century* (Oxford, Oxford University Press, 1994).

[33] Legrand, 'Against a European Civil Code' (ibid). It is very interesting to read Legrand now.

[34] R Brownsword, HW Micklitz, S Weatherill and L Niglia (eds), *The Foundations of European Private Law* (Oxford, Hart Publishing, 2011).

[35] H Beale, B Fauvarque-Cosson, J Rutgers and S Vogenauer, *Cases, Materials and Text on Contract Law* (Oxford, Hart Publishing, 2019); DJ Gerber, 'The Common Core of European Private Law: The Project and Its Books' (2004) 52 *American Journal of Comparative Law* 995.

[36] For an overview, see P Sirena and Y Adar, 'Principles vs Rules in European Contract Law: From the PECL to the CESL, and Beyond' (2013) 9 *European Review of Contract Law* 1; O Lando, H Beale, A Prüm, E Clive and R Zimmermann, *The Principles of European Contract Law* (Alphen aan den Rijn, Kluwer 2019). For critical observations, see MW Hesselink, 'The Politics of a European Civil Code' (2004) 10 *European Law Journal* 675.

On this basis, the project of establishing European private law has also re-energised comparative law as an academic discipline and has given research funding, international recognition and renewed prestige to an elite of European scholars. Some of this work has certainly been driven by intellectual curiosity and a thirst for knowledge. Nevertheless, a large part of the success of this scholarship has been undeniably rooted in the political and financial support for the endeavour of European institutions to harmonise national private laws.[37] On the contrary, comparative law should have prevented the underestimation of cultural differences and dealt with the complexity of a private law having supranational and national sources.[38]

Accordingly, the chapter argues that current criticism may offer an opportunity to debunk the narratives of EU integration with a view to overcoming the monophony of the functionalist doctrine in our discipline.[39] First, we claim that EU private law scholarship has tended to passively accept the conceptual subordination of research and studies in the field to the process of integration and specifically market integration.[40] Secondly, we note that many scholars have induced the study of private law to focus on institutions, policy-making processes and the EU's normative agenda. Finally, this scholarship has also endorsed the idea of codifying EU private law as the result of a turn to legal positivism that is subject to criticism.

The results are there for all to see. In fact, it is the disintegration, not the integration, of law which seems to be the dominant motive behind contemporary politics in Europe.[41] We refer, in particular, to the fact that the European Commission's proposals were made in a political climate of rising nationalism.[42]

This is, for example, the case of the Proposal for a Regulation on a Common European Sales Law (CESL), which contained rules applicable to cross-border transactions for the sale of goods, for the supply of digital contents and for related services. Clearly, it would have introduced into each Member State an optional common European law governing cross-border contracts for the sale of goods and digital content.[43] We agree with Cygan, who noted that 'the CESL provides a solution to a problem that does not really exist' and proposes that the Commission

[37] MW Hesselink, *The New European Private Law* (Alphen aan den Rijn, Kluwer 2002). See also M Van Hoecke and F Ost (eds), *The Harmonisation of European Private Law* (Oxford, Hart Publishing, 2000).

[38] Cappelletti et al, *Integration through Law* (n 11). The authors focused their work on a comparison with the US federal system of law.

[39] In music, monophony is the simplest of musical textures, consisting of a melody (or 'tune'), typically sung by a single singer or played by a single instrument player (eg a flute player) without accompanying harmony or chords.

[40] J Weiler, 'Epilogue' in Augenstein (n 16) 178.

[41] D Kennedy, 'Thoughts on Coherence, Social Values, and National Tradition in Private Law' in MW Hesselink (ed), *The Politics of a European Civil Code* (Alphen aan den Rijn, Kluwer 2006) 9.

[42] G Comparato, *Nationalism and Private Law in Europe* (Oxford, Hart Publishing, 2014).

[43] Commission, 'Proposal for a Regulation on a Common European Sales Law' COM (2011) 635 final.

prioritise the modernisation of the legislation on enforcement, which was considered part of the review of Regulation No 2006/2004 on consumer protection cooperation.[44] The withdrawal of the CESL in 2014 marked the end of the heyday of the endeavour to harmonise European private law after decades of enthusiasm, which included other Commission-backed proposals such as the Principles of European Contract Law (PECL) and the Draft Common Frame of Reference (DCFR). Although the withdrawal of the CESL in December 2014 suggested that there would be a period of inaction in the field of EU consumer and contract law, there were indications that there would be a new initiative in the context of one of the EU Commission's priority areas: the Digital Single Market.[45]

In early May 2015, the EU Commission published its Digital Single Market Strategy, which contained a set of proposed actions. Surprisingly, in the proposals of December 2015, the EU Commission followed the approach that had failed with the CESL and the Consumer Rights Directive.[46] Then, after several years of uncertainty, in 2019 the EU adopted directives on the sale of goods (Directive 2019/771) and distance sale of content and services (Directive 2019/770).[47]

In our view, the Commission's argument is unlikely to convince the opposition because it still focuses exclusively on the internal market. The reason is that it fails to address the main unanswered question about the division of competences between the EU and the Member States in private law matters. To be clear, there are sectors of private law that – probably – do not require full or minimum harmonisation at the European level. Until recently, saying this was tantamount to heresy.

Indeed, for too long a time, any criticism of EU proposals in the field was dismissed as the outcome of a kind of critical legal studies exercise. According to some scholars, criticism was the result of 'an age of rising nationalism' and 'ignorance, myopia or fear of the foreign and the new'.[48] For example, according to a scholar, the process of 'Europeanisation' should 'finally' step away from 'the obfuscatory shadow of the Volksgeist'.[49] In other words, if the French prefer their Civil Code to a European equivalent, they are defending a 'pre-modern artefact', while their reaction to a possible European civil code could be compared to the American reaction to Pearl Harbour in 1940.[50] In particular, some scholars also argued that France's reluctance to adopt a European Civil Code could be seen as

[44] A Cygan, 'Introduction: EU Consumer and Contract Law at a Crossroads?' in C Twigg-Flesner, *Research Handbook on EU Consumer and Contract Law* (Cheltenham, Edward Elgar Publishing, 2016).

[45] Commission, 'A Digital Single Market Strategy for Europe' (Communication) COM (2015) 0192 final. See also Directive (EU) 2019/771 of the European Parliament and of the Council of 20 May 2019 on certain aspects concerning contracts for the sale of goods [2019] OJ L136/28.

[46] Directive 2011/83/EU of the European Parliament and of the Council on consumer rights [2011] OJ L304/64.

[47] Directive (EU) 2019/770 on certain aspects concerning contracts for the supply of digital content and digital services [2019] OJ L136/1.

[48] Kennedy (n 41).

[49] Comparato (n 42).

[50] Weatherill (n 19) 211, quoting Ralf Micheals.

evidence of a 'crypto nationalistic' discourse, containing hidden Europhobic rhetoric and resting on 'sentimental and irrational argumentation'.[51] Lastly, one author was also right to argue for a 'democratic contract law', insisting that legal experts should not exclusively create rules of contract law, but must participate in an inclusive democratic debate.[52]

One may easily note that very few academics have had the courage to recognise the limitations of the previous analysis by seriously challenging the 'market integration functionalism doctrine'.[53] Our main point here is the following: the logic of private law is not necessarily the logic of market integration, and academic analysis has failed to advance the autonomy and self-standing of our discipline. There are some notable exceptions, however; for example, when two authors note that 'Europe is in troubled waters. What does the unfortunate state of the European Union (EU) reveal about the state of the scholarly study of the integration project?' In this regard, they conclude that 'legal scholarship is in short supply of normatively convincing theoretical paradigms'.[54]

D. Early Critical Thinkers

In such a context, early critical voices that attempted to theorise EU private law differently (ie a private law with a certain distance from the EU's political agenda, not necessarily subordinated to the needs of the internal market and formally imposed from above) and advocated another European trajectory have gone unheard in discussions over the past decades of scholarship and analysis.

In the words of one author:

> Cinderellas have always tended to flock to court balls, whether or not pleased with the prince's looks or intentions. Private law departments throughout the Union are the home of Cinderellas of an intellectual type, whose esoteric expertise in either legal history or comparative law is rather tangential to mainstream legal education. Having long been accorded only marginal positions in the conventional hierarchy of law schools, they now welcome opportunities for change.[55]

Indeed, mainstream scholarship has broadly, though often implicitly, accepted the premise that Europeanisation is a one-way process for national private laws. While scholars have considered themselves to be 'pluralists', this self-reading only makes sense within a narrow conception of the scope (ie the subordination to a political agenda) and the methodologies (ie full harmonisation by imposition)

[51] Weatherill (n 19) 211 ff, quoting Ruth Sefton-Green.

[52] MW Hesselink, 'Democratic Contract Law' (2014) 11 *European Review of Contract Law* 81. See also JM Smits, 'Democracy and (European) Private Law: A Functional Approach' (2010) 2 *European Journal of Legal Studies* 26.

[53] Jorges and Kreuder-Sonnen (n 9).

[54] ibid.

[55] Caruso (n 18) 23.

for sectors of domestic private laws. By contrast, scholars working from a critical perspective adopt a variety of standpoints, such as arguments grounded on very different opinions concerning pluralism (Rasmussen),[56] national cultural defence (Legrand) and criticism against the market-driven nature of EU private law and the consequent lack of any social dimension (Joerges and others).

This criticism focuses on the sovereignty of national law, its 'integrity' and 'coherence'; and it considers that the changes brought about by European law jeopardise 'essential' elements of national identity and social justice. The criticism of which we speak raises a question of another kind: how can we prevent a normative strategy designed to promote cohesion and emancipation on a continental level from eventually producing division and alienation?

The birth of this current of thought came late in the history of integration, and Hjalte Rasmussen was undoubtedly its precursor. The book entitled *Law and Policy in the European Court of Justice*, published in 1986, was the first to clearly describe the signs of activism by the European Court of Justice (now the CJEU), a factor in delegitimisation of the European project.[57] This earned Rasmussen the recognition of his peers, but also a form of banishment. The scope of this criticism, however, remained limited since it was content to focus on interpretation of the law by the court. Nevertheless, at the time it was formulated, this criticism went against the grain. Indeed, the dynamic interpretation of the law by the CJEU at that time reflected a commitment on behalf of European governments to integration. Since they could expect long-term benefits for their economies and nationals from the creation of the European Single Market, they gracefully accepted that court interpretations might conflict, in some cases, with their interests. This dialectic has now ceased to flourish. In the context of a broader integration into non-market domains (European citizenship is the best example), the teleology of integration no longer enjoys a consensus. This explains why Rasmussen's criticism moved on from the university to resurface in political speeches.

Criticism developed by authors such as Joerges and Everson, to name but two, is not restricted to an attack against the interpretations of the CJEU. Their critiques have an otherwise profound meaning.[58] Such criticism concerns the consequences of the law on integration for the cohesion of national societies and the structuring of populations in the EU. According to Joerges and Everson, EU law, rather than fully fledged EU citizens, produces 'de-socialized market citizens'.[59]

[56] L Azoulai, 'Solitude, désœuvrement et conscience critique. Les ressorts d'une recomposition des études juridiques européennes' (2015) 4(50) *Politique européenne* 82.

[57] H Rasmussen, *Law and Policy in the European Court of Justice* (Leiden, Martinus Nijhoff Publishers, 1986).

[58] M Everson and C Joerges, 'Reconfiguring the Politics–Law Relationship in the Integration Project through Conflicts–Law Constitutionalism; (2012) 18 *European Law Journal* 644.

[59] More recently, the concern for a social justice deficit of the EU appears in F de Witte, 'Transnational Solidarity and the Mediation of Conflicts in Europe' (2012) 18 *European Law Journal* 694; A Sangiovanni, 'Solidarity in the European Union' (2013) 33 *Oxford Journal of Legal Studies* 1. See generally D Kochenov, G de Búrca and A T Williams, *Europe's Justice Deficit?* (Oxford, Hart Publishing, 2015).

While different, all these critical views start by noting that, since its beginnings, the study of EU private law has had a dominant set of discursive, intellectual and academic practices, which they seek to challenge. The message is that the law of the EU is unable to live up to the ideals (prosperity, justice and freedom) that it has set for itself. Early criticism was based on affirmation of the legitimacy of the integration project and its right, and argued that the right of the Union is to serve legitimate interests, building new collective solidarities and desires for individual emancipation. The problem is that EU law had not been properly able to pursue these interests in recent decades.[60] This is true for political and institutional reasons, but also for a deeper-lying one. What is lacking in this construct can be put simply: it is a theory of justice. It is quite clear that European institutions have had the opportunity to develop arguments on the fairness of the objectives of the European Treaties and the consequences of their interpretation. Nevertheless, the criticism made is that these are theoretically incomplete arguments. The CJEU and the Commission and Council need to develop clearer and stronger criteria for justice in order to regulate the interpretation of European private law.[61] Modern schools of thought tend now to stress that the project of 'integration through private law' has not been able to prevent subordination, inequality and alienation becoming an integral part of the process. This situation points to a need for an analytical critique.[62]

III. Modern Schools of Thought

We point out that modern schools of thought are different from classical schools because they are not openly subordinated to the integration narratives.[63] We provide some examples in the following sub-sections by focusing on pluralism theories and economic and justice traditions in private law scholarship.

A. EU Private Law and Constitutional Values

We note that many legal scholars have addressed the task of identifying the role that EU constitutional values play, or should play, in the field of European private law.[64]

[60] Everson and Joerges (n 58).

[61] Kochenov et al (n 59).

[62] Azoulai, '"Integration through Law" and us' (n 4).

[63] Besides the traditional actors, new ones have emerged, such as the European Law Institute (ELI), an independent organisation set up in 2011 that aims to enhance the quality of the European legal integration process.

[64] S Tridimas, *The General Principles of EU Law* (Oxford, Oxford University Press, 2017); MW Hesselink, 'Private Law and the European Constitutionalisation of Values' (2016) Amsterdam Law School Research Paper No 2016-26; S Grundmann (ed), *Private Law and EU Constitutional Values* (The Hague, Kluwer Law International 2008).

The central idea is that the laws of contract, tort or property have to be designed or developed by the CJEU and national judges in a way that aligns all fields of private law with constitutional traditions of the EU and Member States.[65] This approach requires that, although private law does not have to duplicate constitutional rights exactly, it should not contradict or subvert constitutional rights. In practice, the requirement of alignment means that courts should interpret and develop private law rules and doctrines in a way that ensures that their content conforms to, and is consistent with, the rights that are protected as constitutional values.[66] By contrast, some legal scholars are concerned about theory on the constitutionalisation of private law for various reasons: they underline, for example, the risk that the application of fundamental rights to private law may prove extremely disruptive, lead to uncertainty and foster litigation.[67]

B. Pluralism and EU Private Law Scholarship

The idea of pluralism has gained attention also with respect to the development of EU private law.[68] Here, we are referring to Michaels, who has scrutinised the concepts of legal pluralism used by three of its most prominent proponents: Pierre Legrand, Jan Smits and Thomas Wilhelmsson.[69]

Michaels has attempted to offer a fully fledged criticism of their theories (each of which are among the most fascinating and helpful in the European private law debate). His contribution has mainly addressed the use of ideas of legal pluralism by the above-mentioned authors in the academic discussion about pluralism and EU private law.[70]

More recently, Mak has also reconsidered legal pluralist thinking in private law by examining the concept of 'ordered pluralism', recognising that multiple sources of rules may coexist in EU law. Specifically, her article assesses some of the leading theories of legal pluralism in European private law. It analyses how these theories of pluralism may be ordered and applied by considering what space they give to deliberation between lawmakers at different levels of regulation.

[65] H Micklitz (ed), *Constitutionalization of European Private Law* (Oxford, Oxford University Press, 2014).

[66] Charter of the Fundamental Rights of the European Union [2012] OJ C326/391.

[67] The main objections are indicated by H Collins, 'Private Law, Fundamental Rights, and the Rule of Law', (2018) 121 *West Virginia Law Review* 1, 9.

[68] R Michaels, 'Why We Have No Theory of European Private Law Pluralism' in L Niglia (ed), *Pluralism and European Private Law* (Oxford, Hart Publishing, 2013) 139.

[69] Legrand, 'European Legal Systems' (n 32); T Wilhelmsson et al (eds), *Private Law and the Many Cultures of Europe* (The Hague, Wolters Kluwer International, 2007); JM Smits, 'European Private Law and the Comparative Method' in C Twigg-Flessner (ed), *The Cambridge Companion to European Union Private Law* (Cambridge, Cambridge University Press, 2010) 33–43.

[70] Michaels (n 68).

The author argues in favour of developing a 'strong legal pluralist theory for European private law'.[71]

For the purposes of this chapter, we stress that central to the various concepts of legal pluralism is the issue concerning power relations between the Member States and the EU. While legal scholarship appears confused on this point, the basic question of legal pluralism remains unresolved despite constituting the central node of Europeanisation with respect to private law. To be clear, the questions are the extent to which private law should be harmonised on the European level, the extent to which law should remain within the Member States, and how relations between the European and domestic levels should be organised to overcome the shortcomings of current approaches.

In particular, we note that recent political developments have confirmed the degree of resistance of domestic private laws and cultures to Europeanisation and their ability to contain EU rules so that they do not undermine the coherence of domestic private law systems. Indeed, we hope that it is now clear that private law not only regulates markets, but also takes part in the construction of national identities in the Member States. This connection may not be reduced to an exercise of nationalism.[72] Our point is that this is a simplistic reconstruction of the historical development of Member States' private laws and the role that these laws still have in shaping our identities as jurists.

C. The Law and Economics Perspective

From a different perspective, EU private law scholarship also draws on the economic tradition in approaching the matter. Indeed, the application of empirical methods and the conceptual toolbox of economics to the study of law – commonly known as 'law and economics' – has been praised as one of the most successful interplays between applied economics and the legal field.[73] In its very essence, law and economics considers efficiency to be the main standard of evaluation of legal rules. As such, efficiency is regarded as a constituent part of justice, because 'in a world of scarce resources waste should be regarded as immoral'.[74] Even though the precursors of this school of thought were identified in Europe during the early nineteenth century, it is widely acknowledged that contemporary law and economics dates back to the USA in the 1960s and the seminal works of Ronald Coase, Richard Posner and Guido Calabresi.[75]

[71] V Mak, 'Pluralism in European Private Law' (2018) 20 *Cambridge Yearbook of European Legal Studies* 202.

[72] Comparato (n 42).

[73] E Posner, 'Economic Analysis of Contract Law after Three Decades: Success or Failure?' (2003) 112 *Yale Law Journal* 829; F Parisi, 'Positive, Normative and Functional Schools in Law and Economics' (2004) 18 *European Journal of Law and Economics* 259.

[74] R Posner, *Economic Analysis of Law*, 6th edn (Slough, Aspen Law & Business 2003) 27.

[75] R Coase, 'The Problem of Social Cost' (1972) 3 *Journal of Law and Economics* 1; R Posner, 'A Theory of Negligence' (1972) 1 *Journal of Legal Studies* 29; G Calabresi and D Melamed,

As a result of these contributions, the subject of economics was found to be relevant not only to regulation initiatives (such as antitrust, tax and labour), but also to both positive and normative analysis of the entire private law domain.[76] Accordingly, the methodological breakthrough engendered by this early stage of research enabled insightful applications in the fields of contract, tort and property. It is no surprise that, as far as private law is concerned, modern economic analysis of law has gained ground in transatlantic legal scholarship.[77] From a methodological perspective, the influence of economic analysis in the study of law makes it possible to investigate legal systems as working systems rather than as a coherent body shaped on the basis of systematic internal consistency. This development has implied a striking departure from the old-fashioned Langdellian tradition, as well as from the 'mainstream' continental historical school.[78]

Such a change of approach helps to explain the initial reluctance of European scholarship to accept and implement this new view. Within continental civil law countries, legal scholarship was considered a hermeneutic science used to interpret the law according to principles of the system's internal consistency in terms of language and value judgments.[79] Policy arguments remained outside the scope of the legal endeavour.[80] In fact, one of the main (and controversial) theses put forward by Posner was that common law is inherently better suited than civil law to deploying economic logic since judges are driven by an invisible hand nudging them to shape the law according to efficiency.[81] Since the continental European concept of separation of powers implies that a judge may only 'interpret' the law, policy arguments such as those provided by law and economics fell outside the scope of the legal discipline.[82]

The development of law and economics in continental European scholarship started only in the late 1980s with the seminal works of Mattei, Pardolesi, Schäfer and Ott.[83] In contrast to the USA, law and economics scholarship in Europe

'Property Rules, Liability Rules, and Inalienability: One View of the Cathedral' (1972) 85 *Harvard Law Review* 1089.

[76] GS Becker and RA Posner, 'The Future of Law and Economics' in F Parisi (ed), *The Oxford Handbook of Law and Economics, Volume 1: Methodology and Concepts* (Oxford, Oxfor d University Press, 2017) 5.

[77] E Posner, 'Economic Analysis of Contract Law' (n 73).

[78] According to the Langdellian tradition, legal research should look at the model of science. Accordingly, it hinges on a close analysis of black-letter texts in order to identify high-level principles and then apply argumentation and interpretative tools to criticise judicial decisions. The historical school argued that the task of jurisprudence is to uncover one nation's customary law and investigate through historical methods its social provenance. See JH Merryman and R Pérez-Perdomo, *The Civil Law Tradition* (Stanford, Stanford University Press, 2018); FC Beiser, *The German Historicist Tradition* (Oxford, Oxford University Press, 2011).

[79] M Gelter and K Grechenig, 'History of Law and Economics' (2014) Preprints of the Max Planck Institute for Research on Collective Goods Bonn No 5.

[80] ibid.

[81] R Posner, 'Utilitarianism, Economics, and Legal Theory' (1980) 8 *Journal of Legal Studies* 103.

[82] TJ Miceli, 'Economic Models of Law' in Parisi, *Oxford Handbook* (n 76) 9.

[83] U Mattei and R Pardolesi, 'Law and Economics in Civil Law Countries: A Comparative Approach' (1991) 11 *International Review of Law and Economics* 265; H-B Schäfer and OC Lehrbuch, *Der ökonomischen Analyse des Zivilrechts*, 5th edn (Berlin, Springer, 1986).

was more formal (both theoretical and empirical) and was primarily driven by economists – a feature that, to some extent, still persists today.[84] At the same time, non-formal law and economics scholarship kept growing in law faculties thanks to the establishment of research centres: namely, the Max Planck Institute for Research on Collective Goods in Bonn, the Rotterdam Institute of Law and Economics, the Center for European Law and Economics and the Tilburg Institute of Law and Economics. Moreover, several European universities established graduate courses and PhD programmes specifically based on law and economics.[85]

This steady growth culminated with the academic contribution to the codification process of European private law. In fact, the debate on the role of civil law and European integration witnessed a wide use of arguments based on law and economics.[86] Advocates of both sides (harmonisation versus regulatory competition) relied heavily on economic reasoning to sustain their views and, as a result, drove widespread adoption of this school of thought throughout European scholarship.[87] This wide adoption of law and economics arguments proves that this school of thought has been recognised in recent years as a well-established methodology within the realm of European private law.[88]

Somewhat surprisingly, the core arguments against the harmonisation of European private law have been grounded in law and economics as well.[89] For instance, by relying on the empirical findings provided by Eurobarometer surveys, Hubbard questioned the essential premise of the European codification movement by highlighting that, since contract law is not a substantial hindrance to cross-border trade in the internal market, there is no economic need for a European body of private law.[90] Eric Posner stressed that not only would an optional instrument such as the CESL increase transaction costs for market players, but it was also inherently unfit to help foster a common European identity.[91] Two authors

[84] B Depoorter and J Demot, 'The Cross-Atlantic Law and Economics Divide: A Dissent' [2011] *University of Illinois Law Review* 1593.

[85] To mention just a few: the Joint European Doctorate in Law & Economics set by the Universities of Bologna, Haifa, Hamburg and Rotterdam; the IEL 'Institutions, Economics and Law' International PhD Programme established by University of Turin and Collegio Carlo Alberto. Several other universities set up courses focused on law and economics, such as the 'Law and Economics of Corporate Transaction' within the MSc in Law and Finance at the University of Oxford, which focused on the role of 'business lawyers as transaction cost engineers', according to RJ Gilson, 'Value Creation by Business Lawyers: Legal Skills and Asset Pricing' (1984) 94 *Yale Law Journal* 239.

[86] A Marciano and J-M Josselin (eds), *The Economics of Harmonizing European Law* (Cheltenham, Edward Elgar Publishing, 2002).

[87] C Mak, 'Unweaving the CESL: Legal-Economic Reason and Institutional Imagination in European Contract Law' (2013) 50 *CML Rev* 277.

[88] O Ben-Shahar, 'Introduction: A Law and Economics Approach to European Contract Law' (2013) 50 *CML Rev* 3.

[89] L Bernstein, 'An (Un)common Frame of Reference: An American Perspective on the Jurisprudence of the CESL' (2013) 50 *CML Rev* 169.

[90] WJ Hubbard, 'Another Look at the Eurobarometer Surveys' (2013) 50 *CML Rev* 187.

[91] E Posner, 'The Questionable Basis of the Common European Sales Law: The Role of an Optional Instrument in Jurisdictional Competition' (2013) 50 *CML Rev* 261. The author argues that the underpinning rationale of the European legal integration project is strictly political rather than economical.

have argued that the project to harmonise private law risks seriously jeopardising the regulatory competition dynamics between Member States, ultimately leading to a race to the bottom.[92] Whittaker pointed out that the legal uncertainty over the interpretation of the open-ended provisions of harmonised European private law was set to be exacerbated by the different legal cultures of the judges implementing it.[93] This, ironically, could have ended up with non-uniform interpretation and adjudication throughout the internal market. Whittaker also noted that in the USA convergence in commercial and consumer law was achieved by means of convergence rather than top-down authoritarian impositions. He warned of the risk that harmonisation efforts might be twisted by organised interest groups to the detriment of European social interests at large.[94]

This intense debate proves that law and economics has attracted a high level of attention in the European scholarship in recent years and will continue to be the backbone of European private law's analytical methodologies. In this regard, an increasing number of edited books, treatises, specialised journals and textbooks devoted to law and economics have been published in the European arena.[95]

New theories of private law dealing with the economisation of private law are flourishing: from transnational private regulation[96] to contract governance.[97] Indeed, since the seminal works on civil liability, law and economics scholars have stressed the regulatory functions of private law.[98] At the same time, the EU governance has incorporated such changing patterns into its policy strategies aimed at building the internal market.[99] As a result, many commentators maintain that the divergence between American and European law and economics is set to disappear.[100] As recognised by Ben-Shahar, the law and economics methodology 'has taken a stronghold in European legal academia'.[101]

[92] H Eidenmüller, 'What Can Be Wrong with an Option? An Optional Common European Sales Law as a Regulatory Tool' (2013) 50 *CML Rev* 69; S Grundmann, 'Costs and Benefits of an Optional European Sales Law (CESL)' (2013) 50 *CML Rev* 225.

[93] S Whittaker, 'Identifying the Legal Costs of Operation of the Common European Sales Law' (2013) 50 *CML Rev* 85.

[94] S Levmore, 'Harmonization, Preferences, and the Calculus of Consent in Commercial and Other Law' (2013) 50 *CML Rev* 243.

[95] The *European Journal of Law and Economics* was launched under the editorial direction of Jurgen Backhaus and Frank Stephen in 1999. T Ginsburg and N Garoupa, 'Economic Analysis and Comparative Law' in M Bussani and U Mattei (eds), *The Cambridge Companion to Comparative Law* (Cambridge, Cambridge University Press, 2012).

[96] F Cafaggi, 'Transnational Private Regulation. Regulating Private Regulators' in S Cassese (ed), *Research Handbook on Global Administrative Law* (Cheltenham, Edward Elgar Publishing, 2016).

[97] S Grundmann, F Moslein and K Riesenhuber (eds), *Contract Governance: Dimensions in Law and Interdisciplinary Research* (Oxford, Oxford University Press, 2015).

[98] G Calabresi, *The Cost of Accidents* (New Haven, Yale University Press, 1977); S Shavell, 'Liability for Harm versus Regulation of Safety' (1984) 13 *Journal of Legal Studies* 357; S Rose-Ackerman, 'Tort Law in the Regulatory State' in P Schuck (ed), *Tort Law and the Public Interest: Competition, Innovation, and Consumer Welfare* (New York, WW Norton, 1991).

[99] J Weiler, 'The Transformation of Europe' (1991) 100 *Yale Law Journal* 2403.

[100] Depoorter and Demot (n 84).

[101] Ben-Shahar (n 88).

Nevertheless, it goes without saying that this methodological school is still more influential on the mainstream legal judicial discourse in the USA than in the European Union.[102] As is known, continental courts and non-specialised lawyers are not accustomed to deploying economic arguments when evaluating the outcomes and effects of rulings.[103] In this regard, failure to deliver a European Civil Law Code or a Common European Sales Law finally leaves law and economics free from the constraints artificially imposed by the mantras and narratives centred on European integration.[104] Legal scholarship is no longer subject to political constraints and can deploy economic analysis of private law by focusing on market failures involving private transactions (such as principle-agent problems, asymmetric information, unequal bargaining power and bounded rationality).[105]

D. The Behavioural and Empirical Analysis

The current discourse concerning law and economics has incorporated many of the insights and critiques brought by psychology, neuroscience and empirical research to the concept of rationality.[106] Indeed, economists and early law and economics scholars grounded their analysis on the rational choice theory, ie the simple premise that a rational player selects actions so as to promote outcomes that satisfy his or her motives, objectives, emotions or sentiments to the best of his or her understanding of the causal relationship between the action taken and the outcome generated. However, empirical and experimental data suggest that, in many instances, individuals behave in ways which systematically conflict with models based on the theory of rational choice.[107]

Therefore, behavioural law and economics relaxes those rational assumptions and builds on the biases and heuristics targeted by cognitive psychology and neuroscience. From this perspective, behavioural insights do not disrupt the

[102] For a critical view on the current relevance of Law and Economics, see U Mattei, 'The Rise and Fall of Law and Economics: An Essay for Judge Guido Calabresi' (2005) 64 *Maryland Law Review* 220.

[103] C Jolls, 'Bounded Rationality, Behavioral Economics, and the Law' in Parisi, *Oxford Handbook* (n 76) 3.

[104] M Faure, 'Harmonisation of Private Law in Europe' in J Klick (ed), *The Law and Economics of Federalism* (Cheltenham, Edward Elgar Publishing, 2017) 30–54; F Gomez and J Ganuza, 'How to Build European Private Law: An Economic Analysis of the Lawmaking and Harmonization Dimensions in European Private Law' (2012) 33 *European Journal of Law and Economics* 481; R Van den Bergh, 'Towards a European Private Law: To Harmonise or Not to Harmonise, That Is the Question' in H-B Schäfer and HJ Lwowski (eds), *Konsequenzen wirtschaftsrechtlicher Normen. Ökonomische Analyse des Rechts* (Deutscher Universitätsverlag, 2002); F Parisi, 'Harmonization of European Private Law: An Economic Analysis' (2007) Minnesota Legal Studies Research Paper No 41.

[105] F Cafaggi, 'From a Status to a Transaction-Based Approach? Institutional Design in European Contract Law' (2013) 50 *CML Rev* 311.

[106] E Zamir and D Teichman, *Behavioral Law and Economics* (Oxford, Oxford University Press, 2018).

[107] TS Ulen, 'The Importance of Behavioral Law' in E Zamir and D Teichman (eds), *The Oxford Handbook of Behavioral Economics and the Law* (New York, Oxford University Press, 2014).

methodology of law and economics. Rather, by recognising that welfare maximisation is still a valid goal from a normative perspective, it complements it by fine-tuning the economics model of rational players according to the bounded rationality paradigm. More specifically, legal rules should be evaluated and designed by considering potential biases affecting individuals' behaviour.[108]

A growing body of legal literature, therefore, has started to shed light on this area by making use of empirical evidence such as field data, experimental data and laboratory experiments that demonstrate how human conduct occurs under legally relevant circumstances.[109] Consumer protection is likely to be one of the legal fields most impacted upon by these findings: regulatory remedies would have to be shaped by taking due consideration of consumers' (bounded) rationality. In this respect, product governance in retail banking has delivered better results than mandatory disclosure rules. The pro-competitive data sharing regimes introduced by the Competition and Market Authority in the UK are in the same vein.[110] According to this empirical methodology, legal scholarship should focus on market-based remedies (primarily competition and reputation) and legal measures (primarily disclosure and mandatory regulations) to tackle the issues afflicting consumer contracts.[111]

In many respects, even if empirical behavioural studies are still in their infancy, the years to come will see extensive interactions between legal theory and empirical social analysis.[112] It should come as no surprise, therefore, that legal scholars,

[108] D Pi, F Parisi and B Luppi, 'Biasing, Debiasing, and the Law' in Zamir and Teichman, *Oxford Handbook of Behavioral Economics and the Law* (ibid).

[109] CR. Sunstein, C Jolls and RH Thaler, 'A Behavioral Approach to Law and Economics' (1998) 50 *Stanford Law Review* 1471; CR Sunstein, *Behavioral Law & Economics* (Cambridge, Cambridge University Press, 1998); G Gigerenzer and C Engel (eds), *Heuristics and the Law* (Cambridge, MA, MIT Press 2010); C Engel, 'The Multiple Uses of Experimental Evidence in Legal Scholarship' (2010) 166 *Journal of Institutional and Theoretical Economics* 199; EV Towfigh and N Petersen, *Economic Methods for Lawyers* (Cheltenham, Edward Elgar Publishing, 2017).

[110] The product governance requirements provide that firms which manufacture, design and distribute financial instruments act in the best interests of consumers at all stages of the product's development and distribution life cycle. This mechanism is enshrined in Directive 2014/65/EU of the European Parliament and of the Council of 15 May 2014 on markets in financial instrument [2014] OJL173/349 (MiFID II). For an overview of pro-competitive data sharing regimes, see O Borgogno and G Colangelo, 'Consumer Inertia and Competition-Sensitive Data Governance: The Case of Open Banking' (3 January 2020), a revised version of which is forthcoming in *Journal of European Consumer and Market Law*, https://ssrn.com/abstract=3513514, http://dx.doi.org/10.2139/ssrn.3513514; O Borgogno and G Colangelo, 'Data, Innovation and Transatlantic Competition in Finance: The Case of the Access to Account Rule' (2020) 31 *EBLR* 5.

[111] Moreover, such an approach seems perfectly suited to going hand in hand with the emerging application of experimentalist governance to law making in European private law. According to V Mak, 'Who Does What in European Private Law – and How Is It Done? An Experimentalist Perspective' (2017) Tilburg Private Law Working Paper Series No 5, experimentalism can be understood as a 'a set of practices involving open participation by a variety of entities (public or private), lack of formal hierarchy within governance arrangements, and extensive deliberation throughout the process of decision making and implementation'. Against this background, law and economics can provide a common and workable toolkit to scholars and policy makers to engage withing current private law debates.

[112] C Engel, 'Behavioral Law and Economics: Empirical Methods' in Zamir and Teichman, *Oxford Handbook of Behavioral Economics and the Law* (n 107); TS Ulen, 'The Importance of Behavioral Law' in Zamir and Teichman (ibid).

as Becker predicted, are going to acquire the rudiments and basics of econometric and empirical methods so as to update private law consistently with the most recent behavioural and economic findings.[113]

E. Justice and EU Private Law Scholarship

The call for a 'theory of justice' broadly refers to the development of clearly articulated foundational principles adjusted to the different contexts in which EU law intervenes (ie the national, transnational and supranational contexts). Depending on the diagnosis and context of the critique, this approach develops as political theory, theory of values or social justice theory for the EU.

In particular, with regard to EU contract law, in 2004 a group of academics issued a manifesto exploring the challenging agenda of social justice and regulatory legitimacy in European contract law.[114] The authors argued that existing initiatives had failed to address this agenda adequately. As a consequence, they claimed, EU institutions had failed to sufficiently consider the appropriate methods with which to help construct a European contract law. The narrowness of focus combined with the inadequacy of methodology in current initiatives posed a threat to the successful achievement of a suitable set of fundamental principles that could serve as a legitimate basis for the governance of social and economic relations among the citizens of Europe. Or perhaps, if these initiatives continued in their current orientation, they might result in the creation of a European contract law that ignored the demands of social justice and regulatory legitimacy, thereby increasing scepticism in regard to the value of European unity and its multilevel governance structure. The document was therefore both a plea for reconsideration of the current trajectory towards harmonisation of European contract law and an exploration of an appropriate way forward which fulfilled the twin objectives of social justice and regulatory legitimacy.

More recently, Micklitz has also highlighted the differences among the Member States' concepts of social justice, which have developed historically, and the distinct European concept of access justice.[115] Contrary to the emerging critique of Europe's justice deficit in the aftermath of the euro crisis, Micklitz argues that developing beneath the larger picture of the monetary union is a more positive and more promising European concept of justice. European access justice is thinner than national social justice, but access justice is a distinct conception of justice.[116]

[113] Becker and Posner (n 76) 3.

[114] U Mattei, 'Social Justice in European Contract Law A Manifesto' (2004) 10 *European Law Journal* 653.

[115] H-W Micklitz (ed), *The Many Concepts of Social Justice* (Cheltenham, Edward Elgar Publishing, 2011).

[116] H-W Micklitz (ed), *The Politics of Justice in European Private Law. Social Justice, Access Justice, Societal Justice* (Cambridge, Cambridge University Press, 2018).

IV. The Paradigm Shift: The End of a Noble Narrative

In this chapter, we have provided an early-stage overview of the main schools of thought that have emerged to date in the realm of European private law. Furthermore, we have warned about the risk that a debate excessively biased by political goals could exclude theories and approaches diverging from the discipline of orthodoxy.[117] Two authors have noted how far European scholars have not kept enough professional distance from their object of research.[118] This is because classical schools of thought have accepted the instrumentalisation of EU private law to the goal of EU integration and its subordination to the rationales of the internal market. Modern schools are attempting to theorise private law independently of the paradigm of integration through law, and we think that such an effort is necessary after Brexit and the most recent developments. The classical approach has resulted in a lack of scholarly criticism of EU projects for law codification and a sort of wishful thinking about the impact of EU-driven regulations and directives on the everyday practice of the law in domestic courts and national legal professions.

Accordingly, we believe that the future of private law in Europe depends on a new private law scholarship that is detached from the integration paradigm and the market-driven rationale. In this regard, we note that, for example, both Zimmermann[119] and Joerges[120] have repeatedly called for a new legal science breaking down the barriers between any combination of private law doctrine, comparative law, EU law, legal history and international private law. As Jürgen Basedow approvingly notes: 'legal scholars transcend the traditional limits of the analysis of legal development and try to shape the future European law themselves'.[121]

Here, we have gone further by trying to imagine the form that EU private law scholarship should assume while benefiting from the freedom resulting from the collapse of the integration paradigm depicted above. In particular, we are in favour of directing the study of private law away from legal positivism and towards methodology, away from legal rules and towards principles and shared values.

[117] Brownsword et al (n 34).

[118] R van Gestel and H-W Micklitz, 'Revitalizing Doctrinal Legal Research in Europe: What About Methodology?' (January 2011) EUI Working Paper LAW No 2011/05, https://ssrn.com/abstract=1824237, http://dx.doi.org/10.2139/ssrn.1824237.

[119] R Zimmermann, 'The "Europeanization" of Private Law within the European Community and the Re-emergence of a European Legal Science' (1995) 1 *Columbia Journal of European Law* 63; R Zimmermann, 'Savigny's Legacy: Legal History, Comparative Law and the Emergence of a European Legal Science' (1996) 112 *LQR* 576.

[120] C Joerges, 'The Challenges of Europeanization in the Realm of Private Law: A Plea for a New Legal Discipline' (2004) 14 *Duke Journal of Comparative and International Law* 149.

[121] J Basedow, 'The Renascence of Uniform Law: European Contract Law and Its Components' (1998) 18 *Legal Studies* 121.

In particular, two authors have noted that 'what is desperately needed is more reflection on methodology and theory building in European legal scholarship'.[122] Legal scholarship in the field should adopt the opposite perspective with respect to the processes of full harmonisation of statutory law in the Member States. On the contrary, the discipline may benefit by focusing on the coexistence of the different cultures, ideas and approaches to the study of private law that have been developed by legal scholars in recent decades. National laws do not constitute an obstacle to the harmonisation and uniformity of EU private law to the extent that legal science, as a cognitive activity, has no boundaries. Indeed, this argument clearly draws on European history.[123]

Thus, we put forward the idea that EU scholarship in this field of law primarily consists of theories and approaches – for example, pluralism, justice, efficiency – that are different from those of the past, when the integration and harmonisation rationales drove research. The paradigm shift from classical schools and modern schools mainly consists in the end of the (noble) integration narrative briefly mentioned in the first sections. Put differently, the driving force of EU private law scholarship is the diversity of perspectives and the sharing of ideas, tools and methodologies. Furthermore, rapidly emerging in the field are new perspectives that may be understood in terms of modern (or post-modern) schools of thought. To provide an example, we cite the recent technological turn of private law scholars in the EU: they increasingly examine the impact of technological change and disruptive innovation in the field with a specific focus on big data and personalisation (ie granularity theory).[124] EU private law is characterised by the heterogeneity of the actors (eg consumers, retail investors). While special rules exist for certain subgroups of actors, the members of these legal categories still exhibit marked differences in behaviour, degrees of rationality, vulnerability and economic endowment. This new scholarship draws on behavioural economics and big data analytics to develop a comprehensive framework for the personalisation of EU private law through different regulatory tools such as disclosures, nudges and mandates. In brief, these authors argue that, by harnessing big data techniques, laws can be tailored to individual characteristics of addressees.[125]

Having noted the above, our purpose in this chapter has not been to definitively address one theory among the many that have been briefly mentioned, but rather to point out the various perspectives of the past and the present that many wrongly believe are bound to decline because of Brexit and the rise of nationalism.

[122] van Gestel and Micklitz (n 118).

[123] T Wallinga, 'The Common History of European Legal Scholarship' (2011) 4 *Erasmus Law Review* 3.

[124] C Busch and A De Franceschi, 'Granular Legal Norms: Big Data and the Personalization of Private Law' in V Mak, E Tjin Tai and A Berlee (eds), *Research Handbook on Data Science and Law* (Cheltenham, Edward Elgar Publishing, 2018).

[125] P Hacker, 'Personalizing EU Private Law. From Disclosures to Nudges and Mandates' (2017) 25 *European Review of Private Law* 651.

In the same vein, it is also important to underline that, unlike in the past, we have not pursued a sole understanding of the goals and tools of private law as an instrument to advance the EU political agenda. It is also important that this chapter has not opposed the economic and justice perspectives on private law theory because both are important for the future of this field of law.

V. Conclusion

We have argued in this chapter that scholars have the responsibility to rise to the challenge. The latest developments in the EU, together with the processes of pluralisation, differentiation and trans-nationalisation of the past 20 years, have arguably challenged the centrality of law to European integration. However, these developments also furnish opportunities to gain new understandings of private law triggered by European integration.

Thus, the chapter has tracked the reassertion of legal scholarship as an autonomous source of European private law. First, we hope that studies in the field of law will benefit from the recently achieved freedom from the narratives of EU market integration and mainly from the enchantment with full harmonisation and codification. We stress that this change of paradigm also represents the end of the noble narrative of integration through (private) law. EU private law scholarship can no longer rely on the traditional assumption that law is the natural cement that holds the Member States, their citizens, and social and legal structures together. Secondly, the past tendency in EU scholarship has been to view every critical voice as a Eurosceptic threat. This is no longer the case, and we now enjoy the benefit of freedom and diversity in scholarship. Thirdly, the various theories briefly examined in this chapter can now follow a path which is not bound to the precarious routes of European integration and stick to their arguments in a rigorous and consistent way.

Our answer to the main research question of the conference is as follows: the future of private law in Europe should be based on a legal scholarship more diverse and robust than both of the economic and justice traditions mentioned above. In particular, we stress that EU private law scholarship consists of the various views, approaches and methods from a wide variety of theoretical perspectives that our chapter has explored in order to analyse and reconstruct the classical and modern schools of thought in the field. Instead of basing our scholarship on classical approaches, we suggest that we should take courage and develop our methodological approaches to private law in Europe.[126] Finally, if legal scholarship is to become

[126] The concept may be better understood with respect to the experiences of third countries: see M Cremona and H-W Micklitz, *Private Law in the External Relations of the EU* (Oxford, Oxford University Press, 2012).

the engine of EU private law, it must leave behind the market integration narrative which characterised scholarly debates in the classical period and embrace a plurality of methodologies and theories.[127] We think that a field of study that is diverse, productive, inclusive, robust and engaged would be able to make a greater contribution to the debate regarding a healthier EU private law and provide a firm foundation for further exploration of private law theories.

[127] S Grundmann, H Micklitz and M Renner, *New Private Law Theory. A Pluralist Approach* (Cambridge, Cambridge University Press, 2021).

4

The Geo-blocking Regulation and the Digital Single Market Strategy

VALERIA FALCE AND GIUSELLA FINOCCHIARO*

I. Introduction

As an explicit goal of EU competition policy, market integration has been traditionally fostered against business strategies aimed at fragmenting national markets along their borders through territorial restrictions.[1]

In particular, Articles 101 and 102 TFEU apply to both multilateral and unilateral business behaviours leading to market partitioning. As a direct remedy, the Block Exemption Regulation for Vertical Restraints[2] bans agreements

* This chapter was jointly conceived with, and is inspired by, V Falce and J Monnet, 'EU Fight against GEOFACTORS: Towards a Circular Interplay between Regulation and Competition' [2018] *European Journal of Privacy Law & Technologies* issue 1. Giusella Finocchiaro authored section III and Valeria Falce authored all the other sections.

[1] G Monti and G Coelho, *Geo-blocking between Competition Law and Regulation* (CPI, 2017). On the urgency to update the internal market concept, see I Lianos, 'Updating the EU Internal Market Concept', CLES Research Paper No 1/2018, https://ssrn.com/abstract=3116384 or http://dx.doi.org/10.2139/ssrn.3116384. The literature is extensive for the internal market objective: see, eg C Barnard, *The Substantive Law of the EU. The Four Freedoms*, 3rd edn (Oxford, Oxford University Press, 2010); C Barnard and J Scott (eds), *The Law of the European Single Market* (Oxford, Oxford University Press, 2005); D Chalmers, G Davies and G Monti, *European Union Law* (Cambridge, Cambridge University Press, 2011) 674; P Craig and G de Búrca (eds), *The Evolution of EU Law* (Oxford, Oxford University Press, 1999); K Mortelmann, 'The Common Market, the Internal Market and the Single Market, What's in a Market?' (1998) 35 *CML Rev* 101; A McGee and S Weatherill, 'The Evolution of the Single Market: Harmonisation or Liberalisation?' (1990) 53 *MLR* 578; W Molle, *The Economics of European Integration: Theory, Practice and Policy*, 5th edn (Aldershot, Dartmouth, 2006).

[2] Regulation 330/2010 of 20 April 2010 on the application of Article 101(3) of the TFEU to categories of vertical agreements and concerted practices [2010] OJ L102/1, replacing Regulation 2790/1999 of 22 December 1999. For a comment, see R Wish and D Bailey, 'Regulation 330/2010: The Commission's New Block Exemption for Vertical Agreements' (2010) 47 *CML Rev* 1757. Note that, in line with the Better Regulation Principles, the review of the Regulation is ongoing, the procedure being divided in two steps: (i) an evaluation phase; and (ii) an impact assessment phase. The evaluation phase was launched on 3 October 2018 and its progress can be followed on the website of better regulation (https://ec.europa.eu/info/law/law-making-process/planning-and-proposing-law/better-regulation-why-and-how_en). The evaluation roadmap was published on 8 November 2018. The deadline for stakeholders' feedback expired on 6 December 2018 (http://ec.europa.eu/competition/consultations/2018_vber/index_en.html).

restricting the territories or the customers to whom a distributor may sell as 'hardcore restrictions',[3] tolerating exclusive distribution agreements insofar as passive sales[4] are allowed. At an indirect level, EU competition law operates as an incentive to enter into cross-border trade, insofar as it facilitates distributors to sell their goods online.[5] Also, unilateral behaviours designed to fragment national markets may fall within the scope of competition law when undertaken by enterprises holding a dominant position in the relevant market.[6]

With the emergence of e-commerce, more and more goods and services are being traded worldwide over the Internet. In this new context, the internal market objective was expected to speed up, the online ecosystem having the potential to make it simpler for consumers to purchase products from other EU Member States, overcoming any possible territorial border.

However, the 2017 sector inquiry[7] proved that cross-border online sales within the EU are growing more slowly than predicted: traders tend to rely heavily on digital technical measures, such as 'geo-blocking'[8] and 'geo-filtering'[9] behaviours, to erect different types of borders in order to limit the ability of consumers to make cross-border online purchases.

To respond to these new challenges and in order to advance the Digital Single Market, exploiting the opportunities flowing from the '4th industrial revolution',[10] the EU adopted a comprehensive e-commerce framework[11] with

[3] An individual exemption being highly unlikely: Regulation 330/2010 on the application of Article 101(3) of the Treaty on the Functioning of the European Union to categories of vertical agreements and concerted practices [2010] OJ L102/1, Art 4.

[4] Consisting in selling goods on the Internet without automatic rerouting of customers to another website. See eg Case COMP/37.975 *Yamaha* (16 July 2003) paras 107–09, https://ec.europa.eu/competition/antitrust/cases/dec_docs/37975/37975_91_5.pdf.

[5] Case C-230/16 *Coty Germany GmbH v Parfümerie Akzente GmbH* ECLI:EU:C:2017:941; Commission, 'Competition Policy Brief – EU Competition Rules and Marketplace Bans: Where Do We Stand After the *Coty* Judgment? (April 2018), http://ec.europa.eu/competition/publications/cpb/2018/kdak18001enn.pdf; Case C-439/09 *Pierre Fabre Dermo-Cosmétique SAS* [2011] ECR I-09419, para 47, where the Court found a requirement that the buyer may only sell goods through a physical store to be restrictive by object for not affording distributors the chance to use the Internet.

[6] Joined Cases C-468/06 to C-478/06, *Sot Lelos kai Sia EE* [2008] ECR I-07139; Commission Decision from 14 April 2010 in Case 39351 *Swedish Interconnectors*.

[7] 'Final Report on the e-Commerce Sector Inquiry', COM (2017) 229 final. For a complete overview, see http://ec.europa.eu/competition/antitrust/sector_inquiries_e_commerce.html. See also https://publications.europa.eu/en/publication-detail/-/publication/8bde2f8d-0251-11e7-8a35-01aa75ed71a1/l anguage-en/format-PDF.

[8] Blocking access to websites, rerouting customers to websites targeting other Member States or refusing to deliver cross-border or to accept cross-border payments.

[9] Commercial practices whereby online retailers allow consumers to access and purchase goods or services cross-border, but offer different terms and/or conditions if the customer is in a different Member State. More extensively, DG Internal Policies, 'The Geo-blocking Proposal: Internal Market, Competition Law and Regulatory Aspects' (January 2017).

[10] European Council conclusions, Brussels, 23 June 2017 (OR. en) EUCO 8/17 CO EUR 8 CONCL 3, Consilium.europa.eu.

[11] N Duch-Brown and B Martens, 'The European Digital Single Market: its Role in Economic Activity in the EU' (2015) Joint Research Centre of the European Commission, Institute for Prospective Technological Studies, Digital Economy Working Paper 2015/17, https://ec.europa.eu/jrc/sites/default/files/JRC98723.pdf.

the view to ensuring better access to goods and services offered online, building trust for consumers and greater certainty for businesses, and reducing transaction costs and administrative burden for businesses when trading online across borders.[12]

As part of it, on 3 December 2018 the EU Geo-blocking Regulation entered into force,[13] introducing a new veto against relevant forms of commercial practices based on geo-factors such as the nationality or place of residence of the demand side at intra-Community level.[14]

Since the Geo-blocking Regulation is centered on the obligation imposed on each trader[15] to treat EU customers (including consumers and other end users)[16] in the same manner when they are in the same situation, regardless of their nationality, place of residence or place of establishment, the aim of this chapter is to analyse the new legal system in its interplay with competition law so as to claim that in the digitised ecosystem, both competition policy and regulation are necessary, neither of them being sufficient alone to fully unlock e-commerce in the EU.

II. The Rationale, Ambit and Scope of the Geo-blocking Regulation

The Geo-blocking Regulation addresses unilateral traders practices where there is no objective justification for different treatment of consumers based on

[12] Details on the actions undertaken are available at https://ec.europa.eu/digital-single-market/en/news/76026/3786.

[13] Regulation (EU) 2018/302 of the European Parliament and of the Council of 28 February 2018 on addressing unjustified geo-blocking and other forms of discrimination based on customers' nationality, place of residence or place of establishment within the internal market and amending Regulations (EC) No 2006/2004 and (EU) 2017/2394 and Directive 2009/22/EC. For more data underpinning the analysis for the Geo-blocking Regulation, see 'JRC Technical Report on The European Digital Single Market, Its Role in Economic Activity in the EU', https://ec.europa.eu/jrc/sites/jrcsh/files/JRC98723.pdf; JRC-IPTS based on Mystery Shopping Survey 2015 (GfK Mystery Shopping, https://ec.europa.eu/info/publications/geo-blocking-consumers-online-findings-mystery-shopping-carried-out-european-commission_en); the European Commission's 2015 public consultation on 'Geo-blocking and Other Geographically Based Restrictions When Shopping and Accessing Information in the EU', https://ec.europa.eu/digital-single-market/en/news/public-consultation-geo-blocking-and-other-geographically-based-restrictions-when-shopping-and; and the impact assessment accompanying the proposal for a Regulation on addressing geo-blocking and other forms of discrimination based on place of residence or establishment or nationality within the single market, http://ec.europa.eu/newsroom/dae/document.cfm?doc_id=15953.

[14] Commission, 'Geo-blocking Regulation Impact Assessment' SWD (2016) 173 final.

[15] Trader means any natural or legal person who is acting for purposes relating to his or her trade, business, craft or profession.

[16] For the purposes of the Geo-blocking Regulation, a consumer is any natural person who is acting for purposes which are outside his or her trade, business, craft or profession; a customer is a consumer who is a national of, or has his or her place of residence in, a Member State, or an undertaking which has its place of establishment in a Member State and receives a service or purchases a good, or seeks to do so, within the Union, for the sole purpose of end use.

nationality, residence or place of establishment, hence discriminating against them when they try to avail themselves of best offers, prices or sales conditions compared to nationals or residents of the trader's Member State.

In so doing, the regulation implements the principle of no discrimination, which is at the foundation of the European Union. Article 18 TFEU and Article 21(2) of the EU Charter of Fundamental Rights, as well as the specific provisions of the above-mentioned Treaty related to internal market freedom, clearly include the prohibition of discrimination on grounds of nationality, which also covers indirect discrimination. In addition, as far as the provision of services is concerned, that general principle is specified by Article 20(2) of the Services Directive,[17] according to which Member States shall ensure that the general conditions of access to a service, which are made available to the public at large by the provider, do not contain discriminatory provisions relating to the nationality or place of residence of the recipient, but without precluding the possibility of providing for differences in the conditions of access where those differences are directly justified by objective criteria.[18]

In particular, the Geo-blocking Regulation addresses three different and interconnected phases of a transaction: access to sites and interfaces, access to goods and services, and means of payment. Traders are free to design their website, carry out marketing activities and set the prices across the EU, but the pole star to follow at intra-Community level shall consist in disconnecting their business choices from any nationality, residence or establishment criteria.

In terms of access to online interfaces, the Regulation bans the blocking of access to websites and rerouting without the customer's prior consent. In terms of access to goods or services, the Regulation defines specific situations when there can be no justified reason for geo-blocking or other forms of discrimination based on nationality, residence or establishment. In these situations, customers from another EU Member State must have the same access to goods and services as local customers.

As regards non-discrimination for reasons related to payment, while traders remain free to accept whatever payment means they wish, the Regulation includes a specific provision on non-discrimination within the range of means of payment the traders accept.[19] Article 5 of the Regulation applies to payment transactions

[17] Directive 2006/123/EC of the European Parliament and of the Council of 12 December 2006 on services in the internal market.

[18] See Recital 95 of Directive 2006/123/EC. Additional indications on the application of Art 20(2) are included in Commission, 'With a View to Establishing Guidance on the Application of Article 20(2) of Directive 2006/123/EC on Services in the Internal Market ('the Services Directive')', SWD (2012) 146, https://eur-lex.europa.eu/legal-content/EN/ALL/?uri=SWD:2012:0146:FIN.

[19] The provision of (non-audiovisual) copyright protected content services (eg e-books, online music or videogames) is not covered by the Regulation. These services, however, remain subject to the Regulation's prohibition to block or limit access to online interfaces on the basis of the nationality, residence or establishment of the customer. Audiovisual services are also not covered by the Regulation.

made by means of an electronic transaction by credit transfer, direct debit or a card-based payment instrument of the same brand and category of card, where the authentication requirements are met and the payment transactions are in a currency that the trader accepts. However, once this choice has been made, traders should not discriminate against customers within the EU by refusing transactions or applying different conditions of payment based on the customer's nationality, place of residence or establishment, or in relation to the location of the payment account, the establishment of the payment service provider or the place of issue of the payment instrument.

Traders can therefore decide to offer different conditions on several of their websites. However, if they accept a specific payment means on a specific website, they should also accept that payment means from consumers from outside the Member State that the specific website is targeting.

In practice, this means that if a trader accepts debit cards of a particular brand, they do not need to accept credit cards of that same brand or debit cards of other brands. It also means that the trader does not have to accept commercial credit cards of a given brand when he or she only accepts consumer credit cards of that brand. However, it means that if a trader accepts credit cards of a given brand issued in one Member Sate, they have to accept the same type of credit card of the same brand issued in another Member State.

Because of this limited scope, services linked to copyright-protected content or works in an intangible form – such as music streaming services and e-books – fall outside the ambit of the regulation, as well as other services such as financial, audio-visual, transport, healthcare and social services.

III. Regulatory Safe Harbours

Unlike price discrimination, price differentiation is not prohibited by the regulation. Therefore, traders are free to offer different general conditions, including prices, and to target certain groups of customers in specific territories. Moreover, traders are not obliged to deliver goods to customers outside the Member State to which they offer delivery.

The new provisions also do not impose the 'unbundling' of offers for nationals or residents of another Member State where the trader provides goods or services combined with services that do not fall within the scope of the Regulation. What the new legal system requires in fact is that, if products or services are bundled but only one product or aspect falls within its rules, then the whole bundle will be subject to the rules of the Regulation. If, on the other hand, the trader decides to unbundle the package, then the price and conditions for such goods or services will no longer be restricted, provided that nondiscriminatory conditions based on nationality, residence or establishment are applied.

Likewise, the Regulation does not oblige the trader to sell or deliver products or services in Europe. Rather, its scope prohibits traders from selling across Europe while discriminating on the basis of the customer's nationality, residence or establishment.

Nor does the Regulation prohibit 'tailored offers'. Traders can propose different versions of online interfaces in order to target different customers from different Member States. The different version of the website might have a different layout, another language or other characteristics that make it, or part of it, specific to customers with a specific nationality, place of residence or place of establishment. Of course, in line with Article 3 of the Regulation, redirecting customers from one version of the online interface to another version is banned if carried out on a discriminatory basis and without their explicit consent. For the same reason, such a website or parts of it need to be accessible for customers from different Member States.

As a natural consequence, the Regulation does not address 'dynamic pricing' as such, where traders adapt their offers over time. However, to comply with the Regulation, dynamic pricing shall be dependent on factors unrelated to nationality, residence or establishment (such as offers for young people or for consumers as opposed to professionals).

Also, 'seasonal promotions' are not specifically considered by the Regulation, meaning that such promotions should be accessible for consumers or end users from other Member States in a non-discriminatory manner.

What is more important is that the Regulation does not question the trader's pricing policy, as the harmonisation of price levels is beyond its scope. Traders therefore remain free to set different prices for instance on websites targeting different customer groups. However, these websites should be accessible to all EU customers and – in the specific situations described above – EU customers should be able to purchase goods or services under the same conditions as nationals of the Member State of the trader, including net prices.

For the same reason, the Regulation also does not preclude the freedom of traders to offer, on a non-discriminatory basis, different conditions, including different net sale prices, at different points of sale, such as shops and websites, or to target specific offers only at a specific territory within a Member State. However, under the Regulation, these offers need to be accessible to consumers from other Member States on a non-discriminatory basis.

Under the Regulation, traders are therefore free to have sales, promotions or other types of price campaigns on their selected e-commerce websites as long as they act in a non-discriminatory way.

The Regulation does not impact consumers' rights in such cases. The Regulation's main concern is to ensure cross-border access to goods and services on a non-discriminatory basis in the situations covered. It does not contain any rules on remedies, for instance, where the goods in question later turn out to be defective.

IV. Geo-blocking Practices and Competition Policy

Whereas the Geo-blocking Regulation has been adopted to dismantle geo-barriers,[20] competition law also challenges market segmentation as a possible result of territorial restrictions in vertical distribution and licence agreements. In fact, under EU case law, agreements or concerted practices which are aimed at partitioning markets according to national borders or which make the penetration of national markets more difficult – and in particular those which are pointed at preventing or restricting parallel exports – have been deemed restrictive per se pursuant to Article 101(1) TFEU.[21]

In addition, and while awaiting the review of the Block Exemption Regulation for Vertical Restraints (VBER),[22] contractual restrictions of the territory in which a distributor may sell relevant goods are generally considered a hardcore restriction of competition, with only a limited number of exceptions (see Article 4(b) VBER). In this context, active sales restrictions are allowed insofar as they concern sales in an exclusive territory reserved for the supplier or allocated by the supplier to another distributor, whereas passive sales restrictions provide absolute territorial protection and are normally unlawful.

Within a selective distribution system, neither active nor passive sales to end users may be restricted. As a result, undertakings are generally free to set up the distribution system that best suits them, including selective distribution systems, where the products can only be sold by pre-selected authorised sellers. However, these systems must comply with EU competition rules, with the consequence that consumers must be free to purchase from any retailer authorised by a manufacturer, including across national borders. At the same time, authorised retailers must be free to offer the products included in the distribution contract online, to advertise and sell them across borders, and to set their own resale prices.[23] Despite

[20] In line with Art 2(2) of the Services Directive, financial retail services, audiovisual services, transport services, electronic communication services and healthcare services are excluded from the scope of the Geo-blocking Regulation. On the intersection with intellectual property, see M Trible, 'Geo-blocking and "Legitimate Trade"' in C Heath, A Kamperman Sanders and A Moerland (eds), *Intellectual Property and Obstacles to Legitimate Trade* (Wolters Kluwer, 2018).

[21] See, eg judgment in Joined Cases 56/64 and 58/64 *Établissements Consten S.à.R.L. and Grundig – Verkaufs-GmbH v Commission of the European Economic Community*; judgment of 6 October 2009 in Joined Cases C-501/06 P, C-513/06 P, C-515/06 P and C-519/06 P *GlaxoSmithKline Services v Commission* ECLI:EU:C:2009:610; judgment of 4 October 2011in Joined Cases C-403/08 and C-429/08 C Football *Association Premier League and Others* ECLI:EU:C:2011:631.

[22] For more details, see http://ec.europa.eu/competition/consultations/2018_vber/index_en.html.

[23] However, according to the e-Commerce Sector Inquiry, certain of the reported active sales restrictions are not limited to territories that have been exclusively allocated to other distributors or reserved for the supplier. Moreover, certain suppliers operating a selective distribution system across several Member States are reported to have limited the ability of authorised retailers to sell to all customers within the territory where the selective distribution system is applied: 'Final Report on the e-Commerce Sector Inquiry' COM (2017) 229 final, paras 50–53.

the enforcement of competition law, restrictions on selling in online marketplaces have increased in the digitised world.[24]

At the judicial level, and with regard to online sales restrictions, in the *Pierre Fabre* case the ECJ held that a contractual provision prohibiting de facto the Internet as a method of marketing amounts to a restriction of competition by object within the meaning of Article 101(1) TFEU. It has at the very least as its object the restriction of passive sales to end users wishing to purchase online and located outside the physical trading area of the relevant member of the selective distribution system.[25]

On the same subject, in 2017 the ECJ rendered an important judgment. In the *Coty* judgment,[26] the ECJ largely confirmed the Commission's position that (absolute) marketplace bans should not be considered as hardcore restrictions within the meaning of Articles 4(b) and 4(c) VBER.[27]

In particular, the ECJ held that a selective distribution system compliant with Article 101 TFEU can also be operated for luxury goods in order to preserve the luxury image of those goods, provided that the so-called '*Metro* criteria'[28] are met. This is an important clarification of the ECJ's 2011 *Pierre Fabre* judgment, dealing with distribution contracts for cosmetics and personal care products, which stipulated that all sales had to be made exclusively in a physical space. In its reasoning, the ECJ deemed that the 'aim of maintaining a prestigious image is not a legitimate aim for restricting competition'. The *Pierre Fabre* judgment dealt with distribution contracts.

In other words, in *Coty* the ECJ clarified that the findings in *Pierre Fabre* are confined to the goods (cosmetics) and contractual clause (prohibition of all

[24] For an excellent analysis, see P Manzini, 'Le restrizioni verticali della concorrenza al tempo di Internet' [2018] *Diritto del commercio internazionale* 289; J Hederstrom and L Peeperkorn, 'Vertical Restraints in On-lines Sales: Comments on Some Recent Developments' (2016) 7 *Journal of European Competition Law & Practice* 10. With specific reference to the role of platforms, see S Wartinger and L Solek, 'Restrictions of Third-Party Platforms within Selective Distribution Systems' (2016) 39 *World Competition* 291; A Erzachi, 'The Ripple Effects of On-line Marketplace Bans' (2017) 40 *World Competition* 47.

[25] Judgment of 13 October 2011, Case C-439/09 *Pierre Fabre Dermo-Cosmétique* ECLI:EU:C:2011:649, para 54.

[26] Judgment of 6 December 2017, Case C-230/16 *Coty Germany GmbH v Parfümerie Akzente GmbH* ECLI:EU:C:2017:941; Commission, 'Competition Policy Brief' (n 5). The case concerned a contractual restriction included in a selective distribution agreement between Coty Germany GmbH, which is one of Germany's leading suppliers of luxury cosmetics, and one of its distributors, Parfümerie Akzente GmbH. The contractual clause prohibited the discernible engagement by Parfümerie Akzente of a third-party undertaking which was not an authorised retailer of Coty. Coty sought to prohibit Parfümerie Akzente from distributing its products on Amazon.de through Amazon's marketplace, which enables third-party sellers such as Parfümerie Akzente to sell products alongside Amazon's offerings. Based on the diverging interpretations of the applicable EU competition rules in Germany, the Higher Regional Court of Frankfurt am Main decided to stay the proceedings and submit several questions to the ECJ for a preliminary ruling.

[27] 'Final Report on the e-Commerce Sector Inquiry', COM (2017) 229 final, para 42.

[28] Judgment of 25 October 1977 in Case 26/76 *Metro I, Metro SB-Großmärkte v Commission* ECLI:EU:C:1977:167.

forms of selling via the Internet) in question rather than to selective distribution systems in general. The *Pierre Fabre* reasoning therefore applies to absolute bans of online sales only, and not to marketplace bans or selective distribution systems as such.

Secondly, in *Coty* the ECJ provided guidance on the application of the *Metro* criteria to the scenario in question. According to the *Metro* judgment, resellers must be chosen on the basis of objective criteria of a qualitative nature, laid down uniformly for all potential resellers and not applied in a discriminatory fashion; the characteristics of the product in question must necessitate such a network in order to preserve its quality and ensure its proper use; and the criteria laid down must not go beyond what is necessary.

In *Coty* the ECJ specified that the marketplace ban at stake was appropriate for the legitimate objective of preserving the luxury image of the goods concerned, as it allowed the supplier to verify that the goods would be sold in an environment that corresponds to the qualitative criteria that the supplier has agreed with its authorised distributors. The ECJ also considered the marketplace ban to be proportionate as it only limits online sales via discernible third-party platforms and does not contain an absolute prohibition to sell online.

Finally, in *Coty* the ECJ found that marketplace bans do not amount to hardcore restrictions within the meaning of Article 4 VBER and are therefore block-exempted, provided that the shares of the parties are not above the 30 per cent market share threshold of Article 3 VBER. The ECJ found that marketplace bans have to be differentiated from a prohibition of the use of the Internet as such and therefore neither amounts to a restriction of the customers to whom distributors may sell within the meaning of Article 4(b) VBER or to a restriction of passive sales to end users by authorised distributors within the meaning of Article 4(c) VBER.

The ECJ also emphasised that in the case at hand distributors were allowed to advertise the products via the Internet on third party platforms (eg price comparison websites) and use online search engines with the result that customers were usually able to find the online offer of authorised distributors. These findings are consistent with the information obtained in the e-commerce sector inquiry, which indicates that the importance of marketplaces as a sales channel varies significantly depending on the size of the retailers, the EU Member States concerned and the product categories concerned. On that basis, in the final report on the e-commerce sector inquiry the Commission considered that marketplace bans do not generally amount to a de facto prohibition on selling online and could not be considered to restrict the effective use of the Internet as a sales channel irrespective of the markets concerned. This does not mean that absolute marketplace bans are generally compatible with the EU's competition rules. The Commission or a national competition authority, in fact, may decide to withdraw the protection of the VBER in particular cases when justified by the market situation.

At the EU level, the European Commission has recently fined four consumer electronics manufacturers for engaging in so-called 'fixed or minimum resale price maintenance' by restricting the ability of their online retailers to set their own retail prices for widely used consumer electronics products such as kitchen appliances, notebooks and hi-fi products.[29] The four manufacturers intervened particularly with online retailers, who offered their products at low prices. If those retailers did not follow the prices requested by manufacturers, they would face threats or sanctions, such as blocking of supplies. Many, including the biggest online retailers, use pricing algorithms which automatically adapt retail prices to those of competitors. In this way, the pricing restrictions imposed on low pricing by online retailers typically had a broader impact on overall online prices for the respective consumer electronics products. Moreover, the use of sophisticated monitoring tools allowed the manufacturers to effectively track resale price setting in the distribution network and to intervene swiftly in case of price decreases. The price interventions limited effective price competition between retailers and led to higher prices, with an immediate effect on consumers.[30]

Even more recently, the Commission has fined Guess, a company which designs, distributes and licenses clothing and accessories, for having restricted authorised retailers from selling online to consumers or to retailers in other Member States.[31] The Commission found that the agreements allowed Guess to partition European markets, thus making retail prices of Guess products in Eastern Europe on average 5–10 per cent higher than in Western Europe. On this basis, the Commission concluded that Guess's practices were illegal, depriving European consumers of one of the core benefits of the European Single Market – namely, the possibility to shop across borders for more choice and a better deal.

Recently, the Commission investigated two separate sets of agreements to assess if certain online sales practices prevent, in breach of EU antitrust rules, consumers from enjoying cross-border choice and being able to buy video games and hotel accommodation at competitive prices.

In connection to agreements between European tour operators on the one hand and hotels on the other hand, the Commission investigated whether the agreements contain clauses that discriminate between customers based on their nationality or country of residence, with the result that customers would not be

[29] See http://europa.eu/rapid/press-release_IP-18-4601_en.htm.

[30] http://europa.eu/rapid/press-release_IP-18-4601_en.htm.

[31] Case COMP/AT.40428 *Guess* Commission Decision of 17 December 2018, http://ec.europa.eu/competition/elojade/isef/case_details.cfm?proc_code=1_40428: in particular, the Commission found that Guess's distribution agreements restricted authorised retailers from: (i) using the Guess brand names and trademarks for the purposes of online search advertising; (ii) selling online without a prior specific authorisation by Guess. The company had full discretion for this authorisation, which was not based on any specified quality criteria; (iii) selling to consumers located outside the authorised retailers' allocated territories; (iv) cross-selling among authorised wholesalers and retailers; and (v) independently deciding on the retail price at which they sell Guess products.

able to see the full hotel availability or book hotel rooms at the best prices.[32] The conclusion reached was that a violation had occurred, thus a fine was applied.[33]

In connection to video games, the Commission is investigating bilateral agreements concluded between Valve Corporation, owner of the Steam game distribution platform, and five PC video game publishers, Bandai Namco, Capcom, Focus Home, Koch Media and ZeniMax. The investigation concerns geo-blocking practices, where companies prevent consumers from purchasing digital content, in this case PC video games, because of the consumer's location or country of residence.

Similarly, another set of investigations dealt with licensing and distribution practices of Nike, Sanrio and Universal Studios that may restrict their licensees from selling licensed merchandise across borders and online within the EU Single Market.[34] The Commission examined whether the licensing and distribution practices of these companies might be denying consumers access to a wider choice and better deals in the Single Market, and came to a positive conclusion.[35]

V. Connection with Consumer Protection Regulation, e-Commerce Regulation and GDPR

As well as competition law, the Geo-blocking Regulation has major impacts on consumer protection regulation, data protection regulation and electronic commerce, which need to be coordinated with the new Regulation.

Consumer protection is pursued through EU action. The legal basis that legitimises the EU intervention is to be found in Article 169 TFEU, according to which,

> in order to promote the interests of consumers and to ensure a high level of consumer protection, the Union shall contribute to protecting the health, safety and economic interests of consumers, as well as to promoting their right to information, education and to organise themselves in order to safeguard their interests.

[32] Commission press release IP/17/201 (2 February 2017). Following complaints from customers, the Commission investigated agreements regarding hotel accommodation concluded between the largest European tour operators on the one hand (Kuoni, REWE, Thomas Cook, TUI) and hotels on the other hand (Meliá Hotels). The Commission welcomes hotels developing and introducing innovative pricing mechanisms to maximise room usage, but hotels and tour operators cannot discriminate between customers on the basis of their location. The agreements in question may contain clauses that discriminate between customers based on their nationality or country of residence – as a result, some customers would not be able to see the full hotel availability or book hotel rooms at the best prices. This may breach EU competition rules by preventing consumers from booking hotel accommodation at better rates offered by tour operators in other Member States simply because of the consumer's nationality or place of residence. This would lead to the partitioning of the Single Market.

[33] Case AT. 40528 *Mlia (Holiday Pricing).*

[34] Case AT.40432 *Licensed merchandise – Sanrio*; Case AT.40433 *Licensed merchandise – Universal Studios*; Case AT.40436 *Licensed merchandise – Nike*. See IP/17/1646 of 14 June 2017, http://europa.eu/rapid/ press-release_IP-17–1646_en.htm.

[35] Case AT.40436 *Ancillary sports merchandise.*

Indeed, consumer policy is part of the EU strategy to improve the life quality of European citizens and contributes to the achievement of the broader programme for the creation of the internal market and the free circulation of goods, services and people.

The regulatory framework on consumer protection is particularly broad and covers a number of different provisions that range from the protection of consumers' health and safety[36] to the regulation of their legal[37] and economic interests. The latter include, in particular, the provisions on electronic commerce, on distance selling contracts and off-premises contracts, on unfair terms and unfair commercial practices, and on the modernisation of consumer law.[38]

The common objective of these regulations is to harmonise the legal framework on consumer protection in line with the ultimate goal of pursuing the growth and good functioning of the internal market, which would be severely undermined by the differences in the national legislations.

Regulation (EU) 2018/302 shares the same objective. It aims to remove the obstacles to, and eliminate any form of discrimination that is incompatible with, the four freedoms of the internal market.

To date, the principle of non-discrimination has only implicitly guided the adoption of consumer protection laws. Now, the Geo-blocking Regulation focuses entirely on this principle and makes it an essential requirement for each Member State to respect. The changed approach can be inferred, on the one hand, from the wording of the title that, in declaring the purposes of the Regulation, explicitly states that it addresses 'unjustified geo-blocking and other forms of discrimination'. On the other hand, the new trend can be derived from the choice of the regulation as the preferred legislative instrument which, unlike the directive, is directly applicable and therefore does not require an implementing act by the Member States.

[36] This set of rules includes, for example, regulations on hygiene of foodstuffs and food and animal feed labelling (see, respectively, Regulation EC 853/2004 of 29 April 2004 and Regulation EU 1169/2011 of 25 October 2011), and on procedures for the evaluation, market authorisation, classification and labelling of medicines, medical devices and alternative therapies (see, *ex multis*, Directive 2001/83/EC of 6 November 2001, Regulation EU 2017/745 of 5 April 2017, Regulation EU 2017/746 of 5 April 2017), but also those rules which set security requirements for cosmetic products (Regulation EC 1223/2009 of 30 November 2009), explosives for civilian use (Directive 2014/28/EU of 26 February 2014) and toys (Directive 2009/48/EC of 18 June 2009).

[37] Among these rules are those which have settled alternative dispute resolution procedures and online dispute resolution (see, respectively, Directive 2013/11/UE and Regulation EU 524/2013, both issued on 21 May 2013). Similarly, Decision 2001/470/EC established a European judicial network to simplify the life of citizens facing cross-border litigations by improving the mechanisms for judicial cooperation between Member States in civil and commercial matters and providing them with practical information to facilitate their access to justice.

[38] See, Directive 2000/31/EC, Directive 2011/83/EU, Directive 93/13/EEC and Directive 2005/29/EC of 11 May 2005, and now Directive (EU) 2019/2161 amending Directive 93/13/EEC and Directives 98/6/EC, 2005/29/EC and 2011/83/EU of the European Parliament and of the Council as regards the better enforcement and modernisation of Union consumer protection rules. For an overview of the 'New Deal for Consumers', see https://ec.europa.eu/info/law/law-topic/consumers/review-eu-consumer-law-new-deal-consumers_en.

In this way, the European legislator has applied an extremely effective instrument to the described objective that, thanks to its direct applicability, drastically reduces the risk of regulatory differentiation in the sector, by allowing the highest degree of uniformity among the Member States.

The necessity to strengthen the effectiveness of the mentioned Regulation originates from the insufficient impact of Directive 2006/123/EC on internal market services.[39] Despite its national implementation, the Directive remained substantially unfulfilled and was unable to reduce the legal uncertainty in this field. The Directive already prohibits, in the context of the free circulation of services, any form of discrimination on grounds of nationality or residence of the recipient of the service, and specifies that

> the principle of non-discrimination within the internal market means that access by a recipient, and especially by a consumer, to a service on offer to the public may not be denied or restricted by application of a criterion, included in general conditions made available to the public, relating to the recipient's nationality or place of residence …[40]

In a similar way, Article 20 of the Directive requires Member States to ensure

> that the recipient is not made subject to discriminatory requirements based on his nationality or place of residence … and that the general conditions of access to a service, which are made available to the public at large by the provider, do not contain discriminatory provisions relating to the nationality or place of residence of the recipient, but without precluding the possibility of providing for differences in the conditions of access where those differences are directly justified by objective criteria.

As described below, the EU Geo-blocking Regulation supports these provisions but, unlike the Directive,[41] has a limited scope of application: it exclusively addresses 'customers', a category that includes not only consumers[42] who are nationals of or have their place of residence in a Member State, but also undertakings established in a Member State that receive a service or purchase a good within the Union for the sole purpose of end use.[43]

Furthermore, as Recital no 4 of the Regulation specifies, in the event of conflict with the provisions of the Directive, the Regulation should prevail.

[39] Directive 2006/123/EC of the European Parliament and of the Council of 12 December 2006 on services in the internal market [2006] OJ L376.

[40] See, respectively, recital nos 94 and 95.

[41] The Directive addresses instead 'recipients' who are natural persons, nationals of a Member State or legal persons established in a Member State that, for professional or non-professional purposes, use or wish to use a service.

[42] Pursuant to the definition of Art 2, no 12 of the Regulation, consumer means 'any natural person who is acting for purposes which are outside his or her trade, business, craft or profession'.

[43] Recital no 16 of the Regulation specifies that the 'protection should not extend to customers purchasing a good or a service for subsequent resale, transformation, processing, renting or subcontracting … This Regulation should, therefore, be without prejudice to non-discriminatory practices of traders limiting transactions or repetitive transactions, in order to prevent undertakings from purchasing quantities exceeding their internal needs, taking due account of the size of the undertakings, with a view to identifying whether the purchase is for end use only'.

Last but not least, it is worth noting that each Member State is required to set up a specific body to provide practical assistance to consumers in disputes with traders resulting from the application of the Regulation.[44] On this point, the provision is rather concise. Recital no 36 adds only that these functions could be carried out by the same entities provided for by the European Regulation on Online Dispute Resolution for Consumers.[45] The legislation is silent on further details. Therefore, an implementing regulation of the European institutions or a delegated act to the Member States is expected, even though the last option would jeopardise the intent of standardisation pursued by the new Regulation.

As previously anticipated, the provisions on geo-blocking should also necessarily coordinate with Regulation (EU) 2016/679 of the European Parliament and of the Council of 27 April 2016 on the protection of natural persons with regard to the processing of personal data and on the free movement of such data (also known as the General Data Protection Regulation, or GDPR).

Indeed, information and data belonging to the recipient of a service (or, in the Regulation's words, the 'customer') are an important source of knowledge that the trader can exploit and misuse in order to perpetrate discriminatory acts at the customer's expense.

From the processing of data, even when their collection is apparently unharmful, traders could extrapolate information on the nationality, place of residence or establishment of customers and, on this basis, tailor specific terms and conditions of their products or decide to block or limit the access to the online services they provide. For instance, a piece of information could indicate

> the physical location of customers, such as the IP address used when accessing an online interface, the address submitted for the delivery of goods, the choice of language made or the Member State where the customer's payment instrument has been issued.[46]

Hence, the processing of these data must also comply with the principles and requirements of the GDPR. In particular, the trader, as the data controller, shall respect and apply the principles of purpose limitation and data minimisation.

According to the principle of purpose limitation, the trader shall ensure that the personal data are collected for specified, explicit and legitimate purposes, such as for the performance of a contract, for the supply of a requested service or – for information society services – in order to improve the user browsing experience (for example, in terms of language setting or other kinds of customer preferences) or to control the web traffic and prevent fraud or illegal activities to the detriment of the website. The application of the GDPR could thus prevent traders from

[44] See Art 8 of the Regulation.

[45] Regulation (EU) 524/2013 of the European Parliament and of the Council of 21 May 2013 on online dispute resolution for consumer disputes and amending Regulation (EC) No 2006/2004 and Directive 2009/22/EC.

[46] See recital no 6 of the Regulation.

carrying out data misuse and pursuing unlawful and implicit purposes, such as a discriminatory restriction of access to a website or an unjustified refusal of an electronic payment system.

In addition, the data minimisation principle requires that personal data shall be collected only insofar as they are relevant and limited to what is necessary in relation to the purposes for which they are processed. This means, for example, that if a product is ordered online and the customer chooses to pay cash on delivery, the trader will not be entitled to collect further information about the customer's alternative electronic payment methods (eg the place of issue of the payment instrument). This information would be excessive and irrelevant to the purpose of providing the requested service.

Artificial intelligence (AI) systems and AI-based profiling activities must also be considered. These technologies are able to extrapolate further information about individuals by exploiting the data that the same individuals had previously made available. This could allow the mass categorisation of individuals, which may, in turn, lead to different forms of discrimination, including economic discrimination.[47]

For this reason, it is important to ensure both a careful and aware employment of these powerful tools and the quality of the raw material that these technologies are fed with: the data. The use of low-quality, outdated, incomplete or incorrect data may lead to poor predictions and, consequently, to distorted perceptions, discrimination and bias, which can eventually result in the infringement of the fundamental rights of individuals.[48]

Due attention should also be paid to the electronic commerce context, where the trader could exploit these technologies in order to obtain additional customer information, for instance the physical address or the IP address, and to prevent access to a website or present customers with priorly arranged prices based on the specific country of location.

In brief, despite following different paths, the GDPR and the Geo-blocking Regulation are moving in the same direction, in terms of building a Digital Single Market and removing the legal obstacles represented by the lack of uniformity of the applicable rules and by the traders themselves. Therefore, coordination between the two Regulations seems highly desirable and, if correctly fulfilled, the GDPR could contribute upstream to the avoidance of the establishment of geo-blocking and other forms of discrimination.

The EU Geo-blocking Regulation is also a complementary set of rules to Directive 2000/31/EC on E-commerce. The E-commerce Directive was created with the aim of strengthening consumer – or, more generally, customer – protection,

[47] See Declaration by the Committee of Ministers on the manipulative capabilities of algorithmic processes, adopted by the Committee of Ministers on 13 February 2019 at the 1337th meeting of the Ministers' Deputies, para 6.

[48] See European Parliament resolution of 12 February 2019 on a comprehensive European industrial policy on artificial intelligence and robotics.

in particular by increasing trust and certainty in the electronic commerce sector. Indeed, electronic transactions are affected by the lack of certainty about the identity of the contractors, a fact that often discourages online negotiations.

Recital no 2 of the Geo-blocking Regulation already provides for the application of the new legislation to electronic commerce, considering that in this context discriminatory practices contribute 'to the relatively low level of cross-border transactions within the Union'.

In particular, the Regulation introduces a new obligation upon traders, who now shall mandatorily request the customer's expressed consent to be redirected to a version of the trader's online interface that is different from the online interface to which the customer initially sought access. This case occurs when different interfaces are realised for customers according to their nationality or when the redirection is necessary in order to ensure compliance with a legal requirement laid down in EU law, or in the laws of a Member State.[49] In the latter case, the Regulation enhances the informational obligations[50] that the Directive imposes on traders, who now shall

> provide a clear and specific explanation to customers regarding the reasons why the blocking or limitation of access, or the redirection is necessary in order to ensure such compliance. That explanation shall be given in the language of the online interface that the customer initially sought to access.[51]

VI. Conclusions. Towards a 'Circular' Interplay between Regulation and Competition

While the new framework operates despite and beyond competition law, the Geo-blocking Regulation is fully complementary to competition policy in tackling business strategies pointed at partitioning the Digital Single Market.[52]

As a follow-up of the e-commerce sector inquiry, in the context of the Digital Single Market strategy and as proven by the very recent case law, EU competition rules and the Geo-blocking Regulation are allies in preventing business practices that have evolved as a result of the growth of e-commerce and that pose a risk to competition and cross-border trade within the European Single Market.

[49] See Art 3, para 2 of the Regulation.

[50] Arts 5 and 10 of the Directive 2000/31/EC require service providers to supply a set of information in general and before the recipient of the service places the order, mainly aimed at guaranteeing the provider's identity and the transparency in the supply of services.

[51] See Art 3, para 3 of the Regulation.

[52] 'Implications of e-Commerce for Competition Policy – Note by the European Union', DAF/COMP/WD (2018) 61.

At first sight, there seems very little overlap: apart from applying to traders irrespective of the establishment of their business,[53] the Directive addresses unilateral acts carried out within business-to-consumer relations,[54] whereas the Vertical Block Exemption Regulation applies to multilateral behaviours undertaken within business-to-business relations.

Upon a closer look, however, both the Geo-blocking Regulation and competition law contribute a lot in shaping a Single European Digital Ecosystem. In particular, the sound interplay between them can be appreciated in relation to both passive and active sales.

Under Article 6 of the Geo-blocking Regulation, a supplier cannot contractually prohibit a trader from responding to unsolicited customer requests, meaning that it cannot prohibit so-called 'passive sales' in the specific situations covered by the Regulation. In such a case, the contractual requirement is automatically void, with the result that traders are free to serve all customers independently of their nationality or place of residence. That is why if a supplier prohibits traders from delivering products outside their allocated territory, one should verify whether such form of prohibition amounts to a restriction of passive sales under Article 6(2) of the Regulation or whether the legality of such restrictions shall be determined under the competition rules and not under the Regulation.

On the other hand, the Geo-blocking Regulation does not affect agreements restricting active sales, that is, actively approaching and targeting individual customers, for example through advertising. However, restrictions on active sales need to be compliant with EU competition rules.

Overall, the Regulation provides legal certainty and improves enforceability insofar as its provisions are directly applicable and very clear in defining some blacklisted unilateral behaviours that as such do not need a case-by-case assessment in order to verify whether they are justified. Besides, the new rules operate ex ante, affecting, on the one hand, the potential for cross-border trade, and encouraging, on the other hand, the full use of the Single Market, leaving competition law and policy to foster the same objectives at the market level.[55]

Considering that in several Member States, including Italy, Ireland and UK,[56] competition authorities are in charge of supervising compliance with the

[53] Unlike the e-Commerce Directive, the Regulation endorses a substantial approach, neither containing nor implying an obligation to sign up to the business register or to electronic waste schemes in each Member State where customers are willing to buy goods or services. Each trader operating in Europe is affected by the new regulation, and of course is subject to EU competition law.

[54] The Directive applies to business-to-business (B2B) transactions to the extent that the latter take place on the basis of general conditions of access (ie they are not individually negotiated) and the transaction is for the sole purpose of end use (ie made without the intention to resell, transform, process, rent or subcontract).

[55] D Gerard, 'Fairness in EU Competition Policy: Significance and Implications' (2018) 9 *Journal of European Competition Law & Practice* 211.

[56] For an updated and accurate list, see https://ec.europa.eu/digital-single-market/en/policies/geo-blocking.

geo-blocking rules (including the imposition of fines), the interplay between competition and regulation is expected to be even more fruitful and successful. The new provisions against geo-factors are therefore likely to enrich what has been defined as 'smart'[57] economic integration through technology, regulation and competition law, thus confirming the need for a 'circular' and integrated approach in applying regulation and competition policy[58] in the digital datasphere.

[57] L Ioannis, 'Updating the EU Internal Market Concept' (2018) CLES Research Paper No 1/2018, https://ssrn.com/abstract=3116384 or http://dx.doi.org/10.2139/ssrn.3116384.

[58] More broadly, V Falce, G Ghidini and G Olivieri (eds), *Informazione e big data tra innovazione e Concorrenza* (Milan, Giuffrè editore, 2018).

5

The Case Law of the Court of Justice of the European Union on Directive 98/34/EC Laying Down a Procedure for the Provision of Information in the Field of Technical Standards and Regulations (Directive 2015/1535) and Its Impact on Private Law Relations

EILEEN SHEEHAN[1]

I. Introduction

In this chapter I wish to highlight a number of judgments of the CJEU (or Court) on Directive 98/34/EC laying down a procedure for the provision of information in the field of technical standards and regulations[2] and their importance in the private law sphere.

The procedure for the provision of information in the field of technical standards and regulations referred to in the title of Directive 98/34 was first adopted in Council Directive 83/189/EEC of 28 March 1983 laying down a procedure for the provision of information in the field of technical standards and regulations.[3]

[1] The views expressed in this article are personal to the author and may not be attributed to the CJEU or any of its members.

[2] Directive of the European Parliament and of the Council of 22 June 1998 laying down a procedure for the provision of information in the field of technical standards and regulations [1998] OJ L204/37, as amended by Directive 98/48/EC of the European Parliament and of the Council of 20 July 1998 [1998] OJ L217/18.

[3] [1983] OJ L109/8.

As is clear from the recitals to that directive, its purpose was inter alia to set up a procedure involving the Commission and the Member States in order to prevent barriers to trade resulting from the adoption by Member States of technical regulations relating to products. Member States were thus required to notify the Commission – which, in turn, notified the other Member States – of contemplated 'technical regulations' and to postpone their adoption during specified periods in order to allow the Commission and the other Member States sufficient time in which to propose amendments in order to remove or reduce any potential barriers to the free movement of goods.

It is clear from the Commission's proposal[4] that it considered that it was easier to prevent or pre-empt the emergence of barriers to trade from technical regulations rather than to take action to remove them once such regulations had been adopted.

The essence of this notification and standstill procedure laid down by the Union legislature and its purpose have not changed over time. However, with the amendment of Directive 98/34 by Directive 98/48, the scope of application of that procedure was extended to include Information Society services,[5] which were beginning to emerge at that time. Given the inherent cross-border dimension of those services and the fact that they were emerging in an environment lacking coherent regulation, the Commission feared that the adoption by different Member States of regulations in relation to these new services would hinder their cross-border exchange and lead to fragmentation of the market. The Commission thus sought to forestall that fragmentation by proposing a directive amending Directive 83/189 and expanding its scope.[6] This proposal ultimately led to the adoption of Directive 98/48 amending Directive 98/34. Moreover, the definition of 'technical regulations' which are subject to this procedure has been the object of considerable legislative refinement and judicial interpretation since the entry into force of Directive 83/189.

Despite their title, Directive 83/189 and Directive 98/34 (original version), in addition to the notification and standstill procedure, which is the focus of this chapter, contained a number of provisions on standardisation.[7] Moreover,

[4] Commission, 'Proposal for a Council Decision laying down a procedure for the provision of information in the field of technical standards and regulations' COM (1980) 0400 final.

[5] Rather than services in general.

[6] Commission, 'Proposal for a European Parliament and Council Directive amending for third time Directive 83/189/EEC laying down a procedure for the provision of information in the field of technical standards and regulations' COM (1996) 392, 2. See Joined Cases C-213/11, C-214/11 and C-217/11 *Fortuna and Others* ECLI:EU:C:2012:495, para 34.

[7] These provisions will not be discussed is this chapter as they were repealed by Art 26(2) of Regulation (EU) No 1025/2012 of the European Parliament and of the Council of 25 October 2012 on European standardisation, amending Council Directives 89/686/EEC and 93/15/EEC and Directives 94/9/EC, 94/25/EC, 95/16/EC, 97/23/EC, 98/34/EC, 2004/22/EC, 2007/23/EC, 2009/23/EC and 2009/105/EC of the European Parliament and of the Council and repealing Council Decision 87/95/EEC and Decision No 1673/2006/EC of the European Parliament and of the Council [2012] OJ L316/12. The rules on European standardisation were fragmented over three legal instruments and Regulation No 1025/2012 thus seeks to simplify and rationalise those rules.

Directive 98/34 sought to increase transparency in the field of technical regulations and to ensure a favourable environment for the competitiveness of undertakings.[8]

Directive 83/189 was repealed and replaced by Directive 98/34,[9] which, in turn, was repealed and replaced by Directive (EU) 2015/1535 of the European Parliament and of the Council of 9 September 2015 laying down a procedure for the provision of information in the field of technical regulations and of rules on Information Society services.[10,11] It must be noted, however, that Directive 2015/1535 codifies Directive 98/34, which, in turn, codified Directive 83/189, in the interests of clarity and rationality rather than amending the substance of the previous directive to any great extent.[12]

Given the wealth of case law on Directive 98/34 (rather than on the more recent Directive 2015/1535 or, indeed, the older Directive 83/189), I shall refer more generally to Directive 98/34 for the sake of simplicity.

In this chapter, I shall examine the impact of the case law of CJEU on Directive 98/34 on private law relations, which I believe is twofold. First, that case law has ensured that failure by Member States to comply with the notification/communication and standstill procedure laid down in Directive 98/34 may have a unique and profound impact on both public and private law relations. Given this impact, the very definition of 'technical regulations' is of paramount importance. I will examine these issues in turn. Secondly, with the extension of the scope of application of Directive 98/34 to Information Society services,[13] the interpretation provided by the Court on the definition of such services and the rules on such services can greatly affect the operation of and the legal rules applicable to new technologies and business platforms.[14] These issues have arisen recently in a number of cases before the Court and I will touch on them briefly.

II. Background to Directive 98/34

The main objective of Directive 98/34 is to promote the smooth functioning of the internal market by increasing transparency in relation to the adoption by

[8] See recital 7 to Directive 98/34.

[9] See Art 13 of Directive 98/34.

[10] [2015] OJ L241/1.

[11] See Arts 10 and 11 of Directive 2015/1535.

[12] See recital 1 of Directive 2015/1535 and recital 1 of Directive 98/34. Despite the important similarities between Directive 98/34 and Directive 2015/1535, they are not identical, and certain differences may become relevant in future cases. I would note that Annex IV of Directive 2015/1535 contains a correlation table in respect of the provisions of the two directives in question, thereby facilitating the reading of the case law of the Court. A similar correlation table is provided in Annex IV to Directive 98/34 in respect of the provisions of Directive 83/189.

[13] See the definitions on services and rules on services in Art 1(2) and (5) of Directive 98/34.

[14] This results from the fact that Art 2(a) of Directive 2000/31/EC of the European Parliament and of the Council of 8 June 2000 on certain legal aspects of Information Society services, in particular electronic commerce, in the Internal Market ('Directive on electronic commerce') [2000] OJ L178/1)

Members States of national technical regulations as defined in Article 1(11)[15] of that directive.

This objective is achieved in a twofold manner.[16]

First, Directive 98/34 seeks to ensure that the Commission and the Members States are informed prior to the adoption of such national technical regulations and a specific, detailed procedure is established involving those actors in order to prevent or pre-empt the emergence of barriers to trade and the fragmentation of the internal market. This procedure has been referred to as 'preventive monitoring'.[17]

In accordance with Article 8(1) of Directive 98/34, Member States must immediately communicate to the Commission any draft technical regulation[18] and any significant alterations to that draft.[19] The Commission, in turn, must immediately notify the other Member States of the draft technical regulation and all documents that have been forwarded to it. Pursuant to Articles 8 and 9 of Directive 98/34, Member States must postpone, save for urgent reasons, the adoption of a draft technical regulation for a minimum initial period of three months[20] from the date of receipt by the Commission of the communication referred to in Article 8(1). Depending on the circumstances, that initial 'standstill' period may be extended to a maximum standstill period of 18 months.

A number of exceptions to the communication and standstill requirements are laid down in Article 10 of Directive 98/34, for example, where a Member States adopts technical regulations in order to comply with binding EU acts or a judgment of the CJEU.[21] It is clear from paragraph 20 of the judgment in

(the e-Commerce Directive) provides that, for the purposes of that directive, 'Information Society services' means services within the meaning of Art 1(2) of Directive 98/34. There is thus a form of cross-fertilisation between the two directives.

[15] See Art 1(1)(f) of Directive 2015/1535.

[16] Case C-336/14 *Ince* ECLI:EU:C:2016:72, paras 82 and 83.

[17] *Fortuna and Others* (n 6) para 26.

[18] Except where it merely transposes the full text of an international or European standard.

[19] At paras 40 and 41 of the judgment in Case C-279/94 *Commission v Italy* [1997] ECR I-4743, the Court ruled that, in accordance with the last sentence of the first subparagraph of Art 8(1) of Directive 98/34, the full text of a draft law containing technical regulations must be communicated to the Commission in order to enable that institution to evaluate the exact scope of any technical regulations contained therein.

[20] This initial standstill period may be three, four or six months, depending on the nature of the draft technical regulation.

[21] There are other limitations to the scope of Directive 98/34 and certain of its provisions 'peppered' throughout that directive. Directive 98/34 does not apply to radio broadcasting services or certain television broadcasting services. See Art 1(2) of Directive 98/34. An indicative list of services not covered by the definition of Information Society services pursuant to Art 1(2) of Directive 98/34 is set out in Annex V thereof. See Case C-89/04 *Mediakabel* [2005] ECR I-4891 on the indicative nature of that list. In addition, Directive 98/34 does not apply to rules in the field of telecommunications services and financial services. See Art 1(5) of Directive 98/34. An indicative list of such excluded services is laid down in Annex VI to that directive. Moreover, only Art 8(3) of Directive 98/34 (which requires Member States to communicate the definitive text of a technical regulation to the Commission, rather than the full text of Art 8 of that directive) applies in respect of rules enacted by or for regulated markets. See Art 1(5) of Directive 98/34.

Case C-299/17 *VG Media*[22] that the 'binding' EU act in question must be applicable *ratione temporis*. Thus, a Member State will choose 'at its peril' not to communicate draft technical regulations to the Commission in anticipation of the entry into force of EU legislation on the matter.

The purpose of the communication requirement and standstill periods[23] is to afford the Commission and the other Member States the possibility of ascertaining whether any draft technical regulation may create obstacles to the free movement of goods or Information Society services or the freedom of establishment of services operators within the internal market and, where opportune, to make comments or deliver a detailed opinion thereon. The Member State communicating a draft technical regulation must take the comments into account as far as possible but is not required to respond to those comments. If no detailed opinion is delivered, the draft technical regulation can be adopted after the expiry of the minimum initial standstill period. If the Commission or another Member State delivers a detailed opinion within three months of the communication of the draft technical regulation stating that it considers than the draft measure may create obstacles to free movement, the minimum initial standstill period is extended. The Member State communicating the draft technical regulation must report to the Commission on the action it proposes to take on the basis of the detailed opinion and the Commission must comment on that reaction. The Commission may also indicate that it intends to propose adopting legislation on the matter, in which case the communicating Member State must postpone the adoption of the measure for 12 months from the date of communication.

Secondly, while only the Commission and Member States have specific procedural rights pursuant to Directive 98/34 – most notably to comment on and deliver a detailed opinion in respect of any draft technical regulation in accordance with Article 9 of Directive 98/34 – the possibility for economic operators to be informed of the impending adoption of such measures undoubtedly enables them to make their possible concerns known to the relevant Commission services and, indeed, those of the Member States.[24]

In its judgment in *Ince*,[25] the Court noted that

> it is important that the economic operators of a Member State be informed of draft technical regulations adopted by another Member State and of their temporal and

[22] ECLI:EU:C:2019:716.

[23] See para 50 of the judgment in Case C-194/94 *CIA Security International* [1996] ECR I-2201.

[24] Economic operators may obtain information in respect of and comment on proposed national technical regulations via the European Commission's Technical Regulation Information System. In 'Report from the Commission to the European Parliament, the Council and the European Economic and Social Committee on the operative of Directive (EU) 2015/1535 from 2014 to 2015, of 19 December 2017' COM (2017) 788 final/2, the Commission stated: 'One of the objectives of [Directive 2015/1535] is to inform economic operators, including small to medium-sized enterprises (SMEs), in advance of planned technical regulation in the Member States, to allow them to make their voices heard and to adapt early their activities to future technical regulations. The high number of contributions on notifications sent by stakeholders shows that this right of scrutiny is used extensively and helps the Commission and national authorities to detect barriers to trade.'

[25] *Ince* (n 16) para 83.

territorial scope, so as to enable them to be apprised of the extent of the obligations that may be imposed on them and to anticipate the adoption of those texts by adapting, if necessary, their products or services in a timely manner.

III. The *CIA Security* and *Unilever* Judgments – Horizontal Effects of Directive 98/34

Directive 98/34 itself provides no specific sanction for failure to comply with the obligation to communicate any draft technical regulation or respect the relevant standstill period pursuant to Articles 8 and 9 thereof.

The first cases decided by the Court concerning non-compliance with those obligations were brought by the Commission against Member States as actions for failure to fulfil obligations pursuant to what is now Article 258 TFEU. Thus, in its judgment in *Commission v Italy*,[26] the Court declared that, by failing to communicate a ministerial decree at the draft stage, the Italian Republic had failed to fulfil its obligations under Articles 8 and 9.[27] A Member State is required pursuant to Article 260(1) TFEU to take the necessary steps to comply with a judgment of the Court under Article 258 TFEU finding a failure to fulfil obligations; however, that 'declaratory' judgment does not render any technical regulation per se inapplicable.[28]

It is perhaps unsurprising that failure by a Member State to notify draft technical regulations to the Commission in accordance with Article 8 of Directive 98/34 would render those technical regulations unenforceable in actions by that Member State (or emanations thereof) against individuals[29] or vice versa where, for example, a private party seeks a declaration that such regulations are inapplicable.[30] In effect, the Member State should not benefit from its own wrongdoing or inaction. In such circumstances, failure to respect Articles 8 and 9 of Directive 98/34 can be used by private parties in judicial proceedings as both a shield and a sword against the recalcitrant Member State (vertical relationship).

The judgment *CIA Security International*,[31] however, ensured that the failure by a Member State to communicate any draft technical regulations to the

[26] Case C-139/02 [1993] ECR I-4707.

[27] See also, eg the judgments in Case C-317/92 *Commission v Germany* [1994] ECR I-2039; Case C-52/93 *Commission v Netherlands* [1994] ECR I-3591; Case C-61/93 *Commission v Netherlands* [1994] ECR I-3607.

[28] See, by analogy, para 148 of Opinion of AG Szpunar in Case C-390/18 *YA and Others* ECLI:EU:C:2019:336.

[29] I would note in that regard that many of the cases before the Court concerning failure to communicate laws containing technical regulations in accordance with Art 8(1) of Directive 98/34 have arisen in the context of national criminal proceedings against individuals who have failed to comply with the national laws on gambling. Failure by a Member State to communicate such laws in accordance with that procedure renders those technical regulations and any (criminal) sanctions foreseen by national law unenforceable. See, eg para 37 of Case C-255/16 *Falbert and Others* ECLI:EU:C:2017:983.

[30] See judgment *Fortuna and Others* (n 6).

[31] *CIA Security International* (n 23).

Commission would have the effect of rendering them unenforceable in purely private actions between individuals (horizontal relationship). The case that gave rise to that judgment concerned a dispute between three security firms that competed in the manufacture and sale of alarm systems and networks. On 21 January 1994, CIA Security applied to the referring court for orders requiring Signalson and Securitel to cease alleged unfair trading practices. CIA Security claimed that Signalson and Securitel had libelled it by claiming, in particular, that the alarm system which it markets did not fulfil the requirements laid down by Belgian legislation on security systems. Signalson and Securitel, in turn, lodged counterclaims, the main one being for an order restraining CIA Security from continuing to carry on business on the ground that it was not authorised as a security firm and that it was marketing an alarm system which had not been approved in accordance with a procedure for the approval of alarm systems which security firms may make available to consumers laid down in a 1991 decree law. The case file showed that the 1991 decree law had not been notified to the Commission in accordance with Directive 83/189.

The main question the referring court asked the Court was in effect whether Articles 8 and 9 of Directive 83/189 (subsequently Articles 8 and 9 of Directive 98/34) are sufficiently precise and unconditional that individuals may rely on those provisions before a national court, which must, in turn, decline to apply a national technical regulation which has not been notified.

The Court considered, first, that the terms of Article 8 and 9 are unconditional and sufficiently precise, and may be relied upon by individuals before a national court. The Court then proceeded to examine the legal consequences to be drawn from the failure to notify the national technical regulations in question – a failure that was deemed a 'procedural defect'.[32] Despite the submissions of the German, Netherlands and UK governments that Directive 83/189 solely concerned relations between Member States and the Commission, the Court considered that the objective of that directive of preventing the emergence of barriers to trade would be more effectively obtained if the substantial procedural defect of failing to notify national technical regulations would render them inapplicable to or unenforceable against individuals.[33] The Court further held that the claim that the inapplicability of such unnotified national technical regulations would create a legislative vacuum was unpersuasive, as Members States could adopt technical regulations pursuant to the urgent procedure outlined in Article 9 of Directive 83/189 (Article 9 of Directive 98/34).[34]

[32] ibid para 45. See also *Ince* (n 16) para 67 and case law cited.

[33] In its judgment in *Ince* (n 16) para 68, the Court stressed that while Art 8(1) of Directive 98/34 requires the entire draft of a law containing technical regulations to be communicated to the Commission, the non-applicability which results from the breach of that obligation extends only to the technical regulations contained in the law. See also Case C-144/16 *Município de Palmela* ECLI:EU:C:2017:76, para 38.

[34] It must also be noted that despite the fact that failure to notify national technical regulations will render them unenforceable against individuals, this does not necessarily render the use of products

Although the reasoning of the Court in *CIA Security International*[35] referred to both Articles 8 and 9 of Directive 83/189, the operative part of that judgment was confined to finding that technical regulations which have not been notified in accordance with Article 8 of Directive 83/189 are inapplicable. The Court confirmed, however, in Case C-443/98 *Unilever*,[36] that a national court is required, in civil proceedings between individuals concerning contractual rights and obligations, to refuse to apply a national technical regulation which was adopted during the standstill period prescribed in Article 9 of Directive 83/189 (Article 9 of Directive 98/34). In that regard, the Court, citing its judgment in Case C-91/92 *Faccini Dori*,[37] noted that while a directive cannot of itself impose obligations on an individual and cannot therefore be relied on as such against an individual, that case law does not apply where a technical regulation is inapplicable due to failure to comply with the procedures laid down in Articles 8 or 9 of Directive 83/189 as that directive does 'not in any way define the substantive scope of the legal rule on the basis of which the national court must decide the case before it. It creates neither rights nor obligations for individuals.'[38]

It is worth noting that in his Opinion in the *Unilever* case,[39] Advocate General Jacobs advised that the scope of the judgment in *CIA Security International*[40] should be considerably limited. He stressed that Directive 83/189 was not intended to confer rights on or create obligations for individuals, but 'merely lays down the respective rights and obligations of the Member States and the Commission within a procedure in which individuals are in principle not involved'.[41] Thus, while he agreed that a Member State should not be able to enforce against an individual[42] a technical regulation which was not communicated to the Commission in accordance with Article 8 of Directive 83/18, he stated that the fact that a Member State had not complied with the procedural requirements of that directive should not entail detrimental effects for private individuals. He considered that there was no reason for the other party to proceedings to profit, entirely fortuitously, from a Member State's failure to comply with Directive 83/189.

complying with those regulations unlawful. Thus, in Case C-226/97 *Lemmens* [1998] ECR I-3711, the Court held in effect that failure to notify pursuant to Art 8 of Directive 83/189 (Art 8 of Directive 98/34) a technical regulation on breath-analysis apparatus did not render inadmissible evidence obtained by means of such apparatus and the reliance thereon in proceedings against an individual charged with driving while under the influence of alcohol.

[35] Above n 23.

[36] [2000] ECR I-7535.

[37] [1994] ECR I-3325.

[38] *Unilever* (n 36) para 51.

[39] Opinion of AG Jacobs in ibid.

[40] Above n 23.

[41] Opinion of AG Jacobs in *Unilever* (n 36) para 86.

[42] AG Jacobs considered that the unenforceability of unnotified technical regulations may indirectly create windfall benefits for some traders as they can rely against Member States on the breach of a procedural rule which was not intended to confer rights on them. Moreover, they may do so independently of whether the technical regulation in question creates an unjustified barrier to trade. Opinion of AG Jacobs in *Unilever* (n 36) para 93.

Advocate General Jacobs considered in the alternative that should the Court decide that technical regulations adopted in breach of the procedural requirements laid down in Directive 83/189 were unenforceable in all types of proceedings between individuals, the standstill requirement should not constitute such a procedural requirement and failure to comply with that requirement should thus not entail the unenforceability of the technical regulations in question. He stated that it would be 'disproportionately severe' to impose such a sanction for failure to observe the standstill clause in Article 9 of Directive 83/189.

Despite the two alternative solutions proposed by Advocate General Jacobs, the Court has never departed from the solution it adopted in its judgments *CIA Security International*[43] and *Unilever*.[44] In that regard, the Court has recently restated, in Case C-122/17 *Smith*,[45] that Directive 83/189 (Directive 98/34) does not create rights or obligations for individuals and does not determine the substantive content of the legal rule on the basis of which the national court has to decide the case before it. The Court considered, in effect, that Directive 98/34, as with all other directives, does not produce horizontal direct effects.[46] Thus, at paragraph 49 of that judgment, the Court stated that EU law does not 'extend the possibility of relying on a provision of a directive that has not been transposed, or that has been incorrectly transposed, to the sphere of relationships between private persons'.

While the failure of a Member State to comply with the procedural requirements contained in Articles 8 and 9 of Directive 98/34 does not produce horizontal direct effects per se, it can certainly nonetheless have an enormous impact on the legal situation of individuals seeking to rely on the national technical regulations in question. In that regard, one could perhaps forgive an individual who cannot rely on national technical regulations for failing to understand the subtle legal distinction between the absence of horizontal direct effects of directives and the clear horizontal implications resulting from a Member State's failure to comply with the procedural requirements contained in Articles 8 and 9 of Directive 98/34.

In my view, however, the best explanation for this matter is not to be found in any analogy with the case law on the horizontal direct effects of directives, but rather in the compulsory legislative and procedural steps that must be completed in order for a national law to be validly adopted.[47] In essence, the national measure is rendered unenforceable or inapplicable as a key procedural step has been omitted due to failure by the Member State to comply with Articles 8 and 9 of Directive 98/34. Indeed, it is clear from the judgment in Case C-267/03 *Lindberg*[48]

[43] Above n 23.

[44] Above n 36. See, eg *Ince* (n 16) para 67 and case law cited; see most recently *VG Media* (n 22) para 39.

[45] ECLI:EU:C:2018:631, para 53.

[46] For a very recent (re)statement of the case law on primacy and direct effects and the interaction of those two concepts, see Case C-573/17 *Popławski* ECLI:EU:C:2019:530.

[47] To that effect, see *Smith* (n 45) para 53.

[48] [2005] ECR I-3247, paras 51 and 52.

that a Member State must comply with the procedure laid down in Articles 8 and 9 of Directive 98/34 as failure to do so will, in principle, render the technical regulations inapplicable irrespective of their actual effect on the free movement of goods or services.[49] The Court's consistent and unwavering approach to the legal nature and effect of the failure to comply with the communication and standstill requirement was also evident in its judgment in Case C-98/14 *Berlington Hungary and Others*.[50]

In that case, the Court held that, given that Directive 98/34 does not in any way define the substantive scope of the legal rule on the basis of which the national court must decide the case before it, individuals cannot rely on the failure by a Member State to comply with the procedure laid down in Articles 8 and 9 of that directive in order to establish liability on the part of that Member State on the basis of EU law. In accordance with the judgment in Joined Cases C-46/93 and C-48/93 *Brasserie du pêcheur and Factortame*[51] and its progeny, EU law only confers a right to compensation where three conditions are met, namely: the rule of law infringed must be intended to confer rights on individuals; the infringement must be sufficiently serious; and there must be a direct causal link between the breach of the obligation resting on the Member State and the damage sustained by the injured parties. However, given that the first condition highlighted above is not met, as Articles 8 and 9 of Directive 98/34 are not intended to confer rights on individuals, their infringement by a Member State does not give rise to a right of individuals to obtain from that Member State compensation on the basis of EU law for the damage suffered as a result of that infringement.[52]

The impact of Directive 98/34 in the sphere of the valid formation of national law and on private law relations in particular was, to my knowledge, unique up until the judgment in Case C-390/18 *Airbnb Ireland*.[53] I am unaware of any example prior to that judgment in which a failure by a Member State to comply with

[49] In that case, the Court stated that the possible effects of technical regulations on intra-Union trade do not constitute a criterion for the definition of the scope of Directive 98/34 and that justifications necessary to fulfil overriding public interest requirements may not be relied on by Member States as they do not constitute a criterion laid down by Directive 98/34 for defining its scope. The Court stressed that such 'considerations are alien to the concept of technical regulation'.

[50] ECLI: EU:C:2015:386.

[51] [1996] ECR I-1029.

[52] While a right to compensation under EU law is excluded, it is open to question whether such a right, based on concepts akin to the tort of misfeasance, might possibly be available under certain national legal systems. In *Ogieriakhi v Minister for Justice* [2017] IESC 52, [2018] 2 IR 504, the Irish Supreme Court, after finding that a plaintiff did not have a right to damages under EU law as the conditions in Joined Cases C-6/90 and C-9/90 *Francovich and Others* [1991] ECR I-5357 were not met, examined whether domestic law could grant damages for loss due to a breach of EU law on the part of the state. The Irish Supreme Court found that there is no free-standing right to damages under national law where the criteria laid down in the previously mentioned case are not satisfied and the cause of action arose purely in the context of EU law. In effect, 'the wrong done is a wrong under EU law' and the remedy must thus be found in EU law. The Supreme Court left open the possibility of damages under Irish law where the breach of EU law was accompanied by features giving rise to an independent claim under that law.

[53] ECLI:EU:C:2019:1112.

an obligation laid down in EU legislation to communicate national legislation in advance to the Commission and/or other Member States would render the national legislation in question per se inapplicable in private law relations regardless of the actual content and effect of that legislation. I would note, however, that the procedure laid down in Articles 8 and 9 of Directive 98/34 has been 'co-opted' or 'borrowed' by other EU legislation which specifically requires Member States to comply with that procedure.[54]

In the light of certain procedural analogies drawn by Advocate General Szpunar in his Opinion in *Airbnb Ireland*[55] between the prior notification procedure under Article 5(1) of Directive 2015/1535 and the second indent of Article 3(4)(b) of the e-Commerce Directive,[56] he considered that failure by a Member State to notify measures adopted pursuant to the latter provision that restrict Information Society services 'entails the non-enforceability of a measure against the provider of those services'. The Court endorsed that approach in its recent judgment in that case. It noted, in particular, that the second indent of Article 3(4)(b) of the e-Commerce Directive imposes a specific notification obligation on Member States in respect of their intention to adopt measures restricting the freedom to provide Information Society services which is sufficiently clear, precise and unconditional to confer on it direct effect. The Court thus held, by analogy with the judgment in *CIA Security International*,[57] that the second indent of Article 3(4)(b) of the e-Commerce Directive may be invoked by individuals before the national courts and that failure to comply with the notification requirement contained therein rendered the non-notified measure unenforceable even in disputes between private parties.

Given that measures adopted pursuant to Article 3(4) of the e-Commerce Directive are inherently restrictive of the freedom to provide Information Society services from another Member State, the impact of the judgment in *Airbnb*

[54] See, eg Art 8 of Directive 2014/53/EU of the European Parliament and of the Council of 16 April 2014 on the harmonisation of the laws of the Member States relating to the making available on the market of radio equipment and repealing Directive 1999/5/EC [2014] OJ L153/62; Art 83(5) of Regulation Regulation (EU) No 1308/2013 of the European Parliament and of the Council of 17 December 2013 establishing a common organisation of the markets in agricultural products and repealing Council Regulations (EEC) No 922/72, (EEC) No 234/79, (EC) No 1037/2001 and (EC) No 1234/2007 [2013] OJ L347/67.

[55] ECLI:EU:C:2019:336, para 150. This case concerned criminal proceedings with an ancillary civil action.

[56] According to Art 3(1) of the e-Commerce Directive, each Member State must ensure that the Information Society services provided by a service provider established in its territory comply with the national provisions applicable in the Member State in question which fall within the coordinated field as defined by Art 2(h) of that directive and which refers, inter alia, to the requirements laid down in Member States' legal systems applicable to Information Society service providers or Information Society services. In addition, Art 3(2) of the e-Commerce Directive provides that Member States may not, for reasons falling within the coordinated field, restrict the freedom to provide Information Society services from another Member State. Art 3(4) of the e-Commerce Directive provides for the possibility of adopting derogating measures to Art 3(2) of that directive provided, inter alia, they are in the public interest (Art 3(4)(a)) and that prior notification is given to the Commission and the Member State referred to in para 1 of the intention to take such measures (second indent of Art 3(4)(b)). See also Arts 3(5) and 3(6) of that directive.

[57] Above n 23, para 54.

Ireland[58] is less far reaching than the case law on Directive 98/34, where such a negative impact is not required. Failure to comply with the notification and standstill procedure in Directive 98/34 is in itself sufficient. What, however, is striking in the judgment in *Airbnb Ireland*[59] is the obligation on Member States to notify such restrictive measures even where they predate (by many years) the e-Commerce Directive.[60]

While there is clearly a very close relationship between Directive 98/34 and the e-Commerce Directive, given their common definition of Information Society services,[61] I consider that the ratio in the judgments of the Court in *Airbnb Ireland*[62] and *CIA Security International*[63] could be extended in the future to other cases where a Member State fails to comply with a notification requirement under EU legislation granting procedural rights to the Commission and Member States in an analogous fashion to Directive 98/34 and the e-Commerce Directive.

IV. Article 1(2) of Directive 98/34 – The Concept of a 'Technical Regulation'

Given the profound legal implications which the failure of a Member State to comply with the requirements of Articles 8 and 9 of Directive 98/34 can have on both public and private law relations, there is a wealth of case law of the Court which focuses on the definition of 'technical regulation' contained in Article 1(11) of that directive and thus whether the provisions of national legislation fall within those terms and the procedure in question. To state that the 'devil is in the detail' when trying to ascertain whether provisions of national legislation constitute technical regulations is, at times, an understatement. Moreover, technical regulations may be found in essentially all fields of law, ranging from intellectual property law[64] to criminal law.[65]

[58] Above n 53.

[59] ibid.

[60] At para 87 of the judgment, the Court stated that the 'EU legislature did not make provision for a derogation authorising Member States to maintain measures predating [the e-Commerce Directive] and which could restrict the freedom to provide Information Society services without complying with the conditions laid down for that purpose by that directive'. Van Cleynenbreugel predicts that Member States will have to, in effect, audit their existing legislation in order to determine whether to notify them to the Commission. See P Van Cleynenbreugel, 'Accommodating the Freedom of Online Platforms to Provide Services through the Incidental Direct Effect Back Door: Airbnb Ireland' (2020) 4 *CML Rev* 1201.

[61] See point 2 of the first paragraph of Art 1 of Directive 98/34, Art 1(1)(b) of Directive 2015/1535 and Art 2(a) of the e-Commerce Directive.

[62] Above n 53.

[63] Above n 23.

[64] See *VG Media* (n 22) para 38, in which the Court stressed that technical rules on intellectual property are not expressly excluded from the scope of the rules on services contained in Art 1(5) of Directive 98/34. See also the judgment in Case C-20/05 *Schwibbert* [2007] ECR I-9447.

[65] See *Falbert and Others* (n 29).

Given the potential scope and effect of the notification and standstill requirements, Advocate General Bobek in his Opinion in Case C-303/15 *M and S*[66] warned against an overinclusive interpretation of the concept of 'technical regulation'[67] and what he termed 'notification creep'.

Before examining the concept of a 'technical regulation' in some detail, it must be noted that the Court has reiterated on numerous occasions that

> national provisions that merely lay down the conditions governing the establishment or provision of services by undertakings, such as provisions making the exercise of a business activity subject to prior authorisation do not constitute technical regulations within the meaning of Article 1(11) of Directive 98/34.[68]

Thus, at paragraph 87 of the judgment in *Lindberg*,[69] the Court stated that technical regulations are not specifications concerning economic operators. They are, in effect, national rules concerning products and certain services.

This crucial distinction can, at times, be difficult to operate. Moreover, I believe it imposes a higher standard than the line of case law first developed by the judgment of the Court in Joined Cases C-267/91 and C-268/91 *Keck and Mithouard*,[70] which deems that certain selling arrangements do not constitute barriers to trade and thus fall outside the scope of Article 34 TFEU. By way of illustration, the requirement under national law to hold a licence to operate a gaming casino does not constitute a technical regulation.[71] However, the Court has held that a prohibition on operating slot machines outside casinos, which thus regulates the activity of undertakings providing services in relation to those machines, can significantly influence the nature or the marketing of those machines[72] by reducing the number of outlets in which they can be used, constitutes a technical regulation within the meaning of Article 1(11) of Directive 98/34 and must be communicated to the Commission in accordance with Article 8(1) of that directive.[73]

How can I reconcile this case law? Simply put, the requirement to comply with the procedure laid down in Articles 8 and 9 of Directive 98/34 is not directed at whether national rules in fact constitute barriers to trade. The Court has deemed that such an assessment is irrelevant in that procedural context. Rather, those

[66] ECLI:EU:C:2016:771.

[67] More specifically 'other requirements' pursuant to Art 1(4) of Directive 98/34.

[68] *Falbert and Others* (n 29) para 16 and the case law cited. This limitation on the scope of 'technical regulation(s)' was first referred to in *CIA Security International* (n 23) para 25.

[69] Above n 48.

[70] [1993] ECR I-6097.

[71] See also para 40 of the judgment in Case C-137/17, *Van Gennip and Others* ECLI:EU:C:2018:771, in which the Court held that Belgian legislation which makes the sale of pyrotechnic articles with a pyrotechnic composition exceeding 1 kg subject to the buyer acquiring an authorisation does not constitute a requirement in respect of the product concerned, but rather a requirement for potential buyers and, indirectly, for economic operators selling pyrotechnic articles. Such legislation does not therefore constitute a technical regulation.

[72] Which, according to the Court, constitute goods that may be covered by Art 34 TFEU.

[73] To that effect, see *Berlington Hungary and Others* (n 50) para 99; Case C-303/15 *M and S* ECLI:EU:C:2016:771, paras 25–29.

provisions seek to intervene upstream prior to the actual adoption of such national rules in order to pre-empt the adoption of measures that constitute barriers to trade. In order to carry out this function, objective and broadly drawn criteria are established regarding the national measures which must be notified and subject to the standstill requirement.

In that regard, it is settled case law that the concept of a 'technical regulation' pursuant to Article 1(11) of Directive 98/34 extends to four categories of measures, namely: (i) 'technical specification', within the meaning of Article 1(3)[74] of that directive; (ii) 'other requirements', as defined in Article 1(4)[75] of that directive; (iii) the rules on 'Information Society services', covered by Article 1(5)[76] of that directive; and (iv) the 'laws, regulations or administrative provisions of Member States prohibiting the manufacture, importation, marketing or use of a product or prohibiting the provision or use of a service, or establishment as a service provider'.[77]

The first category, namely 'technical specifications' as defined in Article 1(3) of Directive 98/34, relates to products and refers to national measures which necessarily refer to the product or its packaging as such, and thus lay down one of the characteristics required of a product, such as the dimensions, the sales description, labelling or marking.[78] In its judgment in *Schwibbert*,[79] the Court held that national provisions pursuant to which the initials 'SIAE' must be affixed to media containing reproductions of intellectual works should be classified as technical specifications as the observance of such labelling requirements was compulsory de jure for marketing those products.

As regards the second category, namely 'other requirements', as defined in Article 1(4) of Directive 98/34, it refers to national measures which constitute 'conditions' which can significantly influence the composition, the nature or the marketing of the product concerned. These conditions relate to the lifecycle of products after they have been placed on the market – for example, conditions on the use of products for the protection of consumers.[80]

The third category refers specifically to rules on Information Society services rather than services in general. In that regard, Directive 98/34 is far less ambitious

[74] See Art 1(1)(c) of Directive 2015/15135.

[75] See Art 1(1)(d) of Directive 2015/15135.

[76] See Art 1(1)(e) of Directive 2015/15135.

[77] See, most recently, *VG Media* (n 22) para 25 and the case law cited. The Court often examines national legislation in the light of each of those four categories in order to determine whether a measure constitutes a technical regulation. See, eg Case C-613/14 *James Elliott Construction* ECLI:EU:C:2016:821. Sometimes the Court refers to three categories when Information Society services are clearly not in question. See Case C-26/11 *Belgische Petroleum Unie and Others* ECLI:EU:C:2013:44, para 52. The Court in effect often uses these categories as a sort of checklist and compares national rules against each category.

[78] Case C-307/13 *Ivansson and Others* ECLI:EU:C:2014:2058, para 19 and the case law cited; Fortuna and Others (n 6) para 28. See, most recently, Case C-727/17 *ECO-WIND Construction* ECLI:EU:C:2020:393, para 36.

[79] Above n 64.

[80] To that effect, see *Lindberg* (n 48) paras 69–71. See also Ince (n 16) para 72.

in scope in relation to services as opposed to products, the definition of the latter being extremely broad and extending to any industrially manufactured product and any agricultural product.[81]

The fourth category[82] concerns national measures prohibiting inter alia the manufacture, importation, marketing or use of a product. There is a certain tension between the scope of the second and fourth categories as regards the use of products. In that regard, the fourth category refers to national measures that go beyond a limitation of certain possible uses of a product and relates to measures which *leave no room for any reasonable use of the product other than a purely marginal one.*[83]

Article 1(2) of Directive 98/34[84] defines 'Information Society services' as any service normally provided for remuneration,[85] at a distance, by electronic means and at the individual request of a recipient of services. The individual components of that definition are further defined in detail in Article 1(2) of Directive 98/34.[86] Moreover, pursuant to Article 1(5) of Directive 98/34, a 'rule on services' is a 'requirement of a general nature relating to the taking-up and pursuit of service activities … *excluding any rules which are not specifically aimed at [Information Society services]*' (emphasis added). In addition, Article 1(5) of Directive 98/34 states that national rules are 'specifically aimed' at Information Society services where 'the specific aim and object of all or some of its individual provisions is to regulate such services in an explicit and targeted manner'. It also provides that a 'rule shall not be considered to be specifically aimed at Information Society services if it affects such services only in an implicit or incidental manner'.

[81] See ArticleArt 1(1) of Directive 98/34. See ArticleArt 1(1)(a) of Directive 2015/1535.

[82] I am conscious that I am dealing with these categories out of order. This is because I wish to discuss the third category, on rules on Information Society services, in more detail.

[83] In Fortuna and Others (n 6) paras 32 et seq, the Court considered that a prohibition on issuing, extending or amending authorisations for operating slot machines outside casinos was, subject to empirical verification by the national court, such as to directly affect trade in those machines and could thereby be classified as 'other requirements' under Art 1(4) of Directive 98/34. It could not, however, be classified as a national measure, which leaves no room for any other reasonable use of those machines as the slot machines can be used in previously authorised gaming sites.

[84] See Art 1(1)(b) of Directive 2015/1535.

[85] The Court noted in Case C-291/13 *Papasavvas* ECLI: EU:C:2014:2209, para 30 that the remuneration did not have to be provided by the recipient of online information services but could be provided to the service provider by income generated by advertisements posted on a website. See also Case C-484/14 *McFadden* ECLI:EU:C:2016:689. The Court held at paras 41–43 of that judgment that a service provided by a communication network operator and consisting in making that network available to the general public free of charge constitutes an 'Information Society service' for remuneration where the activity is performed by the service provider in question for the purposes of advertising the goods sold or services supplied by that service provider. In effect, the cost of the service is incorporated into the price of the advertised goods or services.

[86] I would note, for the purposes of illustration, that the Court has stated that a prohibition on offering games of chance on the Internet or a prohibition of broadcasting advertisements for games of chance on the Internet constitute 'rules on services' pursuant to Art 1(5) of Directive 98/34 as they concern Information Society services. *Ince* (n 16) para 75. Failure to communicate such rules in accordance with Art 8(1) of Directive 98/34 will result in their unenforceability.

The limitation of the scope of application of Directive 98/34 to Information Society services has given rise to legal uncertainty and litigation where national legislation applies or refers to both online and offline services ('composite rules'), or where a given service has both online and offline components ('composite services').

V. 'Composite Rules' – Article 1(5) of Directive 98/34

It is clear from the recent case law of the Court that Article 1(5) of Directive 98/34, which defines 'rules on services' that must be notified as technical regulations in accordance with Article 8(1) of that directive, covers national rules that apply or refer to both online and offline services.

In *Falbert and Others*,[87] the Court examined whether an amendment to a national provision providing for sanctions in respect of advertising for unauthorised gaming, which appeared to extend a pre-existing prohibition on advertising to cover online gaming services,[88] constitutes a 'technical regulation' and is thus subject to notification under Article 8(1) of Directive 98/34. The Court considered that both advertising services and gaming services provided, inter alia, online constitute Information Society services. However, in order for the rule in question to constitute a 'rule on services' pursuant to Article 1(5) of Directive 98/34 and thus a technical regulation, it must be 'specifically aimed' at those services. This is assessed in the light of both the stated reasons and the wording of the rule.[89] The referring court indicated that, while no distinction was drawn in the law itself between online and offline services, the *travaux préparatoires* for the amendment indicated 'that the law was aimed, inter alia, at extending that provision to cover online services'.[90]

The Court held, first, that Article 1(5) of Directive 98/34 does not require that the specific aim and object of *all* the rule be to regulate Information Society services – it is sufficient that the rule pursue that aim or object at least in part. The Court held, secondly, that it would run counter to the objective of Directive 98/48, which amended Directive 98/34 to take into account Information Society services, to exclude a national rule aimed at extending an existing rule to cover such services from the scope of Article 1(5) of Directive 98/34 merely because the national rule made no reference to those services 'but instead covers them through a broader definition of services covering both services provided online and offline'.[91]

[87] Above n 29.

[88] This was a question of fact which lay with the referring court to decide.

[89] Art 1(5) of Directive 98/34 refers to the 'statement of reasons or operative part'.

[90] In this case, therefore, the aim and object of the national law were of paramount importance in assessing whether Information Society services were in question.

[91] *Falbert and Others* (n 29) para 36.

Recently, in *VG Media*,[92] the Court examined whether provisions of the German law on copyright and related rights which prohibit commercial operators of search engines (online services) and commercial service providers that similarly publish content (offline services) from making newspapers or magazines or parts thereof[93] available to the public constitute a 'technical regulation' within the meaning of Article 1(11) of Directive 98/34, thereby requiring the prior notification of the draft of the German law in question to the Commission in accordance with Article 8(1) of that directive in order to be enforceable. Given the mixed nature of the services[94] which were the object of the national provisions in question, perhaps the most important issue which arose in that case was whether the German law in question was 'specifically aimed' at Information Society services as required by Article 1(5) of Directive 98/34. The Court, after citing its judgment in *Falbert and Others*,[95] noted at paragraph 37 of *VG Media* that the main aim and object of the national provisions in question were to protect publishers from copyright infringements by online search engines and that it would run counter to the objective of Directive 98/34 to prevent fragmentation of the internal market in Information Society services to consider that national provisions do not constitute a rule specifically targeting such services merely because those provisions refer to both online and offline services.

In a sense, the cases which gave rise to the judgments in *Falbert and Others*[96] and VG Media[97] were 'easy' ones. First, there was no real doubt that the services which were the object of the national legislation in question in both cases were Information Society services as defined by Article 1(2) of Directive 98/34.[98] Secondly, it would appear from those judgments that there was clear evidence from the file before the Court that the national legislation in question or the amendment thereto was principally aimed at Information Society services.

What would be the case, however, if the objective of the legislation was aimed equally at Information Society services and offline services? Or where the Information Society services were of lesser importance but still of some relevance and were included perhaps in order to avoid discrimination as regards the manner in which services are supplied? In my view, given that in such cases Information Society services are regulated in an explicit and targeted manner and are not merely affected in an implicit or incidental manner, the national measure in question would constitute a rule on services subject to notification pursuant to Article 8(1) of Directive 98/34.[99] Indeed, I consider that any other finding could undermine

[92] Above n 22.

[93] Excluding individual words and very short text excerpts.

[94] See *VG Media* (n 22) para 30.

[95] Above n 29.

[96] ibid.

[97] Above n 22.

[98] See *Falbert and Others* (n 29) para 29; *VG Media* (n 22) para 30. By contrast, see Case C-434/15 *Asociación Profesional Elite Taxi* ECLI:EU:C:2017:981; Case C-320/16 *Uber France* (ECLI: EU:C:2018:221.

[99] See fn 25 of the Opinion of AG Hogan in Case C-299/17 *VG Media* ECLI: EU:C:2018:1004.

the objectives of Directive 98/34 in the field of Information Society services and potentially the internal market for such services. This broad approach is, however, subject to the caveat that the services in question are indeed qualified as Information Society services, which is not always evident when faced with composite services.

VI. 'Composite Services'/Intermediation Services? – Article 1(2) of Directive 98/34

In Case C-434/15 *Asociación Profesional Elite Taxi*,[100] the Court found that the Uber service which connects, by means of a smartphone application and for remuneration, non-professional drivers using their own vehicle with persons who wish to make urban journeys was not an Information Society service as defined by Article 1(2) of Directive 98/34[101] but a service in the field of transport. The Court accepted that an intermediation service consisting of connecting a non-professional driver using his or her own vehicle with a person who wishes to make an urban journey is, in principle, a separate service from a transport service consisting of the physical act of moving persons or goods. As such, the intermediation service would, in principle, fall within the definition of an Information Society service contained in Article 1(2) of Directive 98/34.[102]

However, the Court considered that in the case at hand Uber was offering more than an intermediation service and was simultaneously offering or rendering accessible urban transport services provided by non-professional drivers using their own vehicle and 'whose general operation it organises for the benefit of persons who wish to accept that offer in order to make an urban journey'.[103] The Court added that given

> that the intermediation service provided by Uber is based on the selection of non-professional drivers using their own vehicle, to whom the company provides an application without which (i) those drivers would not be led to provide transport services and (ii) persons who wish to make an urban journey would not use the services provided by those drivers

and in the light of the decisive influence exercised by Uber over the conditions under which the transport service is provided by those drivers,[104] Uber's

[100] Above n 98, para 40.
[101] See also *Uber France* (n 98) para 26.
[102] See also para 109 of the judgment in Case C-324/09 *L'Oréal and Others* [2011] ECR I-6011, in which the Court stated that 'an Internet service consisting in facilitating relations between sellers and buyers of goods is, in principle, a service for the purposes of the e-Commerce Directive'.
[103] *Asociación Profesional Elite Taxi* (n 98) para 38.
[104] Such as fares. This, of course, begs the question for future cases as to which conditions are relevant and what weight is to be accorded them.

intermediation service formed an integral part[105] of an overall service whose main component was a transport service and must thus be classified as 'a service in the field of transport'[106] rather than an Information Society service.

The importance of that finding is that it ensured that the conditions for the provision of the overall or composite service in question are regulated by the Member States, subject to conformity with the general rules of FEU Treaty, rather than, for example, by the e-Commerce Directive.[107] Those composite services fall outside the scope of, inter alia, the latter directive despite their undisputed and highly relevant online element.[108] The case thus establishes guidelines in order to determine the applicable rules and the scope of the competences of the Member States and the EU in relation to composite services.

In the judgment in *Ker-Optika*,[109] a clear delimitation was drawn between, first, the online sale and physical supply of the lenses, and, secondly, the online sale of the lenses and the physical medical examination – and thus the applicable rules – with the e-Commerce Directive remaining applicable in respect of the online element of the transaction. By contrast, in the judgment in *Asociación Profesional Elite Taxi*[110] – which makes no reference to the former judgment – the potential for the conditions of supply of the online element of the composite service to be regulated in accordance with, for example, the e-Commerce Directive was eliminated as the offline element was deemed the dominant or main component of the composite service. In effect, the offline service 'consumed' or 'absorbed' the Information Society service even though the latter could hardly be described as irrelevant or incidental in the context of the composite service. The Court referred to an 'overall' service and did not attempt to ascertain whether certain elements were separable. Schaub criticises this approach by the Court.[111] He considers, by analogy with the judgment in *Ker-Optika*,[112] that 'the division that can be made between the booking-app and the performance of the transportation is comparable to the division that is made between online selling of goods and the subsequent delivery of those goods'.

[105] The Court also stated that the services in question were inherently linked.

[106] The Court noted that the intermediation service did not come under Directive 2006/123/EC of the European Parliament and of the Council of 12 December 2006 on services in the internal market [2006] OJ L376/36, since services in the field of transport are among those expressly excluded from the scope of that directive pursuant to Art 2(2)(d) thereof.

[107] Or, indeed, Art 56 TFEU or Directive 2006/123.

[108] See, by analogy, the judgment in Case C-108/09 *Ker-Optika* [2010] ECR I-12213, where the Court distinguished between national rules relating to the sale of contact lenses online, which fall within the coordinated field laid down in the e-Commerce Directive, and the rules on the supply of those lenses, which do not. In addition, the Court noted that while the requirement of prior medical advice, in the form of a precautionary ophthalmological examination, is justified, that examination can be carried out independently of the act of sale and the online sale can proceed on the basis of a prior medical prescription.

[109] ibid.

[110] Above n 98.

[111] See MY Schaub, 'Why Uber is an Information Society Service' [2018] *Journal of European Consumer and Market Law* 109, 112.

[112] Above n 108.

More importantly, however, in the context of the present chapter, it is also clear from the judgment in *Uber France*[113] that, where an Information Society service is part of an overall service, the main component or dominant aspect of which is not an Information Society service and the provider of the Information Society service exercises a decisive influence over the conditions for the provision of the other service, the notification and standstill requirements contained in Directive 98/34 (Directive 2015/1535) are not applicable. Thus, the French legislation at issue in the main proceedings which made the organisation of a system putting customers in contact with persons carrying passengers by road without authorisation subject to criminal penalties was not subject to notification pursuant to that directive and was thus in that regard applicable and enforceable.

In the more recent *Airbnb Ireland*,[114] the Court held that the intermediation service provided by Airbnb which, by means of an electronic platform, connects, for remuneration, potential guests with professional or non-professional hosts offering short-term accommodation services was an Information Society service rather than the provision of an accommodation service, which comes under another legal classification and is governed by different rules. While the intermediation service complied with the four cumulative conditions laid down in Article 1(1)(b) of Directive 2015/1535,[115] the Court examined whether or not it forms an integral part of an overall service whose main component is a service coming under another legal classification.

In that regard, the Court noted that the service provided by Airbnb could not be separated from the property transaction itself, as it is intended not only to provide an immediate accommodation service, but also, on the basis of a structured list created for the benefit both of the hosts who have accommodation to rent and persons looking for short-term accommodation, to provide a tool to facilitate the conclusion of contracts concerning future interactions.

Moreover, according to the Court, the intermediation service provided by Airbnb was not merely ancillary to the provision of an accommodation service, nor was it indispensable to the provision of such services which have other distribution channels at their disposal. In addition, the Court stated that Airbnb Ireland did not set or cap the amount of rent charged by hosts using its platform. It followed, therefore, according to the Court, that an intermediation service such as the one provided by Airbnb could not be regarded as forming an integral part of an overall service, the main component of which is the provision of accommodation. The other services offered by Airbnb did not call into question this finding. Thus, the Court considered in particular that the other added-value ancillary services

[113] Above n 98.

[114] Above n 53.

[115] This is a necessary but insufficient condition in order for an intermediation service which is part of a composite service to be classified as an Information Society service. Additional conditions or criteria must be satisfied.

offered by Airbnb[116] and Airbnb's payment system or conditions were part of the collaborative model inherent to intermediation platforms and common to a large number of electronic platforms respectively. The Court also considered that no analogy could be drawn between the platform in this case and that in *Asociación Profesional Elite Taxi*[117] and *Uber France*,[118] as Airbnb does not exercise a decisive influence over the conditions for the provision of the accommodation services to which its intermediation service relates, particularly since it does not determine, directly or indirectly, the rental price charged or select the hosts or the accommodation put up for rent on its platform.

In the light of the recent judgments in *Asociación Profesional Elite Taxi*,[119] *Uber France*[120] and *Airbnb Ireland*,[121] I consider that while the relevant criteria to be assessed in order to determine whether an Information Society service forms an integral part of an overall service whose main component is a service coming under another legal classification is becoming clearer, the weight and importance to be attributed to each individual criterion remains uncertain. Ultimately, therefore, the applicable rules are uncertain. There may be cases in practice where the main component of the composite service is perhaps less evident than that in the recent judgments in *Asociación Profesional Elite Taxi*[122] and *Uber France*[123] and any influence of the Information Society service provider over the terms of supply of the other service more diluted or dispersed. These situations may lead to (further) legal uncertainty in relation to who may adopt the applicable rules on services and the scope of their competences, and ultimately private parties will face uncertainty as to which rules are applicable to given services. Indeed, at paragraph 95 of the judgment in *Airbnb Ireland*,[124] the concern that a Member State may impinge on the competences of another Member State was relied upon in order to extend the solution adopted by the Court in the judgment in *CIA Security International* in relation to Directive 2015/1535 to the notification obligation under the second indent of Article 3(4)(b) of the e-Commerce Directive.

In addition, I believe that there may be a temptation on the part of private parties to 'tweak' the format of composite services and the contractual relations between the different suppliers of that service in order to obtain what is perceived as the most favourable or convenient legal regime or environment, perhaps at the

[116] Such as a format provided to hosts for setting out the contents of their offer, an optional photography service for the rental property and a system for rating hosts and guests which is available to future hosts and guests.
[117] Above n 98.
[118] ibid.
[119] ibid.
[120] ibid.
[121] Above n 53.
[122] Above n 98.
[123] ibid.
[124] Above n 53.

expense of the optimal[125] provision of services to the consumer.[126] This situation is, however, hardly novel.

In essence, I believe that there is currently not enough case law on the matter from which to distil a clear, coherent rule applicable in most, if not all, cases. The existing case law is inevitably linked to the highly specific facts of the cases in question and the nature of the corresponding services. More litigation is this field is thus perhaps inevitable. In addition, the legislation in this field, which dates back to 1998 (Directive 98/48) and 2000 (e-Commerce Directive), has proved remarkably agile in dealing with Information Society services. However, 20 years is an aeon in the Information Age and as we embark on the Experience Age, there is, in my view, a need for a new, coherent and comprehensive legislative framework for Information Society services rather than the current fragmented and, dare I say, dated legislative framework.[127]

VII. Conclusion

The recent judgments in *Asociación Profesional Elite Taxi*,[128] *Uber France*[129] and *Airbnb Ireland*[130] on composite services have considerable implications for private parties. While a case-by-case approach is perhaps unavoidable, I consider that more legal clarity on the rules applicable to composite services made up of Information Society and other services is necessary. This clarity, whether it comes from the case law (which is dependent on litigation) or EU legislation, is to be welcomed as it is a truism to state that service providers need to know the rules by which they are bound before they can attempt to comply with them.

[125] Including rules on consumer protection and transparency.

[126] Aside from the obvious implications for the procedures in Arts 8 and 9 of Directive 98/34 and the application of the e-Commerce Directive, I would note, for example, that given that the definition of 'online intermediation services' in Art 2(2) of Regulation (EU) 2019/1150 of the European Parliament and of the Council of 20 June 2019 on promoting fairness and transparency for business users of online intermediation services [2019] OJ L186/57 requires, inter alia, that the services in question constitute Information Society services as defined in point (b) of Art 1(1) of Directive 2015/1535 (formerly Art 1(2) of Directive 98/34), important provisions of that regulation may not apply to certain online platforms, depending on how they are legally designed. This does not mean that other, and perhaps more stringent, rules on consumer protection are not applicable to a composite service deemed not to be an Information Society service. Indeed, Hatzopoulos considers that the CJEU in its judgment in *Asociación Profesional Elite Taxi* (n 98) 'by refusing to acknowledge the special characteristics of the collaborative economy, shifts the regulatory vacuum, hitherto favourable to the platforms, to the benefit of their consumers and incumbents. Such an outcome is at odds with the Commission's intention to support the development of online platforms and the sharing economy': see V Hatzopoulos, 'After Uber Spain: The EU's Approach on the Sharing Economy in Need of Review?' [2019] *European Law Review* 88, 97.

[127] The European Commission is aware of these challenges, as is clear from its announcement to adopt a Digital Services Act package.

[128] Above n 98.

[129] ibid.

[130] Above n 53.

More important, however, is the question whether national rules which are ostensibly applicable in respect of the provision of services are subject to the notification and standstill procedure under Directive 98/34 (Directive 2015/1535) or the notification procedure contained in the second indent of Article 3(4)(b) of the e-Commerce Directive and are thus, in fact, applicable and enforceable, for example, in a private law context.

6

Beyond Regulation: The Collaborative Economy in Need of New General Principles of EU Law?

VASSILIS HATZOPOULOS[1]

I. Introduction

'The advent of the collaborative economy, in combination with artificial intelligence, big data and 3D printing, makes something like a fourth industrial revolution.'[2] However, the collaborative economy is more than an economic model; it is also a cultural and social phenomenon, embodying the rise of the individual against the institutions and the intermediaries. It has roots in technological (5G networks, cloud computing, data analytics and robotics; the extensive use of mobile devices, equipped with elaborate apps and real-time GPS mapping), societal (urbanisation, servitisation, the culture of sharing personal data) and economic factors (global financial crisis, rise of unemployment, need for flexibility and for the use of idle capacity/resources).

One problem with the terminology – particularly topical in view of the growing professionalisation of the platform economy – is the use of the adjective 'sharing'. Indeed, given the economic value gained by some platforms,[3] the term 'sharing' has been called a misnomer, used to mask the essentially commercial nature of their activity: 'while [i]t has become a well-worn truism that little, if any,

[1] This contribution is largely based on a presentation, followed by a publication, in S de Vries and U Bernitz (eds), *General Principles of EU Law and the EU Digital Order* (Kluwer, 2020) 131–49.

[2] K Schwab, 'The Fourth Industrial Revolution: What It Means and How to Respond' *Foreign Affairs* (12 December 2015).

[3] In December 2020, Uber was valued at USD 90,3 billion and Airbnb, after its phenomenally successful IPO reached USD 100 billion; it is also worth noting that incumbent industries have heavily invested into 'sharing' platforms; hence eg General Motors has invested more than USD 500 million on Uber's competitor Lyft, and Expedia has taken over AirBnB's competitor HomeAway for USD 3.9 billion; see US Federal Trade Commission (FTC) Staff Report, 'The "Sharing" Economy: Issues Facing Platforms, Participants and Regulators' (2016) 12, www.ftc.gov/reports/sharing-economy-issues-facing-platforms-participants-regulators-federal-trade-commission.

actual sharing occurs in the "sharing economy"'.[4] Therefore, the more ideologically neutral term, 'collaborative economy', also used in the European Commission literature, is preferred here to 'sharing economy'.

Hence, the definitions of the collaborative economy vary considerably, as some put more weight on the intermediation by the platforms, others on the facilitation of interactions between peers, and still others on the lack of ownership transfer. According to the definition given by the Commission in its 2016 EU Agenda for the Collaborative Economy,[5] the term 'collaborative economy' shall encompass those *stricto sensu* collaborative economy platforms, which facilitate (i) access as opposed to transfer of ownership and (ii) the conclusion of a transaction (contract) between two other parties (hence a tripartite relationship), (iii) parties which are mostly – but not exclusively – peers, regardless of whether they are (occasional) prosumers or (professional) service providers.

Based on the definition above, the following characteristics can be identified, as 'disrupting' the traditional economy. First, platforms operate in multi-sided markets, ie markets where there are 'a) two or more groups of customers, b) who need each other in some way, c) but who cannot capture the value from their mutual attraction on their own; and d) rely on the catalyst (platform) to facilitate value creating transactions between them';[6] shopping centres (malls), stock exchanges and credit cards are examples of 'traditional' two-sided markets.

Secondly, two-sided markets produce network effects or externalities, both at the user level (the more users, the higher the utility of the platform to each one of them) and at the metadata level (the more data is fed into an algorithm, the more efficient it becomes). This allows platforms to develop super-dominant positions, having the characteristics of 'superstar economics'.

Thirdly, matching is ensured by the use of algorithms producing search rankings and recommendations tailored to user preferences. In order to produce the best matching results, improve user experience and reduce transaction costs, platforms create a profile for each user, through data collected, acquired or purchased. Therefore, data – both personal and mass (big data) – are essential for the platforms.

Fourthly, platforms make possible peer-to-peer transactions. The introduction into the economic circuit of these 'consumer-producers' (also called 'prosumers') and the creation of new markets that depend exclusively on the platform is a real legal disruption.

Finally, the booming economy of the platforms would not have been possible in the absence of self-regulation and reputation-rating systems. It is through these means that collaborative platforms convince perfect strangers to trust one another

[4] J Infranca, 'Intermediary Institutions and the Sharing Economy' (2016) 90 *Tulane Law Review Online* 29, 30.

[5] Commission, 'A European Agenda for the Collaborative Economy' (Communication) COM (2016) 356 final.

[6] D Evans and R Schmalensee, 'The Antitrust Analysis of Multi-sided Platform Businesses' (2012) Coase-Sandor Institute for Law & Economics Working Paper No. 623 7.

and share their cars, rooms, sofas and beds. Reputation is the new brand name, but, contrary to trademarks, its acquisition, preservation and protection depend solely on private platforms.

II. The Role of General Principles in the Collaborative Economy

In view of the features discussed above, the collaborative economy both disrupts traditional legal taxonomies and raises new legal issues. The first category (disruption) encompasses contract and tort law, consumer protection law and labour law, as well as data protection rules and competition law. The second category (unprecedented issues) relates to questions raised by the use of algorithms, especially in relation to fairness and fundamental rights. Yet another fundamental question relates to the dominant role that self-regulation and reputation rating have played so far, and by the way these could be made to serve the general interest, rather than that of the platforms.

In this context, it is worth asking whether general principles of law do have a role to play in the collaborative economy. A first answer is clearly in the affirmative: in a context where old rules are being questioned and need be reconsidered, and where fresh rules may be forthcoming in order to tackle new realities, reference to general principles becomes pervasive.

What is more, while self-regulation is hardly a new phenomenon, never in the past has it played such a central role in any economic activity. Legal orders have consistently developed a love–hate relationship with self-regulation, as they have acknowledged both its virtues and its risks. The EU itself has a rich, yet incoherent, approach to it. The CJEU (the Court) has developed quite complex conditions under which public regulation may be assimilated to private (and therefore be amendable under competition law rules),[7] while at the same time it has set equally complex conditions for denaturing private regulation into public, thereby taking it outside the ambit of EU law (as a genuine exercise of official authority) altogether.[8] At the same time, the Court has held that private standard-setting may lead to 'public' measures, amendable under free movement rules,[9] while at the same time it has also held that certification activities by private bodies do not fall within the exercise of official authority under Article 51 TFEU, even if their outcome has a general shaping effect on the market.[10] Meanwhile, the EU legislature, in

[7] Starting with Case 66/86 *Ahmed Saeed Flugreisen* ECLI:EU:C:1989:140, but most importantly with the trilogy of cases, Case C-2/9 *Meng* ECLI:EU:C:1993:885, Case C-185/91 *Reiff* ECLI:EU:C:1993:886 and Case C-245/91 *Ohra* ECLI:EU:C:1993:887.

[8] Case C-309/99 *Woutersea* EU:C:2002:98; more recently Case C-1/12, *OTOC* ECLI:EU:C:2013:127.

[9] Case C-171/2011 *Fra.Bo* ECLI:EU:C:2012:453.

[10] Case C-593/13 *Rina Services* ECLI:EU:C:2015:399.

the Services Directive, the Patient Rights Directive and elsewhere,[11] promotes self-regulation as a credible alternative to proper top-down regulation.

If general principles of law seem, at first sight, useful in backing the development of a coherent regulatory framework, the follow-up question is whether such principles may be developed and brought to fruition in an environment as new and as unsettled as the collaborative economy currently is. The recognition of the value of a general principle of law would, in principle, require that such value be applied with continuity, coherence, duration or repetition. These conditions need not necessarily always be true, however. As Takis Tridimas puts it:

> In the absence of guidance by Community written law, it [ie the principle] must be widely accepted in one way or another in the Member States. As already stated, the approach of the ECJ is selective and creative. It does not look for a common denominator. Nonetheless, to be elevated to the status of a general principle, a proposition must enjoy a degree of wide acceptance, ie represent 'conventional morality'.[12]

Therefore, in the context of the collaborative economy, mostly existing general principles of law will receive a fresh light, while a few new ones may also emerge. Hence, it is appropriate to talk of the resilience of existing general principles of law (section III) and of the (re)invention of new ones (section IV).

III. Resilience: New Light to Old Principles

A. *Effet Utile* – The Effectiveness of EU Law

The principle of effectiveness of EU law has been one of the early 'functional' general principles of law consecrated by the Court. Together with the principles of supremacy and direct effect, it makes the EU unique, different from any other supranational legal order. It guarantees the 'autonomy' of the EU legal order, so much cherished by the Court in its recent case law.[13] The effective application of EU law is seriously questioned by the collaborative nature of the EU economy, and that is true for many of its branches.

(i) Internal Market – Market Access

The law of the EU's internal market as it stands after 60 years of extremely rich (and occasionally incoherent) case law may be summed up as being tuned so as to

[11] See Directive 2006/123/EC of the European Parliament and of the Council of 12 December 2006 on services in the internal market [2006] OJ L376/36, Arts 26 and 37; Directive 2011/24/EU of the European Parliament and of the Council of 9 March 2011 on the application of patients' rights in cross-border healthcare[2011] OJ L88/45, Art 12.

[12] T Tridimas, *The General Principles of EU Law*, 2nd edn (Oxford, Oxford University Press, 2006) 26 (footnotes omitted).

[13] See, inter alia, Opinion 2/13 on the accession of the EU to the Council of Europe ECLI:EU:C:2014:2454; more recently, see Case C-284/16 *Achmea* ECLI:EU:C:2018:158.

secure market access to economic operators. The Court has recently held, in relation to services, that if

> the internal market in services is to be fully achieved, that requires, above all, the elimination of obstacles which are encountered by providers in becoming established in the Member States, whether in their own Member State or in another Member State, and which are liable to affect adversely their ability to supply services to recipients located throughout the European Union.[14]

However, the conditions under which platforms and, to a lesser degree, prosumers have access to the market of one Member State, and thence to those of all the others, are far from clear. This issue was raised in the two *Uber* cases decided by the CJEU.[15] The Court had to rule whether Uber is just an electronic intermediation service (and is therefore provided under the extremely favourable conditions of the e-Commerce Directive)[16] or whether it is a transportation service (and therefore requires the relevant authorisations and permits). The Court held that all platforms offer an intermediation service but that, under specific circumstances, a platform may also be offering an 'overall' service, englobing the underlying service. According to the judgment in *Uber Spain*, the platform is itself participating in the underlying service when two conditions are simultaneously[17] met: (i) the platform makes the provision of that service possible, and thus has a market-maker or 'gatekeeper' function; and (ii) the platform exercises a decisive influence over the different attributes of the new service. These criteria may yield a clear-cut solution for Uber, but not for other transportation platforms such as Blablacar,[18] let alone other platforms in the collaborative sector. Advocate General Szpunar, in his Opinion in *Uber Spain*, clearly distinguished Uber's exploitation model from other, more traditional, platforms, like the ones operating in the field of travel and accommodation, such as Booking.com. Contrary to Uber, these other platforms do not themselves create a new offer, but rather serve as yet another means of promoting pre-existing services. Further, such platforms, contrary to Uber, do not determine the content and/or the conditions of the services offered by the providers promoted through their pages; it is the latter who retain sole responsibility for the kind and level of services they offer to consumers. Last but not least, such platforms do not exercise 'entry control' over providers prior to allowing them onto

[14] Joined Cases C-360/15 and C-31/16 *College van Burgemeester v X and Visser* ECLI:EU:C:2018:44, 105.

[15] Case C-434/15 *Elite Taxi ea v Uber Spain* ECLI:EU:C:2017:981; Case C-320/16 *Uber France SAS* ECLI:EU:C:2018:221; for a discussion of these cases, see V Hatzopoulos, 'After Uber Spain: The EU's Approach on the Sharing Economy in Need of Review?' (2019) 41 *EL Rev* 88.

[16] Directive 2000/31/EC of the European Parliament and of the Council of 8 June 2000 on certain legal aspects of information society services, in particular electronic commerce, in the Internal Market [2000] OJ L178/1.

[17] The fact that the two conditions are cumulative has been clearly spelled out in the *Uber France* judgment, para 21.

[18] See the judgment of the Madrid Commercial Court, *Confebus v BlablaCar* SJM M 6/2017 (2 February 2017) ECLI:ES:JMM:2017:6.

the platform, given that such providers, being professionals (and thus not prosumers), already comply with the applicable rules and regulations.[19]

Many of these arguments have been used by the parties in *Airbnb Ireland*; in that case, however, the question was not whether the platform is active in the underlying market (ie short-term accommodation), but rather whether it is in the same market as that of traditional intermediaries, ie real estate agents.[20] Given that in this case the Court held the platform to be no more than a mere intermediary, it becomes clear that the answer to each specific case will necessarily reflect the facts and the precise question put to the Court, but most importantly, it will vary depending on the exploitation model followed by each individual platform; and there are as many exploitation models as there are platforms!

The above may be summed up as follows: (i) there is great uncertainty concerning the conditions under which platforms (and prosumers) may have access to the EU market; and (ii) in some cases the platform may be given the worst of all worlds, ie it may be assimilated to the underlying service providers, thus being stripped of the advantages offered by the collaborative exploitation model.[21] Both these findings counter the effectiveness of EU internal market law, since they run against both the legal objective of an internal market and the political/economic objective of a Digital Single Market (the EU DSM policy).[22]

(ii) Consumer Protection

By blurring the traditional production/consumption paradigm, the involvement of 'prosumers' in the collaborative economy questions the traditional consumer protection model based on the dichotomy between traders (sellers or suppliers, depending on the text) and consumers. In other words, EU consumer law only applies to business-to-consumer (B2C) relations and not to business-to-business (B2B) or, more importantly for the collaborative economy, peer-to-peer (P2P) relations.

This, in turn, creates a potentially very important void in consumer protection as, in those cases where the providers of the underlying services are not themselves traders, the consumers will be devoid of any claim (other than those based on contract or, worse, tort) against the prosumer who has made them suffer damage. Not only will such claims be unable to benefit from the more favourable rules of jurisdiction and applicable law foreseen in favour of consumers,[23] but they shall also be subject to 'traditional' burden of proof standards, and will require

[19] Opinion paras 57–61. The above distinctions have been broadly upheld by the CJEU in the recent Case C-62/19 *Star Taxi App* ECLI:EU:C:2020:980.

[20] Case C-390/18 *Airbnb Ireland* ECLI:EU:C:2019:1112; for a brief discussion of the hearing of this case, see https://blogdroiteuropeen.com/2019/01/17/laudience-de-de-la-cjue-dans-laffaire-airbnb-ireland-c390-18-continuite-ou-rupture-avec-larret-uber-par-edoardo-stoppoini/.

[21] For a lengthier discussion of this issue see Hatzopoulos (n 15).

[22] See COM (2015) 192 final and the corresponding Commision page, https://ec.europa.eu/digital-single-market/en/policies/shaping-digital-single-market.

[23] Under the Rome I Regulation (European Parliament and Council Regulation (EC) No 593/2008 of 17 June 2008 on the law applicable to contractual obligations (Rome I) [2008] OJ L177/6 and

the violation of a contractual term, or fault. Most importantly, such claims shall be addressed against individuals who may lack any financial means and may be unable to offer any redress to the aggrieved consumer.

While most platforms will qualify as *traders*, ie 'acting for purposes relating to [their] trade, business, craft or profession',[24] the legal qualification of the suppliers of the underlying service is far more delicate. Inspired by the practice followed in several Member States, the European Commission, in its Agenda for the Collaborative Economy, suggests the use of the following thresholds as proxies for the qualification of a 'trader': (i) the frequency of the services, ie whether the services are offered regularly or on a purely marginal and accessory basis; (ii) the profit-seeking motive, as opposed to the aim of exchanging assets or skills; and (iii) the level of turnover from the activity concerned, and whether such turnover is higher or lower than that obtained from other activities pursued by the same person.[25] These criteria only resolve clear-cut extreme cases, being unhelpful in most mainstream situations, which would require further clarifications. In the meantime, the Court, in a recent judgment concerning the occasional sales of goods (in the analog economy), established a long set of criteria which should be met for an individual to qualify as a trader;[26] the Court did, however, qualify its judgment by making clear that these criteria are 'neither exhaustive nor exclusive',[27] and that the capacity as a trader should be evaluated on a case-by-case basis,[28] since it is a functional concept.[29]

(iii) Data Protection

Data are inherently significant for the very existence and function of collaborative platforms: platforms collect and process a great amount of data concerning

the Brussels I Regulation (European Parliament and Council Regulation (EU) No 1215/2012 of 12 December 2012 on jurisdiction and the recognition and enforcement of judgments in civil and commercial matters (Brussels I Regulation (recast)) [2012] OJ L351/1.

[24] Unfair Terms Directive 93/13, Art 2(a).

[25] COM (2016) 356 final, 9.

[26] Case C-105/17 *Kamenova* ECLI:EU:C:2018:50, para 38, according to which 'the referring court will, in particular, whether the sale on the online platform was carried out in an organized manner, whether that sale was intended to generate profit, whether the seller had technical information and expertise relating to the products which she offered for sale which the consumer did not necessarily have, with the result that she was placed in a more advantageous position than the consumer, whether the seller had a legal status which enabled her to engage in commercial activities and to what extent the online sale was connected to the seller's commercial or professional activity, whether the seller was subject to VAT, whether the seller, acting on behalf of a particular trader or on her own behalf or through another person acting in her name and on her behalf, received remuneration or an incentive; whether the seller purchased new or second-hand goods in order to resell them, thus making that a regular, frequent and/or simultaneous activity in comparison with her usual commercial or business activity, whether the goods for sale were all of the same type or of the same value, and, in particular, whether the offer was concentrated on a small number of goods'.

[27] ibid para 39.

[28] ibid para 37.

[29] ibid para 35.

the age, gender, residence, employment, professional qualifications, dietary or other preferences, health condition, medications, location and economic details on both sides of the two-sided market in order to perform better matches. Data are acquired, then analysed through the use of algorithms, then applied in order to fulfil the platform's matching function.

In this context, data act as a currency: they are given away by platform users as consideration for the services received (also known as 'freemium'; see also Article 3(1) of the Commission's Digital Content Directive),[30] while constituting a 'tradeable commodity' for platforms which use them (i) for their own matching functions (the more data, the better the matching);[31] (ii) for allowing third party advertisements and promotions; and (iii) for selling complete data sets to third parties.

Rather than using it as a currency, European law envisions – and protects – personal data and the right to privacy as fundamental rights in Articles 7 and 8 of the EU Charter of Fundamental Rights, Article 16(1) TFEU, Article 8 of the European Convention of Human Rights and Convention 108 of the Council of Europe for the Protection of Individuals with regard to Automatic Processing of Personal Data. The EU General Data Protection Regulation (GDPR),[32] together with the (still draft) 'e-Privacy Regulation',[33] introduces strict data protection rules and tough sanctions. However, few (if any) of the rules contained therein seem to take into account the role played by data in the collaborative economy and the way platforms operate: (i) consent given to platforms is rarely as explicit and specific as the rules require it to be, while it is unclear whether it is always prior, free or even sufficiently informed; (ii) sensitive data, such as disabilities, medications, test results, allergies, mental health information and drug use, are regularly processed by platforms; other data, such as the itinerary often followed by Uber customers may be revealing of their sexual preferences and lives, as the notorious Uber's 'Rides of Glory' scandal has shown;[34] (iii) the right to be forgotten, recognised by the CJEU[35] and consolidated in Article 17 GDPR, is also difficult to apply, especially in relation to data which have been given in consideration of a service already received and consumed (freemium); and (iv) the right not to be subject to decisions based solely on automated processing, or else to profiling (Article 22 GDPR), is clearly not respected by the myriad of automated decisions taken by algorithms

[30] Directive (EU) 2019/770 of the European Parliament and of the Council of 20 May 2019 on certain aspects concerning contracts for the supply of digital content and digital services [2019] OJ L136/1.

[31] Therefore data possession offers a competitive advantage and possibly also market power; see the following section on competition law.

[32] Regulation (EU) 2016/679 of the European Parliament and of the Council of 27 April 2016 on the protection of natural persons with regard to the processing of personal data and on the free movement of such data, and repealing Directive 95/46/EC [2016] OJ L119/1.

[33] COM (2017)10 final.

[34] D Perry, 'Sex and Uber's "Rides of Glory": The Company Tracks Your One-Night Stands – and Much More', *The Oregonian/Oregon Live* (20 November 2014), www.oregonlive.com/today/index.ssf/2014/11/sex_the_single_girl_and_ubers.html.

[35] Case C-131/12 *Google Spain* ECLI:EU:C:2014:317.

on the basis of personal data, such as the ranking of providers, automated payment or the withholding thereof, and even the 'firing' of a service provider.

Therefore, as it currently stands, the GDPR is to a large extent unfit to be applied to the collaborative economy. Unless it is substantially modified in the near future – which is rather unlikely – it will need to be interpreted in a way that acknowledges the specific characteristics of the collaborative economy, while at the same time respecting the basic principles of data protection.

(iv) Competition Law

A proper assessment, under competition law, of the role of collaborative platforms is no easy task: their disruptive nature, their participation in two-sided markets, the network effects produced, the use of sophisticated algorithms processing big data and the plurality of peer-based business models employed test the applicability and sufficiency of existing competition rules. Questions are raised in relation to both horizontal and vertical issues.

At the horizontal level, it is unclear whether the providers of underlying services are undertakings (a qualification which is incompatible with their qualification as employees of the platforms, for which see sub-section v below) and, if so, whether they are in the same or a downstream market from the platform itself. The definition of the market itself is quite delicate as it is not always clear whether the platform operates in one two-sided market or in two separate markets; whether it operates in the same market as traditional providers of the underlying service or of intermediation services (see respectively the *Uber* and *Airbnb* cases discussed above under sub-section i); or how the SSNIP (small but significant and non-transitory increase in price) test is to be applied in markets where many of the services offered are 'free'. Market power is also difficult to assess in an environment so dominated by innovation, where externalities create super-dominant firms which, however, may disappear in the space of a few months[36] and where the possession of data may be key for power not only in the economic, but also in the political arena (as the Cambridge Analytica scandal eloquently illustrates).[37]

Once the basic horizontal concepts have been defined, there remain important questions in relation to the application of the specific Treaty provisions. Hence, for instance, how is Article 101 TFEU to apprehend price parallelism which is not based on collusion, but on similarly built algorithms?[38] What responsibility

[36] This has also been acknowledged by the General Court in Case T-79/12 *Cisco* ECLI:EU:T:2013:635, para 69, where it was held (in relation to consumer communications) that 'in such a dynamic context, high market shares are not necessarily indicative of market power and, therefore, of lasting damage to competition'.

[37] Although the Commission so far has resisted the qualification of big data possession as a barrier to entry: see, eg Case COMP/M.6314 *Telefónica UK/Vodafone UK/Everything Everywhere/JV* [2013] OJ C66; Case COMP/M.7023 *Publicis/Omnicom* [2014] OJ C84, confirming previous practice.

[38] In this respect, Case C-74/14 *Eturas and Others* ECLI:EU:C:2016:42 shows that the Court is ready to apprehend parallelism which is based on electronic means, even when no actual collusion has taken place.

do the platforms bear for parallelism between the providers of the underlying services?[39] Are platform agreements comparable to franchise or agency agreements? Is algorithmic price differentiation (based on profiling or other elements) an abuse when practised by a dominant undertaking? May big data qualify as an essential facility, thus compelling its holder to share it with competitors?[40] When is cross-subsidisation of the different activities of a platform, or their bundling and tying, a violation of Article 102 TFEU? Is the fact that platforms often operate in a regulatory vacuum, without being subject to authorisations or other regulatory and/or fiscal burdens, thus forestalling income from the public purse, not constitutive of a state aid under Article 107 TFEU?

(v) Labour Law

Individuals who depend on the collaborative economy for a living must work at least 12 hours a day, with no fixed or regular schedule, while competing for each minute of their work. The working conditions thus created are characterised by a high level of specialisation, the execution of specific mini-tasks isolated from the corresponding project, work conditions being managed and controlled by algorithms and other automated means (cameras, click-counting, etc), very important asymmetries of information between gig workers and the platforms they work for, precariousness, uncertainty and all the related health problems (stress, depression, etc), in addition to the inherent musculoskeletal disorders, visual fatigue, etc which are typical for online work. Important pieces of EU legislation concerning the protection of workers, eg the Working Time Directive,[41] the Fixed Term Work Directive,[42] the Part-Time Work Directive[43] and occasionally also the Temporary Work Agency Directive,[44] risk being violated. The recent Directive on Transparent and Predictable Working Conditions does make a step towards bringing within the definition of 'worker' many of those engaged through platforms, not least because it recognises the possibility for 'workers' to hold parallel employment (Article 9); however, the material obligations stemming from it are only marginally relevant for platform workers.[45]

[39] In this respect, *Eturas* (ibid) and Case C-194/14 P *AC-Treuhand* EU:C:2015:717 suggest that the platforms are far from immune.

[40] Under the logic of Case C-418/01 *IMS Health v NDC Health* ECLI:EU:C:2004:257.

[41] European Parliament and Council Directive 2003/88/EC of 4 November 2003 concerning certain aspects of the organization of working time [2003] OJ L299/9, Art 2(1).

[42] Council Directive 1990/70/EC of 28 June 1999 concerning the framework agreement on fixed-term work concluded by ETUC, UNICE and CEEP [1995] OJ L175/43.

[43] Council Directive 97/81/EC of 15 December 1997 concerning the Framework Agreement on part-time work concluded by UNICE, CEEP and the ETUC [1998] OJ L14/9.

[44] European Parliament and Council Directive 2008/104/EC of 19 November 2008 on temporary agency work [2008] OJ L327/9.

[45] Directive (EU) 2019/1152 of the European Parliament and of the Council of 20 June 2019 on transparent and predictable working conditions in the European Union [2019] OJ L186/105.

(vi) Conclusion on the Principle of Effectiveness

All the previous sub-sections suggest that the collaborative economy constitutes a new and possibly disruptive economic reality, which in many respects confronts the effective application of EU law. To the extent that no specific rules, accounting for the challenges of the collaborative economy, apply in the areas discussed above, the *effet utile* of European law requires that existing rules and concepts (eg information society service, trader, undertaking, collusion, worker) receive a more dynamic – and often voluntarist – interpretation, in order to allow for the application of EU rules which, on a strict interpretation – such as the one followed by the Court in *Uber Spain* – would be prima facie inapplicable. Otherwise an important body of EU law risks remaining inapplicable or else ineffective, with clear and imminent dangers for the internal market.

B. Proportionality and Subsidiarity

The previous section suggests that some fresh rules may be needed for the collaborative economy to develop and flourish. Indeed, the question of whether, how and when to regulate the collaborative economy is recurrent in legal theory.[46] Up until now, the collaborative economy has grown and flourished despite, or because of, the lack of any public regulation. This gap has been filled, to a large extent, by self-regulation by the platforms and peer reviews between their users. Such self-regulatory instruments, however, may be sufficient for relatively small and 'initiated' numbers of users, but will be insufficient for a phenomenon as dynamic as the collaborative economy proves to be. Moreover, the generalised application of self-regulatory methods has, over time, exposed their flaws. This is why several European states have started introducing regulation. Hence, for example, Italy had put forward (but later abandoned) legislative proposal 3564/2016, while France has introduced the 2017 Digital Republic Act,[47] completed by three decrees.[48]

Such national initiatives occupy the regulatory space left by the European legislator. The void thus left corresponds to the Commission's deliberate choice to show restraint and only propose guidelines, in order to avoid stifling the development of the collaborative economy. It is true that this 'void' is far from being absolute. Besides the two 2016 Communications on online platforms in general[49] and the collaborative economy in particular,[50] other texts, already in force or still in draft, are relevant for the collaborative economy.

[46] For a quite detailed discussion, with numerous references to other works, see V Hatzopoulos, *The Collaborative Economy and EU Law* (Oxford, Hart Publishing 2018). Ch. 7. See, more recently, V Hatzopoulos, 'Vers un cadre de la régulation des plateformes?' [2019] *RIDE* 399.

[47] Loi 2016-1321 of 7 October 2016.

[48] Décrets 2017-1434, 2017-1435 and 2017-1436 of 29 September 2017.

[49] COM (2016) 288.

[50] COM (2016) 356.

First, there is the old e-Commerce Directive,[51] as well as the new 'e-commerce' rules of the Digital Single Market package, notably on geo-blocking,[52] on cross-border delivery of parcels[53] and on digital contracts.[54] Secondly, the Fairness and Transparency Regulation for business users using online intermediation services fills an important gap by regulating the relationship between platforms and their professional service providers (hence P2P relations, as opposed to B2C relations already covered by the consumer laws).[55] Thirdly, the Regulation on the free flow of non-personal data shall complement the GDPR in facilitating the transfer of data.[56] Lastly, the Directive on transparent and predictable working conditions covers several forms of flexible, occasional and on-demand work, such as that offered through platforms, thus addressing some of the labour law issues raised above.[57]

These regulatory texts, as well as all future ones, should respect the principles of subsidiarity and proportionality. In the collaborative economy context, however, these general principles, governing the attribution of powers to, and their exercise by, the EU, should be considered in a fresh light.

Subsidiarity is important because if the collaborative economy is to be regulated in any effective manner, it will need a combination of EU rules dealing with general/horizontal issues (eg fairness and transparency issues, who is a 'trader', data transfers) and sector-specific rules adopted at the national and, most importantly, the local level (such as zoning regulations, operation hours). The fact that one and the same activity will be governed simultaneously at the European,

[51] Directive 2000/31/EC of the European Parliament and of the Council of 8 June 2000 on certain legal aspects of information society services, in particular electronic commerce, in the Internal Market [2000] OJ L178/1.

[52] Regulation (EU) 2018/302 of the European Parliament and of the Council of 28 February 2018 on addressing unjustified geo-blocking and other forms of discrimination based on customers' nationality, place of residence or place of establishment within the internal market and amending Regulations (EC) No 2006/2004 and (EU) 2017/2394 and Directive 2009/22/EC [2018] OJ L601/1.

[53] Regulation (EU) 2018/644 of the European Parliament and of the Council of 18 April 2018 on cross-border parcel delivery services [2018] OJ L112/19; Commission Implementing Regulation (EU) 2018/1263 of 20 September 2018 establishing the forms for the submission of information by parcel delivery service providers pursuant to Regulation (EU) 2018/644 of the European Parliament and of the Council [2018] OJ L238/65.

[54] Directive (EU) 2019/770 of the European Parliament and of the Council of 20 May 2019 on certain aspects concerning contracts for the supply of digital content and digital services [2019] OJ L136/1; Directive (EU) 2019/771 of the European Parliament and of the Council of 20 May 2019 on certain aspects concerning contracts for the sale of goods, amending Regulation (EU) 2017/2394 and Directive 2009/22/EC, and repealing Directive 1999/44/EC [2019] OJ L136/28.

[55] Regulation (EU) 2019/1150 of the European Parliament and of the Council of 20 June 2019 on promoting fairness and transparency for business users of online intermediation services [2019] OJ L186/57.

[56] Regulation (EU) 2018/1807 of the European Parliament and of the Council of 14 November 2018 on a framework for the free flow of non-personal data in the European Union [2018] OJ L303/59.

[57] Directive (EU) 2019/1152 of the European Parliament and of the Council of 20 June 2019 on transparent and predictable working conditions in the European Union [2019] OJ L186/105.

national and local levels, requires the competence share between the three sets of rules to be tuned in an unprecedentedly fine manner.

Proportionality must also come under a fresh light as its necessity test will have to be strongly substantiated when it is applied to an economic activity which has, so far, developed and flourished in the absence of any regulation. Indeed, the singularly important role played by self-regulation and by reputation management sets the collaborative economy apart from any other area previously regulated by the EU.

IV. Reinvention: New Principles

A. Effective Analogy

It has been explained above that the principle of effectiveness of EU law would need to be reinforced in order to bring under EU rules newly created situations which have not been specifically contemplated by – or seem prima facie excluded from – such rules. In this direction, the interpretative principle of *analogy* – not a general principle of law itself – could be of great help. Analogy, however, is inherently limited by the need for some degree of equivalence, or at least comparability, between the situations which are to be treated in an analogous manner. In other words, the 'old' situations described in the existing legal rules should be comparable with the new ones to which the rules are to be extended.

In view of the fact that the platform economy is in many respects disruptive, such analogy between the analog and the digital economy cannot necessarily be taken for granted. In such circumstances, the general principle of effectiveness of EU law, boosted by the interpretative principle of analogy, could lead to the application of EU rules in a way that neither of the two principles taken in isolation allows. The justification for such a 'marriage' would be the acute and immediate need to respond to the challenges raised by the collaborative economy, while preserving the unity and coherence of EU law.

This marriage would lead to the creation of a more specific general principle of 'effective analogy'. This would be an enhanced version of the principle of effectiveness, which would allow EU law to embrace new, unforeseen and disruptive developments. If the platform economy appears today as a disruption, it is just the frontrunner of many more disruptions to come in the near future. Artificial intelligence, robotics, the Internet of things, 3D printing, biotechnology and neurotechnology, to state just a few, are on the way to reshaping our economies and our societies. Law, on the other hand, is, by definition, a conservative institution, while the production of EU law, with its legal meanderings and political bargains, is a complex and time-consuming process. Therefore, the general principle of 'effective analogy' would be a 'technology-sensitive' version of the principle of analogy, which should allow for as effective an application of EU law as possible in the new, challenging, legal environment.

If this hypothetical general principle seems a bit abstract and not absolutely necessary, to the extent that it is based on already existing principles, the one that follows is far more radical and, to that extent, much more indispensable.

B. Algorithmic Fairness

It is not the place here to extensively discuss algorithms and the way they operate. It is enough to restate that they are at the core of the collaborative economy, since it is through them that platforms are able to perform their matching function. Next to the matching function, algorithms may perform a number of other, secondary tasks, such as setting the price for the underlying service (eg in the field of urban transportation), managing the fleet and/or personnel attached to the platform and proposing extra services to meet consumers' needs (or general profile characteristics). Further, algorithms process enormous amounts of data, personal and statistical, in order to create detailed profiles and metadata about users, assess consumption patterns, identify health conditions (eg pregnancy), make predictions about future actions (eg getting married in the foreseeable future), identify behavioural patterns likely to be followed by specific groups of individuals (eg committing a crime), adapt the platform's policy to that of its competitors,[58] etc.

The use of algorithms, despite being essential, is problematic in at least two ways. First, from the examples given above, it is clear that the purpose of certain algorithms may be questionable, illegitimate or plainly illegal. Secondly, even legitimate algorithms risk yielding plainly wrong or, more often, unfair outcomes. The latter problem is often discussed under the theme of 'algorithmic fairness'. Algorithmic fairness has been extensively discussed at the technical/technological level, but less so at the legal level; the latter discussion builds upon the former.[59]

(i) The Problem

Algorithms may yield plainly wrong outcomes. This may be because, inter alia, they are poorly built, the data input to them is incorrect or the process of data gathering has been poorly designed. Hence, for example, an algorithm built to measure street quality through a mobile app which detects pot holes yielded

[58] In this respect, see F Marty, 'Algorithmes de prix, intelligence artificielle et équilibres collusifs' (2017) Sciences Po OFCE Working Paper No 14, www.ofce.sciences-po.fr/pdf/dtravail/WP2017-14.pdf; see also the following footnote.

[59] For approaches which try to combine technical and social/ethical approaches, see, inter alia, S Friedler et al, 'On the (Im)possibility of Fairness', https://arxiv.org/pdf/1609.07236.pdf; P Hacker and E Wiedemann, 'A Continuous Framework for Fairness', https://arxiv.org/pdf/1712.07924.pdf; B Goodman, 'Economic Models of (Algorithmic) Discrimination', paper presented at the 29th Conference on Neural Information Processing Systems, www.mlandthelaw.org/papers/goodman2.pdf.

wrong results because the uneven distribution of smartphone ownership biased the data collection.[60] Another example of a plainly wrong outcome yielded by Google's algorithm is the famous 'gorillas' images, which in actual fact presented two people of colour![61]

This latter example illustrates that the outcomes reached by algorithms may not only be wrong, but unfair or immoral. A further well-known illustration of algorithmic unfairness, which does not immediately strike as plainly wrong (as was the case with the gorillas), is the 'three white/black teenagers' search on Google images: the white teenagers were portrayed holding balls, playing games and being happy, while the black teenagers were portrayed through their arrest pictures taken by police.[62] Other examples of algorithmic discrimination include the finding that Google's ad-serving system showed advertisements for high-paying jobs much more often to men than to women; as well as the finding that despite women holding 27 per cent of CEO posts in the USA, Google's image search for this term depicted only 11 per cent of women.[63]

Before even talking about algorithmic 'unfairness', one has to define what is considered to be 'fair' – a task which is typically riddled with ideology, political choices, gender and race issues, human rights considerations and more. The issue of fairness raises at least three delicate non-technical questions. First, one needs to decide when and to what extent individual fairness (ie that all individuals having the same relevant characteristics should get the same ranking) shall be given prevalence over group fairness (ie that protected groups are treated on the same footing as all other groups).[64] Indeed, these two forms of fairness may run in conflict with each other: if the worst candidate of group A is better qualified than the best candidate of (protected) group B, and we adjust for group fairness by replacing some A candidates with some B candidates, this will necessarily be done at the expense of individual fairness. Secondly, it is worth asking what is a 'fair' objective? And how strong is a deviation to be tolerated before an algorithm qualifies as 'unfair'? In more technical terms, what would be the 'statistical parity' that, once transgressed, would render the algorithm unfair? And how would that statistical parity relate to individual fairness? Thirdly, given that there will often be a trade-off between the performance of the algorithm and the removal of discrimination (ie if one corrects the number of people to be hired by including less skilled people from the

[60] See K Crawford, 'The Hidden Biases of Big Data' *Harvard Business Review* (April 2013), https://hbr.org/2013/04/the-hidden-biases-in-big-data.

[61] It is interesting that in order to 'correct' this problem Google did not find any better solution than to remove the tag 'gorillas' from its algorithms so that no mammal risk being tagged as such, see Tom Simonite, *When it Comes to Gorillas, Google Photos Remains Blind*, Wired, 1.11.18, available at www.wired.com/story/when-it-comes-to-gorillas-google-photos-remains-blind/(accessed 4/6/2020).

[62] M Solis, 'Google "Three Black Teenagers" vs "Three White Teenagers" – See the Problem?' (*Mic*, 7 June 2016), https://mic.com/articles/145485/google-three-black-teenagers-vs-three-white-teenagers-see-the-problem#.LPvvgBWhT.

[63] Both studies were conducted in 2015, the former by the Carnegie Mellon University and the latter by the University of Washington; for a brief discussion, see K Kirkpatrick, 'Battling Algorithmic Bias' (2016) 59(10) *Communications of the ACM* 16.

[64] Also called 'statistical parity'.

less-favoured group, the objective of hiring highly performant workers is partly jeopardised),[65] the question of balancing the one against the other – or, in legal terms, the question of proportionality – arises.

A second, no less delicate, issue related to algorithmic fairness concerns the criteria algorithms are programmed to take into account. Hence, for example, which of the following criteria should be used by an algorithm of an urban transportation platform (eg Uber), aimed at rating drivers (on top of the ratings given to them by users of the service): revenues generated, availability for the platform, hours actually worked, cleanliness of the car, road offences and/or accidents committed?

The choice of criteria to be used by algorithms raises two issues. First, which ones are the most adequate to achieve the set objective? Secondly, not all the criteria are discrimination-neutral; for example, from the criteria set above, the three first are likely to yield favourable ratings for male drivers (who tend to be more available), while the last two are more likely to favour female drivers (who tend to be more orderly and clean, and less risk-prone and confrontational when driving).

This second point raises a third one: if we want the algorithm not to yield discriminatory results, is it better to avoid using any criteria likely to lead to discrimination (but then how directly/indirectly discriminatory should a criterion be in order to be banned?)[66] or is it more secure to create a 'meta-algorithm' correcting ex post the unfair results yielded by the original algorithm? Or, under a more detailed categorisation, which kind of approach should be preferred in order to secure algorithmic fairness:[67] (i) pre-processing approaches (or data massaging), which transform input data into fairer representations; (ii) in-processing approaches, which control the algorithmic process from input to output; (iii) post-processing approaches, which transform output data; or (iv) reality check approaches, which look into the relation between predictions, ie output and real outcomes?

The fourth issue relates to the data fed into the algorithms. Irrespective of how robust, intelligent and fair an algorithm is built to be, it will only yield such results as may be dictated by the data fed to it. Therefore, if the data used contains (direct) discrimination, based on the protected characteristic (colour, gender, etc), such discrimination will be replicated by the algorithm. Even when the protected attribute is not fed into the algorithm (indirect), discrimination may occur in at least three ways.

First, other apparently 'neutral' data may indirectly inform the algorithm of the protected characteristic, eg the name and bodily measurements may inform about gender, the postal code and educational level may inform about colour; these are also called 'proxies'. Secondly, where the data is based on past patterns, during

[65] See, inter alia, B Goodman, 'A Step Towards Accountable Algorithms? Algorithmic Discrimination and the European Union General Data Protection, paper presented at the 29th Conference on Neural Information Processing Systems, www.mlandthelaw.org/papers/goodman1.pdf.

[66] See, eg the three criteria above, which are only indirectly discriminatory.

[67] For this categorization, see Hacker and Wiedemann (n 59).

which the protected group was being discriminated against, it is likely to replicate the bias. If, for instance, admissions to a course are based on prior admission records, the algorithm today is bound to favour white men over black women. Thirdly, algorithms built to be risk-averse (eg for loan approval) will be inclined to better rate individuals or groups for which plenty of information is available rather than those who are less represented or for whom information is scarce; this is also known as the 'uncertainty bias'.[68] In a more general way, since algorithms are based on repetitive patterns and rely heavily on statistical data, they are likely to mirror the majoritarian view/preference on any given issue; therefore, minority views, or people belonging to minorities, are likely to suffer.

(ii) Existing (Partial) Solutions

The data fed into algorithms are typically in the form of statistical, ie non-personal, data. Therefore, at first sight, the rules and principles concerning data protection (such as Articles 7 and 8 of the European Charter of Fundamental Rights, Article 16(1) TFEU and the GDPR) are of no help in this respect. This finding should be qualified, however, in at least three ways.

First, Article 22 GDPR specifically foresees that 'the data subject shall have the right not to be subject to a decision based solely on automated processing, including profiling'.[69] Although the prohibition is not an absolute one and several nuances are attached to it, it remains that 'in its current form, the GDPR requirements could require a complete overhaul of standard and widely used algorithmic techniques'.[70] In particular, Article 22(3) recognises that each data subject has 'at least the right to obtain human intervention on the part of the controller, to express his or her point of view and to contest the decision' taken by an algorithm. Together with Articles 13–15, which recognise the right of data subjects to receive 'meaningful information about the logic involved' in data processing, Article 22 may be yielding a new 'right to explanation'.[71] Such right would focus more on the ethical rather than on the technical aspects of algorithms.

Secondly, Article 22(2) GDPR plainly forbids automated decision-making to be based on sensitive data (revealing racial or ethnic origin, political opinions, religious or philosophical beliefs, or trade union membership, as well as genetic data, biometric data, health data or data concerning a natural person's sex life or

[68] See B Goodman and S Flaxman, 'EU Regulations on Algorithmic Decision-Making and a "Right to Explanation"', https://arxiv.org/pdf/1606.08813.pdf.

[69] Regulation (EU) 2016/679 on the protection of natural persons with regard to the processing of personal data and on the free movement of such data, and repealing Directive 95/46/EC [2016] OJ L119/1; see also the Article 29 Working Party Guidelines on Automated individual decision-making and Profiling for the purposes of Regulation 2016/79, https://iapp.org/media/pdf/resource_center/W29-auto-decision_profiling_02-2018.pdf.

[70] Goodman and Flaxman (n 68) 1, where the authors discuss at length the ways in which the GDPR may be used to help secure algorithmic fairness; for a further discussion, see also Goodman, 'A Step Toward Accountable Algorithms' (n 65).

[71] Idea expressed by Goodman and Flaxman (n 68).

sexual orientation), unless the data subjects have given their consent or such use is justified by the public interest. Therefore, the main grounds of discrimination should be removed from algorithms,[72] or their programmer should explain to data subjects the ways in which such sensitive data are to be used, for their consent to be 'informed' in accordance with Articles 4 and 7 GDPR. It is not clear, however, to what extent the prohibition of having algorithms' decision-making 'based' on sensitive data also covers the use of proxies which could indirectly lead to identifying the protected attribute.[73]

Third, Articles 24 (Data impact assessments), 40 (Codes of conduct) and 42 (Certification) GDPR could oblige algorithm writers to implement algorithm audits, ie third party inspections of algorithmic decision-making.[74]

(iii) Future (More Coherent) Solutions through the Creation of a General Principle

The above suggest that there are already – at least tentatively – some rules guiding algorithmic decision-making. Other than the prohibition of direct use of sensitive data, however, these rules are mostly of a procedural nature: a right for individuals to receive an explanation of the way algorithms operate and an obligation for bodies using algorithms to submit to algorithm audits. Even if these rights/obligations did actually exist – a hypothesis so far nurtured by part of the doctrine – they would only offer some ex post, indirect and imperfect relief to data subjects. Moreover, they would be constrained by the scope of application of the GDPR. To the extent that such rules are not core to the GDPR – and thus lack a direct footing in Article 8 of the EU Charter of Fundamental Rights –they may not make for generalised and coherent application.

More importantly, however, the core issues of algorithmic fairness are not addressed by the GDPR or any other text of EU law. Questions such as (i) what is considered to be fair in each given set-up, (ii) is individual fairness to be given prevalence over group fairness, (iii) what level of unfairness is to be tolerated in return for the facilitation offered by algorithms and (iv) what test of proportionality should be applied to the trade-off between algorithmic fairness and the effective operation of algorithms are not addressed by any text of EU law. These issues, which touch upon philosophical/ideological positions while, at the same time, depending on the specifics of each case, may not be addressed in a comprehensive way by any text of EU law. Sector-specific rules, if or when they come into existence, may provide some guidance in specific circumstances, but may not do more than that.

[72] This is what Goodman, 'A Step Toward Accountable Algorithms' (n 65) 2 calls 'data sanitization'.

[73] And the Working Party on its 'Guidelines on Automated individual decision-making and Profiling' (n 69) is silent on this issue; for a discussion of the 'minimal' and the 'maximal' requirement, see Goodman, 'A Step Toward Accountable Algorithms' (n 65) 3.

[74] See Goodman, 'A Step Toward Accountable Algorithms' (n 65) 4–5.

Even if sector-specific rules on algorithmic fairness did exist, they could not possibly offer all round answers, nor cover situations lying outside their scope. More importantly, such rules, to the extent that they would be impairing the functioning of the market in general and the internal market in particular, would often give way to the requirements of algorithm efficiency.

This is where the existence of a general principle of algorithmic fairness could step in. Such a principle could comprise general and abstract standards, but at the same time it could be the source and/or the tool for the interpretation of specific legal rules.

It is through recourse to general and abstract standards that the principle of algorithmic fairness would help determine what is 'fair' in any given circumstance. The principle would allow measurement of the risks of unfair outcomes and identification of the ways in which these may be avoided. Thus, it would help define, in each case, the degree of deviation from 'fairness' which could/should be tolerated. Since, as explained above, most algorithms need to reflect the majoritarian view (and hence discriminate against minorities) in order to be effective, the exercise proposed here would be akin to a proportionality test: on the one side of the scales should be considered the kind and degree of discrimination procured by the algorithm, while on the other side of the scales would figure the effectiveness of the algorithm in question.

At the same time, the principle of algorithmic fairness could create and/or inform more concrete legal rules, both substantial and procedural.

From a substantial point of view, the said principle could be at the origin of specific rules concerning the way algorithms are built and/or reviewed. Hence, for example, it could result in a list of criteria which should or should not be taken into account in order to achieve specific outcomes. Moreover, since many algorithms learn from the solutions they themselves reach, even though they are built in a fair way, they may become unfair over time. Therefore, a rule requiring the periodic revision of algorithms could ensue from the principle of algorithmic fairness. Further, this same principle could be at the origin of rules concerning the way algorithms are being controlled, both at the technical and at the legal level.

From a procedural point of view, the principle of algorithmic fairness could result in a rule whereby platforms would have to disclose the core criteria which are built into their algorithms. If Uber's surge pricing and Airbnb's 'superhost' status have a direct impact on the remuneration of drivers and hosts, respectively, it is only natural that these people know how the level of their remuneration is being determined and how they can make it better. Algorithmic transparency, however, could not be imposed in a blanket manner as it would run counter to platforms' intellectual property rights while, at the same time, raising concerns about algorithmic collusion.

A second procedural rule, concerning the ban of automatic decision-making by algorithms, is already in place in the GDPR and the e-Privacy Directive. This rule, however, concerns only decisions based on personal – not statistical – data. What is more, it is being plainly ignored by platforms which aim specifically to procure the most effective match to each one of their users – thus, basing said match on the users' personal data. The principle of algorithmic fairness, while acknowledging that algorithms are useful specifically because they take decisions for individuals, could nonetheless impose an obligation of random control of the fairness of such decisions; such control could end up in fines or other penalties. In the recently proposed 'Digital Services Act', the Commission, while not explicitly tackling algorithmic fairness as such, does follow several of the interests discussed above.[75]

V. Conclusion

The collaborative economy started almost a decade ago and, due to its enormous dynamism and the warm embrace given to it by users – both consumers and providers – has developed extremely fast. At the regulatory level, developments have been much slower, but responses both at the local and the European level are on their way. Such responses, however, may only partly address the disruption caused by the collaborative economy; at the same time, they may cause fragmentation within the EU internal market. Both outcomes (lacunary regulation and fragmentation) are not conducive to the proper application of EU law, but are unavoidable in a field as innovative, dynamic and rapidly evolving. In this context, where existing EU rules seem at first glance inapplicable, and where new rules need to be adopted, general principles of EU law may prove to be of the utmost importance: both by allowing existing rules to expand and cover original situations, and by informing the content of new rules.

In the former category, the well-established general principle of *effet utile* of EU law – having as its corollary the much-cherished autonomy of the EU legal order – may need to be revamped, in order to make sure that important bits of EU law are not set aside in the collaborative context. The effectiveness of EU law could be secured either through a radical strengthening of the homonymous principle – in which case one could talk of resilience – or through the creation of a new general principle, enhanced by the interpretative method of analogy, which would be tuned to technological innovation by establishing correspondence between old (analog) and new (digital) realities.

In the latter category, the recognition of a new general principle of EU law seems urgent in order to secure algorithmic fairness. If the actual means of securing fairness are technical, the analytical tools, the definitions and the strategic choices for tackling algorithmic unfairness are legal issues which need to be decided at the European level if fragmentation is to be avoided. Because the very concept of fairness is quite abstract and the means to achieve it are so varied, the recognition of a general principle in this area will benefit both the EU legislature and its citizens.

[75] COM (2020) 825 final.

7

Activating EU Private Law in the Online Platform Economy

MENNO COX[1]

I. Introduction

This chapter follows the adoption by the EU of the world's first horizontal platform regulation: Regulation (EU) 2019/1150 on promoting fairness and transparency for business users of online intermediation services [2019] OJ L186/57 ('Platform-to-Business' or P2B Regulation).

The P2B Regulation imposes contractual transparency, fairness and redress obligations on platforms such as e-commerce marketplaces, app stores and social media for business, as well as on search engines. According to the summary in the Official Journal, the Regulation aims to 'ensure the fair and transparent treatment of business users by online platforms, giving them more effective options for redress when they face problems, creating a predictable and innovation-friendly regulatory environment for online platforms within the EU'. The P2B Regulation started to apply on 12 July 2020.

This chapter explores the novel interplay between government regulation and private law that the P2B Regulation represents. Indeed, by forcing the inherently cross-border online platforms and search engines to 'fill the gap' on key commercial issues in their unilaterally imposed, private law contracts with their professional users, the latter will be able to compare terms, make informed decisions and hold providers to (their contractual) account. The premise of this chapter is that the online platform business model is overwhelmingly beneficial and requires further support, including through (harmonised) rule setting – of which the P2B Regulation represents a first important step. While the insights are the author's own views, they have partly been informed by the author's experience in researching online platforms in the context of the preparatory work on the P2B Regulation.

[1] The views expressed are purely those of the author and do not reflect an official position of the European Commission.

The chapter starts by introducing the P2B Regulation against the background of the rise of the 'online platform economy', or simply economy – online intermediation being the new normal. It then describes some unique features of online platforms to underline that these services are a truly novel phenomenon that warrant an '*ex novo*' approach to regulation. The central part of the chapter covers the interplay between government regulation and private law in the inherently cross-border, and frequently global, online platform economy. It ends with a reflection on the future of EU private law, which the author believes to appear to be bright.

II. Background/The Rise of the Online Platform Economy

Google Maps and Facebook Pages are two examples of what are essentially global directory services.[2] They are starting to fill a gap in the ability of private citizens to efficiently discover and compare local service provision. A logical next step would be to bring on board all handymen, dentists, GPs, lawyers and other professionals, and to subject these to consumer-to-business e-procurement functionalities. Sounds futuristic? There are already multiple online platforms that aim to do just that.[3] Some of these platforms, however, did not (or have not yet) achieve the required network effects, or they operate in specialised niches. As one solution, the 'platform-of-platforms' Alphabet is filling the void by seamlessly integrating the entire ecosystem of reservation marketplaces into its Maps service.[4] Whereas the individual reservation marketplaces serve a specific geography or specialise in a single area, such as concert tickets or personal grooming, their collective integration into a single interface enables users to find any of these 'local services' regardless of their location or specific query. These developments underline the scope for (scale and scope) efficiencies that the online platform-business model continues to offer.

This elimination of information asymmetries will most likely continue across the whole economy, and may, at the local, national and global levels, in some

[2] By indexing millions of (mainly small) businesses, including their location and company details, these services are effectively a global, online version of what used to be known as yellow pages. The functionalities offered to businesses and consumers by these services are, however, fundamentally different due in large part to big-data analyses and web hosting capabilities that enable live updates and direct business-to-consumer (B2C) interactions.

[3] Online labour platforms already come in all shapes and sizes, offering customers the ability to procure everything from cleaning services to specialised consultancy work. Dedicated online platforms in addition exist for services such as removal, home improvement, pet care and beauty services.

[4] For more details, see 'Reserve with Google', www.google.com/maps/reserve/partners.

cases even try to outperform public rules addressing important market failures.[5] The ecosystem-building capacity of online platforms can in addition create entirely new professions, such as app development, social media influencer, E-sports, keyword tracking services, ad verification or – to some extent – food delivery.[6] The COVID-19 global health emergency is likely to accelerate this 'platformisation' trend, as businesses have been forced to build or expand their online presence, for which many tend to rely on the efficiencies offered by online platforms.[7] A telling statistic in this regard is the increasing share of GDP accounted for by e-commerce[8] and the accompanying increase in the value of the largest platform companies, from USD 3.9 trillion in 2015[9] to USD 7 trillion[10] just two years later. All of this means that discoverability online is becoming increasingly akin to entrepreneurship. Knowledge of ranking, advertising and other tools used to facilitate this discoverability will accordingly form part of the most basic digital skillset required to enter any market. In turn, it could be argued that facilitating trust in the private firms running the online platform economy becomes a self-standing public policy objective.

It is indeed legitimate for government to recognise the success of online platforms, as they bring important benefits to society – including the facilitation of (cross-border) entrepreneurship. A prerequisite for doing so, however, is not to mistake regulatory evasion for efficiencies. Another prerequisite is not to cement incumbents and their profit models (eg commission based or ad-funded) into legislation. If private intermediaries continue to be allowed to organise markets in this manner, governments will need to be all the more vigilant and not hesitate to intervene.

Transparency, observation and targeted government intervention have also been identified as the pillars for the EU's approach to online platforms.[11] And

[5] Think, for example, of invoice auctioning as a tool to reduce late payment, which presents a persistent (cash-flow) problem for vast swaths of the economy.

[6] Think of so-called 'dark kitchens', which exist by virtue of the large demand that traditional restaurants can struggle to meet.

[7] In this regard, see, eg the various news reports on stock price increases of big tech: www.ft.com/content/d2e09235-b28e-438d-9b55-0e6bab7ac8ec; www.ft.com/content/496bc09a-4646-407a-a0d4-a22dac55c1e6; www.ft.com/content/844ed28c-8074-4856-bde0-20f3bf4cd8f0. *cf* also the surges in user numbers reported by e-commerce hosting services such as Shopify, where 'New stores created on the Shopify platform grew 62% between March 13, 2020 and April 24, 2020 compared to the prior six weeks'.

[8] In major economies like Japan and Korea, e-commerce is estimated to account for more than half of GDP. More broadly, global e-commerce increased 8% from 2017 to reach USD 25.6 trillion in 2020. See UNCTAD/PRESS/PR/2020/007 (27 April 2020).

[9] 'Staff Working Document accompanying the Communication on Online Platforms and the Digital Single Market' SWD (2016) 172 final.

[10] 'Unlocking the Value of the Platform Economy' (KPMG, 2018).

[11] Commission, 'Online Platforms and the Digital Single Market Opportunities and Challenges for Europe' (Communication) COM (2016) 0288 final.

with the entry into force and application of the P2B Regulation, the EU now has a ranking transparency-rule that should enable government, business as well as consumers to understand how service quality is determined, and whether this is done in a fair manner.

The P2B Regulation should in addition act in synchrony with the case-by-case enforcement of EU competition law, and experts advising Commissioner Vestager (now Executive Vice-President for a Europe Fit for the Digital Age, in her second mandate[12]) on competition in digital markets recently noted that:

> In certain areas, regulation can bolster the role competition law [plays] in protecting competition in the platform economy. This is the case, notably of the transparency regime set out in the draft P2B Regulation or in other areas where similar issues arise continuously and intervention may be needed on an ongoing basis (for example to impose and allow for effective interoperability). Apart from these limited settings, we believe that competition law can, and should, continue to accompany and guide the evolution of the platform economy.[13]

The novel regulatory approach adopted by the EU, and already followed internationally to some extent,[14] is precisely to be found in the interplay between private and public regulation, which brings us to the focus of this chapter: the role of private law in the online platform economy.

III. Some Relevant Findings about Online Platforms

First, I present some findings about the specificities of the online platform business model, to frame the debate. Understanding these characteristics is necessary to appreciate: (i) the case for the P2B Regulation as arguably the world's first horizontal platform regulation; (ii) its Single Market objective; and (iii) its potential to leverage existing EU private law.

[12] See https://ec.europa.eu/commission/commissioners/2019–2024/vestager_en.

[13] See J Crémer, YA de Montjoye and K Schweitzer, *Competition Policy for the Digital Era* (European Commission, 2019) 6, https://ec.europa.eu/competition/publications/reports/kd0419345enn.pdf.

[14] The Japanese Diet adopted the 'Digital Platform Transparency Act' in May 2020. See www.japantimes.co.jp/news/2020/05/27/business/japan-enacts-law-toughening-transparency-regulations-tech-giants/. Similar to the P2B Regulation, this bill imposes contractual transparency obligations, including on search rankings, as well as dispute settlement systems on certain 'Specified Digital Platform Providers'. For more details on the contents of the bill, see www.kantei.go.jp/jp/singi/digitalmarket/pdf_e/documents_200218.pdf. Also, in its 2019 settlement with the Bundeskartellamt, Amazon implemented its commitments beyond the German market, see www.bundeskartellamt.de/SharedDocs/Meldung/EN/Pressemitteilungen/2019/17_07_2019_Amazon.html.

A. Statistics on Business Users – Network Effects, Fragmented User Bases and Dependencies

In 2018, there were a reported 5.7 million professional app developers in the EU.[15] All of these depend on app stores for distribution. In the accommodation sector, 71 per cent of online bookings for independent hotels were already made through online platforms in 2016, with online accounting for 49 per cent of all travel bookings in Europe.[16] Etsy alone accounted for over 2 million sellers of handicraft goods globally in 2018.[17] The position of retailers on platforms recently could even be said to have become something of an election issue in India, when the government introduced new rules on foreign direct investment that prevent foreign owners from both operating a platform and providing retail services through it.[18]

Online platforms are also particularly relevant for cross-border trade, and a recent investigation into Amazon by the Federal Cartel Office (Bundeskartellamt) provided insightful statistics in this regard:

> In 2018 more than 300,000 third-party sellers were active on the marketplace amazon.de. Considering the volume of sales of third-party sellers on amazon.de Marketplace, 60–65 percent were accounted for by German sellers, 20–25 percent by non-European sellers and 10–15 percent by sellers from other European countries, with less than 2 percent by sellers from Austria and much less by sellers from Luxembourg. More than 95 percent of the total volume of sales on amazon.de were sold to German or Austrian customers. In 2018 more than 300 million different items (ASIN) were offered on amazon.de and approx. 1.3 billion products were sold.[19]

B. Specialisation as a Business Model

Specialisation in this sense can occur along many different parameters: segments of intermediated industries (eg retail), territorial coverage (eg regional, pan-EU or global), product range (eg designer shoes, luxury watches or the broadest possible spectrum of consumer goods), etc. Online platforms that successfully corner a

[15] Atomico in partnership with Slush, 'The State of European Tech 2018' (2018) 5, https://2018.stateofeuropeantech.com/chapter/state-european-tech-2018/.

[16] Commission, 'Impact Assessment of the Proposal for a Regulation of the European Parliament and of the Council on promoting fairness and transparency for business users of online intermediation services' (26 April 2018) 27, https://ec.europa.eu/digital-single-market/en/news/impact-assessment-proposal--promoting-fairness-transparency-online-platforms.

[17] See www.statista.com/topics/2501/etsy/.

[18] For more details, see, eg https://inc42.com/buzz/walmart-on-india-fdi-ecommerce-policy/; www.reuters.com/article/us-walmart-india-exclusive/exclusive-walmart-told-u-s-government-india-e-commerce-rules-regressive-warned-of-trade-impact-idUSKCN1U620R.

[19] www.bundeskartellamt.de/SharedDocs/Meldung/EN/Pressemitteilungen/2019/17_07_2019_Amazon.html.

segment of the intermediation space can easily overlap, the idea being that they successfully captured consumer audiences for specific purposes.

On the one hand, even relatively small platforms can capture important audience shares in niche areas: for example, online platforms that host artists' portfolios can be important ways to market as gallery owners may use a particularly niche platform to discover new artists in their field.

On the other hand, the number of platform enterprises in the EU appears to have increased from 7,000 in 2016 to over 10,000 today.[20] This vast number of mainly small firms underlines the success of the platform business model, but also the innovation potential of a competitive online platform economy.

C. Competition Is Not a Click Away – Multi-homing of Business Users

The specialisation by online platforms translates into business users being forced to multi-home. And rather than being a feature of contestability, multi-homing underscores the importance of individual sales channels as firms naturally seek to maximise sales in light of their thin margins.

In this regard, the European Commission's Joint Research Centre has shown for the first time how the vast majority of professionals using app stores, e-commerce marketplaces, social media and other platforms multi-home, and that this 'competitive bottleneck model' enables platforms to 'maximise profits by strategically degrading quality to sellers'.[21]

D. Unilateral Trading Practices – Scope for Abuse

A recent study notes that 46 per cent of respondent business users experienced problems and disagreements with the platforms in the course of their business relationship, and that among business users with more than half of their turnover generated via online platforms (heavy users), this percentage rises to 75 per cent.[22] Note that problems are not necessarily the result of abuse, or oppositional interests between platforms and their business users. However, the mere scope for abuse by the online platforms, who can act unilaterally and have the ability to shut down

[20] European Commission (EC) 2019 estimate based on Dealroom data. This statistic is included in Commission, 'How Do Online Platforms Shape Our Lives and Businesses', https://ec.europa.eu/newsroom/dae/document.cfm?doc_id=61687.

[21] N Duch-Brown, 'Quality Discrimination in Online Multisided Markets' (2017) JRC Digital Economy Working Paper 2017-06, https://ec.europa.eu/jrc/sites/jrcsh/files/jrc109185.pdf.

[22] Ecorys, 'Business-to-Business Relations in the Online Platform Environment FWC ENTR/300/PP/2013/FC-WIFO Final Report' (22 May 2017), https://publications.europa.eu/en/publication-detail/-/publication/04c75b09-4b2b-11e7-aea8-01aa75ed71a1/language-en.

entire businesses by delisting them, negatively impacts trust in the broader online platform economy. A telling statistic is the fact that 25 per cent of app developers responding to an industry survey view the app store operators as the biggest threat to their business, notwithstanding their consensus that competition within the app stores is highly vibrant.[23]

E. Power of Online Intermediaries – The Case for a Tailored Approach

In the run up to the Commission's proposal for the P2B Regulation, detractors of online platform regulation have at times relied on the so-called 'law of the horse' argument to express an alleged problem of principle with what they saw as technology- or company-specific regulation.[24] This argument dates back to the early days of the Internet and arose in discussions on cyber law.[25] It essentially goes as follows in the platform context: online platforms are a type of technology that in no way raise fundamentally new ethical or moral questions, and they are not exempt from existing rules developed through our rich legal traditions. This argument is obviously flawed, and in at least two ways. First, platform-specific legislation already existed at the time the argument was made, namely the virtually globally recognised limitation of intermediary liability from which the operators of certain online platforms themselves can benefit.[26] Secondly, online platforms are not a technology but a business model that enables new cross-border peer-to-peer, business-to-consumer (B2C) and business-to-business relations, and which introduces a novel legal construction frequently involving three separate contractual relations (P2B, platform-to-consumer and B2C) building on generally applicable community standards.

Online platforms do indeed raise important 'novel' questions, and although network effects are not a new phenomenon, their unprecedented scale and scope only strengthen the case for regulatory intervention where problems emerge. It is interesting in this regard to note that computerised reservation systems (CRSs) used for airline ticketing have for decades been subject to a tailored regulation which even imposes a 'ranking standard' – CRSs equally being intermediary business models building on telecommunications technology.[27]

[23] See Commission, 'Impact Assessment' (n 16) 27.

[24] See, eg D O'Connor and M Schruers, 'Against Platform Regulation' (Oxford Internet Institute, University of Oxford, 2016) http://blogs.oii.ox.ac.uk/ipp-conference/2016/programme-2016/track-c-markets-and-labour/government-regulation-of-platforms/daniel-oconnor-matthew-schruers-against.html.

[25] See also https://en.wikipedia.org/wiki/Law_of_the_Horse.

[26] See, eg https://wilmap.law.stanford.edu/map.

[27] Regulation (EC) No 80/2009 of the European Parliament and of the Council of 14 January 2009 on a Code of Conduct for computerised reservation systems and repealing Council Regulation (EEC) No 2299/89, [2009] OJ L35/47.

The most important question in this regard reflects a duality in the nature of the online platform business model; the intermediary power of the marketplace operator allows it to create safe and trusted ecosystems, but it also has scope for abuse.

In sum, healthy and competitive platform ecosystems require kindling of the febrile trust on all sides of these multisided ecosystems. Online platforms of course fundamentally recognise this, and they in fact derive part of their competitive edge from their large user bases that provide continuous, real-time feedback on how to improve their ecosystems. Google Play and the App Store are effectively able to deploy the power of open source software within closed ecosystems to create unprecedented economic opportunities for all participants in their ecosystems – including their own organisations. Think about app developers reporting bugs or being 'rewarded' with testing beta versions of special features, or consider consumers, brand owners and even government reporting illegal content to the platform operators. For Tripadvisor, the veracity of customer reviews equally is its core business, and the implications in terms of resources suggest that its very right of existence may be derived from its users' demand for trust:

> The first step in the pre-posting screening process is an automated review analysis system. This technology employs state-of-the art data analytics to review hundreds of pieces of online information that can flag content that doesn't meet Tripadvisor's guidelines or that might be fraudulent. It uses network forensics and advanced fraud modelling to map electronic patterns that no human could ever identify. If the system detects clear violations of Tripadvisor's guidelines, it will automatically reject the submission. Last year, the system rejected 1.4 million review submissions. If the analysis system detects a potential problem, the review is sent to a content moderation team for further analysis. This dedicated team then assesses factors that the review analysis system cannot. That might include the context in which a review is written, or any cultural nuances in the wording. The analysis system or the moderation team might also, on occasion, reach out to a user to ask them to verify a detail of their review, such as whether it is for the correct location. Tripadvisor employs hundreds of content analysts globally, working 24/7 to maintain the quality of the reviews on the platform, including analysts fluent in all 28 languages that the platform supports.[28]

The preliminary results of the Federal Cartel Office's sector inquiry into consumer reviews underlined the value of these digital 'commodities' for online platforms. They also reveal large differences in the effectiveness of different online platforms' filtering mechanisms, with automated systems or limited review sometimes leading to, for example, a 'disproportionally large removal of negative reviews'.[29]

Online platforms are, however, also driven to diversify both horizontally and vertically, for example by moving into payment, delivery, retail or other adjacent areas, to maintain or capture increasing control over consumer 'control points'.

[28] 2019 Tripadvisor Review Transparency Report, www.tripadvisor.com/TripAdvisorInsights/wp-content/uploads/2019/09/2147_PR_Content_Transparency_Report_6SEP19_US.pdf.

[29] See www.bundeskartellamt.de/SharedDocs/Meldung/EN/Pressemitteilungen/2020/18_06_2020_SU_Nutzerbewertung.html.

Think of Facebook's announced launch of the Libra stable cryptocurrency and its Novi wallet,[30] or Apple's push into digital identification.[31] As they successfully lock in customer groups to holistic solutions, their strength and ability to extract rents also increases.[32] What is more, the simultaneous participation in, and control of, entire markets can occur. Again, a duality between possible consumer efficiencies and conflicts of interests arises. In this context, the European Commission is looking into the role played by particularly large online platform companies acting as gatekeepers, proposing a targeted regulatory framework for such gatekeepers in 2020 – as a complement to the P2B Regulation. In the preparatory roadmap for this initiative that falls under the 'Digital Services Act package', the Commission notes that:

> These large online platforms also increasingly bundle a broad range of platform and other digital services into a seamless, data-driven offer … certain of the features described above may bring advantages to both business users and consumers, their unfettered application is likely to hamper the development of a fully functioning digital single market.[33]

All of the foregoing explains why an apparent duality in platform regulation to support platform innovation can be entirely natural.

IV. Online Platforms Are an Ecosystem-Building Business Model

The services that meet the characteristics set out in the previous section are horizontally referred to as online platforms, or 'online intermediation services' as defined in the P2B Regulation. These services are fundamentally a business model, and it is important to keep in mind that one and the same firm can operate multiple platform services. In fact, a recent study identified that the seven largest 'platform companies' operate more than 50 platforms in the e-commerce area alone, each of which is valuated above USD 100 million.[34]

[30] See https://newsroom.fb.com/news/2019/06/coming-in-2020-calibra/. Calibra has recently been rebranded Novi, see https://techcrunch.com/2020/05/26/facebook-rebrands-libra-wallet-service-calibra-to-novi/; www.novi.com/.

[31] See, eg www.cnet.com/how-to/sign-in-with-apple-will-come-to-every-iphone-app-how-the-new-privacy-login-tool-works/.

[32] See Ecorys, 'Business-to-Business Relations in the Online Platform Environment' (6 June 2017) 15, which notes: 'Unequal bargaining positions can be reflected in high prices for using platforms (which vary in practice between 3.5% to 25% for ecommerce marketplaces, while marginal costs might be close to zero).'

[33] Inception Impact Assessment, 'Digital Services Act package: Ex Ante Regulatory Instrument for Large Online Platforms with Significant Network Effects Acting as Gate-keepers in the European Union's Internal Market' Ares (2020) 2877647, 2, https://ec.europa.eu/info/law/better-regulation/have-your-say/initiatives/12418-Digital-Services-Act-package-ex-ante-regulatory instrument-of-very-large-online-platforms-acting-as-gatekeepers.

[34] 'Unlocking the Value of the Platform Economy' (KPMG, 2018).

Precisely to capture the business model rather than the interface design – note that certain social media seamlessly integrate profiles, business pages and interpersonal communications services with P2P and B2C marketplaces – the P2B Regulation defines these services in a technologically neutral manner. To this end, it identifies the following common features shared by online platforms across categories such as app stores, marketplaces and social media: (i) they are provided using the Internet, normally for remuneration (ie the existing legal definition of 'information society services' of Directive (EU) 2015/1535); (ii) they allow professionals to directly offer goods or services to consumers; and (iii) they are provided to those professionals on the basis of (standalone) contractual relationships.[35]

Given the wildly varying types of online platforms, it is unsurprising that the above legal definition is accompanied by two lengthy recitals providing concrete examples of types of services that fall within and outside its scope. For example, online payment services are not used by consumers to browse for goods or services, and only come in once a transactional decision has been made. Online advertising exchanges, in turn, intermediate between professional sellers of advertising space and professional advertisers.

The second and third elements of the definition, however, identify the crucial element that sets online platforms apart from the millions of 'simple' webshops that the definition of information society services covers. The difference is the capacity to leverage indirect network effects to build ecosystems of businesses and consumers, as mentioned in recital 10 of the P2B Regulation: 'A wide variety of business-to-consumer relations are intermediated online by providers operating multisided services that are essentially based on the same ecosystem-building business model.'

V. Private Law in the Online Platform Economy

The Commission's Impact Assessment underpinning the P2B Regulation notes that in the online platform economy, private contracts are unilaterally determined and imposed on the vast majority of professional users. These contracts take the form of general terms and conditions, including 'community guidelines', and frequently combine detailed commercial requirements with behavioural norms, reflecting that platforms are today's 'public spaces', online.

This centrality of private norm-setting in the online platform economy derives from an imbalance in bargaining power that can exist even where the platform and a specific user are similar in size in absolute terms, reflecting the power that online platforms derive as central intermediaries serving specific customer groups or needs. While sometimes being qualified by the online platforms themselves as

[35] P2B Regulation 2019/1150, Art 2(2).

principal–agent agreements, their general terms and conditions tend to limit the agent's risk and liabilities to an extent that is effectively inverse to that usually seen in principal–agent agreements.[36]

At the same time, in the recent CJEU *Airbnb* case,[37] the court addressed the question of whether the relevant, pre-existing French legislation applicable to real estate intermediaries is enforceable vis-à-vis Airbnb. Interestingly, the French legislator has itself put in place a tailored legal regime for online intermediation services operating in the field of 'home-sharing'.[38] The CJEU ultimately decided that the relevant home-sharing intermediation activities of Airbnb constitute information society services under Directive (EU) 31/2000, given 'the absence of decisive influence on the part of Airbnb over the conditions for the provision of the accommodation services to which its intermediation service relates'.[39] This qualification essentially means that the relevant activities are not to be seen as an integral part of (physical) services that are provided locally, subject to the pre-existing, sector-specific, French legislation on real estate intermediaries. They should rather be seen as cross-border digital services that come within the scope of the 'coordinated field' of Directive (EU) 31/2000, thus benefiting from the 'freedom to provide information society services' in the internal market. The online platform service provided by Airbnb could accordingly be said to be 'real' online intermediation, a novel service targeted by the equally novel P2B Regulation, rather than an integral part of a pre-existing service, as one of Uber's services was found to amount to in the seminal '*Uber* case' of the CJEU.[40]

The *Uber* and *Airbnb* case law of the CJEU are only the first, and very sector-specific, steps to delineating service provision in the online platform economy. No general conclusions as to the status of the various services provided by the multifaceted providers of online intermediation services can yet be drawn.[41] This careful building of sector- or even platform-specific case law is important, given the important implications that the qualification of contracts has in terms of, inter alia, civil liabilities[42] and competition law,[43] and crucially also

[36] See also P Akman, 'Online Platforms, Agency, and Competition: Mind the Gap' [2019] *Fordham International Law Journal* 43.

[37] See Opinion of AG Szpunar in Case C-390/18 *AIRBNB Ireland*, 30 April 2019.

[38] See www.gouvernement.fr/action/elan-une-loi-pour-l-evolution-du-logement-de-l-amenagement-et-du-numerique.

[39] Case C-390/18 *AIRBNB Ireland*, 30 April 2019, recital 68.

[40] Case C-434/15 *Asociación Profesional Elite Taxi*, 20 December 2017.

[41] A Chapuis-Doppler and V Delhomme, 'Regulating Composite Platform Economy Services: The State-of-Play after *Airbnb Ireland*' *European Papers European Forum* (12 May 2020) 14.

[42] C Busch, '"Self-Regulation and Regulatory Intermediation in the Platform Economy", When Product Liability Meets the Platform Economy: A European Perspective on *Oberdorf v Amazon*, Editorial' [2019] *Journal of European Consumer and Market Law* 173.

[43] As part of the ongoing review of the Vertical Block Exemption Regulation, respondents to the public consultation pointed to the increasing importance of online sales, including through online platforms as a major trend motivating the need for a revision. See Factual summary of the contributions received in the context of the open public consultation on the evaluation of the Vertical Block Exemption Regulation (EU) No 330/2010.

for the rights and obligations of both consumers and professionals using online platforms.[44]

Another relevant factor determining the role of private law in the online platform economy is the status of the providers on the 'supply side' of online platforms. Under EU law, a strict legal separation is maintained between the 'trader' and 'consumer' notions. This allows awarding additional protection to the weakest participants in economic life (ie private citizens acting as consumers) without the government interfering, ex ante, in the commercial relations between businesses. Competition law remains the sole horizontal backstop for ensuring optimal outcomes in the latter area. Notwithstanding that some EU Member States apply certain consumer protection laws equally to businesses, this tends to be predicated on those (particularly small) businesses effectively operating as consumers when they buy products and services. These protections can also be more restrained for businesses than for consumers. In its Impact Assessment underpinning the P2B Regulation, the European Commission noted, for example, that some Member States offer only some protections in B2B situations (eg rules on unfair contract terms) or extend these protections only to certain types of businesses (eg small- to medium-sized enterprises (SMEs) or microenterprises).[45] The limited government intervention in commercial relations between businesses is actually a result of governments' required respect for the fundamental right to conduct a business laid down in Article 16 of the EU Charter of Fundamental Rights and the associated freedom to contract. This fundamental right essentially requires government to refrain to the furthest extent possible from interfering in business and free competition, while protecting against abuse (ie within the bounds set by EU law and national law in accordance with EU law).[46]

In this context, courts play a key role in separating genuine innovation from potential definitional abuse, with the former potentially justifying a tailored regulatory approach and the latter rather requiring the enforcement of existing norms. Where professionals are concerned, they would accordingly be expected to autonomously secure their business interests, relying on private law-based, commercial negotiations.

An appropriate delineation of the notion of 'intermediation' done by online platforms should accordingly mean that (i) the 'sell-side' of the platform consist of professionals rather than individuals acting in a private capacity and (ii) these professionals can to some extent manage their customer relationships. Subject to

[44] See also P Iamiceli, 'Online Platforms and the Digital Turn in EU Contract Law: Unfair Practices, Transparency and the (Pierced) Veil of Digital Immunity' (2019) 15(4) *European Review of Contract Law*, DOI: https://doi.org/10.1515/ercl-2019-0024.

[45] 'Impact Assessment Annexes accompanying the document proposal for a Regulation of the European Parliament and of the Council on promoting fairness and transparency for business users of online intermediation services' SWD (2018) 138 final Part 2/2, 90–91.

[46] For more details on the Freedom to conduct a business, see European Union Agency for Fundamental Rights, 'Freedom to Conduct a Business: Exploring the Dimensions of a Fundamental Right' (2015) 21, https://fra.europa.eu/sites/default/files/fra_uploads/fra-2015-freedom-conduct-business_en.pdf. See also Explanations relating to the Charter of Fundamental Rights [2007] OJ C303/2.

those requirements, one could maintain that there is no question of invalidity of the private law contracts used in the online platform economy. This validity and enforceability of contracts is crucial to retain the benefits of online platforms. The unilaterally determined contracts namely form the basis of online platforms' ability to have large communities of sellers and consumers abide by a centrally determined set of rules. This, in turn, is a prerequisite to efficiently 'regulating' online platforms, such that they in themselves constitute safe and trusted ecosystems.

However, those entirely new professions, like app developers, that the online platform economy has created suggest that the answer is not as simple as saying that platforms do not restrict their users' business freedom, as they would always be able to use alternative online and offline sales channels. These professional users invest money and, most importantly, time to develop the necessary skills to build up online customer bases; these investments cannot simply be written off or recouped by shifting volumes to different outlets.

Traditional objectives also change. As mentioned above, healthy and competitive platform ecosystems require the kindling of febrile trust on all sides of these multisided ecosystems. And the central intermediaries are naturally incentivised and best placed to engage in the required continuous regulation of their private marketplaces, something that government could never (or should not want to) replicate through public enforcement. In this context, EU rules can complement private regulation by providing harmonised standards that set the outer bounds of P2B behaviour. EU and national competition rules in addition are used to tackle case-by-case abuse of a dominant position.

In addition to unilateral trading practices, the Commission's Impact Assessment underpinning the P2B Regulation identifies a general lack of redress as a second part of a three-pronged problem statement, with emerging legal fragmentation within the EU's internal market for online services making up the third leg.

This trust-undermining lack of redress results from a multilayered and nuanced legal design of today's cross-border online commerce. First, the business dependency identified above induces a fear of retaliation on the part of the professional users that rely on platforms for reaching their customers. The valid but imbalanced contracts these users have with online platforms in turn reduce the chances of successful court proceedings. An existing barrier to access to justice in particular for smaller businesses, which results from the relatively high cost and long duration of average court proceedings, compounds the ineffectiveness of redress. Added to all of this is the generalised use of exclusive choice of law and forum clauses in the inherently cross-border digital economy.[47] This particularity

[47] Virtually all online intermediation services that are available to EU business users and consumers have at least an office in the EU. However, their providers might still claim that those services are organised outside the EU and therefore, possibly justifiably, apply non-EU law and forum clauses. According to a recent study, around 30% of online intermediation services active in the EU are provided subject to such clauses. See S Krüger et al, 'Study on Contractual Relationships between Online Platforms and Their Professional Users FWC JUST/2015/PR/01/0003/Lot1-02 Final Report' (23 April 2018), https://publications.europa.eu/en/publication-detail/-/publication/b3d856d9-4885-11e8-be1d-01aa75ed71a1/language-en.

of the online platform economy complicates access to justice, as business users face the added difficulty of possibly having to retain specialised private international law counsel even to settle the complex question of whether their home state court, or in fact any EU court, could be competent notwithstanding an exclusive choice of forum clause pointing towards a foreign – or extra-EU – venue. A European Commission study in this regard estimates that international business-to-business cases are normally only brought to (foreign) courts if the amount involved is considerably in excess of €40,000.[48]

Amazon recently agreed to cease the use of exclusive choice of forum clauses in its settlement with the German Bundeskartellamt. The latter authority underlined in its press release the significant impact such clauses have even on businesses' perception of the availability of redress:

> Until now Luxembourg was specified as the only court of jurisdiction in the European terms of business applying to the marketplace as well as in the European terms of business for payment transactions. This provision made it difficult, in particular for smaller sellers, to even attempt to seek legal action.[49]

While they can indeed compound the barriers to accessing justice that professional users of platforms experience, it is important to recognise that the use of exclusive choice of forum clauses is not per se unfair or abusive.[50] This common practice among online platforms may in fact be an important way for smaller, start-up platforms to scale up while managing legal costs. Exclusive choice of court clauses may, moreover, help prevent fragmentation in the form of irreconcilable judgments within the EU's Single Market. EU and national rules of private international law recognise the importance of these contractual freedoms and rather formulate exceptions that serve to protect weaker parties such as consumers.

All of the above brings us to the premise of the present chapter, which entails that:

1. Platforms offer unparalleled efficiencies in terms of access to cross border consumer markets and have become the go-to interface for millions of successful firms;
2. The gateway position of online platforms is efficient: it enables platforms to organise ecosystems of millions of users, unilaterally imposing 'rules of the game' for all;
3. The EU has a vibrant online platform economy comprising over 10,000 platform companies, mainly start/scale-ups.[51]

[48] Commission, 'Accompanying document to the Proposal for a Council Decision on the Signing by the European Community of the Convention on Choice-of-Court Agreements – Summary of the impact assessment' COM (2008) 538 final (SEC (2008) 2389) 47.

[49] www.bundeskartellamt.de/SharedDocs/Meldung/EN/Pressemitteilungen/2019/17_07_2019_Amazon.html.

[50] For more information on this topic, see also Krüger et al (n 47).

[51] For the figure of 10,000 platform companies and further details on the online platform economy in the EU, see Commission, 'How do Online Platforms' (n 20).

However:

4. Online intermediation is a real and new phenomenon, but definitions can be misused;
5. Platforms' 'specialisation as a business model' induces dependencies, characterised by a lack of redress;
6. The cross-border nature of the online platform economy poses enforcement challenges and a fragmentation risk;
7. Important open questions remain.

This premise appears to also be reflected in the original problem statement formulated by the European Commission in its Impact Assessment underpinning the P2B Regulation, which identifies an 'underexploited potential of the online platform economy'. The negative consequences of this 'underexploitation' would directly affect professional users as well as the online platforms themselves – reflecting the large mutual interest that these businesses have in effective, safe and trusted online ecosystems.

VI. The Future of EU Private Law

As explained in the previous section, online platforms both enable and shape cross-border entrepreneurship, marrying efficiency with a scope for abuse.

In this context, one could argue that for the professional participants in the online platform economy, their fundamental freedom to conduct a business takes on a new and different dimension. Instead of a right not to be subjected to undue government interference, they could actually demand that their public government intervenes in order to, in this case, set the outer bounds for platforms' unilateral behaviour – in addition to the existing 'competition law backstop'.

The P2B Regulation makes explicit reference to the freedom to conduct a business,[52] and this public framework for P2B relations indeed effectively rebalances the respective fundamental freedom to conduct a business of platforms with that of their professional users.

The EU's approach taken in the P2B Regulation can in this regard be perceived as 'hands off', although it does recognise the paradigm shift in economic organisation that the online platform economy represents, and in itself constitutes a real solution.[53] Indeed, the P2B Regulation could be said to reflect a careful balance between the right to 'non-interference' and the right to 'non-domination' that are incorporated into the fundamental right to conduct a business,[54] instead of a shift

[52] P2B Regulation 2019/1150, recital 52.

[53] See also J Campos Carvalho, 'Online Platforms: Concept, Role in the Conclusion of Contracts and Current Legal Framework in Europe', https://doi.org/10.20318/cdt.2020.5227.

[54] E Gill-Pedro, 'Freedom to Conduct a Business in EU Law: Freedom from Interference of Freedom from Domination?' (2017) 9(2) *European Journal of Legal Studies* 103, https://cadmus.eui.eu/bitstream/handle/1814/46070/EJLS_2017_Gill.pdf?sequence=1&isAllowed=y.

in favour of either of these two concepts. This careful balancing is also paramount to safeguarding the interests of consumers, which can be affected indirectly by P2B commercial behaviour.[55]

Provided it is effectively enforced, the law seeks to leverage transparency in order to facilitate competition by the EU's strong pipeline of platform start-ups. Precisely for this purpose, the P2B Regulation does not horizontally exempt SMEs. It is indeed vital that all of the EU's 10,000+ platforms are associated with the 'quality label' of the P2B Regulation, which is, moreover, relatively easy to comply with as it mostly requires one-off changes to platforms' general terms and conditions. The additional transparency that the P2B Regulation should yield will then provide additional parameters for platform competition, for example on 'business-friendliness', and it could unleash a serious conditioning pressure in the form of potential and actual competition by this rich pipeline of EU platforms. An interesting example of this effect could already be observed around the time of the adoption of the Commission's proposal for the Regulation, when the so-called 'Marketplace Coalition' was formed, which sought to set its non-vertically integrated platform members apart from those online platforms that both operate the marketplace and compete in it. In its inaugural press release, it indeed mentions:

> The Marketplace Coalition is unique because our members focus on empowering third-party sellers of all sizes. These marketplaces provide access to technology tools and services that enable businesses and particularly small sellers to reach consumers around the globe. Marketplace Coalition members don't compete with these sellers.[56]

This approach is consistent with the premise that the online platform business model is overwhelmingly positive, and requires further support. The Single Market legal basis of the Regulation, Article 114 TFEU, reflects this premise. This logic is, however, no less revolutionary; rather than removing existing legal barriers that hamper the Single Market, the Regulation qualifies the online platform business model as a pillar of the Digital Single Market. It aims to buttress that pillar by preventing emerging and future legal fragmentation that could threaten the ability of start-up platforms to scale up and compete with the incumbents – to the detriment of innovation and consumer welfare.

Another reason the P2B Regulation could be perceived to be light of touch, or hands-off, is that it does not directly address all the constituent elements of the established redress problem. Given that, for example, the widespread use of exclusive choice of law or forum clauses can complicate businesses' access to justice, one could have imagined the introduction of a standalone private international law regime, possibly including an outright prohibition of such clauses. However, in line with its stated objective to promote cross-border trade enabled by online platforms, the P2B Regulation leaves the existing rules of EU and national private

[55] I Graef, 'Differentiated Treatment in Platform-to-Business Relations: EU Competition Law and Economic Dependence' (2019) 38 *Yearbook of European Law* 448, https://doi.org/10.1093/yel/yez008.

[56] See www.themarketplacecoalition.com/blog/launching-a-new-coalition.

international law intact in the online platform economy. The reasoning behind this approach points to two other platform specificities, concerning, first, the type of problems and, secondly, the desired redress. Take the example of app stores; among millions of apps, hundreds of thousands of developers and equally many daily product launches, technical and other problems are constant factors. What both developer and platform need in the vast majority of cases is highly efficient prioritisation and, above all, speedy redress – think minutes rather than weeks. Another specificity is, interestingly enough, the amplification of the fear of retaliation caused by the (frequently) particularly imbalanced relationships between business users and the central intermediaries. This fear of retaliation compounds existing barriers to access justice, both real and perceived, including cost, duration and complexity – the latter especially in the cross-border context of online platform-intermediated trade. Such barriers to accessing justice are indeed a horizontal problem and known from other B2B 'areas' such as late payment, where a recent study notes that:

> Businesses have low incentives for objecting against 'grossly unfair' or 'unfair' contractual terms and practices. The reluctance of companies to bring cases to court and the fear of damaging business relationships remain the main obstacles. Litigation regarding unfair contractual terms and practices normally does not take place, being too costly, ineffective (due to the length of the proceeding) or damaging for smaller companies.[57]

The online platform economy therefore calls for a strong problem-driven approach, which strictly separates online-specific problems and solutions from horizontal ones where digital-only approaches actually do risk creating inconsistencies and uncertainties. In short, government regulation is a prerequisite for a healthy online platform economy, but its ability to precisely circumscribe problems is, arguably, more decisive for innovation than ever before.

The P2B Regulation does indeed address the redress issue in a manner tailored to the online platform economy, by placing bilateral, internal and voluntary dispute settlement at its core. At the same time, it leverages existing rules of private international law for (private) enforcement purposes. By leaving those existing rules of private international law untouched, the P2B Regulation in addition supports the broader interests of EU businesses in maintaining full respect for party autonomy. This lofty diagnosis of course requires explanation. Again, it is important to (re)turn to a specificity of the online platform economy, which is that larger firms, too, tend to accept platforms' unilaterally determined contracts. Such firms equally rely on the existing private international law rules to streamline their legal operations, for example by negotiating exclusive choice of forum and law clauses, for intra-EU as well as extra-EU trade. The P2B Regulation therefore aligns with the EU's broader policy of maintaining the utmost respect for the rule

[57] See, in particular VVA and Milieu, 'Business-to-business Transactions: A Comparative Analysis of Legal Measures vs Soft-Law Instruments for Improving Payment Behaviour' (8 August 2018) 46, https://publications.europa.eu/en/publication-detail/-/publication/c8b7391b-9b80-11e8-a408-01aa75ed71a1.

of law at home, and of allowing this area of freedom and justice to be 'exported' by EU businesses operating abroad. Important international developments are worth mentioning in this respect: the People's Republic of China signed the Choice of Court Convention in December 2017, and the first case under this Convention followed in 2018,[58] while the Netherlands established a 'semi-public' court for private international commercial disputes.[59] The second leg of the explanation concerns enforcement; the P2B Regulation brings infringements of its provisions outside the contractual realm of the P2B relationship by giving representative bodies direct standing in EU courts. Exclusive choice of court clauses pointing to extra-EU venues cannot, therefore, be used to undermine the effective enforcement of the P2B Regulation. By virtue of its direct effect, the P2B Regulation will in addition be an integral part of all Member States' legal systems, which means that online platforms remain free to use exclusive choice of law (and court) clauses within the EU. Finally, exclusive choice of law clauses applying non-EU law will not prevent the applicability – in parallel with online platforms' private law contracts – of the P2B Regulation. This results from the public order nature of the latter. This approach finds its legal basis in the CJEU *Ingmar* judgment,[60] and is reflected in recitals 6 and 7, which include references to the public policy objective and mandatory nature of the rules, as well as in Article 1(2) of the P2B Regulation, which sets out its intra-EU geographic scope as well as its application 'irrespective of the law otherwise applicable'. Similar to the *Ingmar* case, which concerned protections afforded to commercial agents operating within the EU, the P2B Regulation respects party autonomy, but provides a certain minimum 'safety net' for businesses from which private contracts cannot detract. This safety net serves the broader public policy objective of ensuring 'healthy', cross-border online ecosystems as positive drivers of the EU's Single Market. This approach should be consistent with the rules of private international law for the following two reasons: first, the Regulation merely rebalances the respective fundamental freedoms to conduct a business of platforms and their business users, thereby safeguarding party autonomy. The application of the P2B Regulation therefore does not override the substantive matters that platforms' contracts regulate. Secondly, the geographic application of the P2B Regulation is strictly limited to intra-EU online commerce, namely the provision of goods and services by businesses established in the EU to consumers present in the EU (at least for part of the transaction[61]). The fact that online platforms can nonetheless fall within the

[58] See www.hcch.net/en/publications-and-studies/details4/?pid=6616&dtid=55.

[59] See www.rechtspraak.nl/English/NCC/Pages/default.aspx.

[60] Case C-381/98 *Ingmar GB*, 9 November 2000.

[61] This is meant to cover the situation in which non-EU residents are temporarily present in the EU, during which time they consume goods and services. This could, for example, apply to foreign tourists. WeChat's 'WeGoEU' is an example of a non-EU platform that can in this manner intermediate EU businesses and consumers present in the EU. See https://wegoeu.com/.

scope of the P2B Regulation even where they are not domiciled in the EU in this regard simply reflects the global nature of the online platform economy, without implying in any way an extraterritorial effect of EU law.

Ideally, this private enforcement mechanism will allow the necessary case-by-case and gradual developments of de facto standards for platform obligations, such as 'swift and effective complaints handling', 'ranking transparency' and 'contractual predictability'. To prevent conflicting or inconsistent judgments, existing coordination and harmonisation tools will of course be available, including the existing EU rules of private international law and the role of the Court of Justice of the European Union as a harmonising force through preliminary references. To fully vindicate the EU's approach (and to render this chapter even more lofty), an increased use of the existing rules of private international law in the internal market would in the process strengthen mutual cooperation and trust in the EU's area of freedom and justice – for example, through using the possibility to hear and determine related actions together pursuant to Article 30(3) of Regulation (EU) 1215/2012 on jurisdiction and the recognition and enforcement of judgments in civil and commercial matters (Brussels I bis).[62]

Turning to the concrete commercial relationship between a platform and its business users, the P2B Regulation should change the 'private law status quo' in three important ways.

First, it requires online platform providers to fill any contractual 'gaps' that may exist today on key commercial issues, including ranking, ancillary goods and services (eg bundled offers from online travel agents), differentiation, data access and cross-platform restrictions (eg most-favoured nation clauses). Subject to the horizontally applicable requirement of Article 3(1)(a), they should in addition do so in 'plain and intelligible' language. The ranking of businesses' goods and services, platforms' access to and use of data and differentiated treatment applied to equivalent situations, including by using ranking and data access practices, are currently especially 'black-box' items. Additional clarity and competition on these key competitive parameters will be particularly important for fostering trust. Importantly, the EU legislators have explained that online platforms should inform their business users of the main parameters used to determine ranking. By setting out these key determinants in the contract, ranking should also happen in a non-arbitrary manner.[63] What is more, real added value can be provided to

[62] Regulation (EU) 1215/2012 on jurisdiction and the recognition and enforcement of judgments in civil and commercial matters (Brussels I bis) [2012] OJ L 351/1. Art 30(3) reads: 'For the purposes of this Article, actions are deemed to be related where they are so closely connected that it is expedient to hear and determine them together to avoid the risk of irreconcilable judgments resulting from separate proceedings.'

[63] P2B Regulation 2019/1150, recital 24.

business users through the very fact of identifying a limited set of the most heavily weighed parameters out of a possibly much larger number of parameters that have some impact on ranking. This at the same time means that compliance with the transparency obligation is possible without affecting platforms' possibly applicable intellectual property rights. The P2B Regulation rather sets out that 'consideration of the commercial interests of providers of online intermediation services or online search engines should, therefore, never lead to a refusal to disclose the main parameters'.[64]

Secondly, the scope for definitional abuse should be reduced because of increased contractual clarity around the role of the intermediary. In this regard, Article 3(5) of the P2B Regulation is particularly interesting, as it requires online platforms to ensure that business users are afforded the appropriate 'direct exposure' to consumers that the online intermediation business model promises.

Thirdly and finally, as mentioned above, the regulation provides business associations with a right of representative standing before EU courts, which will allow them to ensure platform providers stick to the letter of their (transparent and intelligible) contracts.

Relative to the present situation, this amounts to altogether activating EU private law in a relatively immature area that has so far been characterised by unclear contracts offering virtually no rights and being practically unenforceable before home state (or even EU) courts. In addition to activating EU private law, the enhanced transparency that large online platforms will equally have to provide around key commercial questions such as access to data can help inform competition enforcement and thereby indirectly contribute to achieving the required balance between the respective freedoms to conduct a business of platforms and their professional users. Some argue in this respect that the very fundamentals of platform competition actually contributed to global platform dominance.[65]

Reputational levers will in turn be pushed, to ultimately engender a rebalancing of contractual rights and obligations between online platforms and business users. Elaborating substantive, private 'platform regulation' in this indirect manner should then allow online platform companies to develop balanced rules that duly reflect the interests of all sides of their multisided marketplaces. In this context, private law courts in platforms' home EU Member States could then effectively take up a role similar to that of the CJEU, guiding and harmonising the private regulatory platform case law.

[64] ibid recital 27.

[65] AD Chirita, 'Abusive Global Platform Dominance or Competition on the Merits?' (31 October 2019) Durham Law School Research Paper 2019, 3, https://ssrn.com/abstract=3540987 or http://dx.doi.org/10.2139/ssrn.3540987.

This is not to say that no open questions remain. Illegal content continues to proliferate online, deep learning techniques become increasingly pervasive and the concentration of economic power in the (private) hands of a handful of online platforms could have important implications for innovation.[66] Importantly, however, the P2B approach does not exclude additional, other or complementary rules and enforcement actions by public governments to regulate the online platform economy. The European Commission is reflecting on all of these emerging issues and opportunities, and has already announced an update to the by now decades old e-Commerce Directive, an ex ante regulatory framework for a limited set of gatekeeper platforms, and a legal framework for the ethical use of artificial intelligence.[67]

Is the future already here? Trust issues have arguably held back the large-scale deployment of the online platform business model in industry, as already noted in a Commission study on B2B e-markets from 2007.[68] If anything, the opportunities for achieving efficiencies in linear, sector-specific supply chains make it more likely than in the B2C area that large, multi-service platform ecosystems naturally form around the already centrally operating original equipment manufacturers. Market discovery, B2B procurement, accounting, payment and invoicing, and data-as-a-service could efficiently be packaged into a packaged 'solution' – one which, moreover, coincides in time with a true climate emergency which could accelerate wholesale reform (just think of what 3D printing and factory-as-a-service could mean for logistics and warehousing). What remains unanswered is the question of whether the central intermediary will in that case be a horizontally active software company such as SAP, which could leverage the €3 trillion B2B procurement volume intermediated by its Ariba B2B marketplace, or a sectorial incumbent such as Airbus, which has the potential to bring the entire spare parts market on board its Satair B2B marketplace.[69] The answer will have important implications for competition.

[66] See, in particular, Crémer et al (n 13); Stigler Center, 'Stigler Committee on Digital Platforms Final Report' (2019), https://research.chicagobooth.edu/-/media/research/stigler/pdfs/digital-platforms – committee-report – stigler-center.pdf?la=en&hash=2D23583FF8BCC560B7FEF7A81E1F95C1DDC5225E&hash=2D23583FF8BCC560B7FEF7A81E1F95C1DDC5225E.

[67] The various initiatives are included in the European Commission's Digital Strategy, 'Shaping Europe's Digital Future' COM (2020) 67 final. Specifically on the two initiatives included in the Digital Services Act package, see the respective Inception Impact Assessments: Digital Services Act – deepening the internal market and clarifying responsibilities for digital services; Digital Services Act package – ex ante regulatory instrument of very large online platforms acting as gatekeepers.

[68] S Van Eecke, 'B2B e-Marketplaces – a Legal Analysis of Unfair Trade Practices within the European Union' (26 April 2007), https://publications.europa.eu/en/publication-detail/-/publication/43eab44c-4ae2-4929–8b99-0ee0c8b12eef/language-en.

[69] SAP's Ariba offers what could be considered an online marketplace for B2B procurement. Airbus's Satair offers spare parts services, including what could equally be described as an online marketplace. See www.ariba.com/about; www.satair.com/products.

VII. Conclusion

Regardless of how it will evolve precisely, the online platform economy – or simply the economy – will drive the future of EU private law. The P2B Regulation is an important case study on this effect. EU private law is 'unleashed' in relation to key commercial issues such as online visibility and differentiated treatment, in order to ensure more sustainable outcomes. The fact that the future of EU private law is digital especially holds true if the premise of this chapter continues to apply, entailing that the online platform business model is overwhelmingly beneficial and requires further support, including through (harmonised) rule setting.

8

Blockchain Law: Between Public and Private, Transnational and Domestic

GEORGIOS DIMITROPOULOS*

I. Introduction

Bitcoin and cryptocurrencies emerged during the global financial crisis of 2008.[1] Bitcoin was an effort to bypass the mainstream global financial system. Bitcoin and its background technology, blockchain, are at the same time the product of globalisation; they are a fundamentally global technology purporting to bypass national and physical boundaries. Cryptocurrencies and blockchain technology are both symptoms and promoters of a globalised world.

Since the creation of bitcoin, the importance of cryptocurrencies has been increasing. The price of bitcoin exceeded the price of gold on 3 March 2017.[2] Cryptocurrencies have multiplied exponentially since.[3] This explosion of the cryptocurrency market has led to the expected regulatory backlash: a reaction by governments around the world to protect national interests and re-embed money into national jurisdictions.[4] The response has taken multiple shapes, and largely depends on how the relevant national legal orders perceive the nature of cryptocurrencies and their underlying blockchain technology. While the initial focus of regulators and scholarship was mostly on cryptocurrencies, the focus is

* I had the chance to present an earlier version of this chapter and receive valuable comments from participants at the 'The Future of EU Private Law' conference, 8 February 2019, at King's College London. I am most grateful to Takis Tridimas, Mateja Durovic and Bilyana Petkova for wonderful comments. The usual disclaimer applies.

[1] S Nakamoto, 'Bitcoin: A Peer-to-Peer Electronic Cash System' (2008), https://bitcoin.org/bitcoin.pdf/.

[2] The price closed at $1268, while a troy ounce of gold stood at $1233.

[3] The website CoinMarketCap lists more than 2371: see https://coinmarketcap.com/all/views/all/.

[4] G Dimitropoulos, 'Global Currencies and Domestic Regulation: Embedding through Enabling?' in P Hacker, I Lianos, G Dimitropoulos and S Eich (eds), *Regulating Blockchain: Techno-Social and Legal Challenges* (Oxford, Oxford University Press, 2019) 112.

starting to shift towards the technology supporting cryptocurrencies: blockchain technology and the related blockchain markets are becoming more important.[5] Various types of laws come into play for the regulation of blockchain: most importantly, data protection laws, and, within the European Union, the General Data Protection Regulation (GDPR).[6] There is a potential conflict between blockchain technology and the GDPR when it comes to two of blockchain's most important features: the visibility of information on blockchain for every node that participates in the blockchain network and the non-removable nature of information on blockchain – a subsequent transaction can annul the first transaction, but the first transaction will always remain in the chain.

Blockchain technology is a general-purpose technology that can be used to achieve multiple goals; while it was initially developed as bitcoin blockchain to bypass financial institutions and central banks, it was later adopted by private and public actors. Both the private sector and the government already have or are in the process of adopting the technology. The adoption of blockchain, particularly by government, does not come without its perks. Trust in and through government is in the process of being replaced by trust in blockchain. For this reason, scholars have suggested that blockchain and other distributed ledgers are 'the strongest challenge ever posed to the monopoly of the state over the promulgation, formation, keeping and verification of institutions and the public record'.[7]

Blockchain even goes beyond replacement of trust in and through government. According to one of the developers of the Ethereum blockchain, blockchain creates a 'new kind of legal system'.[8] Drawing on the notion of *lex informatica*,[9] scholars today speak of the development of a *lex cryptographia* within blockchain – defined as 'rules administered through self-executing smart contracts and decentralized (autonomous) organizations'.[10] Blockchain is a case of code as law, but also a new application of law as code.[11] The law of blockchain is shaped by

[5] 'With significant benefits in sight, the overall market for blockchain is expected to boom with some estimates projecting growth of blockchain technology from USD $411.5 million in 2017 to $7.68 billion by 2022': see www.marketsandmarkets.com/PressReleases/blockchain-technology.asp.

[6] Regulation (EU) 2016/679 of the European Parliament and of the Council of 27 April 2016 on the protection of natural persons with regard to the processing of personal data and on the free movement of such data, and repealing Directive 95/46/EC (General Data Protection Regulation) of April 2016.

[7] B Markey-Towler, 'Anarchy, Blockchain and Utopia: A Theory of Political-Socioeconomic Systems Organised using Blockchain' (2 January 2018) 1, https://ssrn.com/abstract=3095343.

[8] 'The Future of the Blockchain: Interview with Ethereum Co-founder Gavin Wood' (*Simpleweb*, 18 September 2017), https://simpleweb.co.uk/the-future-of-the-blockchain-interview-with-ethereum-co-founder-gavin-wood/.

[9] JR Reidenberg, 'Lex Informatica: The Formulation of Information Policy Rules through Technology' (1998) 76 *Texas Law Review* 553.

[10] A Wright and P De Filippi, 'Decentralized Blockchain Technology and the Rise of Lex Cryptographia' (10 March 2015) 4, https://ssrn.com/abstract=2580664.

[11] See generally P De Filippi and A Wright, *Blockchain and the Law: The Rule of Code* (Cambridge, MA, Harvard University Press, 2018); K Yeung, 'Regulation by Blockchain: The Emerging Battle for Supremacy between the Code of Law and Code as Law' (2018) 82 *Modern Law Review* 2017; C Reyes, 'Moving beyond Bitcoin to an Endogenous Theory of Decentralized Ledger Technology Regulation: An

the nature of the technology and its uses, as well as the efforts at various levels of governance to regulate it. It is thus a combination of transnational, domestic and international law; it is, moreover, a combination of public and private law. This chapter focuses on the nature of the interaction between blockchain technology and the *lex cryptographia* of the digital world, on the one side, and the ordinary law of the physical world, on the other. It presents three phases of such interaction: the anarcho-libertarian phase; the mainstreaming phase; and the maturity phase. The different phases present a different mix between public and private, transnational and domestic laws and values. The EU has recently intervened and is in the process of developing an EU-wide blockchain infrastructure. Blockchain law, like the law of the interaction between *lex cryptographia* and the mainstream legal system,[12] is in the process of being developed, and this chapter suggests that it should feature the following three characteristics:[13] enabling public and permissionless blockchains; allowing for trust in blockchain to operate with the support of governmental trust; and bridging the gaps and creating interoperability between the public and the private, as well as the physical and the non-physical world.

The chapter proceeds as follows: section II discusses the rise and the techno-legal nature of blockchain technology and cryptocurrencies, highlighting their global nature. Section III delves into the responses by the legal orders to the development of blockchain technology and the rise of cryptocurrencies. Section IV presents the interaction between the ordinary 'physical' legal order and blockchain technology. After presenting a typology of the interaction between the law of the analogue and the digital crypto-world, it makes suggestions regarding the future development of blockchain law.

II. The Rise of Blockchain Technology and Cryptocurrencies

While cryptocurrencies have helped spearhead blockchain technology, blockchain technology is much more than a technology for cryptocurrencies. Blockchain technology can help transfer any type of data, including the transfer of digitised value. In particular, public permissionless blockchains are a general-purpose

Initial Proposal' (2016) 61 *Villanova Law Review* 191; C Reyes, 'Conceptualizing Cryptolaw' (2017) 96 *Nebraska Law Review* 384. Generally on the interplay between code and regulation (law), see L Lessig, *Code and Other Laws of Cyberspace* (New York, Basic Books, 1999).

[12] *cf* also S Blemus, 'Law and Blockchain: A Legal Perspective on Current Regulatory Trends Worldwide' [2017] *Revue Trimestrielle de Droit Financier* 1; Reyes, 'Conceptualizing Cryptolaw' (n 11); U Rodrigues, 'Law and the Blockchain' (2018) 104 *Iowa Law Review* 679; P Quintais, B Bodó, A Giannopoulou and V Ferrari, 'Blockchain and the Law: A Critical Evaluation' (2019) *Stanford Journal of Blockchain Law & Policy*, https://stanford-jblp.pubpub.org/pub/blockchain-and-law-evaluation.

[13] See also G Dimitropoulos, 'The Law of Blockchain' (2020) 95 *Washington Law Review* 1117, https://digitalcommons.law.uw.edu/wlr/vol95/iss3/3.

technology that can be used to achieve multiple goals. The present section showcases some features of blockchain technology that make it a global technology, as well as the characteristics of cryptocurrencies that make them global currencies.

A. Blockchain Technology as a Global Technology

(i) The Development of Blockchain Technology and Blockchain Types

A blockchain is a digital ledger in the form of a secure sequence – a 'chain' – of blocks.[14] Technologically, it relies on Distributed Ledger Technology (DLT), which can record transactions between parties in a secure and permanent way. Blockchain technology has certain features that differentiate it from other digital technologies. The first defining feature of blockchain is decentralisation. Blockchain relies on a decentralised peer-to-peer network based on DLT. Each participant maintains a copy of a shared ledger of digitally signed transactions. Second, all copies are maintained in synch through a consensus protocol in the form of Proof of Work or Proof of Stake, which is used to achieve consensus. Each node in the network must solve a complex and resource-intensive cryptographic problem to ensure all are in synchrony. Third, the electronic ledger is tamper-proof, in the sense that transactions in blockchain are generally irreversible.

There are two main types of blockchain:[15] public and private. For public blockchains, there is no specific entity that manages the digital platform; in the case of private blockchains, the ledger is controlled by a single entity – or managed by a consortium of companies. There are, moreover, permissionless and permissioned blockchains. Permissionless blockchains are accessible by everyone, whereas for permissioned blockchains access restrictions can be imposed on who can access and change the blocks. Two of the most popular blockchains, Bitcoin and Ethereum, are public permissionless blockchains. They can be accessed and used by any person – with access to a computer – anywhere in the world.

(ii) Range of Applications

Blockchain is a general-purpose technology, particularly in its public permissionless form. Blockchain technology has a very wide range of applications. Blockchain

[14] See generally (on how both bitcoin and, more generally, blockchain technology work) A Narayanan et al, *Bitcoin and Cryptocurrency Technologies: A Comprehensive Introduction* (Princeton, Princeton University Press, 2016); SP Williams, *Blockchain: The Next Everything* (New York, Scribner, 2019).

[15] On the categories of public and private, as well as permissionless and permissioned blockchains, see, eg K Wüst and A Gervais, 'Do You Need a Blockchain?' in *2018 Crypto Valley Conference on Blockchain Technology (CVCBT)* (Zug, 2018) 45, http://ieeexplore.ieee.org/stamp/stamp.jsp?tp=&arnumber=8525392&isnumber=8525381.

can replace paper-based documents with digital documents with the additional advantage that these documents are then also stored as a tamper-proof ledger. Businesses in almost all industries are exploring ways to take advantage of these features of blockchain technology. In addition, governments are also trying to stay on top of these developments and explore the opportunities that blockchain technology may provide for the offering of government services.

In the private sector, blockchain technology is increasingly being used to support smart contracts. The concept of the smart contract was developed in the mid-1990s.[16] A smart contract is a self-executing 'contract', whereby the terms of the agreement between the two parties is directly written into code, reducing transaction costs and facilitating transactions without third-party intervention. However,

> The term 'smart contract' is, in fact, a misnomer: smart contracts are neither 'smart' (there is no cognitive or artificial intelligence component to them, only the automatic execution of a pre-defined task when certain conditions are met), nor are they contracts in a legal sense.[17]

A smart contract using blockchain is a way of making an agreement that is fulfilled as soon as certain predetermined conditions are satisfied, and taking advantage of the features of blockchain.[18] Smart contracts were first introduced in blockchain technology in 2015 by Ethereum, and are being increasingly intertwined with blockchain technology. They have become a functionality of blockchain, currently considered as one of its most promising features. A blockchain-based smart contract can be coded between any party in the world, independent of their physical location.

Another very promising area of application of blockchain technology is that of supply chain management and logistics, and all related applications in international business transactions. According to the World Economic Forum, 'Reducing supply chain barriers to trade could increase global gross domestic product (GDP) by nearly 5 per cent and global trade by 15 per cent'.[19] Global supply chains are

[16] The concept was introduced and developed by cryptographer Nick Szabo in various publications during the nineties: see N Szabo, 'Smart Contracts: Building Blocks for Digital Markets' (1996), www.fon.hum.uva.nl/rob/Courses/InformationInSpeech/CDROM/Literature/LOTwinterschool2006/szabo.best.vwh.net/smart_contracts_2.html.

[17] Deloitte, 'Blockchain, Legal Implications, Questions, Opportunities and Risks' (May 2019), www2.deloitte.com/content/dam/Deloitte/za/Documents/legal/za_legal_implications_of_blockchain_14052019.pdf.

[18] See generally R Brownsword, 'Regulatory Fitness: Fintech, Funny Money, and Smart Contracts' (2019) 20 *European Business Organization Law Review* 5; R Brownsword, 'Smart Contracts: Coding the Transaction, Decoding the Legal Debates' in Hacker et al (n 8) 311; LA DiMatteo, M Cannarsa and C Poncibò (eds), *Cambridge Handbook of Smart Contracts, Blockchain Technology and Digital Platforms* (Cambridge, Cambridge University Press, 2019).

[19] World Economic Forum (in collaboration with Bain & Company and World Bank), *Enabling Trade: Valuing Growth Opportunities* (2013), www3.weforum.org/docs/WEF_SCT_EnablingTrade_Report_2013.pdf.

very complex due to the involvement of diverse stakeholders and intermediaries across many different jurisdictions. Blockchain can cope with this complexity.[20] It can help interconnect the various involved parties independent of the jurisdiction in which they are located, as well as independent of whether they are government or private. All stakeholders can view and have online access to bills of lading and other data related documentation, as well as the status of customs documents. Blockchain technology ensures data exchange in a secure way and a repository of information which is tamper-proof for multiple transactions across various systems throughout the world.

The application of the technology is fast transitioning from the private to the public sector, as governments around the world do not want to be left behind when it comes to the use of the technology. The public sector is responsible for many areas of trust.[21] This type of trust may now be secured by blockchain. Many government-related services could thus be provided without the involvement of government – at least in the same way that government is involved today. As *The Economist* put it a couple of years ago, 'an anti-establishment technology faces an ironic turn of fortune':[22] the use of blockchain by the state apparatus. Important public sector applications are identity management and attestation; the keeping of government records, such as land registration and corporate registration records; citizen services management in areas such as healthcare; and the conduct of government activities, such as voting, taxation, customs and public procurement.[23]

Regarding identity management and attestation, legal documents often require notarisation of signatures attesting to the identity of the signer. More than 1.1 billion individuals do not have any official identity documents at all.[24] Many public and private institutions have been trying to remedy this. For example, the Digital Identity Alliance, or ID2020 Alliance – an organisation affiliated with the United Nations – seeks to provide proof of identity to people without an official form of identification. Blockchain has been used to create secure digital identities and as a proof of identity. The ID2020 Alliance is an initiative of governments, non-governmental organisations and the private sector to provide a blockchain-based framework for digital identity that will be personal, persistent, portable and private. Two private companies involved in the ID2020 Alliance are Microsoft and

[20] 'Just as the Internet began a revolution of communication, blockchain technology could disrupt current business practices and models': DHL Trend Research, 'Blockchain in Logistics' (2018) 4, www.logistics.dhl/content/dam/dhl/global/core/documents/pdf/glo-core-blockchain-trend-report.pdf.

[21] See also section IVB below.

[22] 'Governments May Be Big Backers of the Blockchain' *The Economist* (1 June 2017), www.economist.com/news/business/21722869-anti-establishment-technology-faces-ironic-turn-fortune-governments-may-be-big-backers.

[23] See J Woods, 'Blockchain: Public Sector Use Cases' *CryptoOracle* (2 October 2018), https://medium.com/crypto-oracle/blockchain-public-sector-use-cases-49a2d74ad946.

[24] See www.worldbank.org/en/news/press-release/2017/10/12/11-billion-invisible-people-without-id-are-priority-for-new-high-level-advisory-council-on-identification-for-development.

Accenture. The ID2020 Alliance is expected to assist millions of refugees all over the world over the next few years.[25]

One may separate central bank uses of blockchain technology from other types of governmental uses.[26] Central banks all over the world have been working on the development of Central Bank Digital Currency (CBDC). Central bank-issued digital currency operates in a peer-to-peer and decentralised manner, may be made available for consumer use and could be used to complement or substitute for physical money and be an alternative to traditional bank deposits. Another use central banks have been experimenting with is wholesale CBDC, that is, central bank-issued digital currency that operates in a peer-to-peer and decentralised manner but is only available to commercial banks and clearing houses for use in the wholesale interbank market. The People's Bank of China (PBOC) has been developing the 'digital yuan' with the goal of improving the PBOC's ability to track money electronically as it changes hands, thus helping to combat money laundering and other illegal activities. Other examples include Uruguay's pilot program on the 'e-Peso', which is supported by the International Monetary Fund. Venezuela has developed the 'Petro', and Sweden's Riksbank has long been exploring an 'e-krona'. CBDCs are not cryptocurrencies; rather, they are digital blockchain-based fiat currencies, namely a digital form of blockchain-powered fiat money with legal tender status.

The plan for the creation of the digital yuan is to some extent a reaction to the plans of Facebook to create its own blockchain-based currency, 'Libra'. Libra is designed as a 'stablecoin', which has a steady value that is 100 per cent backed by a basket of securities and real-life currencies, such as the dollar, euro, pound and yen. Libra will be run by the Diem Association, an independent, not-for-profit membership organisation, headquartered in Geneva and supported by private companies, such as Facebook, Uber and Vodafone, and non-profit organisations.[27]

In other countries, blockchain is being used as part of a broader and overarching approach to public service delivery. Estonia was probably the first country to develop a vision for an e-state in the form of https://e-estonia.com/. This coincided with the popularisation of blockchain technology, and the Estonian government has been testing the technology since 2008. As of 2012, blockchain has been in

[25] See European Parliament Research Service (EPRS) – Scientific Foresight Unit (STOA), 'Technological Innovation for Humanitarian Aid and Assistance', PE 634.411 (May 2019) 57–58.

[26] Many more possible central bank uses may be identified, except for the ones mentioned in the body of the text: for example, interbank securities settlement, focused application of blockchain-based digital currency, including CBDC, enabling the rapid interbank clearing and settlement of securities for cash; central banks are, moreover, exploring use of the blockchain technologies for purposes of payment system resiliency and contingency, including cases of technical or network failure, natural disasters and cyberattacks. On this as well as on the central bank uses mentioned in the text, see A Lannquist, '10 Ways Central Banks are Experimenting with Blockchain' (*World Economic Forum*, 3 April 2019), www.weforum.org/agenda/2019/04/blockchain-distrubuted-ledger-technology-central-banks-10-ways-research/.

[27] PayPal, Stripe, eBay, Visa and Mastercard left the association in the last couple of months, despite having originally joined the association.

operational use in Estonia's registries and for a majority of government services, such as national health, judicial, legislative, security and commercial code systems. There are plans to extend its use to other spheres, such as personal medicine, cyber security and data embassies. For example, filing tax returns and buying a car can be done online in Estonia using blockchain for purposes of information accuracy. The vision in Estonia even goes beyond public service delivery; according to the former Estonian President Toomas Hendrik Ilves, 'Estonia is now a blockchain nation'.[28]

In a similar vein, Dubai wants blockchain technology to power its entire government, making Dubai the first 'city built on blockchain'.[29] The plan is to move all government documents to blockchain by 2020, and have 50 per cent of its services operating on a blockchain platform by 2021. Dubai has developed the umbrella initiative of Smart Dubai, which includes such other initiatives as Startup Support, the Happiness Agenda, the AI Lab and the Dubai Blockchain Strategy. It has, moreover, established the Global Blockchain Council founded by the Dubai Future Foundation. The government of the Emirate has also announced that it will introduce its own blockchain-based currency, 'emCash', to facilitate transactions in the public and private sectors in the country.[30]

There are many more cases of governments using the power of blockchain. Another very interesting example of a country embracing blockchain technology is Malta, which in 2018 put in place three legislative instruments for the promotion of new technologies, with an emphasis on the blockchain.[31] Georgia has, moreover, become the first country to register land titles using blockchain technology.[32]

The use of blockchain technology has moved to the international level and international organisations. International organisations have started using blockchain technology to pursue their own goals. In August 2018, the World Bank and CommBank from Australia launched bond-*i*, a blockchain-based debt instrument for bond issuance and bond life cycle management.[33] This concept could be popularised and applied to bonds issued and managed by sovereign states or international organisations.

Blockchain technology is a global technology that facilitates trade and transactions on a global scale. It may offer solutions particularly when it comes to international trade transactions between private parties and potentially also government-to-government interactions. It is, moreover, used to help national

[28] See https://medium.com/e-residency-blog/welcome-to-the-blockchain-nation-5d9b46c06fd4.

[29] See www.smartdubai.ae/initiatives/blockchain.

[30] Government of Dubai, 'Dubai Economy Launches Partnership to Expedite emCash' (*Altcoin News*, 26 September 2017), www.cryptocoinsnews.com/emcash-dubais-first-official-state-cryptocurrency/.

[31] Law 43 of 2018 – Innovative Technology Arrangements and Services Act, 2018; Law 44 of 2018 – Virtual Financial Assets Act, 2018; Law 45 of 2018 – Malta Digital Innovation Authority Act, 2018.

[32] See https://cointelegraph.com/news/georgia-becomes-first-country-to-register-property-on-blockchain.

[33] See www.worldbank.org/en/news/press-release/2019/08/16/world-bank-issues-second-tranche-of-blockchain-bond-via-bond-i.

governments facilitate the offering of services to their nationals, but also foreign citizens wanting to do business in or through countries other than those they are nationals of.[34]

B. Cryptocurrencies as Global Currencies

Domestic legal orders have had great issues in grappling with cryptocurrencies. Being global in nature, cryptocurrencies cannot be identified as legal tender in the same way as national currencies, or the euro in the euro area.[35] Different jurisdictions take different views on the legal nature of cryptocurrencies, sometimes treating them as money, sometimes treating them as commodities.[36] Others identify their nature by focusing on their background technology. This, of course, raises the regulatory question: there are different established practices and needs for the regulation of something depending on whether it is characterised as money, commodity or technology. In a continuum of regulatory approaches, regulation as money will have a tendency to be heavier and regulation as a commodity will have a tendency to be lighter, while regulation as a technology will have a tendency to be not restricting, but rather enabling of the technology, as well as the private companies that develop the technology.[37]

Various regulators around the world treat cryptocurrency as money. According to Financial Crimes Enforcement Network (FinCEN) in the USA, virtual currencies are mediums of exchange that operate like a currency without having all the features of real currency – above all, legal tender status; in particular, 'convertible' virtual currencies have an equivalent value in real currency, or may act as a substitute for real currency.[38] Similar approaches may be found in the EU as well. The German Federal Financial Supervisory Authority (Bundesamt für Finanzdienstleistungen) took a similar view as FinCEN in a communication on Bitcoins in December 2013, according to which Bitcoins are legally binding financial instruments in the form of units of account that are similar to foreign currencies.[39] Her Majesty's Revenue

[34] On Estonia's blockchain-based e-residency programme, see CL Sullivan and EW Burger, 'E-Residency and Blockchain. TPRC 44: The 44th Research Conference on Communication, Information and Internet Policy 2016' (31 March 2016), https://ssrn.com/abstract=2757492.

[35] Only the euro has legal tender status in the euro area; see Art 128(1) of the Treaty on the Functioning of the European Union (TFEU), which provides for the legal tender status of euro banknotes, as well as Art 11 of Regulation EC/974/98, which provides for the legal tender status of euro coin.

[36] See Dimitropoulos, 'Global Currencies' (n 4); see also N Vardi, 'Bit by Bit: Assessing the Legal Nature of Virtual Currencies' in G Gimigliano (ed), *Bitcoin and Mobile Payments: Constructing a European Union Framework* (London, Palgrave Macmillan, 2016).

[37] See section IIIB below.

[38] US Department of the Treasury, Financial Crimes Enforcement Network, 'Application of FinCEN's Regulations to Persons Administering, Exchanging, or Using Virtual Currencies' (2013) FIN-2013-G001, www.fincen.gov/sites/default/files/shared/FIN-2013-G001.pdf. This definition brings cryptocurrencies very close to actual money, but does not really equate them.

[39] J Münzer, 'Bitcoins: Aufsichtliche Bewertung und Risiken für Nutzer' (*Bafin.de*, 19 December 2013), www.bafin.de/SharedDocs/Veroeffentlichungen/DE/Fachartikel/2014/fa_bj_1401_bitcoins.html.

and Customs (HMRC) in the UK also treats cryptocurrencies as money for tax purposes.[40] In an important decision concerning the nature of Bitcoin and other cryptocurrencies in the EU legal order, the CJEU both implicitly and explicitly recognises them – including for tax (specifically VAT) purposes – as some form of money.[41] The CJEU uses the term 'traditional currency' for national currencies such as the Swedish krona, and the term 'non-traditional currency' for cryptocurrencies. According to the Court, non-traditional currencies are

> currencies other than those that are legal tender in one or more countries, insofar as those currencies have been accepted by the parties to a transaction as an alternative to legal tender and have no purpose other than to be a means of payment.[42]

It moreover explicitly denies them the nature of a good. Finally, it adjudicated that the provisions of the EU VAT Directive applying to traditional money also finds application in the case of virtual currencies.

Other jurisdictions – mostly outside of the EU – follow yet another approach by identifying cryptocurrencies as commodities.[43] The People's Bank of China (PBOC), together with four other Chinese regulators, issued a 'Notice on Precautions Against the Risks of Bitcoins'.[44] This notice denies cryptocurrencies the nature of money, as well as their ability to circulate in the market through financial institutions. In the USA, the Commodity Futures Trade Commission has also classified virtual currencies as commodities for the purposes of the Commodity Exchange Act of 1936.[45]

When identified as money or commodities, cryptocurrencies would generally be regulated in a restrictive way with legal orders limiting the ways they can be used, or imposing other types of restrictions. But cryptocurrencies, even when identified as money or commodities, are more than just that. Some countries, or certain regulators within some countries, have opted to focus on the underlying technology of cryptocurrencies. As will be highlighted in the next section, the jurisdictions that focus on the technology have adopted a more favourable approach to cryptocurrencies and their presence within their jurisdiction.

[40] HMRC, 'Bitcoin and Other Similar Cryptocurrencies' (*Gov.uk*, 3 March 2014) 9, www.gov.uk/government/publications/revenue-and-customs-brief-9-2014-bitcoin-and-other-cryptocurrencies.

[41] Judgment of the Court in Case C-264/14 (22 October 2015).

[42] ibid para 49.

[43] Bank of England economists have also identified virtual currencies as commodities: see R Ali, J Barrdear, R Clews and J Southgate, 'The Economics of Digital Currencies' (2014) Q3 *Quarterly Bulletin* 276.

[44] People's Bank of China, Ministry of Industry and Information Technology, China Banking Regulatory Commission, China Securities Regulatory Commission and China Insurance Regulatory Commission, 'Notice on Precautions against the Risks of Bitcoins' (2013) YIN FA, 2013, No 289, www.miit.gov.cn/n1146295/n1652858/n1652930/n3757016/c3762245/content.html.

[45] A Guadamuz and C Marsden, 'Blockchains and Bitcoin: Regulatory Responses to Cryptocurrencies' (2015) 20 *First Monday*.

III. The Law's Response

Even when blockchain technology is identified as a technology for regulatory purposes, different types of regulation will kick in. This is particularly the case with regard to privacy and data protection regulation. This section presents the response of legal orders to the rise of blockchain technology, and then to the rise of cryptocurrencies. Overall, a careful observation of the developments discussed in this and the previous section show a clear transition of the approaches by regulators from indifference, to recognition, to control and eventually to adoption by some of them.

A. Response to the Rise of Blockchain Technology

Data protection has been elevated to the status of a fundamental right in the EU, as well as elsewhere in the world. The protection of natural persons in relation to the processing of personal data is inscribed in Article 8(1) of the Charter of Fundamental Rights of the European Union, as well as Article 16(1) TFEU. The CJEU has famously adopted a broad interpretation of data protection. In the *Breyer* case, the relevant data protection-related legislation has found application in cases of dynamic IP addresses.[46] At the same time, the Court has acknowledged that storage of online data by government authorities might be necessary for protection from cyberattacks. Data protection laws may thus find application vis-à-vis the blockchain technology as well.[47]

The legally relevant question is to what extent data protection laws are applicable in the case of blockchain. The GDPR, which has applied in the EU since 25 May 2018, has a very broad scope of application. According to its Article 3, it applies in the 'processing of personal data in the context of the activities of an establishment of a controller or a processor in the Union, regardless of whether the processing takes place in the Union or not'. Article 3(2) GDPR moreover expands the applicability of the EU data protection regime to controllers without an establishment in the EU. The GDPR applies to such controllers if the processing concerns: (i) 'the offering of goods or services … to … data subjects in the EU'; and (ii) 'the monitoring of their behaviour as far as their behaviour takes place within the EU'. The Members States of the EU have also developed national data protection laws, and have in place (independent) agencies for the management of data protection laws.

[46] Case C-582/14 *Patrick Breyer v Bundesrepublik Deutschland*, 19 October 2016.

[47] See M Finck, *Blockchain Regulation and Governance in Europe* (Oxford, Oxford University Press, 2019); M Finck, 'Blockchains and Data Protection in the European Union', 4 European Data Protection Law Review 17 (2018); P De Filippi, 'The Interplay between Decentalization and Privacy: The Case of Blockchain Technologies' [2016] *Journal of Peer Production.*

Article 4(1) GDPR defines the term personal data:[48]

> 'personal data' means any information relating to an identified or identifiable natural person ('data subject'); an identifiable natural person is one who can be identified, directly or indirectly, in particular by reference to an identifier such as a name, an identification number, location data, an online identifier or to one or more factors specific to the physical, physiological, genetic, mental, economic, cultural or social identity of that natural person.

A fundamental question arises regarding the data stored in blockchain: are data subjects identifiable on blockchain?[49] According to an Opinion of the Article 29 Working Party, encrypted data will often qualify as personal data and not as anonymous data.[50] The threshold for anonymisation under the GDPR is very high and only results 'from processing personal data in order to irreversibly prevent identification'.[51] The encryption technique of hashing used in blockchain is a technique of pseudonymisation, not anonymization, as it remains possible to connect the dataset with the data subject.[52]

A second set of issues regarding the coexistence of the GDPR and blockchain technology in the EU arises with regard to the identification of the categories of the 'data controller' and the 'data processor', the two categories of natural or legal persons that are subject to the regulatory ambit of the GDPR. According to Article 4(7) GDPR,

> 'controller' means the natural or legal person, public authority, agency or other body which, alone or jointly with others, determines the purposes and means of the processing of personal data; where the purposes and means of such processing are determined by Union or Member State law, the controller or the specific criteria for its nomination may be provided for by Union or Member State law.

According to Article 4(8) GDPR, '"processor" means a natural or legal person, public authority, agency or other body which processes personal data on behalf of the controller'. There is an obvious difficulty to identify who is the controller in a blockchain network. The general concept of blockchain and DLT is to move beyond the idea of centralised management of ledgers and information. Moreover, where nodes hash on the blockchain personal information concerning themselves, they may qualify both as data subjects and data controllers.[53] In addition, nodes

[48] See also Art 9 on 'special categories of personal data'.

[49] Two sets of data stored on blockchains can potentially be defined as personal data for the purposes of the GDPR: transactional data stored in the blocks and public keys; see Finck, 'Blockchains and Data Protection' (n 47) 17.

[50] See Article 29 Working Party, 'Opinion 5/2014 on Anonymization Techniques' (10 April 2014) 0829/14/EN. The Article 29 Working Party (Article 29 WP) was an advisory body under Directive 95/46/EC (Data Protection Directive). The WP was made up of representatives from the data protection authorities of EU Member States, as well as the European Data Protection Supervisor and the European Commission. On 25 May 2018, it was replaced by the European Data Protection Board (EDPB), which was established under the GDPR.

[51] ibid 20.

[52] ibid.

[53] Finck, 'Blockchains and Data Protection' (n 47) 27.

are decentralised entities that cannot respond to the tasks the GDPR requires of centralised agents.

Apart from the issues regarding pseudonymisation, as well as the identification of the data controller and processor, a third set of issues arise regarding the various data protection principles and rights of data subjects identified in the GDPR, and the extent to which they may find application in a blockchain environment. These are: the principles of data minimization;[54] the principle of accuracy and the right to rectification;[55] the principle of storage limitation;[56] the right to withdraw consent to data processing;[57] and the right of access.[58] There are, moreover, information obligations of the controller.[59] Last but not least, the GDPR famously provides for the right to erasure or 'right to be forgotten' of data subjects.[60] The major issue here is whether there is consent by the users for the processing of their data.[61] Overall, there is a potential conflict of these principles and data subject rights with two of the most fundamental features of blockchain technology: the technical rule that information on the blockchain is visible to every node; and the technical feature that information cannot generally be removed from the blockchain as, although a subsequent transaction can always annul the first transaction, the first transaction will nevertheless remain in the chain.

A legal evaluation of the compatibility of blockchain technology with the GDPR may reach two possible conclusions, at least for the public permissionless variant of the blockchain: (i) that blockchain technology is in direct violation of the GDPR, in which interpretative scenario the incompatibility between the technology and the EU legal framework can only be remedied by express derogation from the GDPR;[62] or (ii) that the GDPR does not find application in the case of blockchain. There are, indeed, certain indications that the GDPR may not find application with regard to blockchain technology. One argument can be drawn from the historical development of the GDPR. The GDPR was developed to address different needs and risks than those raised by blockchain technology. It was developed for centralised collection, storage and processing of data, not for the type of processing for which blockchain technology has been developed. Moreover, arguments that blockchains may be exempt from the scope of the GDPR may be drawn from the text and context of the GDPR itself.[63] Article 17(2) GDPR includes the

[54] Art 5(1)(c) GDPR.
[55] Art 5(1)(d) GDPR; Art 16 GDPR.
[56] Art 5(1)(e) GDPR.
[57] Art 7(3) GDPR.
[58] Art 15 GDPR; see also Art 15(2) GDPR ('Where personal data are transferred to a third country or to an international organisation, the data subject shall have the right to be informed of the appropriate safeguards pursuant to Art 46 relating to the transfer').
[59] Arts 13 and 14 GDPR.
[60] Arts 13(2)(b) and 17 GDPR.
[61] See Arts 4(11) and 6(1)(a) GDPR.
[62] See section IVB below.
[63] According to Michèle Finck, this is not appropriate, both from a rule of law point of view and from the perspective of incentivizing developer behaviour towards the development of privacy respecting products; see Finck, *Blockchain Regulation* (n 47) 151.

provision that when the data controller receives a request for erasure in the context of the application of the right to be forgotten, the controller shall take 'account of available technology and the cost of implementation'. The GDPR seems to be mindful of the existence of multiple technologies potentially different from that of the centralised management of data. Moreover, one of the main objectives of the GDPR is to allow natural persons to obtain 'control over their own personal data'.[64] Blockchain gives greater control over personal data than the techniques of centralised data storage.

Finally, Article 25(1) GDPR provides for the principles of data protection by design and data protection by default. These are overarching principles of the law of data protection in the EU, according to which the controller shall implement appropriate technical and organisational means designed to implement the data protection principles. Pseudonymisation is recognised as a means to achieve data protection by design and data protection by default. Blockchain technology is based on the logic of encryption through pseudonymisation, and may be recognised as offering a superior means of data protection by design and default. Overall, digital decentralisation offers a completely different paradigm of data management, which could be used to promote data protection,[65] and could thus be interpreted to fall outside the scope of the GDPR.

In conclusion, the two different frameworks for data management – the GDPR and blockchain – can perhaps be regarded as protecting different data uses and thus as complementary rather than conflicting.

B. Response to the Rise of Cryptocurrencies

Different countries around the world have developed legal frameworks for the regulation of cryptocurrencies. These countries have realised the potentially disruptive nature of cryptocurrencies functioning as currencies, and have mainly developed two approaches to their regulation: command and control, and various intermediate interventions; other countries focus on the benefits of blockchain technology in the frame of developing new cryptoasset applications, and have adopted more favourable approaches to cryptocurrencies, namely enabling the background technology in an effort to spearhead innovation in the financial and other sectors.

(i) Command and Control and Intermediate Approaches

Some countries have adopted an approach of command-and-control regulation to cryptocurrencies. China has been the main example of a jurisdiction attempting a

[64] See recital 7 of the GDPR; see also M Mainelli, 'Blockchain Could Help Us Reclaim Control of Our Personal Data' (5 October 2017), https://hbr.org/2017/10/smart-ledgers-can-help-us-reclaim-control-of-our-personal-data.

[65] G Zyskind, O Nathan and A Pentland, 'Decentralizing Privacy: Using Blockchain to Protect Personal Data', paper presented at the 2015 IEEE Security and Privacy Workshops, San Jose, CA, 2015, 180–84 https://ieeexplore.ieee.org/document/7163223.

major ban on the use of cryptocurrencies. The PBOC issued jointly with four other government agencies the 'Notice on Precautions Against the Risks of Bitcoins' disallowing banks and other financial and payment institutions from using and trading in Bitcoin.[66] This is not a direct prohibition of Bitcoin in China, as Bitcoin and other cryptocurrencies can still be used. The notice restricts most of the money-like functions of Bitcoin, since Chinese banks and payment institutions are prohibited from dealing in Bitcoins. Moreover, in September 2017, a committee led by the PBOC imposed a ban on fund raising for new cryptocurrency ventures, known as Initial Coin Offerings (ICOs) 'or token sales'.[67] The Qatar Central Bank in 2018 also issued a circular that has a similar effect as the notice issued by the Chinese regulators.[68] While the circular only explicitly disallows banks operating in Qatar from trading in Bitcoin, it may be interpreted as applying to all cryptocurrencies.

Other countries have adopted softer approaches to the regulation of cryptocurrencies. Three main intermediate responses can be identified: first, subjecting cryptocurrencies to related 'neighbouring' regulatory regimes. One of the first measures adopted in the USA with regard to cryptocurrencies was the imposition of an anti-money laundering regime. FinCEN issued in 2013 a guidance specifying that 'decentralised' virtual currencies should comply with money laundering regulations.[69] While a user of virtual currency is not a money services business (MSB) under FinCEN's regulations and therefore not subject to MSB registration, reporting and record-keeping regulations, an administrator or exchanger of virtual currency is regarded as an MSB and should generally be considered as a 'money transmitter'. At the same time, an administrator or exchanger is neither a provider or seller of prepaid access nor a dealer in foreign exchange, under the regulations of FinCEN. The SEC has successfully placed cryptocurrencies under its regulatory ambit by imposing sanctions on unauthorised traders operating securities online for Bitcoin and Litecoin.[70] According to the SEC, investments in cryptocurrencies may be considered as securities for the purposes of US securities laws.[71] In a 2013 judgment, a US district court followed the interpretation

[66] People's Bank of China et al (n 44).

[67] See K Rapoza, 'China's "Bitcoin Ban" No Match for Stateless Cryptocurrency Market' (*Forbes.com*, 18 October 2017), www.forbes.com/sites/kenrapoza/2017/10/18/chinas-blockchain-bitcoin-ban-no-match-for-stateless-cryptocurrency-market/#2032415e2de6.

[68] Qatar Central Bank, 'QCB Circular No: 6/2018 to All Banks Operating in Qatar on "Trading in Bitcoin"' (7 february 2018).

[69] US Department of the Treasury (n 38).

[70] See US Securities Exchange Commission (SEC), 'SEC Sanctions Operator of Bitcoin-Related Stock Exchange for Registration Violations' (*Sec.gov*, 8 December 2014), www.sec.gov/news/press-release/2014-273.

[71] See also US Securities Exchange Commission, 'Final Judgment Entered against Trendon T Shavers, a/k/a "Piratreat40" – Operator of Bitcoin Ponzi Scheme Ordered to Pay More Than $40 Million in Disgorgement and Penalties' (*Sec.gov*, 22 September 2014) Release No 23090, www.sec.gov/litigation/litreleases/2014/lr23090.htm. *cf* also R Yang, 'When Is Bitcoin a Security under US Securities Law?' (2013) 18 *Journal of Technology Law & Policy* 99.

of the SEC.[72] The same approach has been adopted by the SEC with regard to ICOs.[73]

Secondly, national regulators have been issuing warnings. The SEC has also been involved in cryptocurrency regulation in the form of warnings, having issued a statement warning investors about the dangers of investing in Bitcoin.[74] The European Banking Authority (EBA) also issued a warning in 2013 regarding cryptocurrencies, raising the issues of monetary loss due to fraud, price instability, theft and users' inexperience that makes them unable to adequately assess the risk of purchasing and using cryptocurrencies.[75] Many agencies in EU Member States have followed the lead of the EBA and have issued similar warnings.[76]

Thirdly, many countries have introduced taxation schemes for cryptocurrencies.[77] In the USA again, the Internal Revenue Service (IRS) issued a notice clarifying that while virtual currencies are used by consumers in the same way as legal tender, the disposition of Bitcoin is, unlike cash, a taxable transaction to the consumer.[78] According to the IRS notice, cryptocurrency is 'property' in the hands of a taxpayer, which means that its disposition is a taxable event to the extent that the cryptocurrency's value has changed since its acquisition by the taxpayer.[79] As no traditional intermediaries are involved in the transactions, the collection of such tax will only be possible if the taxpayers voluntarily report transactions.

(ii) Regulation as Technology

Increasingly, countries around the world have started adopting policies directed towards the promotion of FinTech start-ups, prominently also including start-ups working towards the development of blockchain technology and cryptocurrencies. FinTech promotion policies involve predominantly two regulatory measures: launching innovation hubs to help FinTech start-ups comply with the relevant laws

[72] *SEC v Shavers and Bitcoin Savings and Trust* Case No 4:13-CV-416 (E.D.Tex.) (6 August 2013).

[73] SEC, 'Report of Investigation Pursuant to Section 21(a) of the Securities Exchange Act of 1934: The DAO' (25 July 2017) Release No 81207; see also US Securities Exchange Commission, 'Investor Bulletin: Initial Coin Offerings' (*Sec.gov*, 27 July 2017), www.investor.gov/additional-resources/news-alerts/alerts-bulletins/investor-bulletin-initial-coin-offerings. SEC Chairman Jay Clayton has differentiated between the regulation of cryptoassets as means of exchange, securities or commodities; see SEC Chairman Jay Clayton, 'Statement on Cryptocurrencies and Initial Coin Offerings' (*Sec.gov*, 11 December 2017), www.sec.gov/news/public-statement/statement-clayton-2017-12-11.

[74] SEC, 'Investor Alert: Bitcoin and Other Virtual Currency-Related Investments' (*Sec.gov*, 7 May 2014), www.sec.gov/oiea/investor-alerts-bulletins/investoralertsia_bitcoin.html.

[75] European Banking Authority, 'EBA Warns Consumers on Virtual Currencies' (*eba.europa.eu*, 13 December 2013), www.eba.europa.eu/-/eba-warns-consumers-on-virtual-currencies.

[76] See eg the warning of the Bank of France, 'Les dangers liés au développement des monnaies virtuelles: l'exemple du bitcoin' (*banque-france.fr*, 5 December 2013) Focus No 10, https://publications.banque-france.fr/les-dangers-lies-au-developpement-des-monnaies-virtuelles-lexemple-du-bitcoin.

[77] See generally O Marian, 'Are Cryptocurrencies Super Tax Havens?' (2013) 112 *Michigan Law Review First Impressions* 38.

[78] IRS, 'Virtual Currency Guidance' (*IRS.gov*, 25 March 2014) IRS Notice 2014–21, www.irs.gov/pub/irs-drop/n-14-21.pdf.

[79] ibid.

and regulations, and establishing regulatory sandboxes for new financial service participants,[80] including the lowering of licensing barriers – sometimes reaching all the way to FinTech licensing exemptions. Regulatory sandboxes allow businesses to test innovative products, services, business models and delivery mechanisms in a more relaxed regulatory environment. The idea is to provide FinTech and start-up companies with more pathways to start testing the viability of innovative financial services before being subject to the regulations and regulatory costs associated with the development of standard financial products. The underlying rationale is to strike a balance between facilitating innovation and competition, while at the same time ensuring consumer protection and the distribution of the benefits of innovative FinTech products to society at large.

C. From Indifference to Recognition to Control to Adoption

It took many years before governments started reacting to the rise of cryptocurrencies, and even longer regarding their reaction to blockchain technology. The phase of indifference gave way in some countries to a phase of recognition. Recognition did not necessarily translate to any regulatory response. Some jurisdictions, such as the UK, have deliberately made a decision not to intervene – at least restrictively – in the development of blockchain and cryptocurrencies.[81] Recognition, in turn, gave way to a phase of control through the various measures that have been presented in this section. As this and the previous chapter have illustrated, some countries have taken a different step by explicitly adopting the technology not only for the purposes of private transactions, but also for the purposes of transactions in the public sector.

IV. Blockchain between Self-Regulation and External Regulation

Lawrence Lessig has famously explained how code can operate as law.[82] According to Lessig, there are four main ways through which individual behaviour is constrained and regulated: the law, social norms, market forces and architecture.[83]

[80] See generally H Smith Freehills, 'Overview of Regulatory Sandbox Regimes in Australia, Hong Kong, Malaysia, Singapore, and the UK' (*law.ox.ac.uk*, 18 December 2016), www.law.ox.ac.uk/business-law-blog/blog/2016/12/overview-regulatory-sandbox-regimes-australia-hong-kong-malaysia.

[81] See eg UK Parliament, 'Banking: Bitcoins', HL Deb 18 December 2013, col WA201, 4013, www.publications.parliament.uk/pa/ld201314/ldhansrd/text/131218w0001.htm.

[82] Lessig (n 11).

[83] L Lessig, *Code v2* (Basic Books, 2006) 123.

Code is the architecture of cyberspace, and can thus regulate individual behaviour via the means of technology. The nature of blockchain technology makes regulation through blockchain code very powerful. The relative immutability of the ledger, as well as its potential for automating transactions, makes *lex cryptographia* a very efficient code.[84] At the same time, *lex cryptographia* is subject to external regulation coming from the ordinary law, as has been explained in the previous section.

This section identifies three phases in the development of 'blockchain law', ie the law of the interaction between the ordinary law of the physical world and the *lex cryptographia* of the digital world: the anarcho-libertarian phase; the mainstreaming phase; and the maturity phase. All three phases feature different levels and types of interaction between the self-regulatory *lex cryptographia* and external regulation by the ordinary law. The section then discusses some of the features of blockchain law, and considers whether there is a need for a separate and specialised legal regime regulating blockchain.

A. Three Phases of Development of Blockchain Law

The three different phases in the development of blockchain law – the anarcho-libertarian phase, the mainstreaming phase and the maturity phase – are at least partly chronologically overlapping, but each has its own distinct features. A different set of uses and users prevails in each phase, while each of the three phases favours different aspects of blockchain technology and produces a different type of interaction between blockchain and the law – and, accordingly, between self-regulation and external regulation.

Blockchain technology and DLT have their origins in the cypherpunk movement that appeared in the 1980s and 1990s with the goal of promoting as widespread use of cryptography as possible, as well as the adoption of technologies that would protect individual privacy; its final goal was social and political change through the means of cryptography. It is telling that 'The Crypto Anarchist Manifesto' of Timothy May (one of the founders of the crypto-anarchist movement) opens in a way that mimics the Communist Manifesto.[85] Eric Hughes, the co-founder of the cypherpunk movement, speaks in 'A Cypherpunk's Manifesto' of the need for a new social contract largely outside the state and with the goal of protecting privacy; this is to be achieved using the means of cryptography.[86]

[84] Wright and De Filippi (n 10).

[85] TC May, 'The Crypto Anarchist Manifesto' (22 November 1992), www.activism.net/cypherpunk/crypto-anarchy.html ('A specter is haunting the modern world, the specter of crypto anarchy'). The manifesto was circulated in an email of the author in 1988.

[86] E Hughes, 'A Cypherpunk's Manifesto' (9 March 1993), www.activism.net/cypherpunk/manifesto.html.

The crypto-anarchist and cypherpunk movements gave rise to similar movements of online individual independence from the government.[87] Bitcoin and its background blockchain technology follow in the footsteps of the same technological developments and social movements. They were developed by libertarians, anarchists and other opponents of the global financial system in an effort to bypass the institutions of the financial markets, namely commercial banks and central banks.[88] During this anarcho-libertarian phase, blockchains were mostly public and permissionless. Blockchains are, moreover, inherently 'transnational constructs'.[89] They are transnational 'because they bypass the need for a central server (which necessarily needs to be located in a specific jurisdiction)'.[90] The technology remained largely transnational in this first phase of development. In addition, in the first five to seven years of blockchain, there was an absence of regulatory intervention by the state;[91] the technology remained largely unregulated – and still remains so in many countries.

In the last years, the use of blockchains has become more common in multiple spheres of life and business, and the quantity and value of cryptocurrencies – as well as other cryptoassets – has exceeded any initial anticipation. Mainstream organisations such as tech giants and international banks have come to terms with a technology that was developed to bypass them.[92] In what is identified in this chapter as the mainstreaming phase of blockchain, blockchains still remained public and permissionless. The multiplication of uses and increase in value have naturally attracted the interest of regulators, who attempted to fit mostly cryptocurrencies under the traditional regulatory categories of domestic law. It was during this phase that an effort to 'domesticate' blockchains started to take place. Domestication of blockchain is an effort by legal orders all around the world to capture and regulate a technology that is by nature and design

[87] See, eg J Assange (with J Appelbaum, A Muller-Maguhn and J Zimmermann), *Cypherpunks: Freedom and the Future of the Internet* (New York, OR Books, 2012); see also S Levy, *Crypto: How the Code Rebels Beat the Government Saving Privacy in the Digital Age* (London, Penguin, 2002).

[88] Nakamoto (n 1). See generally P De Filippi, 'Bitcoin: A Regulatory Nightmare to a Libertarian Dream' (2014) 3 *Internet Policy Review*; UW Chohan, 'Cryptoanarchism and Cryptocurrencies' (27 November 2017), https://ssrn.com/abstract=3079241 or http://dx.doi.org/10.2139/ssrn.3079241; on the politics of cryptocurrencies, see also the excellent analysis of F Pasquale, 'Tales from the Crypto' *Public Books* (6 December 2020), www.publicbooks.org/tales-from-the-crypto/#fn-36490-6 (discussing three recent books that address cryptocurrencies and their background politics: D Golumbia, *The Politics of Bitcoin: Software as Right-Wing Extremism* (Minneapolis, University of Minnesota Press, 2016); K Pistor, *The Code of Capital: How the Law Creates Wealth and Inequality* (Princeton, Princeton University Press, 2018); F Brunton, *Digital Cash: The Unknown History of the Anarchists, Utopians, and Technologists Who Created Cryptocurrency* (Princeton, Princeton University Press, 2019)).

[89] Finck, *Blockchain Regulation* (n 47) 58.

[90] P De Filippi and S Hassan, 'Blockchain Technology as a Regulatory Technology: From Code is Law to Law is Code' (2016) 21 *First Monday* (special issue on 'Reclaiming the Internet' with distributed architectures).

[91] Finck, *Blockchain Regulation* (n 47) 46.

[92] See eg W Zhao, 'Bank of America Files for 3 New Blockchain Patents' *Coindesk* (1 August 2017), www.coindesk.com/bank-america-files-3-new-blockchain-patents.

global and transnational. This is a process that may be observed with regard to other technologies as well, such as the Internet. The Internet was conceived as a global network, but started developing a territorial dimension, with countries around the world developing domestic laws and other mechanisms to domesticate it.[93] Domestication of blockchain took place through the means of regulation presented in section III of this chapter, mostly regarding cryptocurrencies. Regulatory intervention has been – and still remains – asymmetric; while more often the process to fit them into the mainstream regulatory categories by domesticating them meant restricting the uses of blockchain and cryptocurrencies – particularly as they refer to the transfer-of-value functions of blockchain, domestic regulators sometimes favour the technology through sandboxes and innovation hubs for some users and uses.

The third phase may be characterised as the maturity phase of blockchain. The public permissionless blockchains are spinning off to private and permissioned blockchains that have started booming in the last almost two years. Mainstream tech companies are now actively involved in the development of the technology, and mainstream businesses have started using the technology to improve their operations. In this maturity phase, there are blockchains of all types: domestic, transnational and also international, as governments and international organisations have developed uses for blockchain. As a further sign of maturation of the relationship between the law of the physical world and the digital world, restricting regulation has started shifting more towards enabling regulation, as well as adopting blockchain for government service delivery. Central banks around the world are introducing, or considering introducing, CBDCs. Regulation and adoption now take place at the domestic, international and also regional level of governance. The EU has launched an EU Blockchain Observatory & Forum,[94] and is in the process of developing an EU-wide blockchain infrastructure.[95] The European Central Bank also announced in late 2019 EUROchain, a proof-of-concept project for anonymity in CBDCs.[96]

[93] See generally N Tsagourias, 'The Legal Status of Cyberspace' in N Tsagourias and R Buchan (eds), *Research Handbook on International Law and Cyberspace* (Cheltenham, Edward Elgar Publishing, 2015) 13.

[94] See www.eublockchainforum.eu/.

[95] See R Houben and A Snyers, 'Cryptocurrencies and Blockchain: Legal Context and Implications for Financial Crime, Money Laundering and Tax Evasion' (European Parliament, July 2018) PE 619.024, www.europarl.europa.eu/cmsdata/150761/TAX3%20Study%20on%20cryptocurrencies%20and%20blockchain.pdf; Commission, 'FinTech Action Plan: For a More Competitive and Innovative European Financial Sector' (Communication) COM (2018) 0109 final; 'European Countries join Blockchain Partnership', https://ec.europa.eu/digital-single-market/en/news/european-countries-join-blockchain-partnership; but see 'Spooked by Libra, EU Pledges to Regulate Digital Currencies' (Reuters, 8 October 2019), www.reuters.com/article/us-eu-commission-dombrovskis/spooked-by-libra-eu-pledges-to-regulate-digital-currencies-idUSKBN1WN0O6.

[96] European Central Bank, 'Exploring Anonymity in Central Bank Digital Currencies', *In Focus* (Issue No 4, December 2019), www.ecb.europa.eu/paym/intro/publications/pdf/ecb.mipinfocus191217.en.pdf.

B. New Technologies and New Realities: Towards a Blockchain Law?

Blockchain technology and the applications it supports pose great challenges to law as a system and domestic legal systems. Domestic jurisdictions have been faced with great challenges particularly when dealing with cryptocurrencies. On the other side, blockchain technology is faced with great challenges stemming from data protection-related laws, particularly the GDPR in the EU. The GDPR was developed for the centralised collection, storage and processing of personal data. It becomes very difficult to transpose its logic to decentralised digital ledgers. The greatest challenge for the future is to protect individuals from the risks of cryptocurrencies or cybersecurity breaches while at the same time allowing for much-needed technological innovation.

Apart from the principles and rights provided for in the GDPR, the Regulation also provides for the possibility to legislatively 'restrict' its application under Article 23 for the purposes mentioned in the heads of the Article while at the same time respecting the essence of the fundamental rights and the principle of proportionality as identified in the chapeau. Some values allowing for deviation are framed in a rather broad way; for example, Article 23(1)(e) GDPR provides that the supranational or a national legislator may adopt measures to safeguard

> other important objectives of general public interest of the Union or of a Member State, in particular an important economic or financial interest of the Union or of a Member State, including monetary, budgetary and taxation a matters, public health and social security.

'The protection of the data subject or the rights and freedoms of others' is also identified as a reason to allow deviations from the GDPR under Article 23(1)(i) of the Regulation. Even if the GDPR may be seen as finding application in the case of blockchain technology, as opposed to the view expressed above, these provisions may be interpreted as allowing national laws that introduce uses of blockchain in the field of cryptocurrencies, or for the storage of medical data.

Deviation from privacy and data protection laws is more easily achieved in those parts of the world where data privacy has not reached the same level of protection. Within the EU, the way forward for legal certainty purposes may thus be the development of separate national legal regimes for blockchain, either in general laws on the regulation of blockchains or in sectoral laws dealing with money, public health, taxation, etc. Each legislator will have their own priorities and preferred blockchain applications. Going back to the discussion of the different phases of the interaction between blockchain and ordinary law, one could think of the following three elements as fundamental in the future shaping of this interaction through legislative and regulatory intervention: enabling public and permissionless blockchains; establishing new foundations of trust in society; and achieving new interoperability functions between the public and private sectors, as well as the physical and the digital world.[97]

As has been observed above, there has been a general tendency in the more recent phases of the development of blockchain technology to move away from public and permissionless blockchains and towards private and permissioned blockchains. National legislators and regulators could think of ways to again favour public and permissionless blockchain networks. Providing free access to all network participants has been the major innovation of blockchain technology. Cutting them off from their major attraction may mean removing the major reason for their existence, potentially stifling innovation and creating new dichotomies between those with access and those without access to blockchain.

Law differentiates itself from other social systems as it embodies a trust inculcated into it through mechanisms of government action such as legislation by the legislative branch of government and regulation by the executive branch of government. For certain actions of societal life that are perceived as needing to be infused with such trust, the law lends its trust quality to such transactions. Transactions in land, for example, require notarisation by a notary as well as state intervention by mandating registration with the land registry. So far, government has always operated as the mediator of this type of trust. Government intermediation operated in order to safeguard trust in the relevant system. Blockchain purports to take up some of these roles by being the generator of trust.[98] The question thus arises as to what extent peer-to-peer trust in blockchain can replace trust in and by the government. The interplay between these two systems of trust, and the use of the blockchain trust mechanism by government, is a very fundamental feature of blockchain law. A new legislative intervention should allow for trust in blockchain to operate with the support of governmental trust. The state could intervene to support the blockchain network in cases of failure to react to the needs of the law and the realities of the physical world. One example may be legislative provisions such as in civil codes mandating the reversal of transactions that would qualify as irregular under the ordinary legal system, or the application of consumer law.

One of the main themes of the globalisation of law was the effort to understand new institutions and organisations that present features of hybridity between the public and the private. The fourth industrial revolution also produces a post-industrial globalisation.[99] The new legal questions posed by globalisation through the application of blockchain technology are not issues of hybridity; rather, they

[97] See also – as well as on an overarching theory of law and political economy of blockchain – Dimitropoulos, 'The Law of Blockchain' (n 13).

[98] K Werbach, *The Blockchain and the New Architecture of Trust* (Cambridge, MA, MIT Press, 2018).

[99] K Schwab, 'The Fourth Industrial Revolution: What It Means and How to Respond' (*Foreign Affairs*, 12 December 2015).

are issues of interoperability of different systems:[100] at the private-to-private level; at the private-to-government level; and at the government-to-government level. International trade is a case in point.[101] Blockchain technology can potentially facilitate the various dimensions of cross-border private-to-private, private-to-government as well as government-to-government interactions involved. Blockchain can facilitate technical interoperability, allowing IT systems of private parties and different countries to communicate with each other.[102] The new blockchain law should make it possible for all stakeholders to be up to date on the status of customs documents, as well as view bills of lading, and other data, irrespective of whether they are produced by private parties or public authorities. Blockchain-backed sanitary and phytosanitary certificates can also be envisaged in the case of food, plant and agricultural products, which are usually delivered by ministries of health and agriculture. New legislative interventions could mandate their digitisation and storage on blockchain.

Interoperability may even go beyond that. The digital world of blockchain and the physical world do not always operate in isolation. There are multiple access points of the physical world into the digital blockchain world, and vice versa.[103] Blockchain law needs to also guarantee interoperability between the physical world and the digital world by bridging the gaps between them. This can be done by regulating, for example, the access points between the two worlds, such as miners and mining pools in the case of Bitcoin blockchain, as well as structuring arbitrations resolving disputes arising out of smart contracts.

V. Conclusion

This chapter discussed the idea of the new blockchain law that is in the process of being developed. Blockchain law is a new category of law that operates between the law within blockchain, the *lex cryptographia*, and the ordinary law of the physical world. This is the result of a complex interaction between multiple areas of law, across many different levels of governance, and actors of the digital and analogue worlds. The interaction between the ordinary legal orders and the world of blockchain has passed through different phases of development that have been

[100] On interoperability as one of the tasks for regulation in the field of the blockchain technology, see also Finck, *Blockchain Regulation* (n 47) 152.

[101] See generally E Ganne, *Can Blockchain Revolutionize International Trade?* (WTO, 2018), www.wto.org/english/res_e/booksp_e/blockchainrev18_e.pdf.

[102] ISO is in the process of elaborating technical and interoperability standards for blockchain and distributed ledgers; see ISO/TC 307 – Blockchain and distributed ledger technologies.

[103] Michèle Finck calls these 'bridges': Finck, *Blockchain Regulation* (n 47) 86.

identified in the chapter: the anarcho-libertarian phase, the mainstreaming phase and the maturity phase. In all these different phases, the public and the private, the transnational, the domestic, the international and the regional have found different expressions, in a complex interaction between blockchain self-regulation and external regulation by the ordinary legal orders. In order to allow for simultaneous technological innovation and citizen protection from the risks of blockchain technology, new types of legal regimes may have to be developed. If there is a role for the supranational level of governance, this will have to be the facilitation of this process, allowing for innovative economies of scale to develop, while at the same time protecting individuals in the EU.

9

Civil Liability and New Technologies

MICHEL CANNARSA

I. Introduction

The development of so many digital technologies,[1] in recent years, is having increasing repercussions in the field of law. Although legal experts have traditionally shown little interest in such matters, it has recently become virtually impossible for them to ignore the impact of digital technologies on the law, and more specifically, the question of whether legal rules and regulations can cope with the changes taking place in the economy, which is rapidly turning into a digital economy.[2] In other words, are the current legal rules 'fit for purpose' in terms of the changes taking place in the ecosystem? Or do we need to create a new set of rules that will allow new technologies to develop harmoniously? If we take the view that the existing rules can be adapted, should we envisage interpreting them in new ways? If new rules are needed, how should we define their content and how do we make sure they are suitable for the long term, in a context of rapidly changing technologies?

In the European context more particularly, these questions are all the more pressing in that here there are significant risks of market fragmentation. In the absence of a legal framework applicable to new technologies in most Member States, there is a significant risk that these states will adopt their own divergent national rules. This scenario would lead to major disruption of the internal market.

[1] Though a comprehensive and consistent definition of 'new technologies' or 'emerging digital technologies' is not an easy task, the European Commission (EC) relies, in its various communications and reports, on a quite broad and open-ended approach, relying on the main examples of such technologies: 'the Internet of Things (IoT), Artificial Intelligence, advanced robotics and autonomous systems' (Commission, 'Liability for Emerging Digital Technologies' SWD (2018) 137 final, 2). The key aspects of the said technologies are 'complexity, openness, autonomy, predictability, data-drivenness, and vulnerability' (Expert Group on Liability and New Technologies – New Technologies Formation, 'Liability for Artificial Intelligence and Other Emerging Digital Technologies' 5, www.ec.europa.eu/transparency/regexpert/index.cfm?do=groupDetail.groupMeetingDoc&docid=36608.

[2] See, among many others, P De Filippi and A Wright, *Blockchain and the Law, The Rule of Code* (Cambridge, MA, Harvard University Press, 2018). Needless to say, the recent Covid-19 crisis had a further propelling effect on digitalisation.

Consequently, there is an opportunity, at EU level, to adopt a harmonised legal framework that would enable various objectives to be achieved: not only that of offering an environment that will be favourable to the development of new technologies in Europe, but also that of reviving thinking on the harmonisation of private law within the Union, given that many aspects of private law may be affected by the emergence of new technologies. There can be no doubting the fact that the very heart of this book devoted to the future of EU private law lies in the work in progress within the EU and its forthcoming legislative proposals designed to respond to emerging digital technologies.

This contribution will deal more specifically with the rules governing civil liability in the context of new technologies. Are the legal basis and provisions established by the rules in question in the various Member States and at EU level fit for the changes under way? To answer this question, we will need to test them in light of the main characteristics of these new technologies. If the answer is 'no', even if only to some extent, how will they need to be adapted? What new rules would enable civil liability to continue to fulfil its purpose in a context marked by new technologies? A number of principles and analytical methods will be put forward, with a view to identifying some avenues leading towards concrete solutions.

II. How the Law Views Emerging Digital Technologies and Their Characteristics

If we are to perform an effective analysis, we must first execute a diagnostic assessment of the situation to be analysed, and make it as detailed and exhaustive as possible. This is where legal experts encounter an initial problem, in the context of emerging digital technologies, ie the fact that the nature of the digital revolution means that this phenomenon is fairly far removed from the core skills of legal experts (given the key role played by information technology, computer code, algorithms, etc).

A. The Pace of Change

Technology is developing and changing rapidly (from artificial intelligence (AI) to machine learning, from the Internet of Things (IoT) to intelligent objects such as self-driving vehicles, healthcare applications, smart homes and blockchain to 3-D printers, via robotics, etc). Unlike other milestone developments in industrial history, these various innovations seem to be unfolding rapidly, and in some cases at breakneck speed. It is worth highlighting this feature, given that the pace of change gives rise to levels of concern and incomprehension that cannot easily be resolved. Lawyers in particular, like society as a whole, find it difficult to understand the technological changes taking place and thus to keep up with them.

Moreover, the speed of this transformation also impacts on the regulatory response that the legislator is able to provide. In point of fact, rather than running the risk of new legislation rapidly becoming obsolete, the EU and national authorities prefer to take their time to observe the changes unfolding in current technologies, and to assess their impacts from the legal point of view, before proposing any specific courses of action. It is fairly likely that one preferred course of action will be to put forward a number of general principles, or even soft law instruments, that the industry will have to progressively introduce as these technologies emerge. These principles and instruments could be combined with sectoral instruments relating to the safety of a given product or technology.

B. Disruptive Features

The features of the current technological innovations, which I shall shortly discuss in more detail, are sometimes disruptive enough to potentially give rise to a paradigm shift, including as regards the rules governing civil liability. In fact, one of the main characteristics of the harm that may potentially be caused by new technologies is that it may not necessarily be the result of any wrongdoing on the part of a human agent or the result of any product defect (in the 'traditional' sense of the term). For example, consider the harm caused by autonomous systems which, based on a machine learning process, develop the 'capability' to perform their own analysis and actions that subsequently become far removed from the initial settings put in place by the human developers of the said system.

So how, then, can we evaluate the behaviour of these autonomous systems? Can we talk of 'wrongdoing', or defective behaviour? (Incidentally, this is just one of the conditions that would make it possible to establish liability and an obligation to remedy the harm caused, based on a traditional line of reasoning in terms of civil liability.) At this stage, I shall merely indicate that, in order to answer these questions, the technical assessment required to identify the cause of the problem and to establish a causal link with the harm suffered by the victims of intelligent objects would give rise to disproportionate costs and take a disproportionate amount of time in relation to what is required for the smooth functioning of a civil liability system and of an ecosystem in its entirety. In other words, if each case of harm caused by an intelligent/high-tech object requires the commissioning of an advanced-level technical assessment report, neither the victims nor the legal system will be able to absorb the costs involved. As a result, some people are putting forward the idea of covering the cost of harm caused by new technologies by using guarantee mechanisms that are separate from the rules governing civil liability.[3]

[3] M Monot-Fouletier and M Clément, 'Véhicule autonome: vers une autonomie du régime de responsabilité applicable?' (2018) 3 *Recueil Dalloz* 129.

C. The Centrality of Data

When analysing the characteristics of new technologies, an expert group set up by the European Commission (EC) to consider the issue of liability in relation to new technologies noted the following elements: the autonomous and unpredictable nature of their behaviours and their complexity (arising in particular from an interdependence between multiple components, some of which are tangible and others are not, such as sensors, software programs, etc), and the centrality of digital data within the new ecosystem and their vulnerability to risks linked to cybersecurity.[4] It is important to focus here on one of these features, namely the central position occupied by digital data. Information is what lies at the heart of the ecosystem and the 'revolution' that we are talking about. Digitisation of information is the process underlying the technological developments and innovations that we are talking about, and information is – by definition – intangible. In my opinion, this aspect creates a profound change in the classical conceptual framework of civil liability, insofar as the focus is moving away from a physical and material world (in which products and any harm caused are material and corporeal) into an immaterial world (in which products, the sources of harm and any harm caused are largely immaterial and intangible).

Likewise, information is not currently regarded as a product: this has the effect of excluding any harm caused solely by erroneous and thus potentially 'defective' information from the scope of legislation covering defective products. Information has not traditionally been regarded as a 'product', given that it is intangible, but in connected mode, consumer goods are now increasingly interconnected and need information in order to work. In some ways, we could compare electricity (which comes under the definition of a 'product' within the meaning of the Product Liability Directive (PLD)[5] and therefore comes within the scope of its application) with information because, in order to function, high-tech products, such as smart devices, sometimes have as great a need for information as they do for electricity or another energy source. One French author takes the view that information lies at the heart not only of the new economic system, but also of a new dimensional structure, from which derives the fact that its nature is no longer exclusively tangible.[6] It should also be noted that intangible items are regarded as inanimate

[4] EC Expert Group on Liability and New Technologies.

[5] Council Directive 85/374/EEC of 25 July 1985 on the approximation of the laws, regulations and administrative provisions of the Member States concerning liability for defective products [1985] OJ L210/29.

[6] G Berry, *L'hyperpuissance de l'informatique, Algorithmes, données, machines, réseaux* (Paris, Odile Jacob, 2017). According to this author, scientific thinking structured itself on the basis of a triangular dimension based on energy, matter and waves. This triangle was the basis of the 19th century industrial revolution. But the 20th century saw information and its systematic processing by computers as a new central feature in the previously mentioned triangular dimension, leading to the emergence of new technologies, a new ecosystem and the current industrial revolution (ibid 41–45).

objects in all circumstances, as has been the case in French law in the field of liability for damage caused by inanimate objects.[7]

D. Risks and Opportunities

The difficulty faced by society in general and by lawyers in particular in reaching a measured understanding of the technological changes taking place may be all the more regrettable insofar as these innovations present both risks and opportunities. The risks, and particularly the legal risks, must be appropriately analysed against the background of the current legal framework or in light of any new rules adopted. The opportunities, for their part, must be capable of allowing the ecosystem to keep up with them, notably by ensuring that the legal rules are appropriate and balanced, especially at EU level, so that the Digital Single Market can become a reality. This will mean the adoption of harmonised rules, including as regards civil liability arising from harm caused by new technologies. The internal market has developed on the basis of the fair distribution of development risks between producers and consumers. Producers must be able to enjoy a sufficient degree of legal certainty and consumers must be able to obtain protection and compensation when they suffer harm as a result of defective products. It is this type of equilibrium that the EU legislator is currently seeking to achieve in the development of the Digital Single Market. I shall return to the subject of the EU work currently in progress later in this chapter.

III. Analytical Methods Applicable to Emerging Digital Technologies

A. Looking Backwards

While the technological developments and innovations currently unfolding do indeed constitute a phenomenon of industrial change comparable to other industrial revolutions (and there appears to be no doubt that they constitute such a phenomenon, ie a fourth industrial revolution), it is useful to turn round for a moment and look back to the past. In the analysis performed in this chapter, historical precedents may prove valuable. This is certainly not the first time that the law has had to respond to deep-rooted phenomena involving changes in the ecosystem. The second half of the nineteenth century and the first half of the

[7] Here, it should be noted that the proposed reform of civil liability in France, regarding liability for damage caused by inanimate objects, intends to specify that items that come under this liability regime must be deemed corporeal objects. See draft Art 1243 of the Civil Code.

twentieth century was a period characterised by radical industrial changes, in a context in which societies and the legal rules that governed them were defined by a past that was essentially agricultural in nature, and in which the nature and scale of any damage caused were dependent on this type of economic structure. Needless to say, mass production and consumption, hazardous products and hazardous activities would change things radically. Legal systems, and especially civil liability rules, in countries undergoing industrialisation and developing their industrial base reacted in fairly similar ways in responding to the new types of harm arising in industrial society. We know that sometimes, although they have not been changed, these rules have been interpreted in new and sometimes bold ways by the courts, in order to meet victims' needs for compensation. Conversely, where the scale or nature of harm has so required, the legislators have adopted new legal rules (such as for accidents at work, road traffic accidents and damage caused by defective products). Such precedents are, in my view, valuable sources of learning for deciphering the current phenomena and enable us to analyse the questions raised in a more measured way. These precedents are all the more valuable in that EU legislation covering product liability, ie the PLD, dates back not much further than 30 years, even though the economic context has undergone major upheavals over the past 30 years.

When we consider the response that the legal system must provide to the technological developments under way, from the viewpoint of civil liability, one of the first questions that emerges, whether in a national context or at EU level, is that of establishing whether legal systems need new rules to cope with the harm caused by new technologies and new technological objects. In other words, is the existing civil liability legislation flexible enough to be adapted and to allow satisfactory solutions and remedies to be put forward? If the answer to this question is 'no', or if, at the very least, the current rules will have to be amended without new rules taking their place or being combined with them, then there seems to be little doubt that an opportunity exists to adopt EU rules covering civil liability for damage caused by the technologies in question. Conversely, if EU Member States were to legislate on these matters at national level, there would be a high risk of fragmentation of the Single Market, and particularly of the Digital Single Market. Such domestic regulations would constitute barriers to the free movement of goods with digital elements and the free movement of digital content, therefore impairing the development of an EU industry in the new technologies economic sector.[8]

[8] Directive 2019/770 of 20 May 2019 on certain aspects concerning contracts for the supply of digital content and digital services and Directive 2019/771 of 20 May 2019 on certain aspects concerning contracts for the sale of goods, as far as contractual conformity and remedies are concerned, intend to 'meet the multiple challenges posed today by an increasingly technology-driven economy' (Directive 2019/771, recital 1). A similar approach should be strongly considered regarding rules on extracontractual liability.

B. Looking Forward

As previously mentioned, the speed of the technological innovations currently unfolding is a feature that needs to be taken into account. This factor seems to favour a legal approach and legal rules that are flexible enough (and are not rigid) to prevent a risk of rapid obsolescence. This is also one of the main concerns driving national and EU legislators who, ever since the question of new technologies began to make itself felt, have been hesitating between taking action and adopting a 'stand by and wait and see' position. In addition to the speed of the technological innovations under way, another factor makes it a complex task for the law to grasp them: the absence of uniformity among these technologies and among the products developed by applying them. Systems and products may be more or less autonomous, may or may not have the capacity to learn, may or may not draw on artificial intelligence, etc. However, it is fairly rare for these new products not to be connected to the Internet, and as a result, they will perform fairly frequent updates that will change their initial configuration.

As for the method to be used for analysing these phenomena, an empirical approach appears to be called for. This is the experience we have developed in recent years in Lyon, by creating Future of Digital Technologies Law Clinics: these bring together students, academics, members of the judiciary, lawyers and representatives of the business world and task them with identifying and solving the problems posed by the future development of new technologies. This involves choosing slightly futuristic scenarios (looking 5–10 years ahead) to ensure that we continue to work on highly realistic future planning exercises. This method and our project have recently been selected by the Erasmus+ agency, and our TechLaw Clinic is now an EU consortium whose partners include various EU universities, the bar associations of various European cities and the worlds of business and LegalTech, so that these matters can be considered on a Europe-wide scale. Having this structure enables us to compare the various national legal systems and to evaluate their capacity to respond to the changes taking place. It also enables us to identify any European principles in this area that could be the subject of recommendations made to EU and national legislators. Using this approach, ideally we should be able to 'test', in light of the legal rules, technologies that are being developed before they are marketed. The 'sandbox' approach to ensure regulatory compliance is comparable to this method. We should add that this 'fitness check', performed in light of the law before products are marketed, would appear to be one of the conditions governing the social acceptability of emerging technologies, or at least some of them.

C. The Analysis Conducted at European Level

Although the EU legislator initially opted out of making any regulatory interventions in relation to the technological innovations currently unfolding, it would appear that this attitude changed in 2017 and altered further from 2018 onwards. On 16 February 2017, the European Parliament passed a Resolution on Civil Law Rules on Robotics.[9] The EC then published the Communication from the Commission on Artificial Intelligence for Europe in April 2018,[10] and the Communication from the Commission Plan for Artificial Intelligence 'Made in Europe' in December 2018,[11] followed by the AI Ethics Guidelines in April 2019[12] and the White Paper on Artificial Intelligence – A European Approach to Excellence and Trust in February 2020.[13] These documents are additional to the work referred to above, which was executed under the auspices of the EC and sought to determine whether the current rules governing civil liability, and in particular the product liability rules, need to be adapted or will suffice in their present form, or, on the other hand, whether a completely new set of rules will have to be created. In its report 'Liability for Artificial Intelligence and Other Emerging Digital Technologies',[14] the EC Expert Group on Liability and New Technologies stressed the fact that it is 'necessary to consider adaptations and amendments to existing liability regimes' in order to reach a 'fair and efficient allocation of loss', a 'coherent and appropriate response of the legal system to threats to the interests of individuals' and an 'effective access to justice'.[15] This recent body of initiatives, documents and work will constitute the primary framework of my analyses and proposals.

In the working document entitled 'Liability for Emerging Digital Technologies, which echoes the need for an 'appropriate ethical and legal framework' as expressed in the EC's communication entitled 'Artificial Intelligence for Europe', dated 25 April 2018, the Commission sets about the task of identifying aspects linked to the issue of civil liability and meriting attention. In point of fact, in this communication, the EC points out that

> Like every technology or tool, AI can be used to positive but also to malicious ends. Whilst AI clearly generates new opportunities, it also poses challenges and risks, for example in the areas of safety and liability, security (criminal use or attacks), bias and discrimination.

[9] European Parliament resolution of 16 February 2017 with recommendations to the Commission on Civil Law Rules on Robotics, www.europarl.europa.eu/doceo/document/TA-8-2017-0051_EN.html#title1.

[10] Commission, 'Artificial Intelligence for Europe' (Communication) COM (2018) 237 final, www.ec.europa.eu/transparency/regdoc/rep/1/2018/EN/COM-2018-237-F1-EN-MAIN-PART-1.PDF.

[11] Commission, 'Coordinated Plan on Artificial Intelligence' (Communication) COM (2018) 795 final, www.ec.europa.eu/knowledge4policy/publication/coordinated-plan-artificial-intelligence-com2018-795-final_en.

[12] Commission, 'Building Trust in Human-centric Artificial Intelligence' (Communication) COM (2019) 168 final, www.ec.europa.eu/digital-single-market/en/news/communication-building-trust-human-centric-artificial-intelligence.

[13] 'White Paper on Artificial Intelligence – A European Approach to Excellence and Trust' COM (2020) 65 final, www.ec.europa.eu/info/sites/info/files/commission-white-paper-artificial-intelligence-feb2020_en.pdf.

[14] Above n 1.

[15] Expert Group on Liability and New Technologies – New Technologies Formation (n 1) 5.

It should, however, be noted that here the EC tells us that it will make sure it applies the 'Innovation Principle' precisely in order to protect the capacity for innovation within the EU.

One important issue in defining the legal/regulatory response to the risks created by new technologies is that of the approach to be used, which can be either horizontal or sectoral. The heterogeneous nature of the technologies, as noted above, may appear to make it difficult to adopt a horizontal approach that can embrace the complexity of the situations arising in a way that is satisfactory, systematic and coherent. On the other hand, a sectoral approach, based on different categories of products and technologies, might seem more suitable when it comes to defining safety standards. Likewise, the very nature of the regulatory response may necessitate making a choice between, on the one hand, a hard law-type regulatory response, and, on the other, a soft law approach, on the basis of which a number of general rules and principles would enable the current rules governing civil liability to be adapted, notably by interpreting the current rules, using an approach that is gradual, flexible and evolutive. My view is that a hard law approach makes sense as far as specific products safety regulation is concerned. Imposing safety, privacy and ethical standards to producers seems to be an efficient preventive approach. At the opposite end of the spectrum, when harm occurred, liability rules could be adapted and interpreted in the light of new guidelines drafted in order to take into account the major, disruptive features of new technologies.

What ideas and themes can guide the forthcoming definition of the legal framework applicable to new technologies? In my view, it would be advantageous to structure the debate around a number of themes, such as the transition from man to machine, and more particularly the fact that autonomous systems – and this is something new – have a decision-making capability that is assumed in some ways to reproduce human cognitive capacities. The renewal and updating of long-standing principles of liability to ensure they meet modern requirements may be a theme of interest, such as the rules governing liability for things in custody.[16] Further, in continuity with the expert group's work on the ethics of artificial intelligence,[17]

[16] See Commission, 'Liability for Emerging Digital Technologies' (n 1): 'A first question to assess is whether concepts like the liability of a guardian or similar concepts are appropriate to technologies like AI. While AI cannot of course be assimilated to humans or animals, the autonomy element is an intrinsic feature that is relevant and very prominent in both cases. Within the limits set by relevant safety frameworks, an AI powered robot can, and actually is supposed to, act autonomously and independently, ie without any supervision. The approach on liability for animals is linked to the concept of lack of predictability and therefore interesting to that extent in the context of autonomous behaviour. Safety legislation will have an important role to play in reducing this unpredictability to a socially accepted minimum.' See also MU Scherer, 'Of Wild Beasts and Digital Analogues: The Legal Status of Autonomous Systems' (2019) 19 *Nevada Law Journal* 259.

[17] High-Level Expert Group on Artificial Intelligence, 'A Definition of AI: Main Capabilities and Scientific Disciplines' (April 2019); High-Level Expert Group on Artificial Intelligence, 'Ethics Guidelines for Trustworthy AI' (April 2019); High-Level Expert Group on Artificial Intelligence, 'Policy and Investment Recommendations for Trustworthy AI' (June 2019).

which recommends the principle of human-centric AI,[18] might we not envisage a new basis of liability derived from compliance with a number of ethical rules? Concepts such as ethics by design would make it possible to define the basis for liability and product safety rules. We also need to focus our thinking on the centrality of information and of data in the new ecosystem being formed. The immaterial nature of information also leads to a change in the nature of sources of liability and in the nature of harm. The current civil liability rules are still largely designed for, and interpreted in, the context of a physical world, which renders their conceptual framework partly inappropriate for the purpose of apprehending the virtual world.

Furthermore, we must always be able to bear in mind and think about the interface between the virtual world and the physical world. This seems to be one of the criteria that will enable us to reach an appropriate definition of the relevant rules. A number of technologies have been designed without sufficient consideration being given to their interface with, and the realities of, the physical world, notably the legal rules, which manage to apprehend the virtual dimension only imperfectly. Bearing these aspects in mind also enables us to prevent technology framing the legal rules, or at least to prevent it framing them to an excessive degree. One of the risks posed by the current technological changes is that they encourage the legal experts and the legislators to go 'chasing after' technology to an excessive degree, while forgetting about the founding principles of law, and in particular the laws governing civil liability.

IV. Proposals for Solutions

The following have been identified as being some of the notions most likely to evolve in the face of emerging digital technologies in the various documents published by the EC over the past two years.[19]

A. The Notion of Product

Even though the PLD takes a neutral standpoint vis-à-vis technology, the notion of product contained within it has been conceived in terms of, and is aimed primarily

[18] The EU's strategy in the field of AI intends to place people at the centre of the development of AI, through an appropriate ethical and legal framework. The EC listed seven key requirements in order to achieve the objective of a human-centric AI: human agency and oversight; technical robustness and safety; privacy and data governance; transparency; diversity, non-discrimination and fairness; societal and environmental well-being; and accountability: Commission, 'Building Trust in Human-centric Artificial Intelligence' (n 12).

[19] Commission, 'Liability for Emerging Digital Technologies' (n 1): 'The evaluation process included a preliminary assessment of the continued relevance of the Product Liability's concepts, such as product, producer, defect, damage and the burden of proof. The evaluation results as well as the forthcoming Fifth Report on the application of the product Liability Directive highlight that the Directive continues – to some extent – to be adequate for the current state of technological developments.'

at, tangible objects.[20] Surely there is scope within it to spell out further that the notion of product encompasses both tangible and intangible things? For example, would it not be relevant, given the PLD's silence on this subject, to deem that a software program contained on a physical medium, or incorporated into a tangible object, comes within the category of 'products', but that this is not the case where the software is transmitted without this type of medium (eg where the software emanates from a cloud solution and therefore exists solely in the form of information)? Moreover, given that software programs frequently power the operation of intelligent objects, it seems obvious that we need to limit any doubts regarding the application of the PLD to such situations, otherwise we risk leaving the said PLD with an increasingly residual scope of application. Fortunately, this is the approach that the EU legislator seems to be adopting, notably via the Machinery Directive 2006/42/EC, the Radio Equipment Directive 2014/53/EU and the Medical Devices Regulations (EU) 2017/745 and 2017/746,[21] which regard software programs as products, and the CJEU seems to be doing likewise.[22] Producers also seem to think that software programs should be regarded as products, regardless of the media on which they are held.[23]

[20] ibid: 'The Directive defines products as movable items. Even though most producers consulted during the evaluation claimed that they did not encounter problems in distinguishing products from services so far, a number of open questions were identified related to software be it embedded or non-embedded, that will have to be further explored.' See also Commission, 'The Application of the Council Directive on the Approximation of the Laws, Regulations, and Administrative Provisions of the Member States Concerning Liability for Defective Products (85/374/EEC)' COM (2018) 246 final: 'The evaluation has shown that even though products are much more complex today than in 1985, the Product Liability Directive continues to be an adequate tool. However, when it comes to new technological developments, stakeholders have expressed concerns about the continued relevance of the Directive's concepts as they are currently expressed. There are open questions about what separates a product from a service (eg for the Internet of Things, where products and services interact) …'.

[21] Recital 19 of Regulation (EU) 2017/745 on medical devices states that: 'It is necessary to clarify that software in its own right, when specifically intended by the manufacturer to be used for one or more of the medical purposes set out in the definition of a medical device, qualifies as a medical device, while software for general purposes, even when used in a healthcare setting, or software intended for life-style and well-being purposes is not a medical device. The qualification of software, either as a device or an accessory, is independent of the software's location or the type of interconnection between the software and a device.'

[22] Commission, 'Evaluation of Council Directive 85/374/EEC of 25 July 1985 on the approximation of the laws, regulations and administrative provisions of the Member States concerning liability for defective products Accompanying the document Report from the Commission to the European Parliament, the Council and the European Economic and Social Committee on the Application of the Council Directive on the approximation of the laws, regulations, and administrative provisions of the Member States concerning liability for defective products (85/374/EEC)' SWD (2018) 157 final: 'At European Union level, the CJEU has for some specific cases contributed to the classification of software, which for instance is to be considered a medical device (ie a product) when intended by the manufacturer to be used specifically for one or more of the medical purposes set out in the definition of 'medical devices. In addition, the Radio Equipment Directive, the Regulations on medical devices and on in vitro diagnostic, may include software [CJEU Case C-219/11]. This requires a case-by-case analysis, as demonstrated also in pending judgment (CJEU Case C-329/16) in which the Court has to determine whether a certain type of software should be considered a medical device where that software has at least one function that permits the use of data specific to a patient to help his doctor issue a prescription.'

[23] Ibid: 'Most businesses consider apps, non-embedded software and IoT components to be "products" pursuant to the Directive, while they have diverging views as to whether the liability is adequately

As suggested above, and by analogy with electricity, both as an intangible product and as a source of a product's operation, information must be able to be analysed as a source of harm, at least in cases where this information is defective. Many apps could then be deemed products (think, for example, of healthcare apps). They are used by consumers as everyday objects that are assumed to be working properly. If they are not deemed as such, in the event of a malfunction, especially if the information given or the suggestions made by apps are erroneous, excluding these technologies from the scope of application of the PLD on the grounds that they only involve information seems to me to go against the spirit of the said directive. In the same way that the boundary between the physical world and the virtual world is becoming increasingly blurred, thanks in particular to the development of interfaces, the boundary between products (ie tangible objects) and information seems to me to belong to a different era and a different phase of the ecosystem. The conceptions that held sway in the 1980s and 1990s are, in many respects, no longer valid in the current technological context, in which we might envisage a kind of 'reification' of information and data. Here, the EC would like to see a clarification made between the notion of a product and the notion of a service.[24] Thus, the notion of product might be left 'open', so that it can evolve and adapt to technologies of the future.

Another factor to be taken into consideration when studying the notion of a product in the context of emerging digital technologies is the evolutive, non-static and partly unpredictable nature of new 'smart devices'. First, many consumer goods now require frequent – even daily – updates. This means that, in addition to normal wear and tear, the product is now evolving in relation to its status on the day it was sold. This may have several consequences. The producer might, for example, accuse the consumer of not executing these updates, or of executing them imperfectly. The producer might then be tempted not to accept liability, or at least not to accept full liability. Secondly, so-called 'autonomous' systems, which possess machine-learning capability, present the dual characteristic of being both autonomous (given that their 'behaviour' is not necessarily entirely predictable) and also evolutive (the producer of this type of system might then take the view that it cannot be held liable for any unpredictable and autonomous 'adverse behaviour' on the part of its products). These various features impact primarily on the liability regime binding the producer, and more particularly on the latter's capacity to deny liability, in whole or in part, based on the notion either of development risk or of the victim's wrongdoing. However, it is important to bear the said features in mind in the way we define the product, so that this notion offers as high a degree of coherence as possible.

allocated among the different operators. Furthermore, for them defect is adequately defined as to damages caused by an advanced robot or an autonomous system.'

[24] Ibid: 'with the increasing overlap between products and services, it has been highlighted eg by the Study on emerging issues that the distinction between products and services. for the purpose of the Directive may become difficult in the future. A clarification of the concept "product", eg with regards to software, may therefore contribute to improving effectiveness. This needs further assessment.'

The fact that smart devices are, to some extent, interdependent must definitely be taken into consideration in our thinking regarding the notion of a product.[25] The conception of a product made up of various components corresponds only imperfectly to the IoT. In particular, the interdependence mentioned just above affects the nature of the harm caused by these intelligent objects: in fact, it makes it more likely that they will cause harm to other connected objects, based on erroneous information. Risks linked to cybersecurity are also one facet, and not the least one, to bear in mind when evaluating the 'robustness' of products and of the IoT.

B. The Notion of Producer

Regarding the notion of producer, as defined in Article 3 of the PLD, various questions are also raised by the changes associated with emerging technologies and an ecosystem in which the value chain is being diluted by the intervention of multiple parties and sets of information that all contribute to the functioning of new products in the context of the IoT. The redefinition of roles taking place between these various agents (who are not all 'producers' in the traditional sense of the term) must be carefully analysed insofar as it will become increasingly complex, and incidentally more complex than the distinction between the producer of the end product and producers of components, which was the main question preoccupying the EU legislator at the time the PLD was passed in 1985.

The task of identifying the producer is crucial, obviously for the purpose of determining who will be liable for any harm caused, but also for that of determining which agent shall be responsible for ensuring compliance with horizontal and sectoral legislation in terms of product safety.[26] Compliance with this legislation is all the more critical a requirement in the context of emerging digital technologies in that it calls for compliance with a number of safety standards when it comes to marketing the product, as well as imposing monitoring obligations after the product has been marketed, or even withdrawing products from the market and recalling them from consumers where risks are identified.[27] Faced with products that are assumed to be capable of evolving autonomously or semi-autonomously, especially on the basis of data gathered from within their environment and from

[25] Commission, 'Liability for Emerging Digital Technologies' (n 1): 'In the context of the emerging digital technologies, it may be difficult to identify whether the damage has been caused by the product itself or by other elements interconnected to it in a digital ecosystem. In this respect, it will be necessary to provide for adequate safety levels for all types of products, taking also account of any new risks that may be posed regarding the emerging digital technologies.'

[26] See Directive 2001/95/EC of the European Parliament and of the Council of 3 December 2001 on general product safety [2002] OJ L11/4.

[27] According to Arts 5.3 and 8 of the above-mentioned general product safety directive, if producers become aware that a product that they have placed on the market poses risks to the consumer, they shall immediately inform the competent authorities and take all the necessary measures up to the product recall if needed.

other intelligent objects, the obligation to monitor product changes will become a key feature of managing the new risks created by the technologies in question.

In the context we are considering, the whole question arises of the liability incurred by marketplace-type platforms, where defective products are sold on their websites. In a recent case in the USA, a court held one such platform liable.[28] The US Court of Appeals for the Third Circuit considered the following four factors:

> (1) Whether the actor is the 'only member of the marketing chain available to the injured plaintiff for redress'; (2) Whether 'imposition of strict liability upon the [actor] serves as an incentive to safety'; (3) Whether the actor is 'in a better position than the consumer to prevent the circulation of defective products'; and (4) Whether '[t]he [actor] can distribute the cost of compensating for injuries resulting from defects by charging for it in his business, ie, by charging for it in his business, ie, by adjustment of the rental terms.[29]

The question would not, of course, arise if an online sales platform markets products under its own brand name: they would clearly be regarded as a producer within the meaning of the directive. Moreover, in the case of European legislation, platforms should be regarded as importers/distributors within the EU if products that were sold and potentially defective were manufactured by a producer located outside the EU.[30] Incidentally, it is, of course, the responsibility both of the producer and of persons of comparable status to satisfy themselves that the products being sold comply with EU product safety legislation (both horizontal and sectoral legislation).

[28] *Oberdorf et al v Amazon.Com, Inc*, Third Circuit Court of Appeals, No 18-1041, 3 July 2019; recently though, 'unable to predict whether the Pennsylvania Supreme Court would hold Amazon strictly liable for a third-party vendor's defective product, the US Court of Appeals for the Third Circuit has sent the case to the state high court, asking it to weigh in … The ruling comes after the Third Circuit reheard the case en banc. Prior to that, a split court ruled 2–1 that Amazon could be held liable', www.law.com/thelegalintelligencer/2020/06/03/3rd-circ-sends-amazon-product-liability-case-to-pa-supreme-court/; see a recent update on the case at www.natlawreview.com/article/en-banc-third-circuit-sends-online-marketplace-liability-issue-to-pennsylvania; see also EJ Janger and AD Twerski, 'The Heavy Hand of Amazon: A Seller Not a Neutral Platform (2020) 14 *Brooklyn Journal of Corporate, Financial & Commercial Law* 259; C Busch, 'When Product Liability Meets the Platform Economy: A European Perspective on *Oberdorf v Amazon*' (2019) 8 *Journal of European Consumer and Market Law* 173.

[29] Quoted in Janger and Twerski (ibid).

[30] This is the rationale behind Art 3, para 2 of the PLD, extending the producer's liability to the importer. Moreover, according to Art 3, para 3, 'where the producer of the product cannot be identified, each supplier of the product shall be treated as its producer unless he informs the injured person, within a reasonable time, of the identity of the producer or of the person who supplied him with the product. The same shall apply, in the case of an imported product, if this product does not indicate the identity of the importer referred to in paragraph 2, even if the name of the producer is indicated.' In many cases, marketplace platforms would be the only member of the marketing chain available in the EU to the injured plaintiff for redress. The ELI Model Rules on Online Intermediary Platforms (www.europeanlawinstitute.eu/fileadmin/user_upload/p_eli/Publications/ELI_Model_Rules_on_Online_Platforms.pdf) go in that direction, stating that 'If the customer can reasonably rely on the platform operator having a predominant influence over the supplier, the customer can exercise the rights and remedies for the non-performance available against the supplier under the supplier-customer contract also against the platform operator' (Art 20, para 1). See Busch (n 28).

Furthermore, in its work, the EC has raised the question of the producer's capacity to anticipate how the product will 'behave' when it is equipped with an autonomous and machine-learning system.[31] The eventuality of 'updating' the notion of guardian in the context of liability for damage caused by inanimate objects, which incidentally would create parallels with liability for damage caused by animals, also emerges in this thinking. In my view, these analogies seem to offer the benefit, though this is non-exclusive, of making us understand that, conceptually, in reality we are used to thinking about the rules governing civil liability, so that they can account for the unpredictability and the 'intrinsically' hazardous dimension of some things, or even of some people. In these circumstances, it is not difficult to regard the liability of the producer or of other actors as being based on custody of things that have an autonomous capability to make decisions and to evolve.

The notion of producer is also called into question when a product is printed using a 3-D printer, and in a broader sense, in what are known as decentralised production systems. The status of a consumer who does a 3-D printout of an object after customising the program is unclear, even if, in such cases, the producer will in all likelihood have warned users not to alter the file and will probably refuse to accept any liability. This is how the notion of a 'prosumer' first appeared: it merges the pre-existing notions of producer and consumer. Likewise, where a product is reconditioned or upgraded, etc, who is liable? The initial producer, the consumer or the supplier of the update if they are a third party? The EC seems to take the view that it is the person who altered the product,[32] which is a source of legal risk for the consumer, who will not necessarily assess the consequences, particularly as regards the producer's ability to escape liability. This also gives rise to a major complexity in terms of evaluating individual situations, because it might be necessary to establish distinctions categorised according to the type of defect causing the harm (is it the initial electronic file, the alteration made to the file, the material used to print the object, etc?).

C. The Notion of Defect

A defect is defined in relation to the safety level that we are legitimately entitled to expect. The PLD does not contain any formal distinction between different types of defect (manufacturing, information, design) in the way that US law

[31] Commission, 'Liability for Emerging Digital Technologies' (n 1): 'Concerning the concept of producer, the question arises to what extent the producer maintains control over the features of a product in the context of emerging digital technologies and can therefore be held liable for them. While in many cases the final product and producer may be easy to identify, regardless of whether it includes software or other digital elements, or whether different manufacturers have been involved in the production process, other cases may be less straightforward.'

[32] Commission Notice C/2016/1958, 'The 'Blue Guide' on the implementation of EU products rules 2016' [2016] OJ C272/16.

does, notably in the Restatement of Torts.[33] A clarification of the various defect categories might be beneficial in the current thinking, notably as far as a lack of information or defective information is concerned. Given that information occupies a pivotal position in the new ecosystem, we should look closely at its potential defects. We might also consider a new category of defect, namely that of a 'behavioural' defect. In the presence of autonomous systems whose behaviour is, as their name suggests, autonomous, would it not be useful to take a close look at the said behaviour as soon as it is capable of manifesting itself 'dangerously' and thus in a way that is 'defective'?

The autonomy and the self-learning capability of new products and of all new developments in terms of AI have also been at the heart of recent and current work executed under the auspices of the EC in the area of ethical principles applicable to the development of AI, so that we can ensure that the developments in question are human-centric and trustworthy.[34] It is worth thinking on the consequences, in terms of liability, when ethical guidelines are not adhered to. Ethical guidelines could indeed be part of a general duty of care. A breach of the said duty of care would then be the basis of a negligence-based liability. Alternative theoretical approaches are also worth exploring. For example, in the same way that principles such as privacy by design have developed in terms of personal data protection (and, incidentally, we must think about whether it is opportune to take the view that breaking the law governing personal data protection is indicative of a defective product), we could envisage a notion of the 'ethics by design' type. If a product's design does not comply with the ethical principles developed at EU level, then it might be deemed to constitute a form of design defect: the product would be deemed not to present the level of safety that may be legitimately expected, as it does not achieve a sufficient level of compliance with ethical rules. Whether this 'unethical design defect' would lead to strict liability or fault-based liability should be further discussed. A presumption of defect could be a compromise, whenever the harm suffered by the plaintiff is of a kind that the ethical guidelines were aimed at avoiding. The producer would then have to prove that he complied with ethical guidelines and that, for example, he successfully conducted an ethical impact assessment of the product before putting it on the market.

As with other design defects, the defectiveness analysis would in all likelihood be based on a risk–benefit analysis (what are the benefits for society as a whole and what are the risks, and in particular the ethical risks, for that same society?). Incidentally, this risk–benefit approach is one of the avenues being explored by the EC in its current work. This involves an approach that is fairly traditional in US law, especially as described above, when it comes to identifying and evaluating design defects. I believe that such a risk–benefit approach lends itself quite well to the task of evaluating high-tech products, whose defects, if they exist, may to a

[33] American Law Institute: Restatement (Third) of Torts: Products Liability, § 2.
[34] Above n 12.

significant extent be inherent in their design rather than in their manufacture or presentation.

The increasingly connected nature of products also raises problems of vulnerability to cyberattacks. This being the case, the idea is envisaged of integrating into the notion of defectiveness the level of cybersecurity that may be legitimately expected. As stated previously, and this is not the least of the difficulties arising, we should also bear in mind the fact that the burden on the consumer of providing proof of defectiveness, which may already prove a difficult task for 'conventional' products, may become a task of extreme complexity when dealing with high-tech products. It seems to be essential to envisage mechanisms such as presumptions and deductions in the event of non-compliance with sector-specific technical and safety rules (and a defectiveness analysis in light of these technical standards in terms of safety should be decisive) to provide proof of any possible defectiveness. I will add that producers may be tempted to avail themselves of the argument of the product's intended use in order to try and prove that the origin of the harm caused by the product lies in its misuse, eg via the installation, by the consumer, of external applications. I believe that we need to be vigilant regarding this point, given that, in increasing numbers of cases, the consumer not only uses the product, but is also 'used' by the product, notably via the gathering of data by smart connected devices.

D. The Notion of Damage

Article 9 of the PLD can be interpreted as excluding compensation for non-material damage (moral damage), meaning that this issue is left to national legislators as it lies outside the PLD's scope of application. This may be problematic for several reasons. Since one of the main features of the ecosystem based on emerging digital technologies is its increasingly immaterial and intangible dimension, the harm that may be caused within its context will in all likelihood be of the same nature. The fact that information lies at the heart of the ecosystem in question should encourage us all the more to reflect on the nature of any harm caused by erroneous/defective information. The prejudice suffered as a result of the unauthorised disclosure of personal data comes to mind quite naturally in this context. In addition to questions of how the PLD will work in conjunction with the GDPR,[35] if we were to leave the issue of non-material damage to national law in the different countries, and particularly that of the compensation payable for moral damage, the risk of fragmentation of the internal market is fairly serious. Thus, I believe that it is highly opportune to formally designate moral damage, and especially

[35] Regulation (EU) 2016/679 of the European Parliament and of the Council of 27 April 2016 on the protection of natural persons with regard to the processing of personal data and on the free movement of such data, and repealing Directive 95/46/EC (General Data Protection Regulation) [2016] OJ L119/1.

moral damage caused by a breach of personal data protection laws, as damage that is actionable under the PLD in light of the technological changes taking place.

E. The Liability Regime

In addition to the previously discussed notions and conditions of the PLD, other parts of its legal regime are to be assessed from the perspective of their capacity to adapt to the new context. Regarding the burden of proof, which lies with the consumer, a litigation approach will hardly make sense due to the very high costs and time-consuming nature of expertise in complex cases (because systems are becoming more and more complex, the related costs of expertise will ever increase).This assumption is mainly due to the hard times consumers will face when called upon to prove a defect in very sophisticated products and to prove the fact that the defect caused the damage.

Another aspect of the PLD legal regime is the so-called 'development-risk' defence.[36] One of the crucial issues here is to determine whether the development-risk clause should be maintained. It would be socially unacceptable, and would therefore be negative in an innovation perspective, for a producer to escape liability. Indeed, society as a whole would not accept an unfair allocation of loss to the consumers and would therefore become more and more sceptical about innovation. This would especially be the case in the field of machine learning and autonomous systems if producers were able to rely on the fact that the product was defect-free when put onto the market and that it later became defective, unpredictably, on the basis of its self-learning capacities/features. This would mean that more and more losses, caused by unforeseen consequences of emerging digital technologies and cybersecurity threats, would be supported by consumers. In this context, compensation funds look like a socially, legally and economically optimal option, not least because it would, like in road traffic accidents, remove most cases from the litigation arena.

V. Conclusion

Within the EU, the rules governing civil liability resulting from defective products constitute a horizontal legal framework, which is designed primarily for tangible objects and does not apply to the liability borne by service providers. The unpredictability of the way in which autonomous systems behave presents a number of

[36] According to Art 7 of the PLD, 'The producer shall not be liable as a result of this Directive if he proves … e) that the state of scientific and technical knowledge at the time when he put the product into circulation was not such as to enable the existence of the defect to be discovered'.

similarities to situations of unpredictability that the law has experienced in previous eras, such as those involving animals, industrial machinery, products that are hazardous because they are highly unstable, children and adults with disabilities. The EC Expert Group on Liability and New Technologies suggested, for example, that 'The benchmark for assessing performance by autonomous technology in the context of vicarious liability is primarily the one accepted for human auxiliaries'.[37] Thus, the very concept of the unpredictability of the agent or object for whose actions we are answerable is not new at all, and the liability for damage caused by inanimate objects or by other people is not so far removed, in terms of its basis and its regimes, from what we might imagine in terms of liability for damage caused by new technologies. It means that traditional legal rules and categories can cope to a certain extent with the new situation.

However, the complexity of the technologies in question makes it costly, in terms of both time and expertise, to apply the traditional legal conditions governing liability. This is a cost that consumers, and even the legal system itself, are probably not prepared to pay. Mechanisms involving insurance, or even dedicated warranty funds, would take some of these issues out of the contentious sphere. Such a step might also be regarded as a precondition for the social acceptance of new technologies and thus for their development.

Whereas a regulatory intervention has been decided on at the EU level,[38] the choice between a horizontal instrument, such as the PLD, and sectoral instruments, such as regulations applicable to given product categories, has not yet been made. A horizontal instrument offers the benefit of striving to achieve coherence of the system and avoids treating victims of defective products differently, but may also present the drawback of uncertain application if it is not sufficiently tailored to the specific circumstances of different situations. Sectoral instruments are usually tailored to the products and situations concerned, but they also have the effect of 'breaking up' the regulatory framework. By their very nature, they also constitute 'technical' instruments and reflect not how technology apprehends the law, but how the law apprehends technology. If the choice is made to combine horizontal instruments with sectoral instruments, we then need to reflect on how the two will work together, probably on a basis of *lex generalis/lex specialis* allocation. In view of the various initiatives in the field of the Digital Single Market, the work undertaken to establish coherence between them and the instrument(s) regulating civil liability will have to be particularly painstaking in nature.

For the moment, the absence of any tangible data on the consequences of introducing emerging digital technologies onto the market, in terms of civil liability,

[37] Expert Group on Liability and New Technologies – New Technologies Formation (n 1) 7.

[38] The idea of this intervention seems to be agreed in principle, even though its format(s) have not yet been decided (guidelines for interpretation of the PLD, legislative instruments, general principles, etc). Various EC documents have, however, emphasised the fact that the Directive has adapted fairly successfully to technological changes over the course of time.

means that the nature, content and scale of the regulatory response necessary cannot easily be evaluated. We will, however, also run the significant risk of not being ready when these practical questions arise. Moreover, the negative impact on the Single Market of national initiatives taken in this area, in the absence of an EU framework, would be substantial. The digital economy needs a clear and comprehensive legal framework that will provide a sufficient degree of legal certainty and permit its harmonious development. Such a development cannot be envisaged if consumers are not granted appropriate protection by a new law governing civil liability that is tailored to emerging digital technologies.

10

Harmonising Private Law in Cyberspace: The New Directives in the Digital Single Market Context

ANDREJ SAVIN

I. Introduction

The long-awaited Directive on Content and Services (DCD)[1] and Directive on Sale of Goods (OSG)[2] were published in 2019. Having been first proposed in 2015, they entered into force in June 2019 and Member States will have until July 2021 to implement them. In the flurry of directives, communications, judgments and other documents concerning the Digital Single Market that the EU has produced since 2015, it is easy to overlook the importance of these instruments. The fact that it has been possible to harmonise a significant portion of private law should not escape the attention of both the businesses and the general public. Nor should the fact that civil law has been used as a regulatory tool for the digital world. Both facts deserve attention, irrespective of which side one approaches them from.

This chapter does not intend to analyse the new directives in detail, nor to explore their operation or how their use in different contexts might play out. Much less does it attempt to probe deeply into the debate on what European contract law is.[3] The key question asked, instead, is structurally simpler but ultimately complex: what is the position of private law in the context of the Digital Single Market – or, in other words, is private law, so harmonised, capable of significantly contributing to the achievement of the EU Digital Single Market? This question has two dimensions.

[1] Directive 2019/770 on certain aspects concerning contracts for the supply of digital content and digital services [2019] OJ L136/1.

[2] Directive 2019/771 on certain aspects concerning contracts for the sale of goods, amending Regulation (EU) 2017/2394 and Directive 2009/22/EC, and repealing Directive 1999/44/EC [2019] OJ L136/28.

[3] See R Schulze and F Zoll, *European Contract Law*, 2nd edn (Baden Baden, Nomos, 2018).

First, I would like to throw light on the origin of the effort that preceded the directives and establish that the two texts are not unexpected or surprising, but are descendants of a long and notable family of European civil law codifications. Although the directives were promised in the 2015 Digital Single Market Strategy,[4] they are results of a process that dates back to the late 1980s and early 1990s. More directly, I would like to show that the solutions in the directives predate the actual text. While this is of some historical interest for civil law scholars, it has one important consequence: the EU civil law has not been written from the ground up with the new technologies in mind, but adapted.

Secondly, I would like to place the directives in the context of the EU's efforts to bring about a Digital Single Market. In this sense, the question I seek to answer is: why and to what extent is civil law in its present EU form necessary, and can it be used as a tool for regulating the digital world? In the modern world, which is moving forward at frightening speed, it is not unreasonable to ask if further civil law instruments are needed, or what their purpose might be. It is equally important to ask if full harmonisation is preferable to a partially consumer law-driven approach. Furthermore, the modern user/consumer rarely if ever resorts to suing in civil courts or arbitrating, and is rarely sued. A comprehensive civil law reform has little direct effect on such a consumer. At the same time, new phenomena, such as the use of artificial intelligence or a data-based economy, inevitably challenge the foundations of traditional law of obligations and require the rethinking of concepts such as offer and acceptance. It, therefore, seems legitimate to inquire about the relationship between private law and Digital Single Market regulation.

I begin by outlining the origins of the EU's efforts in private law leading to the Common European Sales Law (CESL), the first EU civil law instrument to address the digital world directly (section II). I map the solutions which have been taken up in the subsequent directives. I continue by looking at the new directives and the tasks that they perform in the EU Digital Single Market policy (section III). The main question in section IV is: to what extent can civil law instruments answer the challenges of the modern digital world? I conclude by outlining which harmonisation efforts might make sense for the future Digital Single Market.

II. The Origins

The words 'EU private law' can have two meanings. A distinction has been made[5] between European private law as a common academic tradition (*acquis commun*) and European private law as a collection of EU legal texts on private law (*acquis communautaire*). The first is the rich and diverse body of academic thought,

[4] Commission, 'A Digital Single Market Strategy for Europe' (Communication) COM (2015) 192 final.

[5] N Jansen, 'European Private Law' in *The Max Planck Encyclopedia of European Private Law*, vol I (Oxford, Oxford University Press, 2012) 637–40.

including the Principles of European Contract Law (PECL) and the CESL as the two 'restatements' discussed below. The other is the multitude of EU secondary laws addressing the private law issues. This distinction is of some relevance since the public perceives the first as the true successor to the great European legal traditions while the second is accorded the status of a pragmatic substitute – not universal, not comprehensive, but necessary. The two, although different, are not divergent, for it is the *acquis commun* that has frequently informed the *acquis communautaire* and led to the adoption of the two directives discussed in this paper. Although it may be tempting, when thinking about the Digital Single Market, only to think about EU private law in the second context, it does, in reality, include both.[6]

The EU *acquis commun* took off in the early 1990s. In an article published in the *American Journal of Comparative Law* in 1992,[7] Ole Lando, the then Chairman of the Commission of European Contract Law, set out to explain to the global audience – in broad strokes – the purpose of and need for the European Code of Obligations. His contribution was twofold. He revived the moribund debate on 'common' European civil law. By pushing the discussion in the direction of 'principles' rather than 'code', he avoided the political pitfalls that the use of the term 'unification' might bring. More importantly, he put the new project on pragmatic grounds. Not seeking grand solutions worthy of Napoleon, he looked instead to provide practical guidance for situations where the lack of common understanding might hamper trade between Member States. As irony would have it, by realistically suggesting that any new European attempt should seek to harmonise laws 'linked to economic integration', he followed in the steps of Napoleon, who sought to overcome fragmented laws and bring the ideals of the French revolution to civil law.

The efforts of the Lando Commission had a lasting impact. The work, which commenced with the publication of the PECL in 1990,[8] continued with the Draft European Common Frame of Reference (DCFR)[9] and led to the CESL[10] and to the two directives which are the main subject of this paper. Birth was thus given to a remarkable red line of continuity. Since the PECL had been incorporated into the DCFR, the drafters of the CESL drew on the DCFR and the drafters of the two directives drew on the CESL,[11] and a clear and unusual EU contract law

[6] In that sense, see the approach in N Jansen and R Zimmermann (eds), *Commentaries on European Contract Laws* (Oxford, Oxford University Press, 2018).

[7] O Lando, 'Principles of European Contract Law: An Alternative to or a Precursor of European Legislation?' (1992) 40 *American Journal of Comparative Law* 573.

[8] O Lando and H Beale, *Principles of European Contract Law: Parts 1 and 2*, combined 2nd rev edn (The Hague, Kluwer Law International, 1999).

[9] *Principles, Definitions and Model Rules of European Private Law (DCFR)*, full edn (Munich, Sellier, 2009).

[10] Commission, 'Proposal for a Regulation of the European Parliament and of the Council on a Common European Sales Law' COM (2011) 0635 final.

[11] More specifically on this, see C Twigg-Flesner, 'Introduction: EU Consumer and Contract Law at a Crossroads' in C Twigg-Flesner (ed), *Research Handbook on EU Consumer and Contract Law* (Cheltenham, Edward Elgar Publications, 2016).

started to emerge. The work of Ole Lando and his successors has had a lasting and direct impact.

The PECL had commenced as a specific kind of a restatement of European private law, an effort to find what is common about it and to initiate a discussion about its origins and its relevance to modern Europe. The PECL, which had been drafted in the early 1990s, had no provisions directly relevant for the digital world, but established a basis for the work that continued with the DCFR shortly after the publication of the last document.

The DCFR openly draws on the PECL.[12] Published a full decade after the PECL, the DCFR covered specific contracts which had a digital element and occasionally mentioned digital phenomena.[13] While recognising the importance of the new economy, it was meant neither as a Digital Single Market instrument nor as an effort to address the multitude of challenges the digital world presented. Put differently, while the DCFR was comprehensive and well received (in spite of some fear that a pan-European civil code was being imposed), it did not have digital economy nor the new industrial revolution[14] as its focus.

The official EU interest in private law as part of *acquis communautaire* can be traced to the Parliament's 1989 resolution.[15] At the same time, some elements of European consumer law were harmonised.[16] Sporadic efforts continued until 2001, when a Communication on contract law was published.[17] The Communication sought to identify the instances where discrepancies between laws of Member States acted as impediments. It looked at market-friendly solutions, non-binding principles, the improvement of the present framework and a possible new instrument. The Communication, while demonstrating an awareness of the growing digitalisation, did not directly focus on it.

As a follow-up, in 2003 the European Commission issued an action plan demanding a more coherent European contract law.[18] Surprisingly, it became clear from the response of the stakeholders that (i) the existing private law directives were vague and (ii) the stakeholders did not believe they were affected by the divergences. On the contrary, it seemed that inaction was preferred to action and that the stakeholders were more worried by inconsistencies in the existing laws

[12] C von Bar et al., *Principles, Definitions and Model Rules of European Private Law*, outline edn (Munich, Sellier 2009) 30–35.

[13] Thus, Art IV.A. – 1:101 covers contracts for the sale of IP rights and contracts for the sale of data (including databases).

[14] See K Schwabb, *The Fourth Industrial Revolution* (London, Penguin 2016).

[15] Resolution of 26 May 1989 on action to bring into line the private law of the Member States [1989] OJ C158/400. See also Resolution of 6 May 1994 Concerning the codification of private law and the Commission on European contract law [1994] OJ C205/518.

[16] Council Directive 93/13/EEC of 5 April 1993 on unfair terms in consumer contracts [1993] OJ L 95/29. For an overview of historic changes, see S Weatherill, *EU Consumer Law and Policy*, 2nd edn (Cheltenham, Edward Elgar Publications, 2014).

[17] Commission, 'European Contract Law' (Communication) COM (2001) 398 final.

[18] Commission, 'Action Plan on A More Coherent European Contract Law' COM (2003) final, [2003] OJ C63/1.

or by the cultural or language barriers than the perceived disparities in the legal system. The Action Plan was criticised[19] for bringing up only anecdotal evidence on the 'divergences' and how these might affect EU businesses and consumers. Furthermore, the 2003 Action Plan suggests that a common frame of reference is needed, but it does not name the PECL or the group of laws that eventually led to the DCFR specifically. The Action Plan also names the standard contract terms as the desirable outcome, but it is vague and undetermined as to how these could be used. The third and final idea was the introduction of an optional instrument of European contract law, which is what the Commission ultimately attempted with the CESL.

Nevertheless, the focused attempt to include the digital world came about in parallel with the preparation for the CESL. The 2011 Loos Report was an academic exercise attempting to address the deficiencies in the existing EU framework for digital content and services and to propose solutions for the future.[20] It based its reasoning on the specificities of the consumer law problems, finding several areas of interest. First, the distinction between content and services was shown not to be of particular importance in practice. Secondly, the obligations arising out of general and sector-specific laws need to be in harmony. Thirdly, conformity problems need to be addressed with care as the simple translation from the offline world might not work. Fourthly, the position of minors needed to be specifically addressed.

In 2011, the Commission published a proposal for a Regulation on a Common European Sales Law (CESL).[21] The instrument was to apply to business-to-consumer (B2C) and business-to-small- and medium-sized enterprise (B2SME) transactions only, and was to be entirely voluntary in that the parties could freely opt in. Three elements are of significance. First, the CESL had been envisaged as an optional instrument, existing in concurrence with the civil law systems of the Member States. Secondly, the CESL directly addressed the changes brought about by digital technologies. For example, part IV of the CESL dealt with obligations of the parties to a sales contract including the supply of digital content. Section 3 of part IV dealt with the conformity of the goods and digital content. Digital content is a recurrent theme in the document. Finally, the CESL directly addressed the division between the digital and non-digital by making digital part of the main part of civil law.[22]

[19] J Smits, 'The Action Plan on a More Coherent European Contract Law' (2003) 10 *Maastricht Journal of European and Comparative Law* 111.

[20] M Loos et al, 'Analysis of the Applicable Legal Frameworks and Suggestions for the Contours of a Model System of Consumer Protection in Relation to Digital Content Contracts: Final Report (Amsterdam, University of Amsterdam, Centre for the Study of European Contract Law, 2011) (Loos Report).

[21] On CESL, see M Loos, 'The Regulation of Digital Content Contracts in the Optional Instrument of Contract Law' [2011] *European Review of Private Law* 729.

[22] This is a debatable choice: see section IV below.

The scope of the CESL was from the start meant to include the supply of digital content, and the CESL addresses five groups of problems relating to it:[23] information obligations, incorporation of standard terms, unfair terms, non-conformity and remedies. The problems with CESL's approach were also evident, however. In relation to the different types of digital content, it was not clear what forms of licensing were covered and how.[24] Digital services were expressly excluded, narrowing the text's usefulness even further. Article 2(j)(vi) simply excluded 'the creation of new digital content and the amendment of existing digital content by consumers or any other interaction with the creations of other users'. Personal data had not been incorporated as a consideration and it was also doubtful to what extent the CESL could be applied to cloud computing. It nevertheless seemed that the CESL had a solid basis for dealing with a significant cluster of problems arising from the digital world.

III. Directives in the Digital Single Market Context

After considerable criticism,[25] the CESL proposal had been withdrawn and the two directives were proposed instead. The purpose, the origin and the general direction of both directives has been stated clearly.[26]

Four points are of note. First, the directives are part of EU consumer law proper. In other words, the Commission sees them as consumer law instruments. This is a step back from the CESL, which was more ambitious in its focus on SMEs, but is in line with the consumer law drive of the EU Digital Single Market Strategy of 2015, which expressly deals with the harmonisation of private law relating to consumers and promises that the two directives will be tabled. Secondly, full harmonisation is chosen over an optional instrument. Thirdly, the Commission's original intent had been to have the same rules for online and offline sales; the proposal had only online sales in mind,[27] but the final directive went back to the original plan and includes all sales. The scope of the instrument on digital services had also changed from 'digital content' in the proposal[28] to 'digital content and digital services' in the final text. Although the text in the proposals and in the final directives is

[23] See M Loos, 'The Regulation of Digital Content B2C Contracts in CESL' (2003) Amsterdam Law School Legal Studies Research Paper No 2013-60.

[24] S Arenerstål, 'Licensing Digital Content in a Sale of Goods Context' (2015) 10 *Journal of Intellectual Property Law* 750.

[25] See R Schulze, *Common European Sales Law (CESL): Commentary* (Baden-Baden, Nomos, 2012).

[26] See L Beil, 'New EU Rules for Digital Contracts' [2016] *Journal of European Consumer and Market Law* 110.

[27] Commission, 'Proposal for a Directive of the European Parliament and of the Council on certain aspects concerning contracts for the online and other distance sales of goods' COM (2015) 635 final – 2015/0288 (COD).

[28] Commission, 'Proposal for a Directive of the European Parliament and of the Council on certain aspects concerning contracts for the supply of digital content' COM (2015) 634 final – 2015/0287 (COD).

roughly of the same size and with similar content, the changes are an example of a rare increase in scope on the way from the proposal to the final text. Finally, the Commission stated that a broad scope was preferred and that a directive would serve the purpose better than a regulation. The broad scope ensured that the laws were technology-neutral and future-proof, while the choice of a directive minimised the risk of political opposition from the Member States.

The explanatory memorandums to the directives clarified that different policy options had been considered:

- targeted full harmonisation for digital content and goods;
- targeted full harmonisation for digital content and application of the trader's law, combined with the existing harmonised rules on goods;
- targeted full harmonisation for digital content and no policy change for goods;
- minimum harmonisation for digital content and no policy change for goods;
- a voluntary European model contract combined with an EU trust mark.

The proposals have been called a 'new European law of contract'.[29] While the laws are broad in scope and would have a notable impact, little direct criticism was voiced compared to the CESL. While I do not give a detailed analysis of each of the directives in this chapter, an overview of the main features of each is important.

A. Directive on the Sale of Goods (OSG)

The Preamble to the OSG (see eg items 4, 5 and 9) makes it clear that the main drive for adoption has been the increased importance of electronic commerce and the disparities in national law that exist in spite of the harmonisation brought about by the Consumer Rights Directive (CRD).[30] The purpose of the OSG is to harmonise the requirements for conformity, consumer remedies and the level of consumer protection, and, as such, complement the CRD. Furthermore, the OSG complements the sister instrument – the Directive on Content and Services (DCD).

As expressly stated in paragraph 13 of the OSG Preamble, the DCD applies to all digital contracts, including those involving the sale of content on a tangible medium. The OSG, on the contrary, applies to contracts for the sale of goods even where digital services are involved as part of the goods[31] (see Preamble, paragraph 14). Therefore, a robot toy operating on pre-installed or downloadable software would be covered by the OSG, whereas the sale of virtual reality software on Blu-ray or DVD would be covered by the DCD.

[29] See C Wendehorts and B Zöchling-Jud (eds), *Ein neues Vertragsrecht für den digitalen Binnenmarkt?* (Vienna, Manz 2016). See also J Smits, 'New European Union Proposals for Distance Sales and Digital Contents Contracts: Fit for Purpose?' (2016) 24 *Zeitschrift für europäisches Privatrecht* 319.

[30] Directive 2011/83/EU [2011] OJ L304/64.

[31] Art 3, Preamble, paras 14 and 15.

Tangible movable items which are incorporated in or are interconnected with digital content or a digital service in such a way that their absence would prevent the goods from performing the designated function are included under the OSG.[32] It is somewhat naively stated that the OSG covers situations where goods contain digital elements that are made part of the contract or the consumer explicitly expects them (incorporated or interconnected content).[33] Unincorporated or independent services, on the other hand, are subject to the DCD.[34] This would mean that the goods the services operate on come under the OSG, while apps or services would be under the DCD. Dependent services, even when supplied by third parties, are covered by the OSG, and would be presumed to be so in cases of doubt.

It is not clear to what extent the explanation given in Article 3 and paragraphs 14 and 15 of the Preamble can be accepted. Smart TV apps are given as examples of tangible incorporated movables, but such apps (eg HBO or Netflix) are often both incorporated into various devices (such as smart TVs) and independent (in particular, where they are not pre-installed) under the definitions, and would without doubt be subject to the DCD as separate services. It would make little sense to subject them to the sales contract. Such apps can, furthermore, be provided by the manufacturer on its own hardware initially, but later on sold or provided for free on different platforms.

Both proposals are targeted full harmonisation texts.[35] The OSG does not affect national law with regard to contract legality, formation, consequences of termination, validity, nullity or effect, nor does it affect the obligation to inform. The scope of the Directive includes B2C contracts only, but can explicitly be extended to SMEs.

The main part of the OSG contains the following rules:

- conformity (Articles 5–7)
- incorrect installation (Article 8)
- third party rights (Article 9)
- seller's liability (Article 10)
- burden of proof (Article 11)
- obligation to notify (Article 12)
- remedies for lack of conformity (Article 13)
- repair or replacement (Article 14)
- price reduction (Article 15)
- termination (Article 16)

[32] Art 2(5)(b).
[33] Preamble, para 15.
[34] Preamble, para 16 and Art 3(3).
[35] Smits, 'New European Proposal' (n 29).

- commercial guarantees (Article 17)
- redress (Article 18)
- enforcement (Article 19)
- consumer information (Article 20)
- mandatory rules (Article 21)

The OSG takes maximum harmonisation and a high level of consumer protection as its fundamental points, the former being new in relation to the CESL but familiar from other consumer laws. There was little publicly voiced criticism, the prevailing feeling being that consumers would be given marginally better protection but that the Directive would bring no dramatic changes to national laws.

B. Directive on the Distance Sale of Content and Services (DCD)

The DCD has been more difficult to pass than anticipated, with the trilogue only being completed in December 2018. At the point of adoption, the UK was the only state with any private rules on digital content.[36] The DCD, which complements the OSG, is essentially a consumer protection instrument dealing with pre-contractual information and withdrawal. The DCD has inherited CESL solutions, a fact which had been expressly acknowledged in the text itself.[37]

The scope of both the original proposal and the final directive is extraordinarily broad, encompassing every possible kind of digital content and service.[38]

While content is defined as data in the digital form (Article 2(1)), digital services are defined (in a somewhat circular manner) as services that enable consumers to create, process, store and access digital data or a service allowing the sharing of user-generated digital data. While the first part of the definition targets commercial digital services, the latter deals with user-generated ones, irrespective of the business model of the platform providing them (eg advertising). The fact that digital content is distinguished from digital services both in the title and in the text body of the Directive is justified. While content refers to raw data, services refer to a product or a platform.

The definitions (Article 2), which match those of the OSG, are essentially also the same as those found in Article 2 CRD or Article 2 CESL. The scope (Article 3) comprises the supply of digital content or service for a price. Importantly (*cf* Article 3 of the Proposal), the DCD also applies where the consumer provides or undertakes to provide data to the trader. This does not include data which are

[36] Consumer Rights Act 2015, UK Public General Acts 2015, c 15.

[37] See Explanatory Memorandum.

[38] See G Spindler, 'Contracts for the Supply of Digital Content – Scope of Application and Basic Approach' (2016) 12 *European Review of Contract Law* 183.

necessary for the successful completion of the contract or data which the law requires, but data otherwise not directly related to that. Specifically excluded are non-digital services with a digital output, telecoms services, healthcare, gambling, financial services, open-source software, non-transmitted general public performances and public-sector information. Where a contract bundles both digital and non-digital content, the DCD provides that it will only apply to the digital.

The inclusion of data as consideration is necessary. A direct consequence, however, will be that any collection of personal data on the seller's side (except where this is necessary data or data required by law) triggers the application of the Directive whether the parties so desire or not. This seems justified in light of the numerous transactions for the supply of content conducted on the Internet.

The scope of the DCD is defined in Article 1 as comprising the conformity of the digital content or service, remedies and the modification of content or services. The DCD does not create a new contract type.[39] The contracts covered are essentially ordinary contracts regulated by national contract law in which the rules on conformity and remedies have been added as a bolt-on. In that sense, it is not wrong to talk of the DCD as yet another consumer law directive.

The DCD contains the following rules:

- supply (Article 9)
- conformity (Article 10)
- subjective and objective requirements (Articles 7–8)
- incorrect integration (Article 9)
- third party rights (Article 10)
- trader's liability (Article 11)
- burden of proof (Article 12)
- remedies (Articles 13–14)
- termination (Articles 15–17)
- time limits (Article 18)
- modification (Article 19)
- redress and enforcement (Articles 20–21)

The criticism of the proposal concentrated on the need for having a separate regime for digital contracts, the confusion the new regime brings to the existing consumer law and the choice of maximum harmonisation.[40] The fear is that the introduction of a separate instrument increases confusion and reduced coherence

[39] K Sein and G Spindler, 'The New Directive on Contracts for the Supply of Digital Content and Digital Services – Scope of Application and Trader's Obligation to Supply – Part 1' (2019) 15 *European Review for Contract Law* 257.

[40] M Lehmann, 'A Question of Coherence: The Proposals on EU Contract Rules on Digital Content and Online Sales' (2016) 23 *Maastricht Journal of European and Comparative Law* 752.

while maximum harmonisation contributes to the feeling that the EU is encroaching on Member States' competences.

Not all issues are covered. For example, it is not clear from the current text to what extent the consumer is entitled to dispose of the acquired content in the second-hand market. Article 17 would suggest that the contract termination also terminates the consumer's entitlement to use the content. This is questionable as intellectual property laws may allow the resale and Article 3(9) DCD specifically says that the Directive is without prejudice to EU or national laws on copyright.

The fact that only B2C contracts have been included has also been criticised.[41] It seems that space is left for future action which would include SMEs, although no specific proposal has been made yet.

Overall, however, it is difficult to deny that there is a need for specific modern rules on digital content and services. This has sporadically been demanded not only in previous EU policy papers,[42] but also directly by various consumer associations in preparation for the final text.[43]

C. Clashes with Other Branches of Law

A particularly important question are the real or potential clashes which can arise between other branches of law and the matter covered in the directives. Since both directives deal directly with digital economy, which, in turn, is regulated by a variety of instruments, potential problems may arise.[44] Article 3(7) specifically gives other sector-specific laws priority, and Articles 3(8) and 3(9) do that directly for data protection and intellectual property (IP) laws.

The DCD allows data to be traded as part of the contract (Article 3) or, in other words, to be offered in payment for content or services. There seems to be nothing problematic with the idea of data being traded, nor with data being used as a consideration in a transaction with the trader. Both are regular activities both in the B2B (business-to-business) and B2C contexts, and can conceivably form part of a sales agreement or the contract for the supply of content or digital services.

The DCD does not replace the General Data Protection Regulation (GDPR) framework, which needs to be adhered to in relevant cases.[45] This means that if there are problems arising out of compliance with the GDPR, there would be

[41] See H Beale, *Scope of Application and General Approach of the New Rules for Contracts in the Digital Environment* (European Commission, 2015).

[42] Including the 2015 Digital Single Market Strategy.

[43] Commission, 'Impact Assessment accompanying the document Proposals for Directives of the European Parliament and of the Council (1) on certain aspects concerning contracts for the supply of digital content and (2) on certain aspects concerning contracts for the online and other distance sales of goods', SWD (2015) 0274 final, 2.

[44] For an overview of e-commerce aspect of digital sale of goods or content see A Savin, *EU Internet Law*, 3rd edn (Cheltenham, Edward Elgar Publications, 2020).

[45] See Art 3(8).

problems with the underlying transaction governed by the DCD. Since the main set-up in which the GDPR is relevant is the act of gathering, processing and keeping the data, the main GDPR framework (the existence of the legal basis for the processing, adherence to principles, etc) is governing the transaction inasmuch as it relates to personal data. Only 'personal data' is expressly mentioned, which matches the GDPR scope, meaning that 'big data', defined in this case as anonymised data, are out of the scope of either the DCD or the GDPR.[46] The DCD expressly includes data minimisation as well as the 'by design' and 'by default' principles (paragraph 48 of the Preamble), and mentions that the violation of any of these may be treated as non-conformity under the DCD. This would mean that the supply of content which violates data protection rules can be used as a basis for remedies on the buyer's side, but also that the buyer's supply of problematic (eg false or another person's) data may produce the same effect.

The problem of sales of tangible versus intangible digital goods has been exacerbated with the expansion of streaming. In many jurisdictions, the sale of tangible media (eg a DVD) would be covered under the sales of goods law, whereas downloads or streaming over the Internet would be under the services/IP regime. The DCD is without prejudice to the Copyright Directive or national law on copyright.[47] The traditional supply of content (in a non-digital context) involved a licensing agreement (dealing with the rights in the content) and the sales contract covering the tangible medium carrying the content. Thus, a music CD purchase would bind the buyer through the licensing agreement, while the sale of the actual medium would be covered under sales law. As streaming and digital downloads overtook the sales of physical media, so did the legal treatment. The CESL already subjected digital content to the sales regime, including downloading, streaming and contracts involving tangible media.

The DCD does not say anything meaningful about the copyright problem. The default position would simply be that contract law is allowed to move within the confines that copyright law allows it. It would seem that, where the consumer enters into a contract with the retail trader (including the end-user licence agreement), the agreement including the remedies for its breach is with the retail trader only. This is consistent with the language of the DCD. Where the rights holder, on the other hand, collects data, the data-as-payment consideration provision would seem to activate the contractual relationship with the rights holder too.

A related question would be the extent of the rights holder's liability. Article 10 DCD concerns restrictions resulting from third party rights and states that such restrictions would entitle the consumer to the usual remedies.

It seems from the above that a contractual relationship governed by either of the new directives cannot modify the data protection or the IP mandatory regime otherwise controlled by other EU or national instruments. It would also seem that

[46] But may potentially fall under the scope of competition, cybersecurity or other laws.
[47] See Art 3(9).

the main position is that the directives' referral to the primacy of other relevant laws is sufficient to limit most, but not all, clashes.

IV. Civil Law as a Tool for Regulating the Internet

However successful one judges the new directives to be – and time will tell – from the cyberlaw perspective, there are two main questions. The first is how adequate is private law for addressing problems in the digital world? The other, related, question is how adaptable is it in the face of new technologies?

A. Private Law as a Tool for the Digital World

The role of private law (as opposed to public law, including criminal law) as a tool for regulating cyberlaw has never been the subject of vigorous debate. Although it was often suggested (eg in the CESL, OSG and DCD) that private law ought to be harmonised because of the challenges brought by digital transformations, it has never been doubted that private law was the right tool and the dynamics of harmonisation has not properly been questioned, at least until the attempt with the CESL. It has equally rarely been claimed by those interested in digital regulation that contract law was the obvious and immediate tool to solve the problems, consumer law being the chosen instrument instead. The majority of the efforts to harmonise private law in the EU context were initiated for the practical purpose of addressing the difficulties that consumers were facing.[48] Even when, as in the case of the CESL, digital issues have been addressed, this was on the assumption that the pre-digital context of civil law could be extended to digital phenomena.

Remarkably little concerning private law is actually found in the DSM, or any other digital EU policy document. Little clarification concerning contract or tort law issues in the existing policy is given. A look at the DSM reveals that section 2, entitled 'Cross-border e-Commerce Rules that Consumers and Business Can Trust', contains a promise to harmonise laws relating to cross-border e-commerce, but concentrates on what can safely be described as traditional consumer laws. The changes have come, instead, from the initiatives to change private law itself, often coordinated by different directorates general. It is these documents that then addressed the issues of digital economy independently, and with but a superficial recourse to EU digital strategy. Only the OSG and DCD have directly been a result of an IT policy, but they are, in fact, based on the CESL.

[48] See Commission, 'A Digital Single Market Strategy for Europe' (Communication) COM (2015) 192 (DSM 2015) and Consumer Rights Directive, 2011/83/EU of the European Parliament and of the Council of 25 October 2011 on consumer rights [2011] OJ L304/64.

There are, in my view, three main reasons why private law may not be enough, even when properly harmonised.

The first is the general lack of direction on the issue of private law in EU digital policy. The Commission's policy statements on the issue are often vague and focused on generic promises to 'unleash the potential', 'remove the disparities' and 'protect the consumer', which are also seen in a number of other initiatives. In the – by title – most explicit document on the subject other than DSM, the Commission is desperately vague as to what the actual difficulties are.[49] Those looking for a firm policy statement on the relationship between private law and digital regulation would be looking in vain.

The second key challenge in expecting too much from private law is the interface between different branches of law required to deal with the problems. I indicated above that the key concept of trading data takes EU law into a difficult area previously not subject to private law. Further clashes may be caused with the IP framework. It may have been relatively easy to transfer the licensing problem into the area of private law, but it will be more difficult to do so with complex streaming models that run on different converged and interconnected platforms and sub-platforms. The reality converged; the laws have not. A cursory look at the themes associated with the law of digital content distribution and digital services reveals that the focus is not on private law, but on an entirely different cluster of problems: copyright, artificial intelligence (AI), privacy, competition, etc.[50] Private law disparities are, furthermore, very rarely named by businesses as being obstacles.

Contracts for the supply of digital content and services are not exclusively in the domain of private law, but are suffering from issues that touch upon a number of other disciplines, including finance, tax, data protection and intellectual property.[51] In that sense, it is no longer enough to have well-written contract laws if the parties entering into a contractual relationship are not well equipped to understand and deal with the issues arising out of the neighbouring disciplines. A contract involving the voluntary transfer of information from the consumer to the merchant seller, for example, is largely subject to privacy laws and depends little on contractual arrangements, however innovative they might be.

Related to this is the EU structure of digital regulation. In the EU, the three 'silos' of regulation – e-commerce, telecommunications and audio-video – coexist, relatively oblivious to the changes made in civil law. The e-Commerce Directive[52]

[49] See Commission, 'Digital Contracts for Europe – Unleashing the Potential of e-Commerce' (Communication) COM (2015) 633 final.

[50] See T Pihlajarinne, J Vesala and O Honkkila (eds), *Online Distribution of Content in the EU* (Cheltenham, Edward Elgar Publications, 2019).

[51] R Schulze, D Staudenmayer and S Lohsse (eds), *Contracts for the Supply of Digital Content: Regulatory Challenges and Gaps* (Baden-Baden, Nomos 2017).

[52] Directive 2000/31/EC of the European Parliament and of the Council of 8 June 2000 on certain legal aspects of information society services, in particular electronic commerce, in the Internal Market (Directive on electronic commerce) [2000] OJ L178/1.

incorporated some elements of civil law, but all the subsequent private law changes have either been made in consumer law or the new civil law (such as the OSG and DCD). This causes the entire EU digital policy to have almost no basis in civil law or, put differently, it leaves the complex problems to national laws. Furthermore, the converged reality of digital life meets the non-converged siloed structure of EU digital laws.

Finally, there are doubts as to whether the digital/non-digital division, which is still encountered in EU directives, continues to be meaningful. A number of directives, including the two discussed in this paper, are specifically written to address challenges in the digital world, while older ones are often generic. The EU lawmaker itself believes this to be a problem, which is obvious from the change in the scope of DSG from general (in the first proposal) to online-only (in subsequent readings) to general again (in the final text). This is not only a question of choice, in the sense that each option is available, but is also one of possibility. In certain cases, it may not be possible to regulate 'digital' and 'non-digital' in a single instrument anymore, while in other cases (such as the OSG) it may be desirable. It has been suggested that the development of special digital rules within general instruments (the original CESL approach) gives the flexibility needed for the digital element while solving the practical problems of making a political compromise in a reasonable time period.[53] At the same time, it is clear that part of the success attributed to the new directives comes from the lack of a need to make political compromises needed to achieve a more general law. A further problem is the level of harmonisation. While the CESL had been made a voluntary instrument, the OSG and DCD are measures that require full harmonisation. This matches the approach taken with the CRD and some other consumer-oriented measures, but brings the risk of politically compromised texts which limited flexibility.

B. New Technologies and EU Private Law

New technologies pose significant challenges to traditional concepts of law. In cases where disruptive technologies emerge, the question is often not how to modify the law to fit the new phenomena, but whether the law framework is adequate at all (or even superfluous). Examples of technology in the modern world are numerous, and some challenge traditional concepts of private law significantly.

Where AI is involved, for example,[54] the use of traditional concepts such as agency or liability may make little sense. Equally problematic are traditional concepts from the arsenal of contract law such as offer and acceptance, good faith

[53] See N Helberger, MBM Loos, L Guibault, C Mak and L Pessers, 'Digital Content Contracts for Consumers' (2013) 36 *Journal of Consumer Policy* 37.

[54] See S Bayern, 'Artificial Intelligence and Private Law' in W Barfield and U Pagallo (eds), *Research Handbook on the Law of Artificial Intelligence* (Cheltenham, Edward Elgar Publications, 2018).

or performance. AI may often take a business or an individual through the entire life cycle of a contract without either side even being aware of what is going on. While this does not remove the need for contract law, it should open the debate on its meaning.

The Internet of Things model is equally illustrative of the challenges. The constantly connected devices create lasting as well as temporal relations that may not be contractual in nature even where they have the outward appearance of a contract. In such cases, the term 'machine-to-machine' is beginning to describe the realities of life. In an example where a smart device automatically orders an item the consumer is running out of, one can conceivably extend the application of traditional contract mechanisms. In a situation where items of clothing communicate with a smart watch which, in turn, communicates with a platform, this is more difficult.

Smart contracts in the blockchain model are meant to enable, verify or enforce the negotiation or performance of a contract. In reality, they are not 'contracts', but technical protocols that perform a particular function if certain conditions are performed. The blockchain facilitates this. The problem, as above, is not in finding ways of making the existing legal framework fit by cleverly modifying it, but in realising that the reality represented by smart contracts may not be subject to contract law. The underlying question that the technology brings is: to what extent does technology itself take the role of rules? While the theory of contract law may meaningfully contribute to this debate, the important question for businesses and consumers will be whether the technology removes some of the clumsiness and uncertainty from the traditional world.

It has been argued that the revolution that blockchain may bring lies not in the originality of any rules that may be overturned or the new ones that may be invented, but in the ability of the technology to automatically and efficiently ensure the enforcement of the existing rules (eg compliance).[55] Blockchain can in that sense be used before the contract to facilitate its conclusion, but also after its conclusion to ensure its performance. The elimination of the middleman and the change in the meaning of trust[56] is the obvious gain in both cases. In some cases, at least, smart contracts may replace traditional ones completely.

V. Concluding Remarks

The apparent failure of the CESL turned into a relatively quick success for the OSG and DCD in the form of harmonisation of parts of consumer law for the digital world. There is little doubt that the OSG and DCD texts in their present

[55] See A Wright, *Blockchain and the Law: The Rule of Code* (Cambridge, MA, Harvard University Press 2018).

[56] See K Webach, *The Blockchain and the New Architecture of Trust* (Boston, The MIT Press, 2018).

form are an improvement on the versions proposed in 2015. There is equally little doubt that the long tradition dating back to the PECL and beyond contributed to the texts being well formulated. Finally, it seems clear that the consumer-law nature of the OSG and DCD project made it specific and focused, and enabled it to avoid some of the political pitfalls that a more general harmonisation would have brought. Nevertheless, there are good reasons to be sceptical of the future.

I indicated earlier that the problem of perceived versus real problems is a complex one in any attempt to harmonise EU private law. Whereas the EU perceives divergence as being a serious problem for the development of the Single Market, businesses are more pragmatic and more sceptical, citing language and culture as real problems. There is still scant empirical evidence that harmonisation of private law really brings significant benefits, and there is even more uncertainty as to what those benefits might be. Of equal concern is the haste with which the Commission had attempted to follow up on the CESL. The sector-specific full harmonisation, similar to the CRD, is also suffering from some of the same problems as its predecessor.

It is unreasonable to expect that the lack of clarity in a legislative instrument will be entirely corrected in courts. It is unlikely that the CJEU will come up with innovative solutions that address problems arising from language and culture, however original the interpretation that one might hope for might be. This is due to two reasons. The first is the Court's constitutionally limited task of interpreting the existing directives. The second is the limits of its vision. As an example, the Court is still struggling with the issue of 'digital' versus 'non-digital' in a variety of contexts, including whether digital rights can be exhausted and the digital product can be resold on the second-hand market. Whereas the distribution right is exhausted after the first transfer of ownership in the case of physical goods, for digital goods the question has been open for many years, with only the 2012 *UsedSoft* case beginning to change the issue.[57] This case seems to pave the way for deleting the difference between offline and online distribution, but the issue has not been settled yet.[58]

To me, however, an overwhelming impression remains: that the apparent and real failures concerning the regulation of the Digital Single Market have little or nothing to do with the disparities in contract law. The reasons for these failures remain empirically unclear, but it seems unlikely that a consumer in a Member State would be put off by differences in the legal system of another Member State or even be aware of them. The harmonisation brought about by the directives in such situations is welcome and legally important, but economically marginal. Instead, a consumer would cut their losses and avoid legal proceedings. If that consumer is to trade more online, more original methods of protection are needed.

[57] C-128/11 *UsedSoft GmbH* ECLI:EU:C:2012:407. In the context of lending of e-books, see, eg C-174/15 *Vereningen Openbare Bibliotheken* ECLI:EU:C:2016:856.

[58] A reference is currently pending on the issue in C-263/18 *Tom Kabinet*.

It can be predicted with some certainty that the two directives will have a mild positive effect. On the other hand, I suggest that an alternative approach is needed. This approach should concentrate on three points already mentioned in the literature.

The first is the recognition of the special status that an SME should have. No SME-specific contract rules exist in EU contract law. The CESL was original at least in recognising that this was a gap in the law, and established that the CESL may be used in B2B situations if at least one party is an SME.[59] The main purpose of the two directives is the harmonisation of contract law across Member States with a view to achieving a more coherent Single Market. While SMEs are normally defined as enterprises with fewer than 250 employees, micro-enterprises employ fewer than 10 but contribute 20.4 per cent of the gross value added.[60] Such enterprises are often similarly weak parties to consumers and may need special rules.

The second point is the wider use of standard contract terms.[61] These have been widely used in other industries (eg regular sale of goods under international commercial terms) but have not been tried in the digital world. As long as standard terms relate to a narrow set of facts and do not require reference to general contract law, their use should be relatively problem-free. The need to use general contract law would bring up the majority of the problems that the present directives are attempting to solve.

The third point is the sector-specific, purpose-oriented legislation targeting specific problems but arising from clear policy choices made at the EU level. When the EU first took interest in the digital world, it passed a number of framework directives (including the 2001 e-Commerce Directive).[62] Due to the political difficulties of achieving a more thorough harmonisation, in recent years the EU has concentrated on drafting sector-specific directives that address narrower, more easily achieved goals informed by specific problems. This has been the case with the regulations on geo-blocking,[63] content portability[64] and transparency on B2C platforms.[65] This recognises that new phenomena may require faster, more flexible regulation, but also that the EU policy on private law and its role in the digital world are still vague.

Modern EU contract law is not superfluous, but its importance today is limited and should be observed in the context of other developments, many of which are not from the legal domain. Having a clear picture of which problems are beyond the scope of contract law is the first step. Making an informed choice

[59] Art 7(2) CESL.

[60] Eurostat, 'Annual Enterprise Statistics by Size Class for Special Aggregates of Activities (NACE Rev 2)' (27 April 2020).

[61] See G Cordero-Moss, 'Standard Contract Terms as an Alternative to Legislation' in Twigg-Flesner, *Research Handbook* (n 11) 487.

[62] Directive 2000/31/EC [2000] OJ L178/1.

[63] Regulation (EU) 2018/302 [2018] OJ L601/1.

[64] Regulation (EU) 2017/1128 [2017] OJ L168/1.

[65] Regulation (EU) 2019/1159 [2019] OJ L186/57.

about where the political energy could best be spent would be the next. Few consumers today would declare that harmonising contract rules makes them more likely to buy online. In certain cases, the opposite might be true. An average EU consumer might be more comfortable with buying from the USA (on the account of the familiarity with the language or culture) than from a neighbouring country. At the same time, most consumers choose convenience over price (in particular, in grocery, clothing or electronics purchases)[66] and would value search engine optimisation, accurate AI and strong privacy, all of which are beyond the scope of contract law. In that sense, the EU's limited intervention is only a small, but still a meaningful, contribution.

[66] See National Retail Federation, 'Consumer View Winter 2020', https://nrf.com/research/consumer-view-winter-2020 3.

11

Epilogue – New Directions, but Which Ones?

HANS-W MICKLITZ

> Wir schmieden dauernd zu viele Pläne
> und denken dauernd zu wenig nach
> We make too many plans all the time
> and we are always thinking too little (Schumpeter 1942)[1]

I. New Instrumentalism and New Functionalism

The editors decided to unite the 10 contributions to this book under the heading 'New Directions in European Private Law'. They point into various directions. The majority (six of the 10) – those by Brownsword, Savin, Cannarsa, Hatzopoulos, Cox and Dimitropoulos – focus on private law and digitisation, either more comprehensively raising theoretical and conceptual questions or discussing particular aspects of the digital market and the existing or envisaged EU regulation. Of the others, Sheehan looks at private law with regard to standardisation, Falce & Finnochiaro focus on geo-blocking, Poncibò & Borgogno discuss the role of legal scholarship and Elizalde proposes a new concept of European contract law which differs from national private law orders.

This immediately begs the question of what is meant by 'directions'. The editors' choice suggests that there is a new direction, but does the title insinuate that European private law should have a direction? When legal scholars discuss the future of Italian or Polish private law, would they use the same language? It is likely that they would not. They would speak of the need for reform, the need to integrate the social dimension, ie labour law and consumer law. They might also refer to 're-establishing freedom of contract', but they would not speak of 'directions'.

[1] This is the opening quote in P Staab, *Digitaler Kapitalismus, Markt und Herrschaft in der Ökonomie der Unknappheit* (Berlin, Suhrkamp, 2019) 7.

National private law is self-standing, embedded in the national political and legal order. Is the search for new directions of European private law a new version of what H Collins termed European private law's instrumentalism, functionalism and incompleteness:[2] instrumental because private law shall serves to build the digital market or in the future the green market, functional in that the new directions continue to not address the person (the legal subject) – but now the new customers, and incomplete as European private law remains a law of bits and pieces?

However, even if the search for new directions adds another layer to instrumentalism, functionalism and incompleteness, the question remains what the new directions could offer and whether it is possible to identify one or more directions that European private law should take. I will first try to structure and discuss the many possible directions that European private law might take. This requires a certain opening and broadening, but serves to locate the contributions in the overall debate. Choosing directions implies a certain intellectual distance from them. Critical legal scholarship has gained ground. Private law changes its outlook like a chameleon, depending on one's understanding of it. The contributions seem to start from a rather broad meaning that reaches beyond contract and tort to include data protection, copyright, technical standards and geo-blocking, and points to my understanding of private law as economic law. Such an opening, however, requires structuring the different layers of economic regulation in terms of their impact on the core of private law. Such a holistic perspective then allows us to draw tentative conclusions on what the new directions should be.

II. Many Possible Directions

The direction can be *geographical* – looking, for example, at the European private law after Brexit, namely after a major common law country has left the EU. Will that mean that the continental legal orders will prevail over the remaining common law countries and that the next round of REFIT[3] will look more continental? If so, what will be the implications of that? In the last decade, the global dimension of EU law and, more recently, European private law gained ground.[4]

[2] H Collins, 'The Revolutionary Trajectory of EU Contract Law towards Post-national Law' in S Worthington, A Robertson and G Virgo (eds), *Revolution and Evolution in Private Law* (Oxford, Hart Publishing, 2017) 315–36.

[3] https://ec.europa.eu/info/law/law-making-process/evaluating-and-improving-existing-laws/refit-making-eu-law-simpler-and-less-costly/refit-platform_de.

[4] J Scott, 'Extraterritoriality and Territorial Extension in EU Law' (2014) 62 *American Journal of Comparative Law* 87; M Cremona and J Scott (eds), EU Law Beyond EU Borders: The Extraterritorial Reach of EU Law (Oxford, Oxford University Press, 2019); A Bradford, *The Brussels Effect: How the European Union Rules the World* (Oxford, Oxford University Press, 2020); A Bradford, 'The Brussels Effect' (2019) 107 *Northwestern University Law Review* 1; M Cremona and H-W Micklitz (eds), *Private Law in the External Dimension of the EU* (Oxford, Oxford University Press, 2016).

It should be recalled that the EU was able to develop a more coherent law on external relations only after the UK had joined the EU.[5] How will the external dimension of European private law look without one of the old colonial powers that has left deep traces in many legal orders around the world and that directly and indirectly helped to spread and strengthen the impact of the EU law beyond its territory?[6]

The direction can be *political* – what kind of European private law is needed for the European integration project as it stands, with its focus on the internal market and its incomplete institutional quasi-statutory structure? Linking private law, the internal market and the European Constitution would require us to finally engage in a debate on the foundations of a European private law without a fully fledged European state. The politically driven project on a European Civil Code,[7] first in the form of the Draft Common Frame of Reference (DCFR)[8] and then in the draft proposal of a Common European Sales Law (CESL),[9] did not tackle the relationship between the necessarily incomplete European private law and the necessarily incomplete European Constitution. The search for new political directions could therefore be understood as a kind of a second chance to draw conclusions from the failure of two grand projects, the European Civil Code and the European Constitution.[10]

The political direction – what can and what should be proposed to the European legislature – is closely linked to the *theoretical-conceptual* direction. A *theoretical* clarification is needed at both ends of the European constitution,[11] which is in fact a constitution constantly in the making, and a private law beyond the nation state fit for a European market but also fit for meeting standards of social justice. The idea of a European private law with a social face raises questions

[5] The banana conflict between the USA and the EU is paradigmatic: J de Melo, 'Bananas, the GATT, the WTO and US and EU Domestic Politics' (2012) Fondation pour les études et recherches sur le développement international Working Paper 54/2012, https://ferdi.fr/dl/df-siD4wkjANUc8dDEWa5k6UMkG/ferdi-p54-bananas-the-gatt-the-wto-and-us-and-eu-domestic-politics.pdf.

[6] H-W Micklitz, G Howells, C Lima Marques and T Naude, 'Dissemination of Consumer Law and Policy in Africa, Asia, the Americas, and Australia' (2018) 41 *Journal of Consumer Policy* 303.

[7] For a helpful reconstruction, see R Schulze, 'Contours of European Private Law' in R Schulze and H Schulte-Nölke (eds), *European Private Law – Current Status and Perspectives* (Sellier European Law Publishers, 2011) 3.

[8] C von Bar, E Clive, H Schulte-Nölke, H Beale, J Herre, J Huet, M Storme, S Swann, P Varul, A Veneziano and F Zoll (eds), *Principles, Definitions and Model Rules of European Private Law. Draft Common Frame of Reference (DCFR)*, prepared by the Study Group on a European Civil Code (Study Group) and the Research Group on EC Private Law (Acquis Group), based in part on a revised version of the Principles of European Contract Law (Munich, Sellier European Law Publishers, 2009).

[9] Commission, 'Proposal for a Regulation on a Common European Sales Law' COM (2011) 0635 final – 2011/0284 (COD).

[10] H-W Micklitz, 'Failure or Ideological Preconceptions? Thoughts on Two Grand Projects: the European Constitution and the European Civil Code' in K Tuori and S Sankari (eds), *The Many Constitutions of Europe* (Ashgate, 2010) 109–42.

[11] N Walker, 'Big "C" or Small "c"' (2006) 12 *European Law Journal* 12.

on the opportunities and limits of building a European society through law[12] and maybe even a European identity that unites the European peoples.[13]

A *conceptual* clarification is needed between what is and what should be understood as private law. Is it the law of obligations, of contract and tort or is it private law as economic law, in its links to competition law, trade law, copyright law, data protection, platform regulation and the like? Whatever understanding is advocated, investigation is required of the relationship between what W Böhm coined the 'private law society' (*Privatrechtsgesellschaft*) and the 'economic constitution' (*Wirtschaftsverfassung*).[14] There are many possible forms of economic constitutions, depending on how the role of the state and the role of the EU are understood and how deeply the state and the EU are interfering in and shaping the economy. At times when the EU has to face the criticism of promoting a neoliberal agenda that undermines national democracies, the search for new directions in private law has to engage with the democratic dimension of the European Economic Constitution and the corresponding European private law.[15]

The direction can be *technological* – the role and function of private law in the digital economy and digital society, a direction which is currently very fashionable. The debate is led at two very different levels.[16] On the one hand, there is the question whether digitilisation must be understood as a rupture which breaks down our understanding of the economy and society, and which entails the need to think about a new private law. The challenge is most visible in the debate about technology by design, where technology might serve as a substitute for 'law'.[17] On the other hand, there is the less dramatic understanding of an evolutionary process, underpinned by the assumption that the existing private law rules are by and large subject to certain adjustments fit to deal with digitilisation.[18] Whilst the new direction remains the same, the outlook of the private law differs considerably.

The direction can be *ecological* – what is the role and function of European private law if tied to sustainability and the circular economy? The UN Sustainable Development Goals[19] were adopted in 2015, translated by the EU into a call for

[12] G Comandé, 'The Fifth European Union Freedom. Aggregating Citizenship … around Private Law' in H-W Micklitz (ed), *Constitutionalization of European Private Law* (Oxford, Oxford University Press, 2014) 61–101.

[13] H Lindahl, 'Europe as Heimwelt and Fremdwelt, Constituent Power and the Genesis of a Legal Order' (2006) 13 *Journal of the European Ethics Network* 493.

[14] S Grundmann, 'Economics and Private Institutions' in S Grundmann, H-W Micklitz and M Renner, *New Private Law Theory – A Pluralist Approach* (Cambridge, Cambridge University Press, forthcoming) ch 3.

[15] Contributions in (2019) 52(4) *Kritische Justiz* (all in German).

[16] R Brownsword, 'Political Disruption, Technological Disruption and the Future of EU Private Law' (ch 1 in this volume); R Brownsword, 'The e-Commerce Directive, Consumer Transactions, and the Digital Single Market – Questions of Regulatory Fitness, Regulatory Disconnection and Rule Redirection' in S Grundmann (ed), *European Contract Law in the Digital Age* Cambridge, Intersentia, 2018) 165.

[17] Brownsword, this volume, ch 1.

[18] In this direction, see M Cannarsa, 'Civil Liability and New Technologies' (ch 9 in this volume).

[19] https://sustainabledevelopment.un.org/?menu=1300.

a circular economy.[20] Whilst the Juncker Commission was extremely successful in adopting a whole series of legislative measures that affect private law, including regulations and directives on geo-blocking, on platforms, on data protection, on copyrights, on sales law and on digital content,[21] those measures fall short from taking sustainability seriously. So far there is a deep gulf between conventional European private law driven by the Internal and Digital Market rhetoric and the political agenda on sustainability.[22] The working programme promoted by the von der Leyen Commission,[23] if taken seriously, would require us to rethink the relationship between the public law rules on environmental protection and sustainability, on the one hand, and the market-based private law, on the other. There is more needed than an instrumental adjustment of the policy goals: a deeper revision of the European legal order, the development of a sustainable economic constitution[24] and, maybe, even the revision of the EU Treaties.

Lastly, the new direction can be *doctrinal* – searching for new legal concepts within the European private law *acquis* to pave the way for new interpretations. There are a lot of new doctrinal directions in European private law. In their work, the Study Group and the Acquis Group took a narrow understanding of the European private law *acquis*, exempting the regulated markets and the relationship between primary EU law and national private laws.[25] The political pressure behind the elaboration of rules did not leave time and space to think through European private law as economic law. Stock taking of the European private law *acquis* requires competence not only in the few pieces of secondary EU law that affect contract and tort, but also in primary EU law, the four freedoms, competition

[20] Commission, The Council, the European Economic and Social Committee and the Committee of the Regions, 'A New Circular Economy Action Plan for a Cleaner and More Competitive Europe' (Communication) COM (2020) 98 final.

[21] Regulation (EU) 2018/302 on addressing unjustified geo-blocking and other forms of discrimination based on customers' nationality, place of residence or place of establishment within the internal market and amending Regulations (EC) No 2006/2004 and (EU) 2017/2394 and Directive 2009/22/EC [2018] OJ L601/1; Regulation (EU) 2019/1150 on promoting fairness and transparency for business users of online intermediation services [2019] OJ L186/57; Regulation (EU) 2016/679 on the protection of natural persons with regard to the processing of personal data and on the free movement of such data, and repealing Directive 95/46/EC (General Data Protection Regulation) [2016] OJ L119/1; Directive (EU) 2019/790 on copyright and related rights in the Digital Single Market and amending Directives 96/9/EC and 2001/29/EC [2019] OJ L130/92; Directive (EU) 2019/771 on certain aspects concerning contracts for the sale of goods, amending Regulation (EU) 2017/2394 and Directive 2009/22/EC, and repealing Directive 1999/44/EC [2019] OJ L136/28; Directive (EU) 2019/770 on certain aspects concerning contracts for the supply of digital content and digital services [2019] OJ L136/1.

[22] B Keirsbilck and E Terryn (eds), *Circular Economy and Consumer Protection* (Cambridge, Intersentia, 2019).

[23] https://ec.europa.eu/info/sites/info/files/political-guidelines-next-commission_en_0.pdf.

[24] There is abundant literature on the deficits in the Lisbon Treaty, eg A Kiss, 'European Environmental Law and the Constitution' (2004) 21 *Pace Environmental Law Review* 103, https://digitalcommons.pace.edu/pelr/vol21/iss1/6; P Beyer, 'The Environment in the Future European Constitution' (2004) 1 *Journal for European Environmental & Planning Law* 143.

[25] This might be partly due to the composition of the two groups which relied on private lawyers by and large without involving EU trade and competition lawyers.

law, state aids, public procurement and the vast body of secondary EU law that surrounds the European contract and tort law – all the rules that come under the umbrella of private law as economy law. There is still much room for new doctrinal directions, for rethinking the pillars of private law as economic law, for developing as yet unknown legal concepts and for elaborating new remedies.

III. European Private Law Scholarship

If appearances could provide guidance, the tone in European private law scholarship has gradually changed over the last decade.[26] I would distinguish three phases: the negligence of private law in the foundational period of the EU; the heydays of private lawmaking after 1986; and the (self)-critical reflection of the European private law *acquis* throughout.

The European Economic Community was built on peace through trade. The Treaty of Rome relies on national private laws to organise and enforce cross-border trade. There were early voices which pointed to the impact of the four freedoms and competition law and private law,[27] but by and large private law was conceived as a matter which was not in the hands of the EU. The Single European Act changed the relationship between EU law and national private law. The new competence rule enabled the EU to adopt European private law rules that were broadly understood, provided they were needed to 'complete the internal market'. In the bunch of regulations and directives, based on what is now Article 114 TFEU, the link between market building and private law as economic law was more presumed than proven, but found support by the European Court of Justice through a broad reading of the EU competence.[28] European private law scholarship was heavily involved in the lawmaking of the 1990s,[29] but was involved to a lesser extent after the Lisbon Summit declaration in 2000, which shifted the required expertise from scholarship to consultancy firms.

The European Civil Code project, launched in 2001, enjoyed a particular status. Roughly 200 scholars in Europe were involved in the elaboration. That is why the DCFR is called '*Professorenrecht*' – professorial law.[30] The European Commission

[26] C Poncibò and O Borgogno, 'Schools of Thought in European Private Law' (ch 3 in this volume), referring to H-W Micklitz and R van Gestel, 'Why Methods Matter in European Legal Scholarship' (2014) 20 *European Law Journal* 292; H-W Micklitz, 'A European Advantage in Legal Scholarship?' in R van Gestel, H-W Micklitz and Ed Rubin (eds), *Rethinking Legal Scholarship: A Transatlantic Dialogue* (Cambridge, Cambridge University Press, 2017) 262–309.

[27] E Steindorff, *EG-Vertrag und Privatrecht* (Baden-Baden, Nomos, 1996); A Hartkamp, *European Private Law and National Private Law*, 2nd edn (Cambridge, Intersentia, 2018).

[28] S Weatherill, *Contract Law of the Internal Market* (Cambridge, Intersentia, 2016) 68.

[29] Including myself: H-W Micklitz, 'The Transformative Politics of European Private Law' in P Kjaer (ed), *The Political Economy of the Law* (Cambridge, Cambridge University Press, 2020).

[30] H Schepel, 'Professorenrecht? The Field of European Private Law' in H Schepel and A Jettinghoff (eds), *Lawyers' Circles. Lawyers and European Legal Integration* (The Hague, Elsevier Reed, 2004) 115–24.

turned the academic project – the DCFR – into a political project – the CESL. Whilst the European Commission submitted the CESL to an impact assessment, in line with the post-Lisbon Summit policy, the impact assessment that should test the efficiency and effectiveness remained rather symbolic. Six Member States stopped the project politically through their joint intervention before the European Commission. European private law scholarship had by and large supported the conceptualisation of a Common European Sales Law as an optional legal order which stands side by side with the national private law orders. Contrary to the pre-2000 era, law and economics gained ground in the analysis of the pros and cons of the CESL.[31]

The third phase could be dated back to the collapse of Lehman Brothers, the financial crisis and the euro crisis in 2008.[32] Looking backwards, the de facto institutionalisation of consultancy firms through the 'better regulation approach'[33] promoted a trifurcation in private law scholarship. The consultancy firms are engaging preferably young or midcareer scholars who are under political pressure of their home universities to raise funds. Insofar, legal scholarship forms an institutional part of the ongoing and rather successful – in terms of output – European legislative machinery. The substitution of legal scholarship through consultancy firms affects the role and function of scholarship in lawmaking. One may wonder whether and to what extent this kind of scholarship can be called 'research' as the European Commission frames the questions and does not leave space for distancing or for even more fundamental questions on the direction of EU private law.[34]

The establishment of the European Law Institute in 2011 marks a break-even point in private law scholarship. I claim that there is a link between the reorganisation of lawmaking in the aftermath of the Lisbon Summit through the 'better regulation approach' and the death of the European Civil Code project. The 'better regulation approach' loosened the ties between European legal scholars and the European Commission. Gradually from 2000 on, but more visibly through the failed European Civil Code project, legal scholarship became marginalised in the political process of EU lawmaking. The Study Group and the Acquis Group succeeded in bundling up the intellectual capacity to form the European Law Institute. The ELI is meant to 'initiate, conduct and facilitate research, make recommendations and provide practical guidance in the field of European legal development'.[35] Today, the ELI reaches out into a wide range of topics of European law and European

[31] (2013) 50 *CML Rev* special issue. All contributions are dealing with the CESL, https://heinonline.org/HOL/LandingPage?handle=hein.kluwer/cmlr0050&div=20&id=&page=.

[32] H-W Micklitz and I Domurath (eds), *Consumer Debt and Social Inclusion in Europe* (Ashgate, 2015).

[33] https://ec.europa.eu/info/law/law-making-process/planning-and-proposing-law/better-regulation-why-and-how/better-regulation-guidelines-and-toolbox_en.

[34] H-W Micklitz and A Villanueva, 'REFIT or Rethink – The Politics of EU research – A Grand Misunderstanding?' in E van Schagen and S Weatherill (eds), *Better Regulation in EU Contract Law: The Fitness Check and the New Deal for Consumers* (Oxford, Hart Publishing, 2019) 37–59.

[35] https://www.europeanlawinstitute.eu/about-eli/.

integration, although private law and economic law still dominate its activities and the emphasis still seems to lie on policy recommendations.[36] However, the ELI is independent; there is no institutional link between the European Commission and the ELI. Its policy recommendations may or may not be taken into consideration by policy makers.[37] In comparison to the pre-ELI and pre-2000 period of scholarly involvement, the establishment of the ELI is an opportunity to gain intellectual distance, which enables and promotes the search for new directions in the aftermath of the European Civil Code project.

The third strand of European legal scholarship is characterised by a critical and rather distant attitude not so much towards European integration and the building of European private law as towards the dominance of the 'neoliberal' market rationale and the instrumentalisation of private law to enhance economic efficiency.[38] I do not want to be misunderstood: legal scholars might work for consultancy firms and take a (self-)critical attitude towards the transformation of private law through the European integration project, but what matters is that the search for new directions requires intellectual independence and a certain distance from the constantly moving political agenda of the EU and the European Commission. Whilst there is definitely a need to follow and accompany the regulatory activities of the European Commission, more is necessary in the search for new directions than following the European Commission. The trifurcation in legal scholarship, its downgrading in the present and ongoing law production and the establishment of the ELI as an institutionally independent research and policy unit enhances and strengthens self-critical legal scholarship without which the search for new directions will necessarily fail. This is the necessary condition for thinking through what the European Union has achieved and how all these regulatory activities have affected private law.

IV. European Private Law as European Economic Law

In terms of quantity and quality, there is a mismatch between EU rules on the core of traditional private law – contract and tort – and the much wider European legal environment in which traditional private law is embedded. From a political and economic perspective, one might somewhat provocatively argue that the EU does not need to establish rules on contract and tort because the European legal framework covers what is economically and politically important for the building of the internal market. The two key parameters around which economic regulation is built

[36] https://www.europeanlawinstitute.eu/projects-publications/completed-projects/.

[37] ELI Model Rules on Online Platforms, https://www.europeanlawinstitute.eu/fileadmin/user_upload/p_eli/Publications/ELI_Model_Rules_on_Online_Platforms.pdf.

[38] M Bartl, 'Internal Market Rationality, Private Law and the Direction of the Union: Resuscitating the Market as the Object of the Political' (2015) 21 *European Law Journal* 572; D Kochenov, G de Búrca and A Williams (eds), *Europe's Justice Deficit?* (Oxford, Hart Publishing, 2015).

are 'economic efficiency' and 'governance'. Under reference to the public–private divide, private law scholarship tends to leave the field of economic regulation either to specialists focusing on particular aspects of economic regulation or to public administrative law. The consequence of such thinking was wonderfully summed up by Otto von Gierke nearly 140 years ago.[39] A new direction would imply finally taking a holistic perspective that unites core private law issues and economic regulation, breaking down the public–private divide and studying the interlink between the two fields.

More systematically, it is feasible to distinguish between three layers that surround the core private law. EU rules which directly affect the core – contract and tort – are first and foremost consumer contract law, product liability and international private law, surrounded by three different layers. The first layer that frames the core rules on contract and tort are those coming under the concept of European regulatory private law. I have tentatively distinguished between four categories of economic regulation that affect the core private law: (i) regulated markets – network law (telecommunication, energy, finance, transport), insurance, company law and capital markets; (ii) commercial practices and contract – standard terms, advertising and sales promotion, as well as intellectual property rights; (iii) competition, state aids and public procurement; and (iv) health and safety, food and the regulation of services through technical standards).[40] The distinction and the attributions are certainly debatable, but the above categorisation allows, with minor adjustments, the integration of the Platform to Business Regulation into network law; the General Data Production Regulation affects intellectual property rights and consumer protection, geo-blocking complements competition, state aids, and public procurement under category (iii); and the regulation of unfair trading practices in the food sector and of digital content affect food supply and digital services under category (iv).[41]

The second layer is the double constitutionalisation of private law through primary EU law (the core of the internal market law, ie the four freedoms and competition law) and through the Charter of Fundamental Rights of the European Union and the European Convention on Human Rights.[42] Both pillars are subject

[39] 'One now obtains two systems dominated by a very different spirit: a system of common civil law, in which "pure" private law is decided, and a wealth of special rights, in which private law, clouded by public law and mixed with public law, prevails. Here living, folkloric, socially colored law full of inner application – there an abstract template, romanistic, individualistic, ossified in dead dogma': O von Gierke, *Die soziale Aufgabe des Privatrechts. Vortrag gehalten am 5. April 1889 in der juristischen Gesellschaft zu Wien* (Berlin, Springer, 1889) 13.

[40] H-W Micklitz, 'The Visible Hand of European Regulatory Private Law – The Transformation of European Private Law from Autonomy to Functionalism in Competition and Regulation' (2010) 28 *Yearbook of European Law* 3; for an update, see H-W Micklitz, G Comparato and Y Svetiev, 'The Regulatory Character of European Private Law' in C. Twigg-Flesner (ed), *Research Handbook on EU Consumer and Contract Law* (Cheltenham, Edward Elgar Publishing, 2016) 35–67.

[41] See references in n 21 and Directive (EU) 2019/633 on unfair trading practices in business-to-business relationships in the agricultural and food supply chain [2019] OJ L111/59.

[42] AC Ciacchi, G Brüggemeier and G Comandé (eds), *Fundamental Rights and Private Law in the European Union*, vols I and II (Cambridge, Cambridge University Press, 2010).

to a high degree of politicisation. The internal market is the preferred target of regulatory initiatives from the European Commission (the capital market, the digital market, maybe the sustainable market). This is obvious with regard to competition law. Competition law has turned into a catch-all mechanisms for promoting competition in the capital market, for securing competition in the digital market and for incentivising the production of sustainable goods and services. The Charter of Fundamental Rights provides a safety net for EU citizens in defending their rights throughout the constant transformations of the internal market into sectorial markets or overall political objectives that should be achieved through redesigning the direction of the internal market developments. The impact of both primary EU law and fundamental rights is subject to an intensive debate in private law scholarship, somewhat biased in that the emphasis is all too often laid on fundamental rights, disregarding the not so obvious impact of primary EU law on private law.[43]

The third layer concerns the interaction of the core rules, the European regulatory private law and the double constitutionalisation of European private law rules with international economic law. The global reach of EU law is in the limelight of legal scholarship. The global reach of contract and tort, the traditional private law, lies in the hands of international private lawyers. The Europeanisation of international private law in Rome I and II leads to tensions with the activities of the Hague Academy, which advocates the development of international instead of regional rules. The link between EU private law and international economic law is most striking at the second layer, in the field of regulated markets through sectorial rules, in commercial practices through TRIPs, in state aids and procurement through the corresponding rules in GATT/WTO, and in the regulation of services through the TBT Agreement. It is difficult to impossible to understand European regulatory private law without the interaction with rules, conventions and codes agreed upon at international level.[44] The third layer, the double constitutionalisation, can equally be traced in international economic law. There are voices that proclaim, albeit subject to strong criticism, that the GATT/WTO order connected to human rights could be conceived of as a constitutional order[45] and that human rights obligation should be imposed on companies that operate internationally.[46] To my knowledge, there are no studies on the potential impact of the decisions of the

[43] H-W Micklitz and C Sieburgh (eds), *Primary EU Law and Private Law Concepts* (Cambridge, Intersentia, 2017).

[44] M Cantero and H-W Micklitz (eds), *The Role of the EU in Transnational Legal Ordering: Standards, Contracts and Codes* (Cheltenham, Edward Elgar Publishing, 2020).

[45] E-U Petersmann, 'Time for a United Nations "Global Compact2 on Integrating Human Rights into Worldwide Organisations' (2002) 13 *European Journal of International Law* 621; P Alston, 'Resisting the Merger and Acquisition of Human Rights and Trade Law: A Reply to Petersmann' (2002) 13 *European Journal of International Law* 815; R Howse, 'Human Rights in Trade Law, Whose Rights What Humanity – A Comment on Petersmann' (2002) 13 *European Journal of International Law* 615.

[46] G Teubner, 'The Anonymous Matrix: Human Rights Violations by "Private" Transnational Actors' (2006) 69 *MLR* 327.

Appellate Body of the WTO or on international human rights committees[47] on private law. This is all the more astonishing as the starting point for litigation is all too often a private law conflict which is fought out through states.

The four layers together indicate the tremendous challenge the search for new directions faces, if one understands private law as economic law. The breadth and depth of the issues might explain the temptation of private law scholarship to shy away from economic regulation, to defend contract and tort against all sorts of economic regulation, to insist on the public–private divide and to break down economic regulation and core private law into legal boxes, not only according to national, European and international layers, but also along the line of specialisations in particular legal fields.

V. Many Directions – Many Options

Out of the many legitimate approaches to handle the search for a self-critical direction in European private law as European economic law and in light of the contributions to this book, I would like to outline three different options.

The first is turning to legal theory and searching for a private law theory that deliberately addresses the complexity and the interaction between the three layers.[48] The second is represented in the contributions of Brownsword and Hatzopoulos. Brownsword is advocating the idea of 'red lines' which cannot and should not be crossed in the digital economy and society. He puts the focus on human dignity.[49] This kind of thinking stands behind the constitutionalisation of private law. The difficulty, however, results from the balancing exercise, as each party to a contract may invoke their own set of constitutional, fundamental and human rights. Brownsword goes further. Red lines are supposed to be those that cannot be crossed even through balancing. D Kennedy would probably argue that in the third globalisation of neo-formalism the balancing exercise is ubiquitous.[50] However, his three stages of globalisations of legal thought do not yet include digitilisation and what it means for the law. In a way, we are back at Alexy's distinction between rules and standards. The idea of red lines is not limited to the

[47] J Zglinski, 'Private Law before the European Court of Human Rights – Doing Too Little or Too Much' (2018) 37 *Yearbook of European Law* 98.

[48] For a first attempt, but with a German-European bias, see H-W Micklitz, S Grundmann and M Renner, *New Private Law Theory A Pluralist Approach* (Cambridge, Cambridge University Press, 2021).

[49] R Brownsword, 'From Erewhon to Alpha Go: For the Sake of Human Dignity Should We Destroy the Machines?' (2017) 9 *Law, Innovation and Technology* 117; R Brownsword, 'Human Dignity from a Legal Perspective' in M Duwell, J Braarvig, R Brownsword and D Mieth (eds), *Cambridge Handbook of Human Dignity* (Cambridge, Cambridge University Press, 2014) 1.

[50] D Kennedy, 'Three Globalizations of Law and Legal Thought: 1850–2000' in DM Trubek and A Santos (eds), *The New Law and Economic Development. A Critical Appraisal* (Cambridge, Cambridge University Press, 2006) 19–73; D Kennedy, 'A Transnational Genealogy of Proportionality in Private Law' in R Brownsword, H-W Micklitz, L Niglia and S Weatherill (eds), *The Foundations of European Private Law* (Oxford, Hart Publishing, 2011) 185–220.

constitutional level. One might consider reintroducing more rules into the body of private law. An example of this are black clauses that leave no room for interpretation or circumvention.[51]

Hatzopoulos advocates the need of new general principles for the collaborative economy. He proposes 'effective analogy' and 'algorithmic fairness' both derived from more general principles and fine-tuned to the particularities of the digital economy. General principles cannot work as read lines. They are necessarily subject to interpretation and balancing. It should be recalled that the attempts of the CJEU to develop 'general principles of civil law' came to nothing. The few judgments in private law cases demonstrate experimentalism through the European judiciary.[52] Scholarly research seems to be more optimistic in distilling general principles out of the existing private law *acquis*.[53] My own take is that general principles could turn into a more powerful tool in connection with a reversal of the burden of proof. It would then be for the potential perpetrator to show that she has not infringed the general principle.

The third option consists in the search for innovative legal doctrines. Elizalde hypothesises that EU law *de lege lata* is developing core rules for the formation of contracts that could end up in a harmonised mandatory system (mass EU contract law (MEUCL)), yet one that is of a different colour to the dominating theories of private autonomy and free will. There are many follow-on questions, about whether and to what extent the hypothesis can reach beyond the formation of the contract and how such an EU private law could be connected to the national private law orders. However, European private law needs more of these attempts to elaborate new doctrinal models that condense the core of European private law and that provide for guidance in the solution of concrete conflicts notwithstanding the problem of an extreme instrumentalisation of private law for particular policy perspectives.

VI. Methodology

I would like to propose a holistic perspective that reaches from the very early stages in the preparation of a contract up to and beyond its completion. Only such a perspective will allow us to do justice to European private law as economic law

[51] P Rott, ‚Rechtsklarheit, Rechtsdurchsetzung und Verbraucherschutz' in H-W Micklitz, L Reisch, G Joost and H Zander-Hayat (eds), *Verbraucherrecht 2.0 – Verbraucher in der digitalen Welt* (Baden-Baden, Nomos, 2017) 221–64.

[52] CF Sabel and O Gerstenberg, 'Constitutionalising an Overlapping Consensus: The ECJ and the Emergence of a Coordinate Constitutional Order' (2010) 16 *European Law Journal* 511.

[53] N Reich, *General Principles of EU Civil Law* (Cambridge, Intersentia, 2014); MW Hesselink, 'The General Principles of Civil Law: Their Nature, Roles and Legitimacy' in D Leczykiewicz and S Weatherill (eds), *The Involvement of EU Law in Private Law Relationships*, Studies of the Oxford Institute of European and Comparative Law No 16 (Oxford, Oxford Institute of European and Comparative Law, 2013) 131–80.

and to connect traditional private law and economic regulation. What I have in mind is a particular methodology and technique that could serve as a starter for considering possible 'new directions'.

When it comes to contract law, the focus is on the conclusion of the contract and its content. Opening contract law to economic regulation would mean going back to the pre-contractual stage and also including the post-contractual stage.[54] What European economic regulation has been doing ever since the adoption of the Single European Act is to regulate the pre- and post-contractual stages and leave – at least in theory – the regulation of the conclusion of the contract and requirements of the content for the national laws. The pre-contractual stage could be broken down into the three faces – the contact building via commercial communication at *incertas* personas (an offer to an undetermined number of persons), the targeting of particular groups of customers through commercial communication and information requirements which precede the conclusion. But even such a broadening does not suffice, as the possibility of customers to conclude contracts in the internal market depends on their accessibility to the market and their skill at mastering the access requirements.[55] The post-contractual stage starts with post-contractual information requirements – aftersales services, complaint handling, dispute settlement, redress, protection against insolvency – and ends with monitoring and inspection duties of the contracting partner. An analysis along these lines would demonstrate how the EU is using not only binding rules, but, in particular, codes of conduct and technical standards, to complement legislative gaps, especially in regulated markets, telecoms, energy and financial services.

VII. Conclusion – Is There a Conclusion?

The search for new directions depends on who is searching for what. The European Commission in particular is under structural political pressure to continually look for better solutions and new directions. The constraints are structural, as the future of the EU and the European integration is open ended. The consequences are visible in the move towards 'procedure' and 'governmental experimentalism' not only in private law. Legal scholarship has two tasks: first, to accompany the ongoing moves in new directions – though held together by the completion of the internal market with a social face; and secondly, to critically reflect the Europeanisation of private law. Nearly 10 years ago, R Brownsword referred beautifully to WH Davies's 'A Time to Stand and Stare' as a metaphor of the philosophical-theoretical foundations of European private law.[56] I could not agree more.

[54] H-W Micklitz, 'Services Standards: Defining the Core Elements and Their Minimum Requirements' (Brussels, ANEC, 2007), www.anec.eu/attachments/ANEC-R&T-2006-SERV-004final.pdf.

[55] See M Cox, 'Activating EU Private Law in the Online Platform Economy' (ch 7 in this volume).

[56] R Brownsword, 'The Theoretical Foundations of European Private Law: A Time to Stand and Stare' in Brownsword et al (n 50) 159–76.

INDEX

www.ingramcontent.com/pod-product-compliance
Ingram Content Group UK Ltd.
Pitfield, Milton Keynes, MK11 3LW, UK
UKHW022212051026
15624UKWH00001B/123

9 781509 935611